Contents

Contents

Contributors

Ray Forrest is Professor of Urban Studies and Head of School for Policy Studies, University of Bristol, UK. He has published widely on housing policy, the sociology of housing and urban change. He is currently co-director (with Professor Ade Kearns, University of Glasgow) of the ESRC Centre for Neighbourhood Research and is co-researcher with Gary Bridge on a project, 'Housing, Taste and Place: The Housing Histories of Gentrifiers'. He is also involved in a number of collaborative projects with colleagues at the City University of Hong Kong. These include 'The Meaning of Neighbourhood in Contemporary Hong Kong Society' (with Adrienne La Grange and Ngai Ming Yip), 'Public Housing, Economic Change and the Shaping of Family Housing Histories' (with James Lee, K.Y. Lau, Adrienne La Grange and Ngai Ming Yip) and 'Reshaping Social Divisions? Wealth Accumulation and Home Ownership in East Asia' (with James Lee and Adrienne La Grange). He is a Visiting Professor in the Department of Urban Studies, University of Glasgow and Adjunct Professor, Department of Public and Social Administration at the City University of Hong Kong. He is a founding member of the Asia Pacific Network for Housing Research.

James Lee is currently Associate Professor at the City University of Hong Kong. He specializes in teaching and research in housing policy and administration. He did his undergraduate studies in economics at the University of Hong Kong and graduate work in social administration at the London School of Economics. He obtained his doctorate in housing policy at the School for Policy Studies at the University of Bristol. He is a founder of the Hong Kong Housing Research Network and the Asian Pacific Network of Housing Research. His recent publications include: *Housing, Home Ownership and Social Change in Hong Kong*, London: Ashgate, and 'Home Ownership under Economic Uncertainty: the Role of Subsidized Sale Flats in Hong Kong' (with Yip N. M.), *Third World Planning Review*, Vol. 23, No. 1, June 2001, pp. 61–78.

Contributors

Rebecca L.H. Chiu is Associate Professor at the University of Hong Kong, specializing in the teaching and research of housing policy and management. Her current research interests include housing reforms and the emergence of housing markets in the former centrally-planned economies; housing policies and sustainable housing development in Hong Kong. She is the Convener of the Hong Kong Housing Research Network, and is on the editorial board of *Housing, Theory and Society.* She also serves on the Town Planning Board and the Home Ownership Committee of the Hong Kong Housing Authority.

Chua Beng Huat is Professor of Sociology at the National University of Singapore. He has wide-ranging research interests which include social and political theory, sociology of housing, state and society in Southeast Asia, consumerism in Asia and cultural studies. He has recently edited the book *Consumption in Asia: Lifestyles and Identities*, Routledge, 2000 and is editor of the *Inter-Asia Cultural Studies* journal. In addition to extensive academic writings, he is a regular social and political commentator on Singapore and Southeast Asian affairs.

Deborah S. Davis is Professor of Sociology and Director of Academic Programs at the Yale Center for the Study of Globalization. She is the author of *Long Lives: Chinese Elderly and the Communist Revolution* (Harvard 1983; (2nd ed.) Stanford 1991) and editor of *Chinese Society on the Eve of Tiananmen* (Harvard 1990), *Chinese Families in the Post-Mao Era* (California 1993), *Urban Spaces in Contemporary China* (Cambridge 1995), and *The Consumer Revolution in Urban China* (California 2000). She has held post-doctoral grants from the National Academy of Sciences, Social Science Research Council, National Institute on Aging, American Council of Learned Societies and the Luce Foundation. Her current research focuses on the new class structure of urban China and on the social consequences of privatizing home ownership. Her primary teaching interests are comparative sociology, inequality and stratification, and contemporary Chinese society.

Yosuke Hirayama is currently Professor of Housing and Urban Studies at Kobe University. He specializes in housing and home ownership policy and his publications appear in both Japanese and international academic journals. His current research focuses on home ownership, market instability and social change. He has recently completed comparative Anglo-Japanese research on the restructuring of home ownership systems.

Harvey Perkins is currently Associate Professor at Lincoln University, Canterbury, New Zealand. He specializes in teaching about and research into the social geography, sociology of human settlement, leisure, tourism and urban planning. He is currently working with Professor David Thorns (below) on a project concerned with housing and home as part of their wider research programme 'Studies in Human Settlement' (http//:www.soci.Canterbury.ac.nz/

shshome.htm). His other research projects currently focus on rural commodi-fication, urban intensification, rural residential settlement, holiday homes, and the influences of tourism on the changing meaning and form of places.

Alan Smart is the Head of the Department of Anthropology at the University of Calgary, Alberta, Canada. He has carried out extensive research on various aspects of housing and social change, focusing particularly on the squatter settlements of Hong Kong. He has also contributed regularly to international journals on the political economy of public housing. His books include *Making Room: Squatter Clearance in Hong Kong.* Professor Smart is currently engaged in research in cross-border investment in Hong Kong and Shenzhen.

Michael A. Stegman is the Duncan MacRae and Rebecca Kyle MacRae Professor of Public Policy and Business at the University of North Carolina at Chapel Hill and director of the Center for Community Capitalism in the Kenan-Flagler Business School's Frank Hawkins Kenan Institute of Private Enterprise. In February 1993, President Clinton nominated him to be Assistant Secretary for Policy Development and Research (PD&R) at the US Department of Housing and Urban Development. He held that position until June 30, 1997. He also served as Acting Chief of Staff at HUD from November 1996 through April 1997. He has written extensively on housing and urban policy. Among the books he has written are: *Savings and the Poor: The Hidden Assets of Electronic Banking*, Brookings Press, 1999; *State and Local Affordable Housing Programs: A Rich Tapestry*, The Urban Land Institute, 1999; and *More Housing More Fairly, Report of the Twentieth Century Fund Task Force on Affordable Housing*, 1991.

Wai Keung Tam was formerly the Senior Research Assistant at the Centre for Comparative Management and Social Policy, City University of Hong Kong. He helped to organize the International Housing Conference in April 2001 and worked closely with James Lee on comparative Asian housing policy research. Since fall 2002, he has begun a doctoral program in East Asian studies at the University of Chicago.

David Thorns is Professor of Sociology at the University of Canterbury and previously taught at the Universities of Nottingham, Exeter and Auckland. He is the author or co-author of eight books. Among the more recent are *Under-standing Aotearoa/New Zealand: Historical Statistics* (with Charles Sedgwick, The Dunmore Press, 1997) and *The Transformation of Cities* (Palgrave, 2002). He has published widely on issues of housing, inequality and the urban and regional implications of economic restructuring. His current research focus is on restructuring and change within advanced capitalist societies and the meaning of house and home.

Ya Ping Wang is currently Reader at Heriot Watt University, Edinburgh. He specializes in comparative planning and housing policy and planning in developing countries. Before working in the UK, he was Lecturer in Geography at the Shanxia Teachers University, Xian, from 1982–5. His current research includes housing reform and the urban poor in China; housing policy and reform in China; urban and regional planning in China; social integration and stratification in Chinese cities. His recent publications include: *Housing Policy and Practice in China* (Macmillan, 1999); 'Social and Spatial Implications of Urban Housing Reform in China', *International Journal of Urban and Regional Research*, 2000; 'The Process of Commercialization of Urban Housing in China', *Urban Studies*, 1996.

Sophie Watson is Professor of Sociology at the Open University, UK. She was previously Professor of Cultural Studies at the University of East London, Professor of Housing at the University of Bristol, Professor of Urban and Regional Planning at the University of Sydney, and Senior Lecturer of Town Planning at the University of New South Wales. Her current research focuses on public space and public sphere. Her books include *Engendering Social Policy*; *Surface City: Sydney at the Millennium*; *Postmodern Cities and Spaces*; *Metropolis Now*; and *Housing and Homelessness: A Feminist Perspective*. Her most recent work is *A Companion to the City* (with Gary Bridge) published by Blackwell.

Christine M.E. Whitehead is Professor of Housing Economics in the Department of Economics, London School of Economics and Director of the Property Research Unit, Department of Land Economy, University of Cambridge. She has been working in the fields of urban and housing economies, finance and policy for many years and was awarded an OBE in 1991 for services to housing. She is author of a large number of academic and policy articles and major reports on housing ranging from the first econometric model of the UK housing market to her new text with Sarah Monk on *Restructuring Social Housing Systems: From Social to Affordable Housing*, published in 2000. She has been advisor to the House of Commons Environment Select Committee on four occasions, latterly with respect to housing.

Peter Williams is Deputy Director General of the Council of Mortgage Lenders, a position he took up in January 1997. He joined the former BSA/CML as Head of Research and External Affairs in January 1994. He has overall responsibility for housing policy issues at the CML and is a regular contributor to conferences along with frequent media comment. He has had a long involvement with housing policy and practice in the UK and abroad. A graduate from Oxford, he has worked in universities in the UK, Canada and Australia. In 1983 he became Assistant and then Deputy Director at the Chartered Institute of Housing with responsibility for education, training and research. In 1988, he joined the University of Wales as the first Professor of Housing Management. He was Chairman of the Secretary of State's Housing Management Advisory Panel and a Board member of Housing for Wales from 1989 to 1994.

Preface

The chapters in this volume are revised versions of plenary papers initially presented at an international conference held at the City University of Hong Kong in April 2001. The conference theme was *Managing Housing and Social Change: Building Social Cohesion, Accommodating Diversity.* We are very much aware that the conference could not have taken place without the organizational skills, patience and financial support of the Centre of Comparative Management and Social Policy (renamed Governance in Asia Research Centre (GARC) in 2002) of the City University. We would like especially to thank Dr Julia Tao, Director of GARC, Professor Anthony Cheung and Professor Ian Holliday, both Associate Directors of GARC, and also staff members of the Centre for their support in making the conference a success. In addition, we would like to thank the Editorial Board of *Housing Studies*, the Chartered Institute of Housing Hong Kong Branch, the Hong Kong Institute of Housing and the Hong Kong Housing Research Network at the University of Hong Kong for their generous sponsorship. Finally, we would like to acknowledge the crucial role played by Joyce Lui in assisting us with the overall production of the book.

Ray Forrest
James Lee

1 Some reflections on the housing question

Ray Forrest

Introduction

In 1867 Engels' construction of the housing question drew on his observations of the 'exploding city' of Manchester (Engels 1988). There was mass migration from the countryside to the city, overcrowding, a massive absolute shortage of housing and generally appalling living conditions in many northern European cities. At the beginning of the twenty-first century, for many Western housing analysts, the question appears to have been mainly answered. The vast majority of households are reasonably well housed. Space standards are generous and amenity provision is of a relatively high standard. It is certainly true that amidst this affluence there is deeply entrenched poverty and systemic homelessness – and this is perceived as a growing threat to social cohesion and stability. But access to decent housing is not a preoccupation of majorities in most of Europe and North America. So what does the housing question look like today? This book focuses on various relationships between housing and social change in the contemporary world. It draws on authors from Europe, North America, South and East Asia and Australasia. This introductory chapter aims to provide a backcloth to the various discussions which follow. In particular it will explore key aspects of the current housing question in relation to processes of globalization, demographic change, rising social inequalities and new social divisions associated with wealth accumulation via home-ownership. The housing literature continues to have a strong bias towards experiences in western Europe and North America. For this reason, and consistent with the strong East/West theme of the book, the emphasis in this chapter will be on aspects of social transformation and housing provision in Asia, particularly South and East Asia. Throughout, however, appropriate reference will be made to current developments and debates in the West. The concluding section will reflect on the extent to which, from an international perspective, the housing question has been transformed over the last century.

Uneven developments

For Western governments, then, absolute housing shortages are seen generally as a thing of the past. Housing policies are now more likely to be targeted on particular groups such as lone parents or lowest income households or at the new housing demands of demographic ageing rather than as general strategies to raise standards or widen access. Western governments are also more likely to be concerned with an ageing infrastructure and urban regeneration than with mass provision for an expanding population of urban dwellers. Most Western housing markets are generally well established with mature institutional structures. While some have been shaken in recent decades by price volatility and wider economic uncertainty, they have generally recovered. Moreover, academic debate about housing in the West is likely to be couched in terms of choice and diversity, in terms of postmodernism and post-fordism, rather than in the starker language of deprivation, exploitation and urban poverty.

Of course, the experience of severe overcrowding, lack of basic amenities such as running water and occupancy of precarious and illegal forms of shelter are only a memory for many households living in places such as Hong Kong, Singapore, Kuala Lumpur and Seoul. But when compared with the post war experiences of households in countries such as Britain or the USA, for many the memories of such conditions are relatively recent. Much of East and South East Asia has experienced a period of remarkable growth rates, dramatic economic and social change and rampant urbanization. The rapid pace of urbanization and industrialization has also produced much more volatile upswings and downswings in the property market – during booms prices have risen by more than 20 per cent compared with a more typical 10 per cent in Western property markets (Bank of International Settlements 1997: 106).

The impacts of these rapid changes in working and living conditions have been highly uneven. Some cohorts have experienced rising real incomes and widening job opportunities. Others have been caught by severe economic downturns or by the more brutal aspects of industrialization. Moreover, this unevenness which was perhaps perceived previously to be a transitional phase in a more widespread transformation of peoples' life chances and opportunities has, since the Asian financial crisis, become more deeply entrenched and problematic. Here there are parallels with shifts in Western social structures with deteriorating conditions and opportunities for some. But the consequences in parts of Asia have been more dramatic. Some members of the newly expanding middle classes found themselves unexpectedly jettisoned by a rapid downturn in economic activity. Some lost their jobs – others saw the value of their savings and assets significantly eroded. The hardest hit were those in the most vulnerable economic situations – typically, those least skilled, younger, casual workers and those in the informal sectors.

In this period of economic turmoil there were severe negative impacts on housing markets and housing opportunities. These housing market consequences were most apparent in the core Asian economy of Japan and in Korea and Thailand. There have, indeed, been striking differences in the dynamics of the housing markets of the two dominant economies of East and West. While the 1990s saw an unprecedented housing market boom in the US (Joint Center for Housing Studies 2002), Japan has wallowed in a seemingly incurable recession with negative equity and price deflation. While the rate of home-ownership in the US rose further and encompassed a wider cross section of the population, in Japan rates remained stable at around 60 per cent with substantial falls in the recruitment of young people into the tenure (Forrest *et al.* 2002).

However, as we shall see in both this chapter and in subsequent chapters, there are many points of contact and commonality between housing debates in Eastern and Western societies. Many of these points of contact are associated with the forces of change bearing down on housing provision – particularly demographic ageing, the impact of the knowledge based economy and globalization, shifts in the nature of the family and the household and changing ideologies and policy discourses. There remain, however, striking differences. Some of these differences are associated with the policies of many Asian states which have accorded priority to economic development and modernization over infrastructural investment in areas such as housing – the so-called productivist welfare state orientation (see, for example, Holliday 2000). Other differences are quite simply to do with the relative poverty of many Asian societies. While the discussions in this book focus mainly on societies which have relatively high standards of living, such as Singapore, Hong Kong and Japan, it is important to note that poverty and subsistence living is still the everyday experience in many parts of Asia.

In the period from 1960 until the Asian financial crisis, both per capita incomes and income distributions continuously improved in the Asian NICs and in some of the ASEAN countries. By the mid-1990s per capita GNP in Singapore and Hong Kong was close to, or above, that of the USA (Tan 2000). Many of the ASEAN and South Asian countries, however, saw little or very unequal progress and suffered a major reversal with the Asian financial crisis. Moreover, the shift from labour intensive, export oriented industrialization to more capital intensive industries has tended to produce more unequal income distributions in many countries. Countries such as the Philippines remain extremely poor and there are sharp contrasts between urban and rural areas in, for example, Thailand and mainland China. As Tan remarks, the grossly uneven pattern of investment and development has 'brought prosperity to Bangkok (and the southeast of the country), but left the rest of the country in a sea of poverty' (Tan 2000: 70). The most recent UN Global Report on Human Settlements (UNCHS 2001) estimated some 278 million people in East Asia and the Pacific were living on less than

US$1 a day – a slight increase from the previous assessment in 1996. The report observes that

> The decline in the numbers of the poor in Asia is almost exclusively due to a reduction in the number of poor people in East Asia, most notably in China. But progress was partly reversed by the crisis and stalled in China.
>
> (UNCHS 2001: 14)

For many households in East and South East Asia, living and housing standards remain far behind the normal expectations of Western societies. But it should be underlined that preoccupations with access to decent quality housing are not limited to the populations of the poorer countries of Asia. Many people in the more affluent countries – including their more affluent members – are second or first generation refugees with a perspective on the precariousness of life that few Europeans would now share – decent housing is very precious. In Hong Kong, for example, that quintessential symbol of economic dynamism, housing remains near if not at the top of the policy and popular agenda. For most ordinary people housing is their number one preoccupation. This is hardly surprising given the very high price-income ratios which have been prevalent in Hong Kong and extraordinarily low space standards. It is still not unusual for households to live in apartments of less than 500 square feet, often in an extended family. And home owners in Hong Kong moving from the rental to the ownership sectors typically experience a reduction in space. In the early 1990s, although Hong Kong ranked with cities such as Paris, London, Melbourne and Oslo in terms of average per capita income, in terms of floor area per person, it sat alongside Harare, Karachi and Bogota (UNCHS 1996: 198). Hong Kong remains *the* high density city – a population packed into high rise towers served by an ultra efficient public transport system – a model perhaps of environmental sustainability and efficient residential living or at least a city which raises some key questions about density, urban form and social cohesion which are currently to the fore in housing debates in many Western societies. The general point is that at an international rather than a European or North American level the housing question still represents an enormous challenge for policymakers and governments, and for many households remains a matter of pressing need rather than one of quality and choice.

Globalization and housing

It is impossible to discuss housing and social change without some reference to processes of globalization. It is, inevitably, a highly contested term with a voluminous literature on the topic devoted to both clarification and obfuscation. Held and McGrew, in their extensive collection on the cultural, social, political and economic dimensions of globalization, offer the following straightforward definition:

> Simply put, globalization denotes the expanding scale, growing magnitude, speeding up and deepening impact of interregional flows and patterns of social interaction. It refers to a shift in or transformation in the scale of human social organization that links distant communities and expands the reach of power relations across the world's major regions and continents.
>
> (Held and McGrew 2000: 4)

They then go on to point to the contradictory nature of these processes which can produce divergence as well as convergence, disharmony as well as harmony. This is a point taken up in a rather different way by McGee (2002) when he argues for an appreciation of both the local embeddedness of these so-called globalizing processes and, in particular, the differential pattern of incorporation of parts of the region into the global system. The issues of exclusion and inclusion of people and places are not restricted to processes at work in East and South East Asia – but the contrasts there are starker than in Europe. It is the mega-urban regions such as Manila and Bangkok where these processes of incorporation and connectivity have been concentrated. This has not only driven a sharper wedge between these expanding megacities and their hinterland but also heightened the vulnerability of the poor living within them (McGee 2002).

Held and McGrew also observe that amidst this discourse of global interconnectedness, 'for the most part, the routines of everyday lives are dominated by national and local circumstances' (p.5). And it is important in this context to remind ourselves that housing provision and housing markets are inherently local in nature in terms of who provides the housing, how it is marketed and how we access it to rent or buy. They require, in the main, local knowledge on the part of both agents and consumers, providers and clients. Moreover, whether we are living in London, Sydney or Singapore, we are more sedentary than we might believe. Most of us are only moderately mobile and a surprising number of households, even in the supposedly hypermobile cultures of the West, live out their lives in very limited geographic space. Everyday lives pivot around the local neighbourhood, the dwelling and place of work. Dwellings are, of course, immobile. The capital within them can be released, traded and securitized but the unique attributes of a dwelling, in terms of location, orientation and other features are fixed in space. However, substantial amounts of capital are tied up in the housing sector, and notably so in many Asian societies. The value of those investments is increasingly vulnerable to the vicissitudes of global financial flows and fickle money markets. Economic downturns, conflicts or natural disasters in one part of the globe can impact on the costs of housing finance in another. The global increasingly bears down on the local.

But there are more specific dimensions of globalization which are relevant to this discussion of housing and social change in both Asian and Western housing markets. First, there is the globalization of policy discourse. While the contexts and consequences vary dramatically between say mainland China, the UK and the USA, nonetheless the globalization of policy communities (shepherded in great measure by global organizations such as the World Bank and IMF) has produced an increasingly global policy language and policy response of privatization, deregulation, marketization and contracting out. It has become axiomatic that large, state housing bureaucracies are inefficient, expensive and distort normal market processes. The Housing Loan Corporation in Japan is being transformed into an independent agency by 2005. The Hong Kong Housing Authority, now the Housing Department, is being progressively fragmented and its functions contracted out to the private sector. The Housing Development Board in Singapore appears to be resisting these pressures but the weight of the still dominant neo-liberal orthodoxy continues to erode institutions which have made a major contribution to housing provision in various countries. This is not to suggest that these organizations were not due for reform and closer scrutiny but that the evidence justifying the need for such institutional transformations often seems to take second place to the ideology.

Moreover, if we are in many national contexts 'moving beyond the state' in terms of housing provision it is not yet clear where we are going or with what consequences for particular groups. A common policy language does not signal a convergence of housing systems or outcomes. But there is no doubt that the policy shifts, which some commentators (Harloe 1995) have portrayed as the transition from a period of exceptionalism of direct state provision and mass housing solutions, have, and are, producing new winners and losers. Very often it is those groups in the population which have been the main beneficiaries of direct state provision or substantial indirect assistance in the past which prove to be the main beneficiaries of a privatized and increasingly deregulated present. The inequalities of bureaucratic allocations systems in which privileged strata get access to the best housing generates an additional layer of rewards when these housing systems are privatized and marketized. This has been true of former state socialist societies and certainly many northern European countries (Danielli and Struyk 1994; Forrest and Murie 1990). It is also, as Davis shows in Chapter 10, evidently the case in the housing reform process in mainland China where blue collar workers gain assets of considerably less value than managers and professionals.

Second, there is a climate of greater risk, insecurity and market volatility. Influential commentators such as Beck (1992) and Castells (1996) conjure up a world where we can no longer assume the old certainties and securities of the past. In particular we can no longer assume job security. Flexible labour markets, essentially easier hire and fire regimes with more casual and insecure contracts, create conditions which are not ideal for the promotion of home-ownership. The best conditions for the development of home-ownership are arguably rising real incomes, growing job security and a good dose of inflation – the conditions prevailing in many industrial societies in the three decades following the end of the Second World War. The pressures of competitive globalization, however, drive down inflation and real incomes (for some) and increase job insecurity. Combine this with greater uncertainties about property values and the foundations of much post war housing policy are seriously shaken. While the fear of job loss or the extent of casualization may be greater than the reality, even this 'manufactured uncertainty' (Doogan 2001) has a powerful impact on popular senses of stability and security. Moreover, house prices which do not rise with expectations produce a collective sense of unease. Negative equity remains pervasive in Tokyo. Hong Kong home owners have been on the streets with placards proclaiming 'Save us from negative equity' demanding some kind of ameliorative action from the government. In Thailand, when the Asian financial crisis hit, many of the aspirant middle classes fell rapidly into debt evidenced by the half built detached houses and in some cases unfinished mansions in central Bangkok. During the late 1980s recession in Britain the government agonized over what to do about the million or so households with negative equity who were overwhelmingly concentrated in the core economic region of the country (Forrest *et al.* 1999). Even if house prices are on the mend in many parts of Asia, consumer confidence is increasingly vulnerable to the uncertainties of the residential property market. If prices are going up, people feel wealthy. They borrow and spend. If prices are moving in the opposite direction general consumption can be rapidly depressed. John Calverley, the Chief Economist with the American Express Bank, has commented that, 'In a diverse range of countries including the UK, Japan, South and East Asia, and recently the United States, booms and busts in property and/or stock prices have played a crucial role in the business cycle' (Calverley 2002).

Third, real estate is deeply implicated in general financial flows, perhaps the most unambiguously global process. Changes in its value can impact significantly on macro economies. This was clearly evident in the Asian financial crisis with the high levels of collateralization of bank loans against real estate. Prior to the bursting of the bubble economy some 70 per cent of lending by some Japanese banks was secured against real estate (Forrest *et al.* 2002). In Hong Kong, real estate accounted for almost half of total lending in 1997 (Fung and Forrest 2002). The investment which fuels those markets is embedded in global processes. Residential property sits within an increasingly global market – sometimes literally as is evident from the adverts for luxury apartments in London or Vancouver in Hong Kong newspapers – but more fundamentally as mortgage portfolios became tradeable assets. Home-ownership embodies this juxtaposition of the local and the global as a use value (locally rooted lived experience) and as something to be traded (exchange value) on the international money markets.

The Asian financial crisis produced the kinds of debates in, for example, Japan and Hong Kong which were prominent in the UK after the late 1980s recession in that property market (Forrest *et al.* 1999). There was the view that the slide in property values had changed attitudes to home-ownership fundamentally. From now on people would regard housing as something to live in rather than as a speculative investment. Given the slow recovery of property markets in East and South East Asia it is difficult to pass judgement on whether attitudes towards residential property investment have changed – especially given the volatility of stock markets as an alternative. But if Western experience is a guide then caution among institutions and households is likely to be relatively short-lived if markets recover strongly. Marginal properties and marginal borrowers may face greater difficulties in attracting finance but it is only a particular cohort of purchasers which will have actually experienced negative equity or more damaging consequences. For the cohorts which preceded the Asian financial crisis and for those which follow the experience of property investment may be considerably more positive.

There is therefore unlikely to be a significant retreat from home-ownership as a result of the economic disturbances of the 1990s – unless, of course, government policies, East and West, change dramatically. There is, however, some evidence that for a younger generation priorities are changing. In Japan, for example, the rate of home-ownership among younger people has fallen notably in recent years (see Forrest *et al.* 2002; Hirayama in this collection). Part of the explanation lies certainly in the greater difficulties faced by young people in the job market. But there may be other factors driven by colder financial judgements about how to best invest one's resources. Changes in the tax regime in the USA, for example, has apparently been one factor which has prompted a move among some younger households from home-ownership to private rental (*Realty Times* 2000). They could realize a capital gain and relocate to a part of the city more compatible with their cosmopolitan lifestyles. And a senior partner in one of the major property firms in Singapore offered this rather postmodern explanation for the apparent retreat from home-ownership by young Singaporeans: he commented that,

> The knowledge based economy will produce a paradigm shift in the way real estate is viewed. ... The KBE stresses the primacy of the immaterial over the material, of the virtual over the real or physical like real estate. The development of capital markets which allows people to own a piece of property through a real estate investment reduces the inherent value of physical property by making it much more of a commodity.
>
> (*Business Times Online* 2000)

In other words, live in a serviced apartment in downtown Singapore and take your pick of real estate globally. To anticipate Harvey Perkins and David Thorns' chapter later in this collection, is that part of the meaning of home in a global world? Will East meet West in increasingly virtual transactions in a global real estate market?

Home-ownership, wealth accumulation and rising inequality

These transformations in the structure of labour markets and in the nature of employment are central to contemporary housing debates – whether in terms of absolute housing shortages and affordability problems, or in terms of changing household structures as patterns of labour force participation change. Linked to these developments is the important issue of the extent to which the housing opportunities which have been available to previous generations will be available to subsequent ones. East and West, the growth of mortgaged, urban home-ownership in a variety of forms created new opportunities for post Second World War generations. In parallel, various governments intervened in the provision of state housing and provided a critical ingredient for the expansion of home-ownership through various privatization policies. For countries such as Singapore, since 1964, this has been part of a conscious, nation building strategy to secure greater social cohesion through state assisted home-ownership. Echoing political statements found in the European, Australasian and North American literature, Lee Kuan Yew writes that, 'My primary preoccupation was to give every citizen a stake in the country and its future. I wanted a home owning society.' He continues,

> After independence in 1965, I was troubled by Singapore's completely urban electorate. I had seen how voters in capital cities always tended to vote against the government of the day and was determined that our householders should become home owners, otherwise we would not have political stability. My other important motive was to give all parents whose sons would have to do national service a stake in the Singapore their sons would have to defend.
>
> (Lee 2000: 96–7)

By contrast, as is well documented (e.g. Castells *et al.* 1990), Hong Kong's housing policy differed significantly from Singapore in involving large scale, public rental housing. Mass provision for rent was, however, gradually combined with schemes to assist directly or indirectly the growth of home-ownership. Policies to encourage tenant purchase have also been introduced in recent years. These sorts of schemes are close in form and content to the kinds of policies favoured in many European countries – fuelled in particular by Margaret Thatcher's neo-liberal Right to Buy policies in Britain. The stated aspiration of the Hong Kong's Long Term Housing Strategy is now to achieve a 70 per cent home-ownership rate by 2007.

State assistance with home-ownership has coincided with periods of rapid house price inflation, relatively high levels of job security and rising real incomes to produce particular cohorts within Eastern and Western societies which have experienced substantial real growth in their asset bases. These relatively privileged cohorts who boarded the policy convoy at the most fortuitous point in the economic and housing market cycle may have housing trajectories in sharp contrast to a new generation (and to others without the same set of opportunities in their own generation) which confront more targeted state subsidies, and changed or less certain economic conditions. While the scale of this wealth accumulation, its history and the social implications vary both within Western and Eastern societies, there is no doubt that it is a significant element of the contemporary housing question specifically and in the emergence of new forms of class divisions more generally (for an extended discussion see Forrest and Murie 1995).

Moreover, as has been argued, it is in the Tiger and Cub economies of South and East Asia, and particularly the major cities, where rapid and compressed economic growth has often produced extraordinary rates of house price inflation (see, for example, Bootle 1996). While the Asian financial crisis saw a slump in property values, over the longer term the more fortunate cohorts of purchasers have experienced novel and substantial wealth accumulation through home-ownership.

What distinguishes this form of home-ownership from other types of residential ownership is the fusion of cultural and material capital. While land and property investment has long been of importance in sustaining economic and cultural elites in Asian societies, these contemporary forms provide the material (through asset appreciation) and symbolic (through location, design) basis for middle class membership. The asset value of residential property provides collateral for general consumption and a cosmopolitan lifestyle, offers the potential for financing social protection where state protection is limited or contracting and is pivotal to social status and economic participation. Talib (2000) in a recent collection on the changing nature and role of consumerism in Asian societies, focuses on the consumption habits of a new, state promoted Malaysian urban middle class and their search for greater economic and cultural capital via investment in education and positional status through house, real estate and car purchase. He observes that the fashionable living shifted from bungalows in the 1960s to downtown condos and apartments by the early 1990s and that the owners of such properties enjoyed substantial asset appreciation – in some cases a doubling of market value in three years. And this is a key feature of housing. Unlike cars, hi-fis, designer clothing and so on, housing is both investment and consumption. The desirable dwelling purchased at the right time can deliver both social status and wealth accumulation.

What is evident from most accounts of the old 'new' middle classes of Europe or North America or the 'new' middle classes of South and East Asia is that whatever else constitutes middle classness, the ownership of a house or apartment is generally a prerequisite. A piece in *Asia Business Times* (1996) titled 'Homes for the "tiger" generation' commented that for Bangkok's increasingly affluent urban professionals and entrepreneurs, 'buying a home is a priority purchase for anyone in the so-called middle class'. And Lee (1999) has addressed the issue in relation to Hong Kong arguing that (at least prior to the fall in property values in the late 1990s) life chances had been transformed to such an extent by the appreciation of residential properties that some middle class families could sell up, move to Canada or Australia and live on the interest for the rest of their lives without having to have a job.

Compared with the European or North American situation, these developments in East and South East Asia have occurred within a highly compressed period and the rate and levels of asset appreciation have been greater. The intergenerational contrasts are starker and the demographic profile of this new residentially wealthy generation is generally younger than its Western counterpart.

Governments, both East and West, have become more interested in the accumulative potential of home-ownership as populations age and public resources become more stretched and pressurized. This has been particularly evident in Japan, with its rapidly ageing population, and in countries such as the UK with very mature home-ownership sectors in terms of their demography and the available financial instruments (Forrest and Murie 1995; Hamnett *et al.* 1991). The relatively early development of mortgaged, urban home-ownership in, for example, the UK or Australia, has created ageing cohorts approaching or past retirement. This has generated debates around issues of inheritance, lifetime transfers and on the extent to which this form of wealth accumulation is modifying or exacerbating existing class inequalities.

The differential accumulation of housing related wealth is overlain on income structures which in many contexts have also shown signs of rising, rather than falling levels of inequality. Various analysts have highlighted the deteriorating employment capital for the low skilled in today's Knowledge Based Economy (for example, Castells 1996). The potential divisions between the haves and have nots across Eastern and Western societies appear to be growing rather than diminishing. In the Asian context it is important to acknowledge the tremendous improvements in the living standards and life chances of significant numbers of households in terms of higher real incomes, better health, better education and better housing. It is also important to bear in mind that current levels of GDP growth in many parts of Asia still far outstrip those in Europe and North America and are expected to grow further, particularly in China. Nevertheless, growing disparities in income and wealth which are to some extent themselves the product of housing market dynamics and which will also produce disparities in access to decent housing, are likely to represent a significant fault line in many Asian societies. Rapid urbanization, perhaps most notably in China, combined with new entrepreneurial freedoms and state assistance in various forms (e.g. low cost housing for urban residents) has produced major disparities of income and wealth between urban and rural areas. The World Bank report in 1997 highlighted 'concern about increasing income inequalities in China and Thailand'. It went on,

> The region faces rapid urbanization, formalization of labor markets, and an aging population, all raising new challenges and posing new risks as people's

earlier informal ways of supporting the sick, disabled, unemployed and elderly fall into decline and the need for formal mechanisms increases.

(World Bank 1997: 51)

And drawing on official statistics a report in *The Economist* (2001: 72) high-lighted the growing social tensions in China as rural income levels diverge from those in the major cities, and as disparities grow within urban areas. The Gini coefficient is now hovering around the 0.4 mark – indicating major inequalities in the distribution of income. 'The richest 20 per cent of urban households receive 42 per cent of total urban income, whereas the poorest 20 per cent receive only 6.5 per cent.' Knowles observes that while economic development raises the overall standard of living, income inequalities also tend to rise in the faster developing economies. 'The relatively high level of economic development in Malaysia and Thailand is accompanied by relatively large disparities between rich and poor. By contrast, income inequality is comparatively low in the poor countries of South Asia' (Knowles 2000: 1).

Evidence from Hong Kong and Singapore also shows that the least skilled are falling behind – raising fears about future social cohesion and the need for greater attention to social security provision and welfare safety nets. A report in the *New Straits Times* refers to Singapore's 'income gap' as revealed by offical government statistics. It shows a significant increase in the average family monthly income of some 60 per cent but 'the 20 per cent of households in the upper income bracket earned 21 times more than the lowest 20 per cent, up from 11.4 times in 1990 and 17.9 times in 1999' (*New Straits Times* 2002). Hong Kong has seen a similar process as the least skilled have fallen behind, as manufacturing has moved across the border and as a result of the corporate restructuring following the Asian financial crisis. A report on labour market conditions in Hong Kong claims that 'The income gap between rich and poor has almost doubled: the ratio of average per capita household income between the richest and poorest deciles rose from 10.8 to 1 in 1990 to 19.2 to 1 in 1999' (Social and Economic Policy Institute 2001). The official census confirms that compared with 1991 the share of overall household income of the lowest decile group has fallen from 1.3 per cent to 0.9 per cent. In parallel, the share of the highest decile group has increased from 37.3 per cent to 41.2 per cent (Census and Statistics Department 2002). The same picture emerges in other countries such as Thailand and Taiwan. These developments were evident long before the Asian financial crisis but the social consequences of that severe economic downturn fell disproportionately on the poorer and least skilled sections of the societies affected (Hewison 2001). In some circumstances, the richer sections of society may have gained. For example, an early analysis of the impact on the Korean income structure (Moon *et al.* 1999) showed that in the immediate aftermath of the crisis 'the degree of reduction [of income] gets larger as the income level decreases'. It continues,

In contrast, the average income of the top 10 per cent of the households actually rose by 3.2 per cent during the same period. Considering the fact that the market interest rate was extremely high during the first quarter of 1998, we can easily guess that this rise in income was mainly attributable to the increased return from their financial assets.

(Moon *et al.* 1999: 38)

Housing systems and demographic change

These trends in income and wealth inequalities coalesce with demographic change. In all societies shifts in the population structure are a primary pressure on housing systems and are certain to become more marked in both Eastern and Western societies in the next decade. Pre-existing housing systems and housing stocks often have to accommodate rapid demographic transformations associated with shifts in social and behavioural norms or in some cases large scale in or outmigration. Indeed, the pace of demographic change need not be that dynamic to outpace the capacity of markets or states to provide appropriate dwellings in appropriate locations. The rate of dwelling replacement or structural adaptation is always likely to lag behind changing household behaviour.

The key trends in demography are declining fertility and greater longevity. It is well established in the demographic literature that the latter almost always precedes the former in what is generally referred to as the first demographic transition. Populations rise as individuals live longer but the birth rate remains high (Bongaarts and Bulatao 1999). The second demographic transition refers to changing patterns of household formation associated with changing social norms such as increased divorce, separation and earlier departure from the parental home. Many Western countries have experienced rapidly falling fertility rates, a substantial increase in single person households, escalating divorce and lone parenthood, and ageing populations. Some of these trends have been most marked in recent years in countries which have long been associated with the more traditional and extended family forms such as Greece, Portugal and Spain. Fukuyama (1999) sees this demographic transformation as a key element of what he refers to as the 'great disruption' of the contemporary social order. He describes a number of Western societies as being in the process of 'depopulating themselves' (p.38). These trends are not, of course, confined to the West. Japan, most notably, has one of the most rapidly ageing populations and very low fertility rates (World Bank 2000). Fukuyama (1999) notes that in countries such as Spain, Italy and Japan fertility rates have fallen so far below replacement that 'their total population in each successive generation will be 30 per cent smaller than the previous one' (p.39). And demographic ageing is a strong feature of Singapore, Hong Kong and South Korea's population structures (ADB 2002). While divorce and separation rates are low by European or North American standards in South and East Asia they are rising nevertheless. The extended family also remains of considerably greater importance in much of Asia but as in countries in the southern Mediterranean such as Portugal or Greece it is gradually withering away. The trend is towards smaller households, later marriage, fewer children and an increase in independent living. If we take Hong Kong as an example all these trends are evident. Comparing 1981 and 1996 the marriage rate per 1000 for females fell from 12.9 to 9.5, the median age of first marriage for males rose from 28.6 to 29.8, average household size fell from 3.7 to 3.3 and the divorce rate rose from 0.56 to 2.42 (Census and Statistics Department 1999).

All these social trends have implications for the way housing systems work. Even with stable or shrinking populations, changing social norms and expectations combined with rising affluence can produce substantially increased housing demand as rates of household formation rise. Divorce, separation and remarriage produce new patterns of household fission and fusion contributing to less predictable housing needs over the life course, and expansions and contractions of space requirements. Moreover, if informal processes of mutual aid within and between families have traditionally been important forms of assistance in both material and non-material ways, new and disruptive processes of family household dissolution can create considerable social stress. This is particularly true in the absence of alternative forms of publicly funded support or where such support networks are being eroded.

The interaction between demographic change and changes in housing policy can also produce varied impacts in different countries. Most obviously, governments are likely to face very different sets of policy issues if they are coping with a nation of rapidly ageing renters compared with a nation of rapidly ageing home owners. The ageing process may have very different implications for social and housing policy, particularly if the ageing cohort of owners have substantial resources to mobilize in their old age. And there are complex relationships between particular population cohorts and the shifts in housing policy and housing provision. Cohorts of varying sizes will have had their housing histories and opportunities shaped in distinctive ways – this coincidence of demography, policy change and shifting economic fortunes will generate uneven impacts on the housing system as these cohorts age and move through the population structure.

Conclusion – old questions, new answers?

This chapter has aimed to provide a general context for the more focused and specific discussions which follow. Inevitably, this discussion will be partial and will neglect or deal only tangentially with some of the key issues which have been raised. The changing nature and role of housing provision links to a wide range of policy areas and theoretical debates. Moreover, the book is dealing with a broad canvas of societies in which there are major differences in policy histories, developmental paths, institutional structures and demographies. Nevertheless, the selected authors draw on their specific examples to address such pressing issues as sustainable development, social exclusion and inequality, economic instability, diversity and social fragmentation and the changing position of state involvement in housing provision. In anticipating these subsequent discussions it is tempting to try and force some uniformity of perspective on the relationships between housing and social change. But that would be premature and, indeed, may be inappropriate and conceptually erroneous. We shall return to that discussion in the final chapter. However, the overall aim of the book was not to force a set of authors into one mould but to offer a variety of windows through which to view the housing question in the contemporary world. Indeed, topics and authors were selected intentionally to expose the very different current preoccupations of housing analysts.

Nevertheless, whether East or West, there would appear to be a current consensus that the old answers no longer seem to work. This applies, for example, to the role of mass rental housing, to the boundaries between the market and the state, to the separation of housing policy from other areas of social policy or, indeed, in terms of the promotion of home-ownership. Social and economic conditions have it seems changed to the extent that we need to move beyond established housing policies and forms of provision. New and more fragmented institutional structures, new financial products, and a greater variation in types of provision are all emerging amidst substantial shifts in occupational and household structures.

But if that is the case, it is debatable how far the fundamental questions have changed. What is gained from drawing on a wide range of societies is a perspective which hopefully avoids an ethnocentric view of the contemporary housing question. While policymakers may spend considerable time fine-tuning the policy details we need to remind ourselves that for many thousands of households fundamental questions of basic, affordable housing remain unanswered. In this context, we can return to Engels' original construction of the housing question. Northern European cities may have been transformed over the last century or so but the housing question overall is still very much about these fundamental processes of urbanization and industrialization. The geography has changed – then it was Manchester, now it is Manila – the exploding cities now are in Asia and Latin America. According to UN projections, by 2015 cities such as Jakarta and Manila will have experienced annual growth rates of 1–3 per cent and Asia will contain more than half of the world's megacities (UNCHS 2001). And the Asian Development Bank has estimated that some 120 million people have moved into Chinese cities from the countryside (ADB 2002). In this context, Sudjic remarks,

> Between 1810 and 1850, Manchester's population increased by 40 per cent every 10 years. It became a gigantic mechanism for the creation of wealth,

and the transformation of rural migrants into city dwellers. Manchester invented the factory, the railway station, the civic university, and the back-to-back house. Asia's vast new cities are doing the equivalent for the next century.

(Sudjic 1996: 37)

And to draw even closer parallels with Engels' commentaries, it is a world in which urban proletarianization remains a dominant force. While much of the Western literature talks of a postindustial world, from an Asian perspective things look rather different. The city states of Hong Kong or Singapore may be dominated by the service and financial sectors but the patterns of urban and employment change elsewhere are very different. As Neil Smith has rather pointedly observed, while Western academics have been preoccupied with postmodernism and postindustrialism,

Since the late 1960s, East and South East Asia especially, from China and Korea round to India and Pakistan, have undergone an industrial expansion unparalleled in human history. The industrial revolution of eighteenth century England, often treated as paradigmatic, pales by comparison.

(Smith 2000: 1014)

He comments more generally that 'In retrospect, the ideology of a "postindustrial society" should come to be seen as one of the grand conceits of "First World" social science' (Smith 2000: 1014).

This new phase of proletarianization has also involved a substantial recruitment of women into the industrial workforce of the region so there has been a change not only of geography but to a significant degree of gender. The general point is that in assessing the housing question at the beginning of the twenty-first century from an East-West perspective it is as much about housing a low paid, urban industrial proletariat as an expanding middle class. Moreover, this expanded Asian proletariat, with their poor working conditions and their often weak position in the housing market, meet their Western counterparts in the low waged, often illegal immigrant workforce in the major cities of the West. Ross (2001) argues that 'wherever globalization unites, in the same industries, labor reserves of workers in richer countries with those in poorer ones, the tendency is for standards of employment in the richer countries to descend, often sinking below nominally legal standards' (p.4).

So the housing question at the beginning of the twenty-first century, from a global perspective, has not changed perhaps as much as we might believe. Moreover, housing remains in a pivotal position in both generating and reflecting wider social and economic changes. This is perhaps most clearly seen in the importance of housing reforms in mainland China or Russia and in the importance of the housing sector in the developmental strategies of the Tiger and Cub economies of South and East Asia.

And for the moment at least, there is a widespread policy commitment to the development of various forms of home-ownership as a basic element of social and economic cohesion. But are we now entering a period where we shall witness a retreat from these policy priorities and perhaps even a significant revival of new forms of market renting in the wake of greater economic turbulence and changing social norms?

The ownership of land and dwellings has particular cultural resonance in this region and links to the continuing if perhaps waning importance of the family. The Asian financial crisis and the continuing depressed state of many residential real estate markets has begged some fundamental questions about the relationship between the property sectors and the wider economy. Most directly, the disproportionate reliance on real estate as a source of corporate profit, as security for bank lending and as a key source of social security and social protection for individual households has been exposed as problematic when economic conditions change. Any substantial shift in faith by institutions or households in the investment value of residential property would indeed signal a major shift in individual priorities and occasion wider social changes. At the time of writing, some residential property markets and submarkets are magnets for growing amounts of footloose capital in search of more secure investments than stocks and shares. At the same time some property markets remain as depressed as the economies in which they are embedded. In this uncertain economic context, the risks are being unambiguously transferred onto individual households through the need for personal mortgage insurance, more stringent subsidies regimes and a general retreat from state intervention. Growing social tensions may force a change of direction. But for the immediate future, at least, the scenario is of differential bargaining power in housing markets which are generally being increasingly privatized.

References

Asia Business Times (1996) 'Homes for the "Tiger" generation'. Available online http://web3.asia1.com.sg/data/ab/docs/ab1055.html.
Asian Development Bank (2002) *Key Indicators 2002: Population and Human Resources*, Manila: Asian Development Bank.
Bank of International Settlements (1997) *67th Annual Report*, Basel: BIS.
Beck, U. (1992) *Risk Society: Towards a New Modernity*, London: Sage.
Bongaarts, J. and Bulatao, R. (1999) 'Completing the Demographic Transition', *Population and Development Review*, 25 (3): 515–29.
Bootle, R. (1996) *The Death of Inflation*, London: Nicholas Brealey.
Business Times Online (2000) 'Rent or Buy?' Available online http://business-times.asia1.com/.
Calverley, J. (2002) 'The Power of Asset Prices', *The International Economy*, 16 (1): 55–7.
Castells, M. (1996) *The Rise of the Network Society*, Oxford: Blackwell.

Castells, M., Goh, L. and Kwok, R.-Y. (1990) *The Skek Kip Mei Syndrome*, London: Pion.

Census and Statistics Department, Hong Kong SAR (1999) *Hong Kong Social and Economic Trends*, Hong Kong SAR: Census and Statistics Department.

—— (2002) *2001 Population Census*, Hong Kong SAR: Census and Statistics Department.

Danielli, J. and Struyk, R. (1994) 'Housing Privatization in Moscow: Who Privatizes and Why', *International Journal of Urban and Regional Research*, 18: 510–25.

Doogan, K. (2001) 'Insecurity and Long Term Unemployment', *Work, Employment and Society*, 15 (3): 419–41.

The Economist (2001) 'Income Distribution in China', 2 June 2001.

Engels, F. (1988) 'The Housing Question', in Marx, K. and Engels, F. *Collected Works Volume 23*, Moscow: Progress Publishers.

Forrest, R., Kennett, P. and Izuhara, M. (2002) 'Home Ownership and Economic Change in Japan', *Housing Studies*, 18 (3): 277–93.

Forrest, R., Kennett, P. and Leather, P. (1999) *Home Ownership in Crisis? The British Experience of Negative Equity*, Aldershot: Ashfield.

Forrest, R. and Murie, A. (1990) *Selling the Welfare State: The Privatisation of Public Housing*, London: Routledge.

—— (1995) *Housing and Family Wealth: Comparative International Perspectives*, London: Routledge.

Fukuyama, F. (1999) *The Great Disruption: Human Nature and the Reconstitution of Social Order*, New York: The Free Press.

Fung, K.K. and Forrest, R. (2002) 'Institutional Mediation, The Asian Financial Crisis and the Hong Kong Residential Housing Market', *Housing Studies*, 17 (2): 189–208.

Hamnett, C., Harmer, M. and Williams, P. (1991) *Safe As Houses – Housing Inheritance in Britain*, London: Paul Chapman.

Harloe, M. (1995) *The People's Home? Social Rented Housing in Europe and America*, Oxford: Blackwell.

Held, D. and McGrew, A. (2000) *The Global Transformation Reader*, Cambridge: Polity Press.

Hewison, K. (2001) 'Thailand: Class Matters'. Paper presented to conference 'On the Roots of Growth and Crisis. Capitalism, State and Society in East Asia', Cortona, Italy, March.

Holliday, I. (2000) 'Productivist Welfare Capitalism: Social Policy in East Asia', *Political Studies*, 48: 706–23.

Joint Center for Housing Studies at Harvard University (2002) *The State of the Nation's Housing*, Harvard.

Knowles, J. (2000) 'A Look at Poverty in the Developing Countries of Asia', *Asia-Pacific Population and Policy*, No. 52, 1–4, Honolulu: East–West Centre.

Lee, J. (1999) *Housing, Home Ownership and Social Change in Hong Kong*, Aldershot: Ashgate.

Lee, K. Y. (2000) *From Third World to First: The Singapore Story: 1965–2000*, New York: HarperCollins.

McGee, T.G. (2002) 'Reconstructing The Southeast Asian City in an era of Volatile Globalization', *Asian Journal of Social Sciences*, 30 (1): 8–27.

Moon, H., Lee, H. and Yoo, G. (1999) *Economic Crisis and Its Social Consequences*, Seoul: Korea Development Institute.

New Straits Times (2002) 'Singapore Rapped Over Income Gap', 20 April 2002.

Realty Times (2000) 'High Income Earners Consider Renting Chic Again', 7 July 2000. Available online http://realtytimes.com/rtnews/rtcpages/20000707_renters.html.

Ross, R. (2001) 'Vulnerable Labour in Global Capitalism'. Paper presented at conference on 'Labour in a Globalising World', City University of Hong Kong, 4–6 January.

Smith, N. (2000) 'What Happened to Class?', *Environment and Planning A*, 32: 1011–32.

Social and Economic Policy Institute (2001) *Current Labour Market Conditions in Hong Kong*, Hong Kong: Social and Economic Policy Institute.

Sudjic, D. (1996) 'Metropolis Now: Hong Kong, Shanghai, Jakarta', *City*, 1 (2): 30–7.

Talib, R. (2000) 'Malaysia: Power Shifts and the Matrix of Consumption', in Chua, B.-H. *Consumption in Asia: Lifestyles and Identities*, London: Routledge.

Tan, G. (2000) *Asian Development*, Singapore: Times Academic Press.

UNCHS (1996) *An Urbanising World – Global Report on Human Settlements*, Oxford: Oxford University Press.

—— (2001) *Cities in a Globalising World*, London: Earthscan Publishing.

World Bank (1997) *Annual Report*, Washington: World Bank.

—— (2000) *World Development Indicators*, Washington: World Bank.

2 Home-ownership in East and South East Asia

Market, state and institutions

James Lee, Ray Forrest and Wai Keung Tam

Introduction

Unlike many Western societies, the rise of individual home-ownership in East Asia is a comparatively recent phenomenon. Except in Singapore where the government began to promote home-ownership in the 1960s, contemporary forms of urban home-ownership existed on only a very small scale in most South and East Asian countries until the 1970s. However, its development path accelerated towards the last quarter of the twentieth century and was closely associated with rapid economic growth of the so-called 'tiger economies'. Indeed, one of the key themes that stands out in any study of East Asian development is this intriguing link between the real estate sector and the wider economy, and how the state has mediated that relationship.

This relationship between government strategies for economic growth and the property and land markets can create a confusing picture for Western observers used to sharper, if sometimes highly contested, distinctions between market and state provision in the housing sector. From a Western perspective, home-ownership is usually placed towards the commodified end of the commodification/ decommodification continuum with forms of social/public housing towards the decommodified end along with informal provision such as squatting. Home-ownership is associated generally with private market processes, perhaps with modest assistance from government in the form of tax breaks or targeted low cost entry schemes. The development of home-ownership has in the main been through the activities of private developers and private households rather than the product of pervasive and direct state intervention and orchestration (although privatization policies such as the Right to Buy in the UK could, of course, be argued to be precisely that). In some parts of South and East Asia, however, the productivist logic of the so-called developmental state has firmly embraced the housing market with the promotion of home-ownership being more closely associated with public intervention than the private market.

This chapter explores home-ownership as a focal point of both household investment and government social and economic policy in South East and East Asia. It focuses particularly on the six nations/city states of Japan, Taiwan, Singapore, Thailand, South Korea and Hong Kong to draw out the different forms and trajectories of home-ownership in the region. The key local institutional arrangements are highlighted as are the exogenous economic effects of the recent Asian financial crisis, local institutional arrangements and the development of contemporary forms of home-ownership. The next section offers an overview of the development of home-ownership. This is then followed by a case-by-case account of the key features of the various housing systems and an assessment of the specific impact of the economic downturn of the late 1990s on the respective housing systems. The chapter concludes with a discussion of the reshaping of these housing systems in the aftermath of the Asian financial crisis and a more general consideration of the position and development of home-ownership in the region.

The rise of home-ownership in East Asia

What has been the general pattern of development of home-ownership in the post war period across our six societies? As Table 2.1 shows, ownership levels vary from around 52 per cent in Hong Kong to 86 per cent in Singapore and 85 per cent in Taiwan. These figures, however, embrace a variety of forms of home-ownership and are the product of a contrasting mix of policies and processes. In particular, as in such European comparisons, traditional rural forms of home-ownership sit with more contemporary, loan financed urban forms in the statistics. So, for example, in Thailand the level of home-ownership in Bangkok is around 50 per cent, much lower than the national figure which encompasses more traditional rural forms. By way of contrast, home-ownership in Hong Kong or Singapore is almost comprehensively contemporary and urban. With that cautionary note in mind it is evident that the overall pattern of development of individual home-ownership varies considerably. While Taiwan, Singapore and Hong Kong have experienced an increase in owner occupation rates, Japan has recorded relatively stable rates over the last decades and South Korea and Thailand have seen rates falling. The table also shows, that as in Europe, the level of home-ownership varies inversely with GNP per capita. In other words, and counterintuitively, the wealthiest societies have the lowest levels of home-ownership. And Hong Kong and Japan, with the lowest levels of home-ownership, also have the highest house price to income ratios.

Table 2.1 A comparison of housing indicators in East Asian economies[a]

	GDP Per capita[a] in US$	% Owner occupier[b]	% Public housing[b]	Ratio house price to income[c]
Japan	34,375	60	7	11.6
Singapore	26,702	86	82	2.8
Hong Kong	24,879	52	45	7.4
Thailand	1,903	82	8	4.1
Taiwan	13,248	85	5	6.1
South Korea	6,908	75	8	5.0

Notes:

a. Figures from Japan: GDP per capita in 1999; Singapore, Hong Kong, Thailand, South Korea: GDP per capita in 1998; Taiwan: GNP per capita in 1999 (GDP per capita was not available for Taiwan). Sources: *Major Statistics of Korean Economy 2000.9*; *Statistical Indicators for Asia and the Pacific*, December 1999; *Taiwan Statistical Data Book 2000*.
b. Figures from Japan: 1998; Singapore: 1999; Hong Kong: 2000; Taiwan: 1997; South Korea: 1995; Thailand: 1996. Sources: *Housing Statistics of Japan 1998*; *Yearbook of Statistics Singapore*; *Hong Kong Housing in Figures 2000*; *Social Indicators of the Republic of China 1997*, p. 98; *Republic of Korea 1995 Population and Housing Census Report Volume 1 Whole Country (2)*; *Thailand Report of Housing Survey 1996*.
c. Ratio of median price of dwelling to median annual household income.

Hong Kong and Singapore as quintessential urban city states have sharply differing housing tenure histories. From encompassing a fifth of the population in the early 1960s, Lee Kuan Yew's determination to create a cohesive, home-owning society (Lee 2000a) had by 1999 produced almost universal home-ownership (86 per cent). In Hong Kong, however, half the population continue to rent, predominantly from the Housing Department (formerly the Hong Kong Housing Authority). Home-ownership has risen among moderate-income households with various state-assisted schemes introduced since the late 1970s but it has been a relatively slow upward trajectory. In both cases, however, direct state provision has been absolutely central to housing and economic policy. This contrasts with the other two tigers of South Korea and Taiwan. Again, in this case, two rather similar approaches to housing policy have produced wildly differing results.

In both Taiwan and South Korea, housing provision has been seen as of secondary importance to the central goal of economic development, or at least government policy has been guided by the view that housing problems would be gradually solved as economic development proceeded and real incomes rose. Yoon (1994) refers to this as essentially a 'filtering up' approach. With limited developmental resources, therefore, the Korean government chose to invest in what it saw as more directly productive areas (mainly heavy industries) although it has taken a directive role in housing provision. An undeveloped mortgage finance system combined with high price-income ratios has meant, however, that prospective buyers have had to fund the purchase outright. These factors, among others, have resulted in a decline in the level of home-ownership, which has only recently seen a modest reversal.

Like Korea, in Taiwan there has been limited state direct provision in housing (5 per cent of total housing). Both countries have very small state rental sectors. Taiwan, however, has had a high level of home-ownership throughout its post war history. As with all the new Asian NICs the label of 'home-ownership' only acquires the ingredients for any meaningful comparison with other industrialized nations of Europe or North America as its economic transformation is also paralleled by the urbanization and commercialization of its housing. In Taiwan, for example, prior to the mid-1960s self-help and squatter housing were dominant with very limited commercial housing production (Li 1998). Substantial housing investment and output occurred, however, throughout the 1970s and 1980s producing a level of home-ownership of over 70 per cent by the mid-1980s. State involvement has been limited to direct provision in response to housing crises occasioned by natural disasters and to quasi-Keynesian economic policies during the early 1980s. During that period public housing construction was boosted to stimulate the economy generally but also to aid the construction sector. Beyond that, government involvement in the home-ownership sector has focused on regulatory measures in relation to mortgage and loan finance. Home-ownership in Taiwan has developed via a system of pre-sale in which the amount of capital tied up by developers is reduced through incremental payments from purchasers as the building progresses (Li 1998). The down payments are supported by mortgage finance from private banks that have generally covered 70 per cent or more of the purchase price.

In Thailand the national level of home-ownership stood at 82 per cent in 1996 – a fall of 7 per cent in two decades (Thailand National Statistical Office 1996). However, contrasts between the urban and non-urban areas are very evident in terms of levels of affluence, tenure and dwelling type. Bangkok in particular experienced a building boom for home-ownership prior to the Asian financial crisis with rapidly rising incomes among an expanding middle class. Nevertheless, home-ownership in the municipal areas of Thailand stood at 51 per cent in 1996 compared with 90 per cent for non-municipal areas (Thailand National Statistical Office 1996). And while 90 per cent of households in the more rural areas live in detached houses, this is true of just over 40 per cent of those in Bangkok and other more urban areas. Private renting, therefore, continues to be an important form of provision in the cities. Public rental housing represents a small (8 per cent) and decreasing proportion of Bangkok's dwelling stock. The principal vehicle of government intervention in housing has been the Government Housing Bank. This was established in 1953 to provide loan finance for both developers and individual purchasers. As the Thai economy developed, its role became more extensive with the rising affluence of consumers, shifts in government policy and the increasing number of private developers. High loan to value ratios, cheap loans and beneficial taxation have all been factors encouraging the growth of commercially mortgaged home-ownership. Unfortunately, as will be discussed later, an increasingly deregulated finance market with lenders competing eagerly for business combined with rampant price inflation in the early to mid-1990s and led to a spectacular collapse. By the end of 1996 it was estimated that some 14 per cent of Bangkok's housing was vacant (Richupan 1999). The property market has remained depressed with only a modest, very uneven and precarious recovery evident by 2002.

Home-ownership trends in Japan reflect a combination of factors. They have fallen less steeply than in South Korea but are lower than in the immediate post war period and have remained relatively stable over the last three decades (Freeman *et al.* 1996). The most potent has been the rapid increase in land costs which has created major affordability difficulties. According to Hayakawa (1987), between 1955 and 1983 the average cost of housing land in the major urban areas increased by 71 times. Even with low interest loans available from the Government Housing Loan Corporation, the major mortgage provider, home-ownership was beyond the reach of an increasing number of households. More recent trends in relation to declining home-ownership rates among young people have been linked to decreasing job security, falling private rental costs and the bursting of the bubble economy in 1989 (Forrest *et al.* 2000).

The nature of home-ownership and the growth and development trajectories of the sector in South East and East Asian societies have therefore been very different. We now turn to look in more detail at these different institutional structures and mechanisms and at the varied impact of the Asian financial crisis on these housing systems.

Housing institutions and the impact of the Asian financial crisis

Hong Kong

The Hong Kong government has always been proactive in the housing sector. This is evidenced by a relatively large public housing sector and the varying measures launched in the last two decades to promote home-ownership. Table 2.2 shows that the housing system in Hong Kong is almost equally divided between the public and the private sector. In the last decade, there has been a clear trend for the government to contract its role in public housing and deregulate the private housing market. The delicate balance between both sectors has sometimes been hard to strike and this has been further complicated by the impact of the Asian financial crisis both on households and the housing market.

Since the initiation of the Ten-Year Housing Plan in 1972 the Hong Kong government has pumped substantial resources into building public rental housing.

Table 2.2 Housing provision in Hong Kong

	Public	*Private*
Actual number of housing units (1999)	970,000 (47.5%)	1,072,000 (52.5%)
Home-ownership rate	32%	71%
Rental rate	68%	29%
Annual housing production (1998/9)	34,200	17,300
Major sources of housing finance	Public funding	Bank mortgage + personal savings

Source: Hong Kong Housing Authority, *Housing in Figures 1999*.

In the period 1983–99, the number of public rental flats increased by 36 per cent from 505,300 to 687,300 (peaking in 1997 at 704,600). These flats have been heavily subsidized, with rents at only a fraction of those in the private sector (Yip and Lau 1997). The Housing Authority – a statutory body existing outside the government bureaucracy – assumed the main responsibility for public housing provision and management, with the Housing Department as its executive arm. Over the years, the Authority was able to make substantial gains from the selling of public flats to cover financial subsidies to the comparatively large public rental sector.

Although the size of the public rental sector has increased in absolute terms over the past 15 years, as a proportion of the total housing stock it has been consistently declining. Between 1987 and 1999 it declined by 10 per cent – from 44 per cent to 34 per cent. This is closely related to an important change in policy direction in 1987 under the Long Term Housing Strategy (LTHS). Under the LTHS, a clear home-ownership policy was adopted. Several initiatives were developed to promote home-ownership, including the Home Purchase Loan Scheme, the sale of public rental units to sitting tenants and the Sandwich-Class Housing Scheme run by the Hong Kong Housing Society (the only NGO in Hong Kong which provides subsidized rental and home-ownership flats).

Government-subsidized sale flats doubled from 7.6 per cent to 15.9 per cent between 1989 and 1999 contrasting sharply with the decline in the public rented sector over the same period. By 1999, the private owner-occupied sector and government Home-ownership Scheme (HOS) accounted for two thirds of the housing stock. This reflects a successful government effort to implement a housing policy biased in favour of home-ownership while leaving the public rented sector to become progressively marginalized (Chan 2000; Yip and Lau 1997). Chiu (1999) contends that Hong Kong has particularly extensive assisted home-ownership schemes and schemes for home financing. This is evident in the increase in assisted home-ownership opportunities offered by the SAR government, rising from an

James Lee, Ray Forrest and Wai Keung Tam

annual average of around 19,000 pre-1997 to more than 88,030 in subsequent years (Table 2.3).

The Hong Kong residential property market did not escape the impacts of the Asian financial crisis. The private residential price index dropped by 40 per cent between the third quarter of 1997 and the end of 1998 (Table 2.4). In the luxury apartment sector, property prices plummeted by 60 per cent from the peak of HK$17,615 per square foot in October 1997 to HK$7,049 per square foot in August 1998. The loss of market value for residential housing was estimated at HK$170 billion (Fung and Forrest 2002). Although the residential price index rose in the first quarter of 1999, it began to fall again afterwards before beginning to bottom out towards the end of 2000.

The decline in market activity was particularly marked in the second hand market with transactions falling to 54 per cent of the October 1997 level. Although there was a temporary uplift in March 1998 for new flats, the second hand housing market continued to nosedive. A clear signal of the weak sentiment in the market was the government's decision to suspend land sales for nine months starting from July 1998. And the initial policies adopted by the Hong Kong Monetary Authority to counteract attacks from speculators combined with the prolonged

Table 2.3 Average annual assisted home-ownership opportunities, pre- and post-1997

Home-ownership schemes and measures	Pre-Oct 1997	Post-Oct 1997
In-kind subsidy schemes		
Home Ownership Scheme/Private Sector Participation Scheme	10,000	30,000
Flats for Sale Scheme	425	930
Sandwich-class Housing Main Scheme	3,000	6,000
Tenants Purchase Scheme	–	25,000
Buy or Rent Scheme	–	10,000
Mixed Development Scheme	–	600
Sub-total	13,425	72,530
In-cash subsidy schemes		
Home Purchase Loan Scheme	4,500	4,500+
Sandwich-Class Housing Loan Scheme	810	5,000
Home Starter Loan Scheme	–	6,000
Tax Deduction for Mortgage Interest Payment	–	Not available
Sub-total	5,310	15,500
Total	**18,735**	**88,030+**

Source: Rebecca L.H. Chiu, 'The Swing of the Pendulum in Housing' in Larry Chuen-ho Chow and Yiu-kwan Fan (eds), *The Other Hong Kong Report 1998*, Hong Kong: The Chinese University Press, 1999, p.336.

26

Table 2.4 The Asian financial crisis and its impact on residential prices on selected East Asian cities 1997–9 (average house price index)

	1997				1998				1999			
	1Q	2Q	3Q	4Q	1Q	2Q	3Q	4Q	1Q	2Q	3Q	4Q
Hong Kong	395	429	433	422	354	321	265	258	264	263	256	242
Singapore	289	287	274	263	238	219	190	173	181	202	219	231
Taipei County	96	96	96	96	90	90	92	88	87	–	–	–

Sources: Hong Kong: *Hong Kong Property Review 2000*; Singapore: *Asian Economic Database*; Taipei: *Taiwan Real Estate Research Center, National Chengchi University* www.housing.nccu.edu.tw

financial crisis in the region resulted in tight liquidity and higher interest rates which in turn affected house prices. The downturn in the economy also affected household incomes. Monthly median household incomes declined from HK$19,200 in the fourth quarter of 1997 to HK$17,500 in the second quarter of 1998. As the decrease in house prices was more rapid than the decline in incomes, housing affordability actually improved for the first time in two decades. The price-income ratio fell from 12.6 per cent in the fourth quarter of 1997 to 8.6 per cent in the second quarter of 1998. However, housing demand continued to contract despite improved affordability. Potential home purchasers were unwilling to enter the market for fear of a bleaker economic and labour market outlook. With rapidly rising unemployment (from 6.3 per cent in March 1999 to 7.1 per cent in May 2002) and a budget deficit looming, this sluggishness in the housing market continues. The Asian financial crisis has apparently changed previous conceptions of household investment in the 1980s and the 1990s with residential property purchase no longer seen as a reliable hedge against inflation.

Singapore

As emphasized earlier, the genesis of Singapore's home-ownership policy dates back to the nation-building period in the early 1960s when having a stake in the country was considered paramount to national stability. In 1959 the Housing and Development Board (HDB) was set up to assume the responsibility for providing adequate home-ownership opportunities for the Singaporeans. Although financially supported by public funds, the HDB was free to set guidelines of eligibility for a range of apartment-type dwellings. Public housing from the start was regarded more as privilege rather than a right. Since housing was not regarded as welfare, individual households were required to pay for it through their own savings (Chua 1996). Currently, 86 per cent of the three million population live in public housing, of which just over 90 per cent is 'owner-occupied' (Table 2.5).

Table 2.5 Housing situation in Singapore

	Public	*Private*
Actual number of housing units (1999)	791,000	184,000
	(81.7%)	(18.2%)
Home-ownership rate	90.5%	89.9%
Rental rate	9.5%	10.1%
Annual housing production (1999)	34,481	11,079
Major sources of housing finance	CPF funds + government subsidies	Bank mortgage + personal savings

Sources: *Yearbook of Statistics Singapore; Monthly Digest of Statistics Singapore, May 1999.*

The HDB also adopted a resale policy which has contributed to the upgrading process of its flats. Under the resale policy, a lease-owner is entitled to resell his/her flat to anyone eligible for public housing at a market price. The seller is permitted a second chance to apply for a new upgraded flat or to trade down and realize significant financial gains. Here market forces are allowed their full impact in determining the resale values of the flats. The resale mechanism has allowed Singaporeans opportunities to build up wealth through home-ownership and this has formed part of the whole 'planned life-long consumption' philosophy of the Singaporean social policy system. To enable this to happen, the housing system has had to be integrated with the key social security institution, the Central Provident Fund (CPF).

The CPF, created in 1955, is a national saving scheme under which both employers and employees are obliged to contribute together an average of 40 per cent of the wage of working individuals to their personal CPF account. Citizens are not allowed to withdraw their savings until they are 58 but can use their savings to pay their monthly mortgage costs. This collective funding is then used to buy government bonds as well as to finance loans and subsidies to the HDB for development. The HDB in turn acts as the mortgagee for all the households living in HDB flats. The government estimates that 90 per cent of Singaporean households are able to meet their monthly mortgage payment for public housing flats through their monthly CPF savings (Chua 2000). Through a progressive adjustment process, the CPF and the HDB have been successfully integrated into an institution which provides both the administrative and financial infrastructure for state-wide home-ownership. The entire process constitutes an internal transfer, with favourable terms of interest on loans for all parties, without involving any of the conventional banking processes, nor competing with capital demands in other sectors of the economy.

To accomplish a 'home owning' nation, the Singapore government has exercised enormous regulatory powers over the housing sector. One notable example was the 1966 amended Land Acquisition Act. The Act enabled the government to acquire all land deemed necessary for the purpose of national development, at compensation rates determined by the statutes themselves, which were invariably drastically below prevailing market values. Accordingly, the government expanded its land holdings from about 40 per cent in the early 1960s to 85 per cent currently.

In Singapore, the effect of the economic downturn in Asia was not felt until very late in 1997. By the fourth quarter of 1998, the private residential price index had fallen by 37 per cent. It hit the lowest point in 1999 and then rose slightly in response to an apparent improving general economic environment. However, continual news of economic decline in the US and the fallout of the technology sector hit house prices in both 2000 and 2001.

The number of private sector written permissions and newly-built dwellings fell by 73 per cent and 77 per cent respectively in 1997 and 1998 and the figures showed little improvement in 1999. Compared with countries such as Thailand, however, Singapore did not suffer from excessive housing supply as the occupancy rate of private residential property remained very stable after the Asian financial crisis. Two reasons might account for this. First, with a monopoly of housing supply, the government is able to maintain a stable housing regime. Second, the government has also made use of the CPF contribution rate to regulate the consumption power of households. A higher CPF rate generates a higher level of savings available for home purchase and mortgage repayment. In sum, the housing market is subject to considerable manipulation by the Singapore government – stable housing prices contribute to political legitimacy.

Taiwan

Unlike Hong Kong and Singapore, Taiwan has a very small public housing sector, accounting for only about 5 per cent of the entire residential housing stock. From 1986, local governments were granted more discretion in planning public housing programmes within their respective domains (Chang 1991). The central government set aside a loan fund in its annual budget for the construction of public housing. Apart from borrowing from this fund, provincial and city governments also levied a land tax, using the money to purchase land and provide loans to individual households (Doling 1999). The main emphasis of the housing programme has been on home-ownership and, as with Singapore, most public housing in Taiwan has been built for sale. Table 2.6 shows that owner-occupied dwellings represent almost 85 per cent of the stock. Chang (1991) argues that in Taiwan the market performs a central role in the three stages of the housing provision, namely construction, allocation and consumption.

A key feature within the Taiwan private housing sector since the late 1960s is the dominance of the system of pre-sale housing. Such a system helps to lower the cost of home purchasing and hence promotes home-ownership. Briefly, the

Table 2.6 Owner occupation in Taiwan (in thousands)

	1981	1985	1987	1989	1991	1993	1995	1997	1999
Owner-occupied	2805.9	3314.5	3595.2	3868	4148.6	4438.2	4963.2	5164.2	5460
	73.3%	77.3%	78.6%	79%	80.4%	81.9%	84.7%	84.6%	84.9%
Renting	589.5	561.7	590.1	616.9	624.4	579.8	561.7	561.6	572
	15.4%	13.1%	12.9%	12.6%	12.1%	10.7%	9.6%	9.2%	8.9%
Employer provided	210.5	128.6	86.9	88.1	72.2	54.2	57.3	42.7	45
	5.5%	3.0%	1.9%	1.8%	1.4%	1.0%	1.0%	0.7%	0.7%
Others	222	283	301.9	323.2	314.8	352.2	326.7	335.7	353
	5.8%	6.6%	6.6%	6.6%	6.1%	6.5%	5.6%	5.5%	5.5%

Source: *Social Indicators of the Republic of China 1999*, p.98.

pre-sale system refers to the sale of houses prior to their completion and generally begins immediately after building land is found to be available (Li 1998). Arrangement for down payments varies according to the market situation. It can be broadly divided into payments before construction and payments during the period of construction. The former includes both a deposit and a payment upon contract signing. The amount of each of these payments will be set in the sales contract by the property developers according to market situation. When many buyers are eager to buy houses, the payment before construction may be set higher. In such situations, with 70 per cent of the price covered by a mortgage, the buyers may be contracted to pay about 15 per cent before the start of construction. The other 15 per cent will be paid by instalments during the period of construction. If the housing market is falling, developers may reduce the payments required before construction, thereby attracting buyers and boosting the sales rate. In order to collect cash quickly from house buyers, property developers will try to speed up construction to obtain these payments, and also to begin to get the house buyers' mortgage payments sooner. Thus, developers will consider the market situation in choosing the building type. For example, high rise (over seven floors) buildings with large sized housing units will be more popular during housing booms (Li 1998: 72).

Pre-sale housing arrangements enable property developers to use less of their own capital for housing production because of the down payments they receive from buyers during the construction phase. This has in turn made it easier for small property developers with limited capital to enter the market. Thus, contrary to Hong Kong where property giants like Cheung Kong Holdings and SHK dominate the market, developers in Taiwan are generally fairly small. In 1989, 86 per cent of property developers in Taipei City had a capitalization of less than NT$60 million. The new houses produced under the pre-sale system play a significant role in the housing market. For example, the total value of pre-sale housing units sold in 1980 was NT$40,300 million which represented 56 per cent of the total monetary value of the housing supply in that year (Li 1998).

The impact of the Asian financial crisis on Taiwan's residential market was relatively modest. Compared with the 50 per cent and 37 per cent drop in the residential price index in Hong Kong and Singapore, Taipei County fell by only around 9 per cent between the fourth quarter of 1997 and the fourth quarter of 1999. Nonetheless, the housing construction sector and residential market were still hard hit. The government tried to revive the stagnant property market by various stimulation measures. For example, at the end of 1998, Taiwan's Central Bank and Finance Minister announced a stimulation package of NT$150 billion of low-interest loans for first time buyers. Any buyer of a new home in 1999 could secure up to NT$2.5 million in financing at a fixed 5.9 per cent interest rate for up to 20 years (*South China Morning Post* 1999). The state of the property market and the measures taken to mitigate its difficulties are reflected in the falling interest rates in the last two years, suggesting the continuing political pressures on the Taiwan government (*China Intelligence Wire* 2001).

Japan

In 1955, the Japan Housing Corporation was set up to tackle the growing serious-ness of the housing shortage which had been caused by excessive concentration of industries and people in large cities. The Corporation was to raise private and public funds to develop large-scale housing sites to construct dwellings for middle-class workers in major urban areas. Postwar housing construction in Japan, however, has depended overwhelmingly on the private sector – housing investment reached 12,990 billion yen in 1978 of which 94 per cent came from the private sector. Compared with Hong Kong, Singapore and even Taiwan, Japan has a tiny public housing sector and is dominated by home-ownership and private renting (see Table 2.7). At the national government level, the Housing and Urban Develop-ment Corporation builds apartment buildings and rents them to tenants. Local government also contributes to public housing and receives central government subsidies to supply low-cost public rental housing to low-income families on a need basis. There is also a limited amount of apartment accommodation for rent that is operated directly by local government. Over the past two decades, the public sector has accounted for around 7 per cent of the total residential units. It is also of relatively low quality. The government has a minimum-housing-standard-index for density. While only 2.7 per cent of private home-ownership and 20.4 per cent of private rental housing are below this standard, 27.4 per cent of public rental housing is well below this standard (Hirayama and Hayakawa 1995).

By and large, home-ownership is still the predominant element of Japan's housing policy. Housing has always been regarded as an individual's responsibility, a personal problem, and therefore the responsibility of the private market rather than the state. Owner-occupied housing and private rented housing have made up more than 85 per cent of the total dwellings since the late 1970s. The Government Housing Loan Corporation (GHLC) has had the major responsibility of providing low-interest loans for home-ownership to most middle class households. From 1950 to 1997, the GHLC financed the construction of 16,820 thousand housing units, representing 31.1 per cent of the accumulated total of housing starts (Government Housing Loan Corporation 1998: 149). The dramatic rise in land and house prices during most of the post war period prompted many Japanese to seek home-ownership as a means of building up family assets (Hirayama and Hayakawa 1995). According to the 1988 Housing Survey, 32 per cent of home-owners acquired their wealth by inheriting housing and land. High house prices have also made it very difficult for the younger generation to purchase homes, thus contributing to an increasing number of cases of *cross-generation mortgaging* where parents' loans can extend beyond their own working life. This is reflected

Table 2.7 Japan: housing tenure (unit: thousands and %)

	Total units	Owner-occupied	Rented housing			
			Total	Public	Private	Employer-supplied
1958	17,432	(71.2)	(28.8)	(3.5)	(18.5)	(6.7)
1963	20,372	(64.3)	(35.7)	(4.6)	(24.1)	(7.0)
1968	24,198	(60.3)	(39.7)	(5.8)	(27.0)	(6.9)
1973	28,713	(59.2)	(40.8)	(6.9)	(27.4)	(6.4)
1978	32,189	(60.4)	(39.4)	(7.5)	(26.1)	(5.7)
1983	34,705	(62.4)	(37.3)	(7.6)	(24.5)	(5.2)
1988	37,413	(61.3)	(37.5)	(7.5)	(25.8)	(4.1)
1993	40,773	(59.8)	(38.5)	(7.1)	(26.4)	(5.0)
1998	43,892	(60.3)	(38.0)	(6.8)	(27.3)	(3.9)

Sources: Takatoshi Ito, 'Public Policy and Housing in Japan' in Yukio Noguchi and James M. Poterba (eds) *Housing Markets in the United States and Japan*, Chicago: University of Chicago Press, 1994, p.223; *Japan Pocket Housing Statistics 1999*, p.33.

in the popularity of the prefabricated two-generation homes where sales have increased rapidly in recent years. To capture this growing market, the GHLC established the 'two-generation housing loan' in 1980.

As the price of housing in Japan is extraordinarily high, affordability and housing finance have been major issues. Tachibanaki (1994) estimated that between 1979 and 1988, the rising price of houses in Tokyo had reduced the proportion of households able to buy from 64 per cent to 39 per cent. The single most important reason is land prices, which are significantly higher than in other countries. They rose continually over a long period prior to the bursting of the bubble economy in the early 1990s. In the major cities the cost of land can constitute over 60 per cent of the housing cost – in central Tokyo this percentage can rise to well over 90 per cent. In such locations, the housing problem is essentially a land price problem.

Public-sector lending plays an important role in the Japanese housing finance system. The GHLC is the largest single mortgage lender in the world and accounts for some 25 to 35 per cent of housing loans in Japan. It draws funds from the Fiscal Investments and Loans budget which derives its income from the postal savings system, from postal life insurance and postal annuities, and from bonds issued for public subscription by government agencies. The amount of money to be loaned and the number of houses to be built with these loans each year are determined by the budget for the Fiscal Investments and Loans programme. It is important to emphasize that capital for housing-purchase loans in Japan is primarily mobilized from the deposit-taking system (i.e. through short-term savings) by both GHLC and commercial banks. Generally, GHLC lending favours new housing, with much stricter limits and lending criteria for older housing. This acts to depress the resale value of homes and discourages the development of a mortgage market in second hand dwellings. Typically, only around 6–7 per cent of GHLC funds has been allocated to the purchase of second hand owner-occupied housing. The other large lenders are the commercial banks and housing loan companies that are subsidiaries of commercial banks.

Japan's housing finance system is characterized by two special features. First, unlike other advanced industrial countries, Japan has had no major private-sector institutions that specialize in housing finance, like the savings and loan associations in the United States (Seko 1994: 49). Second, the mortgage market for second hand houses is virtually non-existent. Mortgages are not bought and sold as commodities. It appears that the government's longstanding informal policy of maintaining low interest rates on housing loans has rendered mortgages unattractive investment instruments. The absence of private-sector institutions specializing in mortgages has also hindered the development of a mortgage market. In addition, there is a limited legal foundation for such a market, since gaining clear title to real estate pledged as collateral on a loan is difficult (Seko 1994: 52).

The housing finance market in Japan has expanded greatly since 1965, marked by a decreasing reliance on public loans and a rapid increase in private loans. During the 1980s, while GHLC loans fluctuated between 20–30 per cent of total housing loans, there was a marked increase in property-related lending by commercial banks. In 1990, the share of bank loans outstanding for households rose to 16 per cent of the total, for the first time exceeding the share for manufacturing firms, while the share for property companies rose from 4 per cent in 1970 to 12 per cent in 1990.

Another distinguishing feature of Japan's housing market was that it was in the doldrums long before the more generalized Asian financial crisis. For more than 10 years it has experienced falling or stagnant land and property prices with only marginal signs of recovery in February 2001. Prior to the bursting of the bubble economy in 1990, price-income ratios were around 9:1 in the main metropolitan areas. Land in central Tokyo was at that time the most expensive real estate in the world. The bubble economy fed off this rampant inflation in land prices with real estate being used as collateral for 70 per cent of loans among financial institutions. When property values tumbled the shock waves ripped through the entire economy with various well publicized bankruptcies. Where property values had risen most steeply, they declined most rapidly and sharply – in Tokyo and the other main metropolitan areas. Some property values fell by as much as 60 per cent and it was estimated that some 280,000 condominium owners were in negative equity in the Tokyo metropolitan area in January 2000 (Forrest *et al.* 2002). Despite various reflationary and rescue measures by the Japanese government and the Housing Loan Corporation, the housing market and the general economy has remained stubbornly depressed. Land prices have fallen by around 50 per cent over the last decade and the main mortgage activity seems to be refinancing as households replace higher interest loans from the GHLC with cheaper loans now available from commercial banks. And while there has been rising demand in the fashionable parts of the major cities, there is still a significant housing glut (*The Economist* 2002).

South Korea

In 1999, South Korea had 11,104 thousand dwellings and 15,444 thousand households. One salient feature of the Korean housing situation is clearly an absolute housing shortage. Between 1960 and 1990 the housing supply ratio, measured in terms of the number of dwellings relative to the number of households, continually fell. Between 1960 and 1990, the number of households expanded by 5.9 million, or 242 per cent, but there was only a net addition of 3.7 million housing units – an increase of 207 per cent (Table 2.8). There were also substantial geographical variations in relation to the shortage of housing supply. In 1990, for example, the housing shortage in urban areas was 38.9 per cent, whereas in rural areas it was only 1.9 per cent. With a substantial increase in the housing stock since the early 1990s the housing shortage rate fell from 40.8 per cent in 1987 down to 25.7 per cent in 1995 in urban areas and 30.8 per cent to 17.3 per cent during the same period for the country as a whole. As a response to the growing shortfall in supply, particularly in the urban areas, in 1990 the government launched the Two Million Housing Construction Plan (1988–92). However, with the slowdown of housing construction after the Asian financial crisis, the shortage rate has again risen to 28 per cent. The limited supply has also contributed to a significant affordability problem with the price of housing rising almost five times between 1975 and 1988, while the nation's real GNP grew less than three times. The housing system in South Korea is almost equally divided between renting and owning. Table 2.9 shows the tenure structure in 1985 and 1995. Owner-occupation accounted for about 53 per cent of the total number of households.

Although the number of owner-occupied households increased from 5.1 to 6.9 million during 1985–95, the relative share of owner-occupation has not changed. The Korean rental system is also rather complex and unique. There are both a monthly rent and a *jonsei* rental system. The significance of the monthly rental system has gradually declined and accounted for 14.5 per cent of total households in 1995, a 4.5 per cent decrease since the mid-1980s. The *jonsei* rental system is a central component of the Korean rental sector and accommodated around 44 per cent of renters in Seoul in 1995. The significance of the *jonsei* system for our discussion is that it is a form of tenure which sits halfway between renting and ownership. Under *jonsei*, households pay a lump sum deposit to their landlords in lieu of rent and the entire sum should be returned when the household moves out. In this way, *jonsei* renters could gradually accumulate their capital for outright purchase while *jonsei* landlords could take advantage of the capital returns from either investing the deposits in home building or simply earning interest from the bank. The amount of the *jonsei*

Table 2.8 South Korea: changes in population and housing (1960–99) (thousands)

	1960	1970	1980	1990	1995	1999
Whole country						
Population	24,982	30,882	37,436	43,411	44,609	46,858
Households (A)	4,198	5,576	7,471	10,167	11,133	15,444
Housing units (B)	3,464	4,360	5,318	7,160	9,205	11,104
B / A (%)	82.5	78.2	71.2	70.4	82.7	71.9
Urban areas						
Population	6,995	12,709	21,434	32,309	35,036	
Households (A)	1,209	2,377	4,362	7,604	8,832	
Housing units (B)	805	1,398	2,468	4,646	6,563	
B / A (%)	66.5	58.8	56.6	61.1	74.3	
Rural areas						
Population	17,987	18,173	16,002	11,102	9,572	
Households (A)	2,989	3,199	3,109	2,563	2,433	
Housing units (B)	2,659	2,962	2,850	2,514	2,642	
B / A (%)	88.9	92.6	91.7	98.1	108.6	

Source: Jeong-Ho Kim and Geun-Yong Kim, 'A Comprehensive Overview of Housing Policies' in Jeong-Sik Lee and Yong-Woong Kim (eds) *Shaping the Nation toward Spatial Democracy*, Korea: Korea Research Institute for Human Settlement, 1998, p.94.

Notes
Population figure of 1999 is estimated. Sources of the 1999 figures come from Korea National Statistical Office, *Major Statistics of Korean Economy 2000.9*, p.100; Korea National Statistical Office, *Monthly Statistics of Korea 2000.11*, p.17.

deposit is significant as the average ranges from 30 per cent to 70 per cent of the purchase value of the housing unit. Underlying the popularity of the *jonsei* system is a lack of other financial alternatives and the absence of a bank mortgage system. Few landlords choose to operate monthly rental units because they believe *jonsei* rental offers more benefits than monthly rental.

In terms of public rental housing, a critical feature of the Korean system is that most of the public rental dwellings are supposed to transfer to ownership within five years. The tenants are given priority to purchase at below market price. Only a very small proportion of the public rental stock (2–3 per cent) is on rental terms of more than five years. Exceptionally, 140,078 public sector dwellings were built for permanent rental between 1989 and 1992, during the era when there was an acute shortage of low-cost housing for the lowest income households.

The main policy-making body for national housing development is the Housing Bureau of the Ministry of Construction (MOC). The MOC formulates and imple-

Table 2.9 Housing tenure in South Korea

	1985 Whole country households %	1985 Seoul households %	1995 Whole country households %	1995 Seoul households %
Owner-occupation	53.0	40.0	53.3	39.7
Jonsei	23.0	36.0	29.7	43.8
Deposit-based monthly rental/ Monthly rental	19.0	19.0	11.9	15.0
Others	5.0	5.0	5.1	1.4

Sources: 1) Juhyun Yoon (2002) Structural changes in the rental housing market, KRIHS Special Reports (2) March 2002, page 21; 2) The Korean jonsei system: effective or defective response? – Paper presented at the Conference 'Major Planning Issues in the 1990s' organized by EAROPH September, 1990, Seoul, Korea; 3) National Statistics Office (1997) The Report of population and housing census for 1995.

ments long-range housing policy and co-ordinates public and private efforts in order to ensure the efficient allocation of housing funds and resources. The Economic Planning Board and the Ministry of Finance are also actively involved in housing policy. The former is related to the National Economic Plan whereas the latter has a direct impact on housing through its circulating funds. The Korea National Housing Corporation (KNHC) was set up in 1962, under the direction of the MOC. Its main functions are to construct new, decent, low-cost housing for sale and to create residential sites in urban areas. KNHC's major financial resources come from tax benefits, participation in acquiring and developing land, and the National Housing Fund (NHF) (Yoon 1994). By 2000, KNHC had constructed one million housing units, roughly equivalent to 11 per cent of the total housing stock (www.jugong.co.kr/web/English/English_index.html). Likewise, both the Korea Housing Bank (KHB) and the NHF act as the key agencies for housing finance. Thus, in the early 1980s about 90 per cent of all funds for housing mortgage came from either the Korean Housing Bank or National Housing Fund. The private banking sector was essentially not involved in the housing finance business.

Although the Korean government maintains only a small public housing sector, it has extensive ways to influence the housing market. It plays a critical role in shaping the building industry as initiator, promoter, and regulator. It also selects large promoters and contractors to buy publicly owned building plots at below market prices. The designated builders can also be given government loans as a reward for meeting output target numbers of housing units. The government also manipulates the financial system to influence the housing market. Unlike most other developed East Asian economies, the private mortgage market was not developed until the late 1990s (Yoon *et al.* 1998). Loan-to-value ratios have been between 20–30 per cent and commercial banks are not equipped to grant housing loans since the mortgages cannot be securitized. Thus, in the early 1980s, about 90 per cent of all funds for housing mortgages came from the state-owned KHB and NHF (Ha 1987: 107).

The South Korean property market and construction sectors experienced a major slump following the Asian financial crisis. Prices for condominium units dropped by as much as 45 per cent for single family detached units in the Seoul Metropolitan Area (Kim and Kim 1998: 119). The value of dwelling construction orders and the number of residential construction permits issued plunged by 46 per cent and 54 per cent respectively in 1998 (Lee 2000b). Although these two figures improved in 1999, they have not regained their pre-crisis level. Many property developers were also hit by the Asian financial crisis. As of 1997, the number of general contracting companies was 3,900 and the number of special contracting companies was 23,925. These figures were four times higher than in 1990. However, as the construction sector went into depression, the bankruptcy rate in general contracting companies increased by 278 per cent and in special contracting companies by 175 per cent in 1998. Between 70 and 80 per cent of home-builders went out of business with a vast oversupply of new units. Only about 200 (out of a total registered home-builders of 2,300) remained in the market (Kim and Kim 1998: 120). It is estimated that the plight of the housing industry caused the loss of some 350,000 jobs.

To stimulate the housing market, the government adopted various measures. First, the house price control system and other market intervention measures were eliminated. Home-builders were allowed to set their own prices. Second, the government channelled sizeable amounts of public funds into the housing market by expanding housing finance credit and by providing subsidized interest loans to new home buyers. For example, it used US$200 million borrowed from the World Bank as seed money to extend credit up to Won$900 billion to enable new home buyers to pay their mortgage instalments on time and thereby help the ailing housing industry.

Thailand

In Thailand, the public sector (i.e. the National Housing Authority) has never played a dominant role in urban housing provision. Rich families build their own houses in the residential areas; poor families build their temporary shacks in rental slums; middle-income families rely on the private sector (Yap and Kirinpanu 2000). The principal vehicle of government intervention in housing has been the Government Housing Bank. This was established in 1953 to provide loan finance for both developers and individual purchasers. As the Thai economy developed, its role became more extensive with the rising affluence of consumers, shifts in government policy and the increasing number of private developers. High-loan-to-value ratios, cheap loans and beneficial taxation have all been factors encouraging the growth of commercially mortgaged home-ownership. Seeking to reinvigorate the flagging economy in the early 1980s, the government made housing a priority area for investment and forced the commercial banks to lend a certain percentage of their credit for low-cost housing projects. And in the mid-1980s the Government Housing Bank broke the cartel of the private commercial banks by offering super-saving schemes to its customers and by reducing interest rates on home mortgage loans. These policies prompted customers to shift their savings or mortgage loans from private commercial banks to the Government Housing Bank, which in turn forced the commercial banks to lower their lending rates. These developments boosted new housing construction in Bangkok by providing private developers with cheaper funds and by providing the middle class with low-cost mortgage loans (Table 2.10).

Initially private developers focused on the lower-middle-income earners by building row houses and town houses at prices affordable to about half the households in Bangkok. By the end of the 1980s, it was no longer possible to produce low-cost row and town houses because of rapidly rising land prices. Accordingly, developers shifted to condominiums for both the middle-income and high-income groups. As a result of the booming property market, the number of developers in Bangkok increased steadily. The ease of selling in such booming conditions also made developers complacent and little market research preceded the building of new developments.

The excessive housing speculation in Thailand prior to the Asian financial crisis caused a dramatic slump in Thai house prices and the property market

Table 2.10 New house construction in the Bangkok Metropolitan Region

Year	Self-built	Developer	Total	Change (%)
1987	22,700	30,653	53,353	
1988	22,276	45,175	67,451	+26.4
1989	22,529	57,502	80,031	+18.7
1990	25,940	76,395	102,335	+27.9
1991	25,275	104,413	129,688	+26.7
1992	23,717	84,284	108,001	−16.7
1993	36,459	97,627	134,086	+24.2
1994	35,150	136,104	171,254	+27.7
1995	32,118	140,301	172,419	+0.7
1996	28,059	138,726	166,785	−3.3
Total	274,223	911,180	1,185,403	

Source: Yap Kioe Sheng and Sakchai Kirinpanu, 'Once Only the Sky was the Limit: Bangkok's Housing Boom and the Financial Crisis in Thailand', *Housing Studies*, Vol.15, No.1 (January 2000), p.14.

experienced some of the worst impacts in the region. An increasingly deregulated finance market with lenders competing eagerly for business had combined with rampant price inflation in the early to mid-1990s to produce a spectacular collapse. By early 1999 there were some 330,000 empty residential units in Bangkok. In many cases, the market value of these unoccupied units was lower than the outstanding loan used to either develop or purchase the property (*Bangkok Post* 1999). The central bank's property index in May 1999 stood at 30.73 points, lower than that in 1992. In 1998 sales of newly-launched property projects were only 31 per cent of the total, and the figure fell further to 23 per cent during the first half of 1999. The total outstanding loans financing property projects dropped from 790 billion baht in 1996 to 619 billion baht in 1997. It remained stagnant in 1998 at 627 billion baht. Total housing loans extended to consumers also declined from 803 billion baht in 1997 to 776 billion baht a year later (Parnsoonthorn 1999). To support this stagnant real estate sector, the National Housing Authority spent 15 billion baht on buying half-finished condominiums and houses built for low or middle-income earners. But analysts estimated that this spending could only absorb up to 15 per cent of the excess housing (Crampton 1999). A recent assessment of housing market conditions noted that only around 250 developers have survived from the 2000 which were active prior to 1997 (*Bangkok Post* 2001). And while there are signs of a modest recovery at the upper end of the Bangkok market, for detached dwellings in particular, the large number of abandoned blocks (some 350) in the city is a reminder of the severity of the 1997 slump.

Discussion

What can we distil from this account of the development of home-ownership systems in these six cases? What are the common features and structural pressures and what are their major differences? As Doling (1999) has emphasized, while there have been significant differences in policy mixes across the 'tiger' economies there is a high degree of commonality in the involvement of governments in organizing the factors of production in the housing sector, primarily through ownership or significant regulation of land supply and through policies designed to encourage larger and more efficient construction companies. The degree to which these efforts have been directed towards the promotion of home-ownership has, however, varied substantially. The Singaporean case is the most exceptional with social and economic policy being closely intertwined in the achievement of both growth and social cohesion. Indeed, Chua (2000) has argued that the essence of the success of the Singapore system lies in the consistently high political priority given to housing within a whole range of socio-economic policies designed to modernize Singapore. In other words, housing development has been an important element of national development policy which, when faced with risks and challenges, the government is always ready to step in and salvage. Price stability and a satisfactory housing environment have been the two foremost policy objectives. The overwhelmingly dominant position of the Housing Development Board has also meant that home-ownership sits within highly controlled and regulated conditions. Dwelling mix, access and price fluctuations are all encompassed by the government's housing policy.

To a much greater extent than in Europe or North America, home-ownership has also been promoted through what would be called in Britain 'build-for-sale' programmes. Again, Singapore's housing provision falls almost entirely into this category. Elsewhere, as in Thailand's rental purchase schemes, Hong Kong's Home Ownership Schemes or the Korean National Housing Corporation's build-for-sale scheme governments have been variously involved in direct provisions for home purchase. While such programmes have been increasing in volume and scope in recent years and have tended to supplant elements of provision for low-cost renting, they have, with the exception of Singapore, remained of secondary importance to private sector-led building for home-ownership.

The orchestration and control of financial institutions has also been a key factor. In Japan the Government Housing Loan Corporation has been the principal mortgage provider as is the Government Housing Bank in Thailand. With Singapore's Central Provident Fund as the prime example, privileged and separate public sector based circuits of housing loan finance have been cornerstones of housing and economic policy. This is in contrast to developments in, say, the UK or other European financial markets where liberalization and deregulation have created more integrated financial circuits in which lending for house purchase or residential development has become part of general commercial lending. Governments have also exercised considerable control over the lending process even where, as in the case of Korea, banks have been going through a process of privatization. The Korean government, exceptionally, while shifting from direct to indirect subsidy arrangements has enforced strict price controls on new apartments to control general price inflation.

In general, the development of home-ownership in South East and East Asia has been far removed from a free market with limited state involvement. The development of the sector has been intimately connected with broader strategies of economic growth and development and in all cases home buying has formed a major element of the growth machine in particular periods. Compared with Europe, Australia or North America the conventional distinctions between the 'public' and the 'private' in housing provision and the links to tenure are much more blurred. Government intervention has been driven by, and in many cases contributed to, extraordinary levels of house price inflation, reflecting underlying processes of accelerated urbanization, sustained and high levels of economic growth and rising real incomes. The Asian financial crisis therefore compromised a policy architecture predicated on a booming housing market and exposed home-owning households to a new and unpredictable deflationary regime. The differences in policy and institutional arrangements, however, meant that when the bubble burst the impacts were uneven both within and between home owning sectors. The existing institutional frameworks appear designed in many cases to work optimally only during periods of positive economic growth. As a result there may have to be a greater emphasis in the future on more protective measures such as insurance in order to create built-in stabilizing effects within the housing system to prevent future collapse.

It is also evident, as Doling (1999) has observed, that Asian societies have been more inclined to adopt a model of housing policy which combines a high level of intervention by the state, in providing the necessary institutions and infrastructure, with the development and consumption of housing largely embedded within a market context. This provides an affinity between the state and market which is not generally prevalent in Western housing systems. Thus in Singapore, while the Housing Development Board assumes an almost monopolistic control of housing provision, most of its properties are in fact flats for sale. Price setting for public sale flats makes frequent reference to both the affordability index as well as the price index of a mature secondary market of public sale flats. In order to maintain effective demand and market domination, the state housing sector provides abundant housing choices through an elaborate housing ladder, culminating in the so-called 'executive condominiums' which are in fact upmarket condominiums geared to the needs of the emerging professional class housing consumers.

A similar situation also applies to the sale of home-ownership flats by the Hong Kong Housing Department where price setting and sales strategy are often in line with competitive strategies used in the housing market. Examples can be found in the sale of middle class home-ownership flats through the state subsidized Home Ownership Scheme (HOS). In other words, public housing organizations see themselves as part of the housing market competing for consumers within a certain sector of the market. In this respect, public housing organizations in Singapore and Hong Kong behave somewhat like a real estate developer competing for market share.

Over-investment in residential and commercial real estate has been deeply implicated in the Asian financial crisis of the late 1990s and in the longstanding difficulties of the Japanese economy (Henderson 1999; Taggart-Murphy 2000; Boyer and Yamada 2000). Overgeared households, undercapitalized banks and a lack of proper monitoring and regulation combined to produce a disastrous cocktail for many institutions and households across Asia. Property prices plummeted, job security was severely reduced, real and nominal incomes fell and established and emergent middle classes suddenly faced a higher risk future. Particular cohorts of homeowners, who had entered the property market or traded up when prices were at their peak, were most adversely affected. Negative equity was pervasive, possession and loan defaults increased and the assumptions of a previous era, when property appreciation seemed assured, were called into question. Home-ownership has been promoted generally if to varying degrees by governments in East Asia. It has been argued that the ownership of land and dwellings has particular cultural resonance in Asia (Chan 2000; Lee 1999) where such assets have important symbolic and material value and link to the continuing, if waning, centrality of the family. In a region in which significant migrations have occurred and with a patchwork colonial history, home-ownership has also been viewed as providing and representing a degree of social stability and security in an uncertain world.

This link between social cohesion and the promotion of home-ownership is perhaps most explicit in Singapore but is also evident in the migrant cultures of Hong Kong (Lee 1999) and Taiwan (Hsiao and Liu 1993; Li 1998). The general point is that the importance of real estate investments both for households, governments and institutions in the East Asian region gave a particular prominence to the impact of the Asian financial crisis on the value of residential assets.

Since the Asian financial crisis more fundamental questions have been asked about the relationship between the property sectors and the wider economy. Most directly, the disproportionate reliance on property as a source of corporate profit and household security has been exposed as a source of weakness in many of the national economies in the region. For more enduring and robust competitiveness, it has been suggested that a higher proportion of capital should flow into technology and human capital investment and that investment loans should not be secured against overinflated real estate. Nonetheless, for many households their dwelling represents their main source of wealth and security and a renewed period of price inflation would be their priority. There is in this sense a tension for some governments between what might be the most sensible economic strategy and popular demands and sentiments. This is all the more difficult when the state of the residential property market has long been seen by many as a more general barometer of the strength or weakness of the wider economy and a guide to individual risk exposure or aversion.

Acknowledgement

We wish to acknowledge the funding support from the Governance in Asia Research Centre (Centre for Comparative Public Management and Social Policy). Project number: RCPM 994: *Economic Downturn and Home Ownership: An Exploratory Study on How Households Cope with Owner-occupation after the Asian Economic Crisis in Selected Asian Cities.*

References

Bangkok Post (1999) 'Housing Oversupply: Lights off in a Fifth of Bangkok's Homes: Few Western Nations have Faced Situation', 12 March: 1.
—— (2001) 'Year-End Economic Review'. Available online www://bangkokpost.net/year end2001/property.html.

Boyer, R. and Yamada, T. (eds) (2000) *Japanese Capitalism in Crisis: A Regulationist Interpretation*, London: Routledge.

Chan, K.W. (2000) 'Prosperity or Inequality: Deconstructing the Myth of Home Ownership in Hong Kong', *Housing Studies*, 15 (1): 29–44.

Chang, C.O. (1991) 'Research on Residential Issues and Policy Framework', *Journal of National Cheng Chi University*, 63: 263–92.

China Intelligence Wire (2001) 'Taiwan's Interest Rate for Housing Loans Drops to 6%', 17 April: 1.

Chiu, R.L.H. (1999) 'The Swing of the Pendulum in Housing', in L.C. Chow and Y. Fan (eds) *The Other Hong Kong Report 1998*, Hong Kong: The Chinese University Press.

Chua, B.H. (1996) *Private Ownership of Public Housing in Singapore*, Perth: Asian Research Centre on Social, Political and Economic Change, Murdoch University.

—— (2000) 'Public Housing Residents as Clients of the State', *Housing Studies*, 15 (1): 45–60.

Crampton, T. (1999) 'Thais Unveil $3 Billion Bid to Stimulate Economy', *International Herald Tribune*, 11 August: 11.

Doling, J. (1999) 'Housing Policies and the Little Tigers: How Do They Compare with Other Industrialised Countries?', *Housing Studies*, 14 (2): 229–50.

The Economist (2002) 'New Loans for Old – A Mortgage Boom in Japan?', 13 July.

Fung, K.K. and Forrest, R. (2002) 'Institutional Mediation, the Hong Kong Residential Housing Market and the Asian Financial Crisis', *Housing Studies*, 17 (2): 189–207.

Forrest, R., Kennett, P. and Izuhara, M. (2000) 'Home Ownership in Japan's Troubled Economy', *Housing Finance*, 46: 50–5.

—— (2002) 'Home Ownership and Economic Change in Japan', *Housing Studies* (forthcoming).

Freeman, A., Holmans, A. and Whitehead, C. (1996) *Is the UK Different? International Comparisons of Tenure Patterns*, London: Council of Mortgage Lenders.

Government Housing Loan Corporation (1998) *Housing Statistics of Japan 1998*, Tokyo: The Housing Loan Progress Association.

Ha, S.K. (1987) 'Korea', in S.K. Ha (ed.) *Housing Policy and Practice in Asia*, London: Croom Helm.

Hayakawa, K. (1987) 'Japan', in S.K. Ha (ed.) *Housing Policy and Practice in Asia*, London: Croom Helm.

Henderson, J. (1999) 'Uneven Crises: Institutional Foundations of East Asian Economic Turmoil', *Economy and Society*, 25: 327–68.

Hirayama, Y. and Hayakawa, K. (1995) 'Home Ownership and Family Wealth in Japan', in R. Forrest and A. Murie (eds) *Housing and Family Wealth: Comparative International Perspectives*, London: Routledge.

Hsiao, M.H.H. and Liu, H.J. (1993) 'Land-Housing Problems and the Limits of the Non-Homeowners Movement in Taiwan', *Hong Kong Journal of Social Sciences*, 2, Autumn: 1–19.

Kim, J.H. and Kim, G.Y. (1998) 'A Comprehensive Overview of Housing Policies', in J.S. Lee and Y.W. Kim (eds) *Shaping the Nation toward Spatial Democracy: Emerging Issues and Lessons from the Past*, Anyang: Korea Research Institute for Human Settlements.

Lee, J. (1999) *Housing, Home Ownership and Social Change in Hong Kong*, Aldershot: Ashgate.

Lee D.S. (2000b) 'The Korean Experience of Public Housing Provision', paper presented at the East and South East Asian Housing Workshop, 8–10 November, Seoul, Korea.

Lee, K.Y. (2000a) *From Third World to First: The Singapore Story 1965–2000*, New York: HarperCollins.

Li, D.H.W. (1998) *Housing in Taiwan: Agency and Structure?*, Aldershot: Ashgate.

Parnsoonthorn, K. (1999) 'Property: Market Still Deep in Slump', *The Bangkok Post*, 22 July: 1.

Richupan, S. (1999) 'Macroeconomic Instability and Housing Finance: Thailand's Experience', *Housing Finance International*, XIV (2): 26–35.

Seko, M. (1994) 'Housing Finance in Japan', in Y. Noguchi and J.M. Poterba (eds) *Housing Markets in the United States and Japan*, Chicago: The University of Chicago Press.

South China Morning Post (1999) 'Housing-industry Support Measures Fail at Building Confidence', 6 January: 4.

Tachibanaki, T. (1994) 'Housing and Saving in Japan', in Y. Noguchi and J.M. Poterba (eds) *Housing Markets in the United States and Japan*, Chicago: University of Chicago Press.

Taggart-Murphy, R. (2000) 'Japan's Economic Crisis', *New Left Review*, Vol. 1, Jan: 5–24.

Thailand National Statistical Office (1996) *Report of Housing Survey 1996*, Bangkok: National Statistical Office.

Yap, K.S. and Kirinpanu, S. (2000) 'Once Only the Sky was the Limit: Bangkok's Housing Boom and the Financial Crisis in Thailand', *Housing Studies*, 15 (1): 11–27.

Yip, N.M. and Lau, K.Y. (1997) 'Housing', in P. Wilding, S. Huque and J. Tao (eds) *Social Policy in Hong Kong*, Cheltenham: Edward Elgar.

Yoon, I.S. (1994) *Housing in a Newly Industrialized Economy: The Case of South Korea*, Aldershot: Avebury.

Yoon, J., Kyung Hwan Sohn, Hye-Seung Kim and Hyeon-Sook Chun (1998) 'Structural Changes in Housing Market and New Directions for Housing Policy', *Korea Research Institute for Human Settlement Research Report: Housing Research 1998*. Available online: http://www.krihs.re.kr.

3 Restructuring social housing systems

Christine M. E. Whitehead

The question

In many countries, especially in Europe, housing policy in the latter part of the twentieth century has been dominated by the growth and then the restructuring of the social housing sector – defined either by ownership (government or non-profit organizations) or by the provision of supply side subsidies.

The rationale for and mechanisms by which this housing has been provided have differed greatly between countries in that period. In some, such as the UK, social housing has generally been restricted to the provision of rented housing for lower income households by public landlords; in some other countries in Europe, notably in Scandinavia, the Netherlands and Germany, it has included assistance across tenures and has been available to all types of household; in others, including many Commonwealth countries, housing has been directly provided mainly for government employees; finally, in countries such as Singapore the vast majority of housing has been built by government as part of wider social policy.

The methods of financing and subsidy have similarly differed, ranging from tenure specific public finance for rented housing to tenure neutral subsidy systems supporting private finance in both rented and owner-occupied sectors. Equally, how much households living in social housing have been required to pay has been determined by very different principles and has varied from nothing up to market rents and prices.

While the starting point for government involvement and the specifics of housing provision have differed greatly across countries, the economic environments in which these policies have operated have tended to converge over the last thirty years. Special circuits of housing finance have, in the main, declined in importance, as have the subsidies relating to general housing investment. Housing financing arrangements have been integrated into wider finance markets, which have themselves become global as they have been deregulated. Controls on rents and security of tenure in private rented sectors have also tended to be reduced as absolute shortages of housing have declined. Government funding for housing has become more limited, especially in Europe, where as part of the development of the European Union, member governments have been required to restrict their public expenditure to meet centrally determined monetary criteria.

More fundamentally, the rationale for government intervention has changed. Incomes across most of the (post) industrialized world, have risen fairly consistently, ensuring that basic shelter requirements have been achieved for the vast majority of households. On the other hand, both the demand for housing and the minimum housing standards regarded as acceptable have increased. At the same time, the resource costs of housing have risen, as land has become more valuable and productivity in housing development and management has not kept pace with increases in improvements in other sectors of the economy. The emphasis has shifted away from new housing production towards affordability as well as to housing as part of the broader definition of neighbourhood and inclusion (Maclennan and Williams 1990a and 1990b; Whitehead 1991 and 1998).

It is in this context that I was asked to discuss the question of whether there is evidence of convergence in social housing systems over the last decades of the twentieth century, particularly with respect to financing, and whether these trends are likely to continue into the twenty-first century. In examining this convergence we need to distinguish three distinct aspects and ask whether there is convergence with respect to (i) a reduced direct role through social sector provision; (ii) a reduced social role overall; and/or (iii) a change in the mechanisms by which that role is implemented – in particular through privatization. Economic principles can help us to understand both why policy change has occurred and whether the underlying pressures are likely to continue. The answers to these questions then lead us to address a more fundamental issue – whether there is or should be a role for social housing in the post-industrial societies of the twenty-first century.

In order to examine what has been happening in social housing systems, it is useful both

- to understand the different elements which make up social housing provision, and
- to set out the economic principles which can be used to explain why governments intervene in housing systems and the attributes of these systems which make such intervention effective.

Looking at principles and practice together in this way allows us to identify both the pressures leading to social provision and the rationale for moving away from that approach.

Christine M. E. Whitehead

Elements of social housing provision

The provision of social housing involves at least three important processes:

- the development, and ultimately the redevelopment, of the social dwelling stock – including in particular land assembly, construction and financing – i.e. how the relevant housing asset is produced;
- the organization of the existing social stock, which includes who owns the stock; how it is managed, including maintenance and improvement investment; how it is financed – by government, owner-occupiers or other institutions; and who bears the risks – i.e. how the asset is maintained; and finally
- the use of the asset, including the principles by which the stock is allocated and paid for, and more generally who benefits from social housing – the owners, the occupiers, other households, tax payers, land owners, government? – i.e. for whom the asset is provided.

Relevant economic principles

Efficiency, equity and macroeconomic rationales

The rationale for government intervention in market economies is to use scarce resources as efficiently as possible and to distribute the resources available in a more equitable fashion. This involves recognising that there is always a relevant opportunity cost to decisions which should be taken into account in order to maximize benefits to society overall. It also requires setting criteria for determining minimum standards and an acceptable distribution of housing services. In addition, because housing is such a basic necessity, not just in terms of shelter but also with respect to security and opportunity, governments, especially within welfare state systems, often regard it as different and more socially important than most other goods and services. Finally, housing takes a large proportion of the household budget – especially for low income households – so is an obvious area for concentrating redistributive policies through kind rather than cash (Hancock 1991; Whitehead 1998).

As important as the efficiency of housing provision itself is the fact that housing is seen as one of the most effective ways of addressing macroeconomic problems, notably with respect to unemployment and income distribution but also in terms of macroeconomic stability (Maclennan *et al.* 1998). Housing programmes have regularly been used by governments as acceptable means of mobilising under-utilized resources, in part because of the perceived social value of the resultant housing investment. Housing provision and subsidies have also been substituted for higher wages or more generous social security to help ensure minimum housing standards (Maclennan and Williams 1990a and 1990b). Housing finance is a significant element in monetary stabilization policies. At the same time housing is one of the areas of public expenditure which it is most easy to cut in times of restraint. Programmes are more readily adjusted than larger scale longer term investments in defence and large scale infrastructure, and affect smaller numbers of voters than most revenue services (Turner and Whitehead 1993).

The attributes of housing, market failure and efficiency

The most important attributes which lead to government intervention in housing systems on efficiency grounds relate to the fact that housing is a long lasting, locationally specific asset which cannot be readily adjusted in response to changes in demand. Markets left to themselves will almost certainly under-provide both new housing and improvement investment because of inadequate information about costs and benefits, high private discount rates, poorly operating finance markets and household risk aversion. Equally economies of scale and scope may be lost because markets are likely to be based on small scale individual decisions. Land assembly by individuals has particular problems relating both to monopoly power and to high transaction costs. Slow adjustment of supply, the heterogeneous nature of the stock and the complex nature of the landlord/tenant relationship all tend to generate problems of relative power and monopoly control. Both locational specificity and the importance of housing as an input into quality of life mean that the social costs and benefits of housing may be very different from those recognized by individual decision makers. Most of these market failures tend to generate lower levels of housing investment, shorter term decisions and higher costs and prices than is desirable – all of which can in principle be addressed by social provision and other forms of intervention. A final argument relates to whether housing is seen as a private good, providing benefits mainly to the owner or occupier of the dwelling, or whether housing is more of a social, or merit, good providing benefits to the community as a whole because members of that community are well housed (Burns and Grebler 1977). In most twentieth century welfare states, housing has indeed been regarded as a merit good making it politically easier to implement policies which improve housing conditions. On the other hand choice with respect to location, housing type and levels of expenditure is fundamental in generating the highest value from housing assets. This generates tensions with respect to which mechanisms are appropriate to achieve the greatest benefits from the resources employed (Whitehead 1983 and 2002).

Intervention and equity

Many of the positive reasons given for government intervention relate not so much to improving the efficiency of markets but rather to this merit good argument and to distributional objectives more widely defined.

There are four main reasons for intervention on equity grounds:

- most societies argue that, because housing is an expensive necessity with a social value, there should be a commitment to ensuring minimum standards for all;
- housing is often seen as a practical and effective way of reducing inequalities because of its importance in individual budgets and its political acceptability;
- because it is difficult to adjust supply as quickly as demand, market allocation will allow owners to use their monopoly power and therefore must be checked; and
- because land and infrastructure are inherently in short supply, the possibility of housing development often generates large scale increases in land prices which may be taxed for the benefit of the community (Barr 2001).

These principles all tend to suggest that there are good economic reasons for increasing investment in housing across the board; for ensuring adequate financing and risk management of that investment; for providing equality of power between landlords and tenants; for assisting lower income households to achieve adequate housing; and for managing housing investment effectively to limit external costs and to provide a positive element in social infrastructure. On the other hand they also suggest that the majority of benefits to well operating housing systems will lie with owners and occupiers – and that freedom of choice is a particularly important aspect in ensuring that potential benefits are fully realized (Whitehead, 1998 and 2002).

European approaches to social housing

There has been much academic discussion during the 1990s about approaches to cross-national research on welfare, including housing. The accepted baseline typology is that of Esping-Andersen (1990) which distinguishes liberal (market oriented), social democratic and corporatist states – to which has been added rudimentary welfare states of the Mediterranean (Leibfried 2001). Barlow and Duncan (1994) have related approaches with respect to housing production and land supply to this typology, finding that within the first group there are large builders undertaking speculative development while the opposite is true of social democratic systems, and corporatist states come somewhere in between. Kemeny (1995a and 1995b) has suggested a two-fold classification of rental regimes – an anglo-saxon dualist system which concentrates assistance in a non-market sector and a germanic unitary market where the division between private and social is more blurred (Figure 3.1). Under each typology some clear relationships can be distinguished – although in most cases the analysis is quite partial, concentrating on particular aspects such as the source of profit rather than all stages from land assembly, through production and management to the allocation of the resultant housing benefits.

In this chapter I concentrate on experiences in the western European welfare states in relation to both the Kemeny classification and the first two elements of

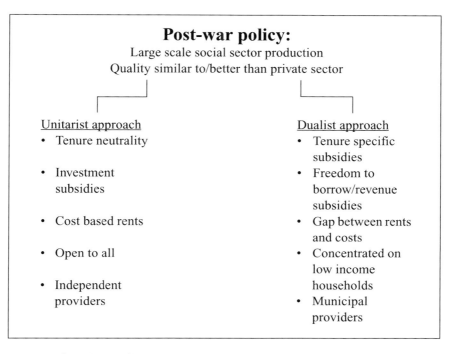

Post-war policy:
Large scale social sector production
Quality similar to/better than private sector

Unitarist approach
- Tenure neutrality

- Investment subsidies

- Cost based rents

- Open to all

- Independent providers

Dualist approach
- Tenure specific subsidies

- Freedom to borrow/revenue subsidies

- Gap between rents and costs

- Concentrated on low income households

- Municipal providers

3.1 Rental regime policy

the Esping-Andersen typology. This is because it is among countries of the European Union that most of the discussion of convergence and divergence has taken place (Kemeny and Lowe 1998; Doling 1997; Gibb 2002). The conclusions from this analysis are then applied to the minimalist welfare states of southern Europe, transition economies and examples across the world to provide a basis for assessing the potential role of social housing in the twenty-first century.

The starting point

The common baseline for almost the whole of Europe after the Second World War was a massive shortage of housing arising from the destruction or major damage to significant proportions of the existing stock together with an almost complete lack of housing investment through the war years. Equally the labour force and other resources had to be redeployed from war to peace production. Housing was seen as an important element of social infrastructure and of political cohesion. It was therefore given high priority. The result was that large scale resources were mobilized for social sector production across Europe, but within at least two quite different general frameworks (Department of Environment 1977; Papa 1992; Boelhouwer and van der Heijden 1992).

The two approaches

The unitarist approach exemplified by Sweden and the Netherlands, and, with somewhat different parameters, Germany, was applied with more or less consistency across much of continental Europe (Lundqvist 1992). It was predicated on tenure neutral subsidies for investment usually in the form of interest rate reductions and guarantees. Rents were generally cost based. Rents in the private sector were controlled and the two systems at least partially linked. In some countries, notably the Netherlands, administrative allocation of the available stock continued for decades.

The wider financial framework, however, remained highly regulated and within this there were special circuits of housing finance. France was in many ways a special case of this model, with a complex range of financial intervention linked more closely to income related assistance (Lefebvre in Turner and Whitehead 1993).

As investment caught up over the years, rents across sectors tended to converge often at or near market levels. These rents were themselves significantly modified by the availability of social investment. Social housing often became open to all households and, in most countries, municipalities took a more strategic role allowing independent providers to develop the social rented stock.

At the same time, while subsidy systems remained broadly neutral, financial deregulation enabled greater choice in housing for many households leading to greater investment in private housing. The pressures for more targeted assistance grew in order to concentrate help on poorer households and areas in an environment where the vast majority of households were well-housed and other priorities, notably health but also macroeconomic stability, started to dominate (Turner and Whitehead 1993).

During the 1990s problems of low demand and particularly of obsolescent stock began to dominate in many European countries – both in metropolitan and more rural areas as population followed employment change. Equally, notably in France but now across most northern European countries, housing became more widely defined to include not just the attributes of shelter and security but also a range of neighbourhood, environmental and service attributes. This often results in a wider role for social suppliers as leaders in urban management (Boelhouwer 2000; *Housing Studies* 2000 and 2002).

The dualist approach, exemplified particularly by the UK, concentrated on tenure specific subsidies to municipalities. These authorities were enabled to borrow at government interest rates and both developed and managed the resultant stock. Housing was allocated to those in poor housing conditions, who were mainly lower income households. Initially authorities had complete powers to build within individual cost limits. Later their borrowing powers became more limited and subsidies were reduced and directed at areas where the costs of managing and maintaining the stock at below market rents could not be covered by revenues

(Department of Environment 1977). The question of how the value of existing assets might be employed to fund new and improvement investment became paramount and led to significant changes in subsidy, ownership, rents and allocation principles. In particular social sector provision became more broadly based with housing associations taking the main role in provision (Department of Environment 1987).

Financial deregulation and a generous tax regime enabled the growth of owner-occupation, as did subsidies to transfer from social housing. This helped reduce the range of households accommodated in housing requiring supply subsidies. Latterly assistance has become even more tightly targeted on lower income tenants (Stephens *et al.* 2002). Equally, many of the problems of obsolescent infrastructure and social exclusion can be found in areas dominated by social provision (Smith 1999; Kleinman and Whitehead 1999). This has led to a growth in area and housing specific policies to improve neighbourhoods and individual opportunities.

Thus, each country's investment experience can be divided into three main stages. The first stage in almost all countries concentrated on new construction. As the stock of dwellings began to exceed the number of households, usually in the 1970s but much later in Germany, the emphasis moved towards management and maintenance of the existing stock and to questions about the appropriate form of subsidy (Hills *et al.* 1990). In this second stage the pressure was on reducing public expenditure and improving the use of existing assets including an emphasis on greater privatization and a shift towards demand side subsidies. Finally, in part because of the very large scale post war building programme, the emphasis in the third stage has now moved on in most European countries to addressing problems of regenerating urban areas and restructuring housing within wider social infrastructures, again often within a framework of privatization and reduced funding (Boelhouwer and van der Heijden 1992; Papa 1992; Boelhouwer 2000).

The development of policy in a dualist system: the UK

The starting point in the UK was an acceptance that public sector organizations, including local authorities and New Towns, were the only agencies able to undertake large scale investment for lower income households in the immediate post war period (Ministry of Reconstruction 1945). In particular, these agencies were the only ones with the powers to clear slums, to redevelop urban areas and to build new settlements. Part of this capacity arose from the 1947 Town and Country Planning Act which nationalized development rights, together with the fact that these agencies owned large tracts of land where they could give themselves permission to build. Part came from their capacity to employ compulsory purchase powers in a political environment where the government was taking control of infrastructure provision across the board. Part also came from the wider development of the welfare state, which included as a major strand of policy adequate housing for all. Most importantly the finance and subsidy system gave these authorities powers to borrow, build and to obtain subsidy for all dwellings that met certain cost and standard criteria – there was no overall limit on borrowing capacity (Department of Environment 1977).

Stage 1, which lasted from the 1950s to the early 1970s, concentrated on removing slums and damaged properties and on overcoming the massive absolute shortfall in the number of dwellings available. Local authorities and New Towns undertook large scale building programmes, sometimes developing themselves, but more usually using private contractors. These programmes involved replacing slums in the urban areas, building large estates on the edge of cites and towns and developing new towns and town extensions. Subsidies were readily available for clearance, infrastructure and new build. The programmes involved public ownership and management, public sector borrowing and control, risks borne by local authorities and central government, and allocations relating not specifically to income but to household needs and particularly existing housing conditions (Department of Environment 1977).

Stage 2, in the 1970s, can be seen as the period of re-evaluation of local authorities as developers and the beginnings of the introduction of independent social landlords. The most important elements of this period included:

- the recognition that in almost all localities the number of dwellings now exceeded the number of households – so that it was no longer the case that any investment anywhere was desirable. Equally clearance and redevelopment programmes became unpopular and were replaced by large scale rehabilitation projects;
- the introduction of demand side subsidies for low income households in rented accommodation first for social and then for all tenants. This shift was associated with the introduction of residual rather than investment subsidies on the supply side;
- controls on local authority borrowing powers and a reduction in supply subsidies as a result of macroeconomic problems which involved borrowing from the IMF. This meant that for the first time the level of total social output was determined by central government;
- a shift in the subsidy system to encourage independent social landlords to develop and, in particular, to undertake large scale rehabilitation projects;
- the introduction of legislation to require local authorities to take responsibility to house particular groups of households, notably through the 1977 Homeless Persons Act, as well as for local housing strategies;
- growing concern about the efficiency of the public sector in general and local authority competence in particular.

The result was lower public expenditure on new investment and an increasing interest in addressing inefficiencies, as local authorities recognized that their main role was to manage, maintain and allocate the existing stock rather than simply to build and replace. There was also growing emphasis on housing lower income and other vulnerable households rather than simply concentrating on those suffering poor housing conditions. However, one element of the efficiency scenario was missing. In the early 1970s the Conservative government had tried to introduce market related rather than historic cost rents (Department of the Environment 1971). However, a change of government, together with worldwide inflation, led instead to the introduction of rent controls in the social sector to support more general income policies together with limits on local authority borrowing powers. Taken together this meant that resultant rent increases were inadequate even to pay for increasing maintenance costs. This led, well before the election of the Thatcher government, to financial problems with respect to investment in the existing stock as well as to a rapid decline in new building programmes (Malpass and Murie 1994; Murie 1997).

Stage 3 developed from this scenario itself in two stages. First, the Conservatives concentrated public expenditure cuts in housing investment: reduced subsidies by ring fencing the housing accounts of local authorities and deeming costs and rent increases; shifted from a right to sell local authority dwelling to a right to buy by sitting tenants; and deregulated housing finance and general finance markets. Taken together this both enabled a large number of households to enter owner-occupation and further restricted local authorities' capacities to improve and maintain their stock. The second stage concentrated on restructuring the social sector by introducing private finance to independent social landlords (RSLs); concentrating new social sector building capacity in these RSLs, who then had to bid for government subsidy; introducing competitive tendering into the local authority sector; transferring ownership from local authorities to newly created RSLs in order to recycle asset values to pay for improvement and maintenance programmes; and concentrating allocations on the most vulnerable households (Whitehead 1993 and 1999).

The outcome was to limit social sector output; increase rents; target the much lower levels of supply subsidies available on the most cost effective RSLs; shift assistance from supply to income related benefits; target allocations to the poorest and most vulnerable households; and place greater emphasis on ensuring affordable, rather than specifically social, housing. The Labour government that came to power in 1997 continued many of the same policies – putting further pressure to restructure the social sector and greater emphasis on private finance, although with rather more subsidy, especially to support improvement and regeneration (Department of Environment, Transport and the Regions 2000).

The results of these changing policies in terms of both new construction and the existing stock can be seen in Tables 3.1 and 3.2. The overall stock of housing has increased quite rapidly but the relative importance of social and particularly local authority housing has fallen equally rapidly. New construction has shifted

Christine M. E. Whitehead

Table 3.1 Housing stock (Great Britain)

	1980 %	1999 %	Increase/ decrease (millions)	Increase/ decrease %
Social sector				
Public sector	30.6	15.4	−2.6	−41.0
Registered social landlords (RSLs)	2.4	5.7	+0.9	+1.8
Private sector				
Owner-occupied	56.0	67.9	+5.0	+43.0
Private renter	11.0	11.0	+0.4	+ 17.0
Total	**20.9**	**24.6**	**+3.7**	**+17.7**

Source: Department of Environment, Transport and Regional Affairs, Housing and Construction Statistics.

Table 3.2 New construction: Great Britain

	1980	1990	2000
Private sector	128.4	154.2	145.1
Public sector	86.0	16.4	0.0
RSL	21.1	16.3	23.3
Total	**235.5**	**186.9**	**168.4**

Source: Department of Environment, Transport and Regional Affairs, Housing and Construction Statistics.

towards the private, fundamentally the owner-occupied sector. Within the social sector almost all new provision is by housing associations.

The current agenda is much more broadly based than thirty years ago. It reflects the increased prosperity of the country; the different position of housing – where it is not so much shelter but security, neighbourhood and services that are required; and the growing role of the private sector in both provision and aspirations. New build is once again important, especially in pressured areas because of the increased number of households associated with immigration as well as indigenous demographic factors. Within the required total more than 30 per cent of new build needs to include some element of subsidy, if standards and affordability are to be achieved (Holmans 2001). There is an emphasis on developing balanced communities, co-locating social and market housing and requiring market providers to contribute to social housing provision. Housing is also seen as a central element in other agendas – reurbanization, regeneration and social inclusion as well as sustainability – and local authorities are regarded as core partners in these agendas (Urban Task Force 1999).

Yet the role of social housing itself in this new environment is unclear. It is still widely accepted by government and commentators that local authorities, and indeed RSLs, have not overcome their administrative failures in managing the existing stock. Equally central government plays the main role in determining pricing and allocation rules. It is a dismal reality that, to a significant extent, policy aimed at social housing is now directed at unwinding the outcomes of stages 1 and 2 when local authorities acted as the main developers and then lost the capacity adequately to maintain their stock, and at addressing the need to manage the neighbourhoods and large estates which are the outcome of that process of rapid development (DETR 2000). Equally they must address changing demand side issues: those in employment clearly aspire to home-ownership and control over their own environment and are generally uninterested in being accommodated by social landlords (Greater London Assembly 2001). Municipal landlords as such are set to disappear to be replaced by arm's length organizations with powers to diversify activities (DETR 2000). The jury is thus out about whether a social sector, as traditionally understood, will continue to exist in the second decade of the twenty-first century.

The development of policy in unitarist systems: the Netherlands and Sweden

The Netherlands

Post war policy in the Netherlands was based on a tenure neutral system of subsidies associated with a heavily controlled private rented sector, reflecting the extreme shortages in provision throughout the country. The Housing Act 1901 had enabled the development of some 700 Approved Housing Corporations, many of which were closely linked to and sometimes owned by municipalities. These municipalities had planning powers to assemble land and provide infra-structure before transferring it to other owners. In the post war period the Housing Corporations played the central role in a large scale industrialized building programme to provide social housing for a wide range of households – not just those on low incomes. Subsidy was provided by government and there was a layered guarantee system provided by municipalities and central government which enabled private finance to be raised at interest rates little different from those available for central government borrowing (Priemus 1995; Priemus and Boelhouwer 1999).

In many ways stage 1 lasted until the late 1980s when the need for public expenditure cuts came together with the fact that housing was now readily available in most parts of the country. The result was a call for significant reductions in subsidy and regulation, culminating in the Heerma policy of 1989. This limited interest subsidies for housing investment in all tenures, increased social sector rents and aimed to target social housing more towards lower income groups. The most important element in financing terms was the 'Brutering' policy by which all outstanding loans to Corporations were written off against the removal of subsidies on the existing social sector stock. Thus the Housing Corporations as a sector had to stand alone, to develop mechanisms of cross subsidy to ensure the survival of those in low demand and low income areas, and to bear the risks of future changes in incomes and costs. Subsidies continued to be available for urban renewal but the general implication was that most of those who could afford it would wish to become owner-occupiers (subject to a formally tenure neutral taxation system, providing interest rate reliefs but charging, limited, imputed income tax) (Boelhouwer and van der Heijden 1992). At the same time the private rented sector, where allocations and rents remained well into the 1980s, was the subject of creeping decontrols (Turner and Whitehead 1993). The outcome of these two stages was first that, by the year 2000, 50 per cent of all housing had been built since 1969, and, second, only 52 per cent of the stock was owner-occupied, while 36 per cent was Corporation owned and the rest was in the private rented sector (Gruis 1997; Dieleman 1999).

Stage 3 is reflected in the new 'Mensen, wensen, wonen' policy enunciated in 2001 (Ministerie van VROM 2000a, 2000b, 2001 and 2002). This reflects a number of important concerns including that Corporations are inefficient; that the increasing demand for owner-occupation is resulting in greater suburbanization and the hollowing of urban areas; and that the quality of the existing stock and particularly of the urban environment is inadequate for the twenty-first century. Owner-occupation is thus seen as the major competitor to social housing provision, and there is concern that, on current trends, the social sector will be bypassed as households become more affluent, leading to the collapse of some, mainly urban, neighbourhoods. To address these issues the policy calls for large scale transfers to save the social sector. Some 500,000 Corporation homes are to be sold off. The proceeds are then to be used to fund improved building and improvement standards in the social sector. An individual voucher scheme will replace rental subsidies. The expected outcome over the next ten years is that owner-occupation will grow to 65 per cent, with around 25 per cent Corporation owned and 10 per cent in the private rented sector. Housing overall will be self-financing, except for subsidies to low income households (van Kempen and Priemus 2002).

Whether or not this vision will be achieved is, as yet, unclear – and there is some evidence already that transfers are not occurring as expected (Haffner 2002). But the underlying pressures are strong – people want control over their own homes and are mainly in the position to pay for it. The concern is to ensure that urban and suburban areas built in the immediate postwar period can meet these requirements rather than to concentrate on the specifics of who owns the available stock.

Sweden

Policies in Scandinavian countries have similarly been based on the ethos of cross tenure interest subsidies, a range of social providers linked to a generous welfare state, and income support.

Stage 1 in Sweden lasted from the 1960s to the 1980s and was characterized by 'The Million Programme' aimed at generating enough homes to meet the short-fall through tenure neutral interest rate subsidies, together with income related subsidies to individuals. Much of the programme was built by municipal housing companies or by co-operatives as well as by private developers for owner-occupation. Rents were set by local negotiation, including unions as well as the companies and the municipalities. The rents set in the social sector then impacted on private sector rents. The outcome by the end of the 1980s was that some 34 per cent of the total stock was owner-occupied, 17 per cent owned by co-operatives and 49 per cent was rented. Within this 49 per cent, half were municipally owned. Equally, half had been built since 1965 (Turner *et al.* 1996).

As in other European countries, the late 1980s brought the need to cut public expenditure at the same time as it was recognized that absolute shortage had been replaced by adequate supply overall, and indeed excess supply in some areas (Turner and Whitehead 1993). A major government Commission (the Danell Commission) report led to the removal of general interest rate subsidies replacing them by far lower levels of assistance targeted at deprived neighbourhoods and low income groups in pressured urban areas (SOU 1992). Municipal companies were expected to be more market oriented and to increase rents, to sell stock and to concentrate on housing the lowest income groups. At the same time maintenance standards were reduced. An important outcome of this approach was to reduce investment in new building across all sections to negligible levels. By the end of the century, there were still low demand areas where there is no incentive to build, but rapidly increasing pressures in the capital and university towns (Englund *et al.* 1995; Turner and Whitehead 2002).

Another Housing Commission was set up in the mid-1990s (SOU 1996). It addressed the question of whether housing subsidies should remain tenure neutral but also pointed the way towards a situation where housing overall would be a net contributor to public funds rather than dependent upon government subsidy. It reiterated that the state retained responsibility for ensuring an adequate housing supply but saw this as being addressed by targeted subsidies more tightly directed at particular areas – especially in the university cities where pressure was so obviously increasing. There was to be a move towards market rents in both the social and private sectors. In the social sector, additional financial constraints were introduced with the aim of increasing the efficiency of housing companies and encouraging sales to individuals and to other landlords. Area based policies of regeneration were also emphasized, based on partnership of housing providers and other local agencies. Again the message was that privatization and partnership were necessary in order to ensure the survival of the social sector.

Convergence or divergence in social housing in Europe

The driving forces for change in the social sector relate to a range of factors observable across countries in Europe:

- the fact that the imbalance of demand and supply has been addressed at least at the national level. The public sector was seen as a necessary force if large numbers of dwellings were to be built to meet absolute shortages across Europe after the Second World War. Whatever the underlying policy ethos, only the public sector could put together the land, the productive capacity and the funding necessary to ensure that enough dwellings would be produced to meet the needs of the total population not just those unable to pay for their own housing. This requirement has now been met – and some of the costs of meeting requirements via administrative means are becoming more obvious;
- the equally important fact that average standards of housing are now high for the vast majority of households, even though there are growing concerns about neighbourhood and particularly fear of crime and anti-social behaviour in some, mainly inner urban areas. The fact that the majority are well-housed removes much of the political pressure to maintain housing as a priority;
- the need to reduce public expenditure across the board – arising from cross national and national macroeconomic policies, together with the capacity to use the large unencumbered housing asset base in the social sector to lever in private finance. This in turn is related to
- a general concern that social sector organisational structures tend to inefficiencies, unless incentives and constraints can be developed which mirror aspects of private sector governance – including incentives to greater consumer orientation, to utilize the asset base more effectively and to minimize costs of management and maintenance; and
- general increases in incomes and wealth, which are associated with growing aspirations to owner-occupation, resulting in greater tenure polarisation observed across countries with quite different approaches to the organisation of government assistance.

The policies that governments from both the unitarist and dualist approaches have employed have had many similar attributes:

- reductions in general subsidies, whether across tenures or specific to the social housing sector;
- a movement away from tenure neutral subsidies towards targeted assistance concentrating on specific groups of households and areas;

- a movement towards market related rents and interest rates linked with increased dependence on income related subsidies;
- increasing the emphasis on housing the poorest households in the social housing sector – generating increased social exclusion within the tenure, if not necessarily in particular localities;
- greater emphasis on increasing efficiency in the social sector, through the introduction of private ownership, finance and management;
- a commensurate increase in the choices available to social sector tenants, particularly through the purchase of their own homes and latterly through choice based lettings; and
- a growing concentration of assistance on neighbourhood regeneration through social housing investment linked with wider programmes to improve both infrastructure and opportunity.

There are, however, continuing differences, notably with respect to the relationship between housing assistance and social security. In the UK, housing assistance remains, in part, a cheap way of achieving minimum income standards by concentrating on those in greatest need of long term assistance in the social sector and those in shorter term need in private renting. In unitarist systems incomes tend to be more evenly distributed, social security is more generous and those with the lowest incomes are more evenly spread across tenures – so the extent of social exclusion is lessened (Stephens *et al.* 2002). But in all countries, general subsidies have been withdrawn, and output levels have fallen, in some cases to the point where shortages are beginning to re-emerge in pressured areas.

Thus the evidence certainly suggests convergence in terms of both policy and outcomes across the different approaches to social housing in western Europe (Doling 1997; Boelhouwer 2000; Turner and Whitehead 2002; van der Heijden and Haffner 2000). First, the role of the state in ensuring adequate housing continues to be a core national policy objective. However, in almost all contexts the direct role of social provision is being reduced and replaced by income related benefits, and more targeted supply subsidies, usually to independent providers. Funding is much reduced across the board, to the point where housing overall may soon become a net contributor to state funding. Delivery mechanisms emphasize private sector provision and incentives – and where social ownership remains, market pressures are being introduced, supplemented by financial constraints aimed at minimizing costs and targeting assistance to specific problems.

Are these patterns mirrored elsewhere?

Similar patterns can be found in other environments. In the 'minimalist' countries of the USA, southern Europe and Australia the state has generally further withdrawn from direct involvement. Instead they tend to concentrate on improving financing systems and market frameworks as well as developing guarantee and insurance systems to support the provision of that funding. In the USA, for example, this has led to greater emphasis on fiscal incentives to expand the supply of affordable housing and provide incentives for regeneration (Holmans *et al.* 2002).

In the transition economies the pressures have been almost wholly on introducing legal frameworks which will enable owner-occupation and private finance to operate more effectively. The major problems of industrial restructuring, increasing social sector rents, and poor management, maintenance and design in the large estates mean that the public sector is generally in crisis – and privatisation, especially the introduction of private finance, is often seen as the only way forward. However, before this can generate many of the projected benefits, notably with respect to private investment, there are often extremely difficult problems of property rights to be addressed, notably with respect to alienation. Funding individual ownership and developing appropriate instruments is seen as fundamental to meeting housing objectives (Struyk 2000).

In Hong Kong and Singapore with their long histories of public provision of land and housing the problem is very different, as government continues to play a central role in organizing markets. In both countries, government has proved its effectiveness in delivering large scale development programmes, including new towns. In Singapore especially, these have been associated with clearance in central areas. As such both countries have experienced a stage 1 similar to that found in Europe, but greatly extended because of the far lower starting point and thirty years of very rapid demographic and economic growth. However, new development is no longer the only priority and some of the problems of management and particularly regeneration are now becoming of greater importance. Both countries are now emphasizing owner-occupation, private finance and private provision as a means of expanding choice and increasing standards (Doling 1999; Chiu 2001). Even countries such as Japan with very little government involvement in housing per se are concentrating more on partnership involvement in neighbourhood and special housing needs (Esping-Andersen 1996).

In countries such as Kenya and South Africa, where much of the housing provision has historically been for government employees, dwellings are being sold off. The aim is to develop finance markets, which will help those able to pay to fund themselves and allow subsidies to be concentrated more directly on the poorest households (Karley 2002). In many developing countries, the policy emphasis is on developing both formal and informal financing systems to enable households to solve their own housing problems. These policies can include reducing formal standards so that they are more in line with what is potentially affordable. Arguably therefore, whatever the starting point, the pressures and the potential solutions are the same – tending towards enabling greater private production rather than direct government involvement in provision and supporting individual and local initiatives.

Social housing in the twenty-first century

So where do we go from here?

The evidence so far suggests that social provision in advanced industrialized countries has been generally effective in ensuring housing development and that social sector leadership is probably the only way of enabling large scale redevelopment and regeneration. Equally, it suggests that, without clear incentive structures and pressures from consumers and funders alike, the social sector is not particularly good at management, maintenance and allocation. This is not necessarily to say that these activities must be privatized, but rather that lessons should be learned from how the private sector system operates within a framework of well defined objectives, incentives and constraints. Most notably, competition and consumer choice are powerful motivators towards efficiency and the better use of resources to provide what households are prepared to pay for.

The fundamental difficulty remains that many households in all societies cannot afford adequate housing either at some stages of their housing careers or at any stage. Most commentators would argue that demand side subsidies, or even loans, may well be the most appropriate means of addressing short term affordability problems but that some form of social intervention is likely to be more effective for households who are vulnerable into the longer term (Galster 1997). This does not necessarily require social ownership, but it certainly implies meeting social objectives, including security of tenure and social inclusion, in part through housing provision (Yates and Whitehead 1998).

In the current European context the most important agenda relates to the regeneration of poor quality and insecure neighbourhoods many of which involve concentrations of socially owned accommodation. This process calls for partnership approaches, which play to the strengths of the different private and social sector actors. It also requires large scale central government resourcing because of the risks involved and the difficulties of coordinating private initiatives. The local social sector is likely to play an increasing role in this process – but not necessarily as housing provider.

Yet, as incomes continue to rise, housing, narrowly defined, tends to be seen as more of a private good, because the benefits go to the owner and/or occupier. In the UK, for instance, average expenditure on housing is now less than for leisure activities – so it is not surprising that people want to choose how much housing they want, above a socially determined minimum standard, as well as the location and other attributes of that housing. Increased incomes and wealth thus tend to be associated with private provision and particularly with owner-occupation. If social sectors cannot meet these aspirations they must fail in terms of long run sustainability and social inclusion – both because of administrative failures in management and maintenance and because they cannot meet reasonable aspirations. This is the pattern we see emerging across much of Europe at the present time.

On the other hand there is no doubt that there is a continuing role for additional affordable housing provision to meet existing and emerging needs. These appear to be on the increase in many countries, in part because of the growing impact of in-migration. Private sectors still appear to be relatively unresponsive in terms of new building, and the filtering process remains highly inefficient. Some subsidy to affordable housing provision appears to be absolutely necessary if shortages are not to reappear, at least in pressured areas. This may well not be in the form of traditional rented housing. It can be shared ownership, shared equity or owned by independent landlords – as such it does not have to involve a social sector per se.

The continuing role of a traditional social sector therefore appears to depend on three main factors: the extent of inequality in income distribution; the commitment to housing as a merit good for households further down the income scale; and, most importantly, the relative efficiency of social as compared to private landlords. The role of the social sector as leading partners in development and redevelopment appears far more secure – because they are the only ones with the planning and compulsory purchase legal powers – and because they are often significant land owners in areas ripe for redevelopment. But to play this role there must be funding – either from cross subsidy within the projects or from central government commitment.

We can therefore put forward two basic scenarios. The optimistic one is where:

- incomes continue to rise and governments operate progressive tax and benefit systems;
- owner-occupation and other forms of private ownership dominate but take a smaller proportion of households' incomes;
- government intervention is concentrated on improving markets, especially housing finance markets, and on bearing large scale and political risks through guarantees, new insurance products and partnership arrangements;
- the social sector has adequate funding to operate as one set of landlords within a broader competitive framework; and
- municipalities and other public agencies play a full role in enabling development and especially redevelopment.

In this version social housing would be one element in provision for mixed communities with growing aspirations, concentrating on their areas of particular expertise, notably with respect to regeneration and social inclusion.

The pessimistic one is where:

- incomes, at least in some countries, decline, economies become more volatile and governments do not address income inequalities;
- owner-occupation and private ownership dominate but take a larger proportion of households' incomes – leaving a far higher proportion of households in need of assistance to achieve adequate housing;

- governments assume that finance and regeneration markets can manage their own risks;
- Nimbyism dominates new housing provision, limiting the expansion of the total housing stock;
- planning and other powers are not developed in a way which enables effective regeneration; and
- there is inadequate funding for social housing so that there are queues, lower standards and a lack of choice – so that the sector becomes more residualized.

Many commentators in the UK and in other parts of Europe, particularly in the transition economies, recognize the second scenario as more than a possibility. Even in the richer unitarist economies the pressures are there. If this is the social sector's future it will be bypassed and those who have the chance to opt out will do so, leaving a costly and politically undermined social housing system.

The potential for the first scenario does, however, exist, and the fundamentals of income growth, demographic change and our growing understanding of the nature of housing as linked to its neighbourhood and local services make it overwhelmingly important that it be achieved. Equally, it makes sense in terms of the fundamental market failures associated with housing provision, even in wealthy societies.

What, however, is most likely is something in between – perhaps with the social sector playing different roles within each country depending upon the extent of pressure in local housing markets. In low demand areas the case for significant social sector restructuring will be strong, while in areas of pressure it will continue to play a more traditional, if declining, role in ensuring provision. Even this diminished role depends upon rebuilding political faith in social housing and reversing the growing perception across advanced economies of social housing as a second class system, inappropriate for those able to exercise housing choice.

References

Barlow, J. and Duncan, S. (1994) *Success and Failure in Housing Provision – European Systems Compared*, London: Pergamon.

Barr, N. (2001) *Economic Theory and the Welfare State*, Northampton: Edward Elgar Publications.

Boelhouwer, P. (2000) *Financing the Social Rented Sector in Western Europe*, Delft: Delft University Press.

Boelhouwer, P. and van der Heijden, H. (1992) *Housing Systems in Europe: Part I. A Comparative Study of Housing Policy*, Delft: Delft University Press.

Burns, L. and Grebler, L. (1977) *The Housing of Nations*, London: Macmillan.

Chiu, R.L.H. (2001) 'Housing in the Social Development Perspective', in Estes, R.J. (ed.) *Social Development in Hong Kong*, London and New York: Oxford University Press.

Department of Environment (1971) *Fair Deal for Housing*, Cmnd 4728, London: HMSO.

—— (1977) *Housing Policy Review*, Cmnd 4728, London: HMSO.

—— (1987) *Housing: the Government's Proposals*, Cm 214, London: HMSO.
Department of Environment, Transport and the Regions (2000) *Quality and Choice: a Decent Home for All*, London: TSO.
Dieleman, F.M. (1999) 'The Impact of Housing Policy Changes on Housing Associations: Experiences in the Netherlands', *Housing Studies*, 14 (2): 251–9.
Doling, J. (1997) *Comparative Housing Policy: Government and Housing in Advanced Industrialised Economies*, London: Macmillan.
—— (1999) 'Housing Policy and the Little Tigers: How Do They Compare with Other Industrialised Countries?', *Housing Studies*, 14 (2): 229–50.
Englund, P., Hendershott, P.H. and Turner, B. (1995) 'The Tax Reform and the Housing Market', *Swedish Economic Policy Review*, 2: 318–56.
Esping-Andersen, O. (1990) *The Three Worlds of Welfare Capitalism*, Cambridge: Polity Press.
—— (1996) *Welfare States in Transition*, Sage.
Galster, G. (1997) 'Comparing Demand-side and Supply-side Housing Policies; Sub-market and Spatial Perspectives', *Housing Studies*, 12 (4): 561–77.
Gibb, K. (2002) 'Trends and Change in Social Housing Finance and Provision within the European Union', *Housing Studies*, 17 (2): 325–36.
Greater London Assembly (2001) *Key Issues for Key Workers*, London: Greater London Authority.
Gruis, V. (1997) 'The Netherlands', in P.J. Boelhouwer (ed.) *Financing the Social Rented Sector in Western Europe*, Delft: Delft University Press.
Haffner, H. (2002) 'Dutch Social Rented Housing: the Vote for Associations'. Paper presented at the 9th European Real Estate Society Conference, Glasgow.
Hancock, K. (1991) 'The Economic Principles of Affordability'. Paper given at Housing Studies Association Conference, York.
Heijden, H. van der, and Haffner, M. (2000) 'Housing Expenditure and Housing Policy in the West European Rental Sector', *Journal of Housing and the Built Environment*, 15 (1): 71–92.
Hills, J., Hubert, F., Tomann, H. and Whitehead, C. (1990) 'Shifting Subsidies from Bricks and Mortar to People', *Housing Studies*, 5: 147–67.
Holmans, A.E. (2001) *Housing Demand and Need in England 1996–2016*, London: Town and Country Planning Association.
Holmans, A., Scanlon, K. and Whitehead, C. (2002) *Fiscal Policy Instruments to Promote Affordable Housing*, Research Report VII, Cambridge: Cambridge Centre for Housing and Planning Research.
Housing Studies (2000) 'Special Issue: Housing and Health', *Housing Studies*, 15 (3).
—— (2002) 'Special Issue: Opportunity, Deprivation and the Housing Nexus; Trans-Atlantic Perspectives', *Housing Studies*, 17 (1).
Karley, K. (2002) 'Mechanisms for Mobilising Private Funding towards the Development of a Sustainable Housing Finance System'. Unpublished PhD, University of Cambridge.
Kemeny, J. (1995a) *From Public Housing to the Social Market: Rental Policy Strategies in Comparative Perspective*, London: Routledge.
—— (1995b) 'Theories of Power in Esping-Andersen's Three Worlds of Welfare Capitalism', *Journal of European Social Policy*, 5 (2): 87–96.
Kemeny, J. and Lowe, S. (1998) 'Schools of Comparative Housing Research: from Convergence to Divergence', *Housing Studies*, 13 (2): 161–76.

Kleinman, M.P. and Whitehead, C.M.E. (1999) 'Housing and Regeneration: the Problem or the Solution', *National Institute Economic Review*, 170: 78–86.

Leibfried, S. (2001) *Welfare State Future*, Cambridge: CUP.

Lundqvist, L.J. (1992) *Dislodging the Welfare State? Housing and Privatisation in Four European States*, Delft: Delft University Press.

Maclennan, D. and Williams, R. (eds) (1990a) *Affordable Housing in Britain and America*, York: Joseph Rowntree Foundation.

—— (1990b) *Affordable Housing in Europe*, York: Joseph Rowntree Foundation.

Maclennan, D., Muellbauer, J. and Stephens, M. (1998) 'Asymmetries in Housing and Financial Market Institutions in the EU', *Oxford Review of Economic Policy*, 14 (1): 54–80.

Malpass, P. and Murie, A. (1994) *Housing Policy and Practice*, London: Macmillan.

Ministerie van VROM (2000a) *Cijfers over Wonen 2000/2001. Feiten over mensen, wensen, wonen*, Den Haag.

—— (2000b) *Mensen, wensen, wonen. Wonen in de 21ᶜ eeuw*, Den Haag.

—— (2001) *What People Want. Where People Live. Housing in the 21st Century. Summary*, Den Haag.

—— (2002) *Cijfers over wonen 2002. Feiten over mensen, wensen, wonen*, Den Haag.

Ministry of Reconstruction (1945) *Housing*, Cd 6609, London: HMSO.

Murie, A. (1997) 'Beyond State Housing', in Williams, P. (ed.) *Directions in Housing Policy: Towards Sustainable Housing Policies for the UK*, London: Paul Chapman.

Papa, O. (1992) *Housing Systems in Europe: Part II. A Comparative Study of Housing Finance*, Delft: Delft University Press.

Priemus, H. (1995) 'How to Abolish Social Housing? The Dutch Case', *International Journal of Urban and Regional Research*, 19 (1): 145–55.

Priemus, H. and Boelhouwer, P. (1999) 'Social Housing Finance in Europe: Trends and Opportunities', *Urban Studies*, 36 (4): 633–46.

Smith, G.R. (1999) 'Area-based Initiatives: the Rationale and Options for Area Targeting', LSE CASE paper no. 25, London School of Economics, London: Centre for the Study of Social Exclusion.

SOU (1992) *Avreglerad bostadsmarknad*, SOU 1992:24 (del 1) and SOU 1992:47 (del 2), Stockholm: Swedish Government Publishing Office.

—— (1996) *Bostadapolitik 2000 – fran productions – till boendepoltik*, SOU, 1996:156 (Final Report of the Housing Commission), Stockholm: Swedish Government Publishing Office.

Stephens, M., Burns, N. and Mackey, L. (2002) *Social Market or Safety Net?*, Bristol: Policy Press.

Struyk, R.J. (ed.) (2000) *Homeownership and Housing Finance Policy in the Former Soviet Bloc*, Washington: Urban Institute.

Turner, B. and Whitehead, C. (1993) *Housing Finance in the 1990s*, Research Report SB:56, Gavle: The National Swedish Institute for Building Research.

—— (2002) 'Reducing Housing Subsidy: Swedish Housing Policy in an International Context', *Urban Studies*, 39 (2): 201–17.

Turner, B., Whitehead, C.M.E. and Jakobsson, J. (1996) 'Comparative Housing Finance', Swedish Government Housing Commission, Bosdstadspolitik 2000, Expertrapporter, SOU.

Urban Task Force (1999) *Towards an Urban Renaissance*, London: E. and F.N. Spon.

Van Kempen, R. and Priemus, H. (2002) 'Revolution in Social Housing in the Netherlands: Possible Effects of New Housing Policies', *Urban Studies*, 39 (2): 237–53.

Whitehead, C.M.E. (1983) 'The Rationale of Government Interventions', in Dunkerley, H. (ed.) *Urban Land Policies: Issues and Opportunities*, Oxford: Oxford University Press.

—— (1991) 'From Need to Affordability: an Analysis of UK Housing Objectives', *Housing Studies*, 28 (6): 871–87.

—— (1993) 'Privatising Housing: an Assessment of UK Experience', *Housing Policy Debate*, 4 (1): 104–39.

—— (1998) *The Benefits of Better Homes*, London: Shelter.

—— (1999) 'The Provision of Finance for Social Housing: the UK Experience', *Urban Studies*, 36 (4): 657–73.

—— (2002) 'The Economics of Social Housing', in O'Sullivan, T. and Gibb, K. (eds) *Housing Economics and Public Policy*, Oxford: Blackwell Science.

Yates, J. and Whitehead, C.M.E. (1998) 'In Defence of Greater Agnosticism: a Response to Galster's "Comparing Demand-side and Supply-side Subsidies"', *Housing Studies*, 13 (3): 415–23.

4 Housing provision and management of aspirations

Chua Beng Huat

Introduction

Social welfarism is now largely a negative concept; unemployment insurance has been substituted with 'workfare' and 'co-payment' by user and state has been instituted in other services, such as healthcare, primary and secondary education and public transportation. However, to the extent that market failures to provide employment, housing, and healthcare for all are inevitable, so too is the fact that there will be a segment of the population that will fall through the market net – some form of welfarism is unavoidable in capitalist market driven economies. This would entail that no capitalist states can reject the idea of welfarism out-of-hand or totally. Nevertheless, there is a tendency for analysts to take a 'fiscal' outlook: due to its drain on the national economy, the state will always maintain provision at the minimal levels, and get out completely if it were possible. For example, in the case of public housing, the trajectory of state provision has been characterized as a four-step process: intervention, provision, quality improvement and withdrawal (Power 1993: 3–4). Such a conceptualization fails to explain the Singapore instance, where the long-ruling government espouses 100 per cent home-ownership, overwhelmingly by state provision, through sales of 99-year leasehold high-rise apartments built on state land. Since the mid-1980s, the state housing sector has completed more than 700,000 flats, accommodating 85 per cent of the population of three million, of which more than 85 per cent of the households own their 99-year leasehold flats. The Singapore case suggests that a narrow fiscal view of state provision of any goods is inadequate.

Analytically, state provided goods and services should always be viewed primarily as a 'political' good, while the ability to provide, the fiscal question, is always a contingent issue. As political good, it is analytically crucial that one examines the political pay-offs of provision, of which the most immediate, if not the most obvious, is the ruling government's legitimacy to rule. It would seem to be both logically and substantively the case that a well-implemented program of provision of any goods will accrue to the ruling government political capital, thus enhancing its legitimacy to rule. Instead of waiting anxiously to withdraw from state provision, the possibility of enhancing legitimacy may even push the ruling government to implement universal provisions if this would entrench its political longevity in government, as exemplified by universal provision of state-subsidized housing in Singapore.

In this chapter, I will attempt to draw out the social, political and economic effects of universal provision of housing by Singapore's long-ruling People's Action Party (PAP).

Universal/monopolized housing provision by the state

Formed in 1954, the PAP consisted of two ideologically different groups, joined by the common political desire for decolonization. One group was ideologically influenced by social democracy, which they imbibed during sojourn in post-war Britain as students; the other by the winds of communism and socialism in Asia. The Party captured electoral majority in the first general election in 1959 and has governed Singapore since then without any discontinuity. Influenced by both social democracy and socialism, the first generation leaders of the PAP, upon election, spent the little national wealth that it had on the three conventional 'welfare' items of education, health and housing expansions; this 'redistribution before growth' (Lim 1989: 173) marks state-subsidized housing, along with other welfare measures, as a political good.

The public housing authority, the Housing and Development Board (HDB), started modestly, in 1961, with minimal, emergency, one-room rental flats. The subsequent massive expansion of state housing provision was not envisaged as a grand plan at the outset. It is a process that grew with the momentum of each clearly identifiable policy turn. For example, when the 'sale' of 99-year leases for the apartments was introduced in 1964, the take-up rate was abysmal. It was only after citizens were allowed to use their compulsory social security savings, the Central Provident Fund, to service both down-payment and monthly mortgage that sales took off; by 1970, 63 per cent applied to purchase the 99-year lease, and by 1986, the figure reached 90 per cent of all applicants.[1] The program has expanded continuously in the last 40 years, providing the nation with apartments of internationally comparable high standards of quality and space, of between 65 and 145 square meters for average family sizes of between 3.5 and 4.5 persons.[2]

Nationally, the materially tangible and highly visible presence of the state-subsidized housing estates is a powerful substantive and symbolic monument that attests to the efficacy of the PAP government. This has contributed very significantly to its longevity and legitimacy to govern, as housing has become a covenant between the people and the PAP government (Chua 1997: xi), in which the latter is obligated to provide housing for all in exchange for political support. Beyond domestic politics, Singapore's success in housing the nation in state-subsidized housing has been duly noted internationally; the financing scheme for home-ownership, through a 'provident fund', has been emulated in Shanghai, PRC (Chiu 2000: 459). Now possibly abandoned, Hong Kong's policy to increase home-ownership rapidly to 70 per cent within a short span of five years, formulated during the early days of Tung Chee Hua's installation as the first chief executive of the Special Administrative Region (SAR), was obviously influenced by Singapore's success.

Monopoly provision and social control

Part of the national development process of Singapore involved the near total nationalization of land, through bequests by the colonial administration, extensive land reclamation of the coastal areas and compulsory acquisition of land, often settled by either farms or squatter housing.[3] By the early 1990s, the state owned close to 90 per cent of the land. With the demolition of squatter housing and the progressive lifting of rent control in pre-war dwellings, the entire citizenry of Singapore, except those at the highest end of the income strata, is now dependent on the HDB for housing. In this sense, renting or purchasing of HDB flats contains within it an element of involuntary, if not coerced, behavior. This is true especially for very poor families, as the flexibility of rent in the informal housing sector that suits the uncertainty of income is lost when one moves into the formal state-housing sector with its rigid monthly payments, which can be met only through regular incomes.[4] In this sense, home-ownership contributes as one of its significant effects the active proletarianization of the population, transforming it into an industrial workforce (Tremewan 1994: 49). Thus, if improved housing environment is a pull factor in Singaporeans availing themselves of HDB housing, absence of alternative housing is undoubtedly the push factor. The result is the phenomenal expansion of the HDB housing estates and of the HDB itself as a housing agency and a bureaucracy,[5] transforming it into virtually a monopoly provider of housing to the nation.

In spite of the citizens' near absolute dependency on state provision, the PAP government remains ideologically adamant that access to public housing is not a 'right' but a 'privilege' of citizenship. This conceptual distinction has very consequential political and juridical advantage for the government. Since it is not a 'right', access to subsidized housing is not an 'entitlement' of citizenship; instead citizens must pay for the access to subsidized housing. This allows the state-subsidized housing to be commodified and priced according to affordability under changing national economic conditions. Being able to vary sale-prices of the apartments enables the HDB to recover much of the construction costs of the apartments, which in turn enables it to refinance the next cycle of construction, with each cycle carrying a tolerable margin of subsidy. Concurrently, the government is able to impose consumption discipline on the households; the accommodation obtained by a household is entirely dependent upon its ability to pay, rather than on established scales of needs. The level of subsidy being dependent on the size of the flat rented or bought from the HDB. Access to the subsidy is reserved only for citizens and permanent residents as a 'privilege'. Furthermore, the 'privilege' is granted to citizen-purchasers under conditions of sales specified by the vendor, the HDB, on the basis of 'willing buyers and willing seller', which again, politically and administratively, exempts the government from the obligation to provide the housing on terms other than those it itself specifies.

The 'reality' for the Singaporeans is neither one of 'entitlement' nor of 'privilege'. Absolute dependency has effectively reduced Singaporeans to the status of being 'clients' to the HDB, a 'patron-client' relation in which they depend on the HDB for shelter, in the total absence of alternative, affordable housing. They are thus obliged, or even coerced, to accept restrictions on their rights and behaviors, exercised on them through conditions of sales and rental meted out by the HDB as part of tenant/lessee and landlord agreements. This opens up a floodgate for the government to introduce social control measures, often unrelated to housing issues, as conditions of rent and sales.

The battery of social controls piggy-backed on housing provision includes: at the national level, housing is used to promote pro-family policies. New state-subsidized flats are only sold to households. It was not until 1991 that singles over 35 years old, deemed to be 'out' of the marriage market, were allowed to buy higher-priced resale three-room flats – two bedroom, sitting room, kitchen and washroom – out of the central area. Single, unmarried mothers are denied access to new, state-subsidized flats although each with her child(ren) constitutes a household. They will have to buy resale flats, punished for their 'immorality'. Conversely, multi-tier families that choose to live in the same flat or in close proximity to each other are given higher cash subsidies and priority of allocation.

Also at the national level, housing provision has been used to break up spatial/residential racial or ethnic concentrations and working class neighborhoods and redistribute the residents into high-rise housing estates, with the salutary effect of achieving spatial integration of the different races and social classes.[6] However, simultaneously, it increases the hardships of ethnic minority groups in the routines of their everyday life. This becomes apparent in the way the racial mixing is executed at the estate and block of flats level. Distribution of the three major 'races' in the population – Chinese, Malays and Indians – is regulated by quota in the allocation of new flats by the HDB. This practice is in turn transferred to the block level, where the number of households of each 'race' is controlled by quota for each block. The effects of this allocation/control procedure are unevenly suffered. Constituting approximately 75 per cent of the population, Chinese suffer little because the quota is quite large, thus new or resale flats remain readily available. On the other hand, the quota often prevents Malay and Indian households from purchasing flats in desired blocks or estates, particularly resale flats in established estates, even if they are choosing to live in close proximity with their aging parents.[7] This exposes an instance of the plethora of contradictions in housing policies taken as a whole system.

At household level, housing is used to control a string of possible personal criminal offences by the threat of eviction, thus punishing the entire family. The activities proscribed include gambling, engaging in unauthorized businesses, renting of rooms to illegal migrants and throwing of 'killer litter', that is, throwing objects out of the flat with the risk of hurting someone. In each of these, not only the perpetrator of the offence is subject to criminal punishment, including caning and jail, but the entire household risks being evicted from the flat, whether rental or leasehold. Thus, revealing that having a lease is not 'ownership' of the apartment; as opposed to 'freehold' property in which the owner of the house also owns the land upon which it is built in perpetuity, in the leasehold public housing flat, the land is owned by the state which can revoke the lease, with negotiated compensation. Fortunately, the monopoly of provision renders all eviction rules inoperative because its execution would produce homelessness, which will only worsen and/or multiply social problems; nevertheless, families with leaseholds can be subject to enforced downgrading to rental flats.

Finally, the cost of dependency on state provision is fully exposed in the political sphere. In the 1997 general election, in the face of a very closely contested constituency, the PAP in its desperation warned that constituencies that elected non-PAP MPs would be the last to be 'upgraded' – the sprucing up of public areas and improvements to existing flats in old housing estates under a cost-sharing scheme between tenants and the government, which will be discussed later. HDB residents were held hostage politically in terms of their material interests by the PAP; only those who believe in democracy at all costs would have voted for non-PAP candidates and risked jeopardizing the value of their properties. Eighty-five per cent of Singaporeans are consequently severely constrained in their ability to fully exercise their electoral rights as citizens. In the end, the PAP regained some of the lost electoral grounds and the Prime Minister attributed this to the success of this 'vote in exchange for upgrading' strategy.[8]

Obviously, Singaporeans pay a social and political cost for the quality housing they obtain from the state. Conversely, state provision has become and constitutes a very significant part of the instruments of governance in Singapore. However, exchange of good housing and secure property values for political and social compliance to the ruling government is not a one-way street. The costs to the latter in developing a housing monopoly that contributes directly to popular political support, whether freely given or coercively extracted, should not be underestimated. To maintain mass support, the ruling government has to intervene constantly to take care of the living conditions of the population, ensuring that the environment is well maintained and property values preserved for the entire nation. Such interventions constitute the 'burden' of the ruling government in exchange for mass loyalty of compliant citizens. As demonstrated below, it is a task that is never done.

Monopoly, resale and profits

Details of Singapore's public housing program are by now readily available, thus only some of its components relevant to the issues at hand will be highlighted here.[9] Two of these have already been mentioned; the use of CPF to finance down-payment and monthly mortgage and the sale of 99-year leases by the HDB to recover capital cost that enables reinvestment. In addition, of greater significance to its success, is the market mechanism that is built into the consumption side of the program.

After five years of tenancy, a household can sell the 99-year lease in the market to other households who are eligible to purchase within the regulations of HDB, keep any profit derived and avail itself of a new, subsidized flat for a second and final time. All subsequent changes of residence will have to be bought in the resale market or the more expensive private sector. Opportunity for profit has the virtuous consequence of increasing a household's propensity to upgrade housing consumption. As its financial condition improves, a household living in a small three-room flat is likely to sell it and use the profit obtained towards payment for a larger flat. Such self-upgrading produces the desired trickle-down effect, where older and smaller flats are sold to lower-income households, singles or other fresh entrants into the housing market and home-ownership.

The success of this upgrading trickle-down process is reflected in the fact that HDB has by now demolished most of the first generation one-room flats and stopped building flats with less than three bedrooms – four and five-room flats – since 1987. Also, in the decade 1990 to 2000, 42 per cent of heads of households who stayed in three-room flats had moved to four-room or larger flats or private sector housing,[10] while 24 per cent of those living in four-room flats had similarly upgraded.[11] Parenthetically, such a high level of residential mobility is detrimental to community formation and development, which being greatly desired by the government absorbs much time and effort from all PAP MPs in organizing estate level 'grassroots' organizations.

Due to sustained national economic development since 1964 when leasehold ownership was initiated, all leasehold owners who sold their flats made substantial financial gains that facilitated their upgrading of housing consumption. The highest upgrading mobility is to be found among the three-room flat leaseholders, where the propensity to upgrade is matched by a ready market of newly married couples and singles beyond 35 years of age. In 1995, a three-room flat that was purchased in the early 1980s from the HDB for about $20,000, would be selling at between $100,000 and $140,000, depending on age of the flat and location, giving the seller more than $100,000 profit. Little wonder that in addition to households who were upgrading, others sold their flats and moved into another, same size, resale three-room flat to realize capital gains: having already fully paid up the $20,000 for the flat, one would sell it, make a substantial profit, then finance the mortgage for the second flat by CPF, leaving one with plenty of cash in hand (*Straits Times*, 30 September 1995).[12]

Obviously, prices of all sizes of public housing flats were rising at significant rates. In the decade of 1985–95, those of four-room resale flats jumped from $62,000 to $121,200 and five-room flats from $77,000 to $191,000. The profit was so good that even a sober economist and ex-PAP MP had this advice to offer:

> The fact is that we can take full advantage of asset appreciation. Consider a five room HDB flat-owner: his flat is worth $450,000. He could sell it and buy a resale three-room flat for $150,000. With the remainder he could buy two bungalows in Perth [Western Australia] and rent them out for 7 per cent net returns a year.
>
> (Tan, 2 July 1996)

The suggestion that the profit be invested in Perth was because property prices in the private sector in Singapore had also risen very significantly, in tandem with and in part caused by rises in HDB flats.[13]

In spite of the very significant differences in prices, commonly in excess of $100,000, many young families choose to buy resale over a new public housing flat for, among others, the following considerations. Buying a resale flat: (i) enables young families to live in close proximity to their parents, if that were what was desired; (ii) avoids queuing time, which can be as long as five years; (iii) allows one to get a specific flat of one's choice, instead of allocation by chance, as HDB flats are distributed via luck of the draw in order to maintain fairness; (iv) allows one to obtain a flat in an established estate that already has all the necessary services, such as shopping facilities, kindergartens, schools, in place rather than waiting for them to be developed in new estates; (v) provides the chance to have better locations as older estates are closer to the central area. The earlier-mentioned rate of residential movements is indicative of a buoyant resale market, with new entrants to ownership anticipating future profits instead of worrying about the immediate additional financial burden of the difference between the cost of new flats and the resale ones they bought. The result is an HDB flat is singularly the most important piece of investment for the majority of Singaporeans.

Burdens of the state 1: ensuring affordability

With government's encouragement, easily obtainable loans facilitated by payments through the use of CPF and the opportunity for profit, public housing prices have risen steadily since the inception of leasehold ownership. Prices for new flats have been increasing also, in tandem with the rise of the economy, after the early 1980s. Until then, rental and sales prices were not adjusted for a period of almost twenty years, resulting in accumulation of debts by the HDB, as the prices of all flats were subsidized, the smaller the flat the greater the subsidy. To reduce subsidy and sustained long term provision, a steep adjustment of prices upwards was introduced in the early 1980s. This led to a rush of applications, as Singaporeans feared that prices would escalate in leaps from then on. However, the one-time radical adjustment enabled the government to build in, subsequently, gradual increases in line with general economic conditions.

By 1995, escalating prices of both new and resale flats led to fears of their affordability for new families, as price rises had outstripped wage rises. Government then re-emphasized its assurance that prices of the lower end public housing flats will always be kept affordable to their respective target consumer households. This it can do easily because prices of new flats are determined by the Ministry of National Development, according to its estimates of affordability within prevailing macroeconomic conditions, subjected only marginally to market discipline. It pledged that the price of three-room flats will be fixed so that 90 per cent of the households will be able to afford one; while that of four-room flats will be fixed at affordability level for 70 per cent of households; prices of new flats will rise and fall with wages for working class Singaporeans (*Straits Times*, 23 September 1996).

It would be remembered that the HDB had stopped building three-room flats since the mid-1980s. Additional measures had to be introduced if one of the pledges were to be honored. One of the measures is the 'buy-back' scheme: HDB will buy back resale three-room flats at market value, refurbish them and sell them at a huge subsidy to households with monthly income of less than $1,000, who are buying a flat for the first time. The subsidy in these flats often amounted to more than 50 per cent of the costs of the buy-back prices. Not surprisingly the queue for such flats is long and HDB has set a target of buying in and reselling 2,000 flats per year, beginning 1995.

Significantly, the government not only has to bear the burden of provision at the low-income end of the society but also at the higher middle class level as well. Symbolically, breaking away from the overwhelming majority who live in public housing and moving into private sector housing has become a desired marker of 'success' among the higher end of the middle class, particularly the younger professional families. Yet, many are unable to afford the prices of private, freehold condominiums. To allay their frustrations, an 'Executive Condominium' scheme was introduced in 1995. Concurrently, HDB stopped developing the largest 'executive flats' within the public housing system. Under the new scheme, state-owned land parcels are to be auctioned to private developers at a discount, in exchange for an agreed price of the flats to be built. Owners of such condominiums are subjected to the same five-year residency rule before being allowed to sell them in open market. The first two projects under this scheme were undertaken by government-linked companies and were grossly over-subscribed; the cost of a flat was about one-third less than comparable cost in the non-subsidized private sector.

State subsidy to the already relatively well-off did not go unnoticed by the population. It gave rise to public complaints that the government is subsidizing people who deemed themselves to be too good for the rest of society in HDB flats. Ironically, in satisfying the aspiration of a rising middle class through the 'executive condominium' scheme, the ruling government has contributed directly to the visibility of increasingly obvious class divisions; contributing to the politicization of housing provision by its own act.

Burdens of the state 2: constant upgrading

The ruling government's commitment to 100 per cent home-ownership is an ideological mechanism aimed at intensifying nationalist sentiments among the citizens, by making them 'stakeholders' of the nation. Having so directly encouraged ownership of HDB flats, it also has to bear responsibility of maintaining the values of the citizens' investments in HDB properties; a responsibility it cannot shirk without serious political costs. One obvious area is to maintain property values of older estates, so that they remain attractive to new entrants to home-ownership. Older estates will have to be upgraded to standards as close to new ones as possible, lest they turn into 'slums' by comparison with the new, devaluing the sitting residents' investments. So, in mid-1989, almost thirty years after the first HDB block was built, the Minister of National Development announced a fifteen billion dollar upgrading program for older housing estates, to be spent over fifteen years. The first flats to be upgraded were those completed before 1975; by March 2001, those completed before 1980 were included. The program is undertaken on cost-sharing basis between affected households and the government. Seventy-five per cent or more of the households in the blocks in the neighborhood selected for upgrading must vote for it, to establish the absence of coercion.

Models of proposed upgrading are exhibited for comments and adoption by the residents through their committees, supervised by their MPs. It generally includes substantial sprucing up of open areas in the neighborhood, such as parks, playgrounds and other shared facilities. Alterations to the blocks include not only aesthetic redesigning, as almost all the older blocks are plain functional slab blocks, but also improvement of corridor lighting and additional elevators, as many of the oldest estates built in the early 1970s were without elevators in spite of being high-rise buildings. Finally, at the household level, additional space, such as additional bedrooms or expansion of kitchens and balconies, is provided. The substance and cost-sharing formulae vary with each upgrading project.

To avoid both cost from being the obstacle to voting for upgrading and excessive financial burden for tenants, payments for their share are made easy through various arrangements. They can use their CPF funds for installments, spread over 25 years. For household heads who are retired, payment can be deferred until their flats are sold or ownership transferred. The program's success is reflected in the immediate rise of resale prices of upgraded five-room flats by a margin of up to $100,000 (*Straits Times*, 16 September 1996). With promise of potential windfall, residents supported enthusiastically the upgrading program, so much so that, as mentioned above, it could be successfully used as a threat to the residents *qua* electorate during the 1997 general election.

If the 'executive condominium' scheme led to dissatisfactions among the majority of the population, the upgrading scheme had led to complaints from the high-end of the middle class, who had paid non-subsidized, high prices for private sector housing. They complained against what they see as yet another, additional subsidy to HDB tenants, paid with their tax dollars. Behind this is also the sense of 'injustice' of the profits that HDB households are able to gain in playing the system of buying, reselling and buying again of HDB apartments. Another segment of the population that lives in the private housing sector began to call for government subsidy in upgrading their own estates, particularly for estates of over 25 years. While they were able to afford the cost of housing at the point of purchase in earlier times, they are not necessarily able to afford the costs of upgrading in a much expanded market economy.

In response to calls for subsidized upgrading of private housing estates, the government agreed, in October 2000, to spend $20.5 million on five estates in a pilot scheme. As to those who object to upgrading subsidies in general, the Minister of Finance pointed out that personal income tax level in Singapore has been declining for over a decade. Thus subsidies for upgrading came from, and will continue to come from, surpluses in the overall national revenue and not personal income tax (*Straits Times*, 19 September 1995). Whether the complaining segment was convinced by the Minister's argument is moot, the politicization of housing along class lines has been reinforced and will likely intensify in future for two reasons. First, upgrading is an endless cycle that will involve greater and greater costs, which may challenge the ruling government's ability to meet them. Second, it should be noted that the ruling government has in fact carried out its threat that constituencies that show 'low' support for the government, measured in electoral votes, will be the last to be upgraded;[14] the level of tolerance of Singaporeans for what is recognized and admitted to by the ruling PAP as using public money to its own ends may yet be politically tested.

Closed market: inter-generational transfer of burden

In the determination to achieve universal provision and to demonstrate that public housing flats are sound investments, the government has through its various policies contributed very significantly to the steady increase in prices of HDB flats, with the sharpest increases registered in the mid-1990s. The then Minister of National Development claimed 'relaxation of public housing rules' and 'government's asset enhancement programmes', along with 'political stability, good economic growth and growing affluence' as primary reasons for the rapid rise in prices (*Straits Times*, 11 July 1996). By 1996, at the eve of the then yet unknown Asian regional financial crisis, measures had to be introduced in allocation and resale rules to cool down the market. The crisis was to expose a much more serious contradiction in the system, with more intractable solutions.

As a privileged provision of the state to citizens, only households of citizens and others with legal permanent resident status can purchase the 99-year leasehold flats. The public housing market is effectively a closed market, in which citizens sell to each other, closed to external investors. Enhanced property values can be realized only when an existing lease-owner sells the lease to another eligible household, who is either a new entrant to ownership or upgrading to a bigger flat. This means, one Singaporean household profits from another Singaporean household; often, one generation from another where older households who had bought their flats earlier gain from younger families who are new entrants into ownership. Herein lies a deep concern: if the new entrants into home-ownership were to stop buying from the resale market, the entire upgrading trickle-down virtuous cycle would come to a complete halt! What might have been a hitherto 'unthinkable' scenario had partially materialized during the 1997 crisis.

Prices peaked in 1997, as Singapore was not affected by the regional crisis until late in the year.[15] After that, prices declined to their lowest point in the first quarter of 1999, and then began to rise slowly as the national economy appeared to be recovering. However, by the first quarter of 2000 prices began to drop again; at the end of the fourth quarter of 2000, they had declined by more than 100 index points from their peak in the first quarter of 1997. What was hitherto a guaranteed investment for all was no more. For the first time, just like private sector housing investments, prices in HDB flats can and will fall in the resale market and a household can end up with negative equities. This has more than a financial consequence. It also has a psychological effect of damping enthusiasm for resale flats. Although prices of resale flats fell close to 5 per cent in 2000, the total number of resale flats fell by a hefty 23 per cent for the year (*Straits Times*, 27 January 2001). Apart from scarce, and perhaps scared, buyers, those who are looking to upgrade also find themselves in a contradictory position: while they may be able to purchase a resale flat at a lower price, they will also have to take reduced price on their existing flat; a situation which is as likely to discourage buying as selling.

On the other hand, the queue of application for new flats from the HDB has extended, indicating that there is a greater willingness to wait for a lower cost new flat, forgoing the advantage of locations of higher price resale flats.[16] Meanwhile, they can benefit from rent subsidy that the HDB provides for its three-room rental flats, as one prong of the pro-family policy of encouraging marriages.[17] Finally, there have been instances in which such newly married couples were unable to take up the flat allocated to them during the year 2000 because the flats had come 'too early' and they had not accumulated sufficient cash and CPF funds to pay for them. How much of this 'refusal' to take up an earlier offer was due to shaken confidence because of the regional crisis and also, increasingly, fear of unemployment through restructuring and retrenchment of the multinational firms that are operating in Singapore remains unclear.

Failure in the resale market is a new phenomenon in Singapore's forty years of national public housing program. It exposes a very serious flaw in the closed market system: if new entrants into home-ownership were to unanimously buy their flats directly from the HDB, there will be no resale market. The reason for buying from the HDB has always been there: prices for new flats have always been lower than comparable resale, older flats; consequently, there is no financial reason to take on additional burden for first time home owners, especially if the quality of the new flats is always improving. On the other hand, existing home owners who sink very significant parts of their life-savings into the flats, looking to 'realize' profits in the resale market, have always been in a position of risk; risk that had been hidden by a sustained buoyant national economy. The negative consequences of this confluence of development will be most serious for heads of households who are looking to finance retirement by realizing capital from selling their flats. They would be in substantial financial difficulties if they were to take sharply reduced resale prices, or worse, a loss.

Failures to keep prices rising in the resale market appear to expose one conundrum: if resale prices kept increasing and found ready buyers, it burdened and relatively impoverished new entrants to home-ownership, likely the younger generation; if ready buyers of resale flats could not be found and resale prices declined, the process relatively impoverished existing leasehold owners, generally the older generation.

Ultimate, ironic solution: buy-back by state

With its commitment to 'always maintain the quality and value of HDB homes' (*Straits Times*, 22 June 1996), and the fact that the state is the landlord, the government has various options for easing the above problem. Two obvious solutions are already being undertaken. First, is to reduce supply of new flats, forcing a segment of the new applicants into purchasing higher price resale flats. There has been a reduction of new constructions since the early 1990s but not entirely for this reason. The reduction is largely determined by the concern to avoid an excess of flats caused by 'inheritance': as the population ages, the head of a household may find himself with two flats, one purchased by himself and the other inherited from the parents. If this happened on a mass scale, prices of resale flats would be greatly affected, in turn, affecting the retirement funds of the older generation. It is therefore essential that HDB does not concern itself exclusively with building new flats for every eligible family but also 'finds a mechanism to recycle older properties',[18] as part of the above-mentioned upgrading process.

Second, is for the state to buy back flats from sitting leaseholders, either in a direct cash buy-out or by a reverse mortgage, which will give them a steady and good income while allowing them to enjoy their flats at the same time (Tan 1996). The latter process can only be undertaken by the state. As it is the landlord, no one else can provide such a facility because as the leases run down to year zero, the land will revert back to state ownership, unlike freehold properties in which the land will be owned eventually by the financial institutions that provide the reverse mortgages. The state can ultimately destroy the re-purchased flats and save the recovered land for future developments.

While the resale market for flats has not yet, and might never, 'collapse', an inkling of the effects of its materialization can be gleaned from troubles in the HDB retail space sector. In 1992, HDB initiated a scheme of selling shop spaces in public housing estates at discounted rates to sitting retailers. The scheme was met with immediate 'success'. A total of 12,000 units of shops were to be sold within seven to ten years and the first 5,000 units were literally snapped up within the first year. It should be noted that this process was initiated at a time when the retailers in HDB housing estates were beginning to feel the impact of keen competition from new 'regional' shopping centers developed as new town centers, each filled by popular chain stores and an entertainment complex. Under such conditions, to take on a hefty mortgage on account of buying the shop space, which is at least twice the existing rental cost, would immediately put a squeeze on the profit margin of the trades. Thus, for most of the affected retailers, especially those in marginal trades such as barbershops, men's tailor shops and small convenience stores, the entire exercise was one of hoping to gain windfalls from the resale of the shops to new retailers and services, such as medical clinics, banks and chain stores.

Anticipation of profits quickly pushed up prices of HDB shops; within two years of the scheme, prices went up by 40 per cent, yet the acceptance rate of the shops placed was 92 per cent because the resale value remained, on average, at least twice the discounted prices set by HDB (*Straits Times*, 3 June 1995). While those who managed to sell their shops did make windfalls, the rest immediately faced financial difficulties. Difficulties intensified after the regional crisis and the sales scheme was suspended. For many, dreams of profit have turned into financial nightmares. As one of these shop owners puts it, 'We bought our shops and we are trapped. Our business is bad, our turnover is low, we cannot rent out the shop or sell it' (*Straits Times*, 5 March 2001), because there are no buyers. They began to cry for help from (who else?) the government, the HDB.

Pressured by sufferings of the many small family-based retailers who can no longer stand up to competition from supermarkets and shopping centers and, very significantly, in view of a forthcoming general election that must be held before August 2002,[19] the government has finally agreed to rescue some of these shops, with various measures through the HDB: it will pay any of the 500 retailers a sum of $48,000 to quit business in selective HDB rented premises with very poor business prospects. If this scheme were well received, it will be extended to all HDB rental retail premises in Singapore. It will allow retailers to sublet up to half the shop space to generate income. Finally, in selective precincts, it will subsidize upgrading undertaken by 50 per cent of the total cost, which hitherto had been borne completely by retailers (*Straits Times*, 15 March 2001). The measures fell short of the ultimate demand of some shop owners, who want the HDB to buy back their shops, so that they can exit with minimal cost.

The shop owners are clearly 'inspired' by the fact that HDB has, indeed, buy-back schemes in other areas. Apart from the above-mentioned buying back of three-room flats at market value to resell them to low-income households, HDB is also undertaking '*en-bloc* buy-outs' of sitting lessees in selected areas. These areas, generally, have older and low-density developments close to the city. The blocks of flats are compulsorily acquired, with each lessee being compensated at estimated market value determined by the government,[20] and given choices to exit the public housing sector or a new 99-year lease for a new flat in the same neighborhood. They will be resettled only after the new flats are completed and ready for occupation. The purpose of this government-initiated scheme is to reclaim the state land for future, intensified development. It is therefore financially likely to be beneficial to the state; benefits that some of the affected families feel that they should have their share of, like other households who profit from selling their HDB flats.

Thus, while the shop owners' demand that HDB buys back their leases is immediately unacceptable, even apparently unreasonable, to the government, there is no telling that the latter will not adopt it. Indeed, this is something that it will have to ponder and may have to adopt in future with reference to excess HDB flats, if it were to maintain the values of the investments of the citizens in public housing, which it has encouraged throughout the past 40 years. There are good reasons for the state to undertake buying back its own housing products. First, in return, the process can generate and maintain mass electoral support. Second, lands recovered by demolition of buy-back flats constitute resource for future and value-added intensified developments; this is all part of the capitalist logic of 'creative destruction', which may be happily undertaken by a highly entrepreneurial ruling government.

Conclusion

The logic of the monopoly position of the state in housing provision in Singapore holds two obvious substantive points. First, the financial cost of achieving the political objective of 100 per cent home-ownership is obviously very high for the ruling government. Second, so too are the costs to Singaporeans as citizens; in addition to escalating costs and thus heftier mortgage burdens, they are subjected to non-housing related constraints in their social and personal activities, including constraints on exercising fully their electoral rights to vote, with threats to the values of their properties in public housing estates. These points may be peculiar to Singapore in terms of the character of the long-ruling PAP government.

The long-ruling PAP government has over the years been very prudent in its management of the national economy and has amassed a very large financial reserve, which enables it to finance the public housing scheme, including guaranteeing the values of public housing properties. In the last forty years, the PAP has developed one version of 'patriarchalism' (Woodiwiss 1998) as the principle of government, which involves not only authoritarianism in politics and social governance but also state responsibility in improvement of the material life of the citizens. Indeed, it may be argued that it is the success of the latter that allows them to finesse the authoritarianism. As a rule, authoritarian or semi-democratic regimes are likely to lead to political instability over the long term, as evidenced in Asian countries such as the Philippines, and in many African and Latin American countries. Elsewhere in Asia, such as South Korea, Malaysia and Singapore, such regimes had been able to gain the legitimacy and longevity to rule only by the 'performance' principle, that is, by 'delivering the goods' in material life, until the 1997 Asian financial crisis. Of course, this specific authoritarian/ semi-democratic politics cannot be easily generalized and readily found application elsewhere; although one should be reminded that there are many cities and countries in Asia that would like to emulate what they see as Singapore's 'success' – a vibrant capitalist economy, with very high standards of living and a ruling political party that does not have to share power – not the least of which is the People's Republic of China.

Beyond these specificities, some general observations may be offered. First, from the history of the long-term development of the public housing sector in Singapore, it would appear that potential dividends for political capital, that may be derived from successful provision of welfare goods and services, may generate momentum in the expansion of provision, contrary to the conventional under-standing that fiscal considerations give rise to a generalized tendency for the ruling government to withdraw from welfare provision. Of course, the degree of expansion or contraction depends significantly on the existing political condition of the countries in question.

Second, the ways through which social control measures are inserted into housing provision in Singapore illustrate a general process of how political capital generated by successful provision can in turn be used to impose social control measures without generating excessive social and political disruptions; that is, the general political support allows the ruling government to withstand any unhappiness that the control measures may generate within specific segments of the population. Successful provision provides the ruling government maneuvering room in political and social control. Indeed, one speculates that the temptation for the ruling government to impose social controls as entailments to the access to welfare goods would be very high, if potential disruptions, including displacement from seats of political power, can be readily contained. In a sense, the idea of 'workfare' operates on the same principle, but in reverse: a generalized mass resentment against abuse of the 'dole' cushions the ruling government from protests of those who need the dole, thus enabling it to impose severe constraints on its distribution. Again, the extent to which social control measures can be imposed is highly dependent on the political culture of the country in question.

Finally, as welfare goods are provided with entailments of social and political controls, political legitimacy and political coercion become confused; a citizen-recipient-consumer becomes alternately grateful and resentful; grateful for the decent housing and resentful of all the constraints that have to be suffered ignobly, beyond the financial burden of the monthly mortgage. Analytically, one can no longer be certain whether the citizens are driven by moral gratitude and give freely their support to the ruling government or support is coercively extracted from them. Substantively, the ruling government is unlikely to be interested in such conceptual subtleties, least of all the PAP government that is determined to retain absolute power in the city-state of Singapore. Either way, the ruling government remains in power.

Notes

1 Details of the Central Provident Fund system are readily available in literature on Singapore; for a comprehensive overall description of the system see Tay (1992).
2 There are already several comprehensive and critical accounts of the HDB and public housing in Singapore, hence there is no need for detailed descriptions; see Wong and Yeh (1985), Tremewan (1994) and Chua (1997, 2000).
3 The state owns approximately 90 per cent of the land in Singapore, partly from land initially bequeathed by the colonial government, partly from land reclamation around the island's main shorelines and partly from a very draconian land acquisition law that allowed the state to appropriate any land 'in the interest of national development' at below market prices that are determined by statute or existing use, whichever is the smaller (Koh 1967). It was not until the early 1990s, when the government had already acquired all the lands it wanted, that the state began to pay market values for the lands subsequently acquired.
4 Difficulties in meeting the demands of monthly payments are most acute in households who are resettled from squatter housing into HDB flats.
5 The expansion of the HDB was abruptly halted and its size and power trimmed, when the PAP government transferred estate management duties from HDB to local town councils, under the care of the elected Members of Parliament; see Ooi (1990).
6 In the 1960s, when politics was at its most competitive, many of these poorer neighborhoods and Chinese squatter areas were supporters of the left-wing Barisan Socialis (Socialist Front); hence the demolition of these settlements and breaking up of the blocks of left-wing supporters was politically advantageous to the PAP (Tremewan 1994: 45–7).

7 For more discussion of dissatisfactions with the quota system see Lai (1995).

8 It was the first time in the history of the PAP that they stooped to self-admitted pork barrel politics (*Straits Times*, 29 December 1996). For detailed discussion of the 1997 general election and housing, see Chua (2000).

9 For comprehensive reviews of the work of HDB, see Wong and Yeh (1985) and Chua (1997).

10 The price in the private sector is at least twice that of a public housing flat of comparable size; however, it can be as high as four times, depending of course on the location of the former.

11 Data is obtained from Singapore Census of Population, 2000, Advance Data Release No. 6: Households and Housing.

12 In one instance, a family has made almost one million Singapore dollars by changing residences within a period of about twenty years: they bought the first public housing flat from the HDB in the early 1970s for slightly more than $30,000 and sold at more than $250,000 about ten years later; they then moved into a freehold private condominium, which they subsequently sold for about $700,000 with a profit of more than $300,000 and bought a resale executive flat in the public sector; finally, they sold this flat for another profit of about $300,000 and downgraded into a resale five-room HDB flat.

13 It should be noted that many Singaporeans do invest in properties overseas. Developers in Canada, Australia and Britain regularly market new developments in Singapore. However, as for investment in Perth, a city that is only four hours flight away, there is very little capital gains to be made, making it unattractive to Singaporeans. A friend who is a developer told me that he was so frustrated by the sluggishness of returns and the troubles of having to deal with poor tenants that he traded with a friend: six houses in a suburb in Perth for an apartment in Singapore.

14 This was clearly stated by both the current Prime Minister and the then Minister of National Development, currently Second Minister of Finance (*Straits Times*, 23 January 1995).

15 The picture in the private sector is even more bleak: in the fourth quarter, 1998, prices fell to the 1993 level, falling more than 180 index points from its peak in the first quarter, 1996. Prices picked up in 1999 and by the fourth quarter, 2000, it remained 23 per cent lower than the peak in 1996 (*Straits Times*, 27 January 2001).

16 Also, in its pro-family social policies, the government will grant to a first time home buying family a cash subsidy if the latter choose to purchase a resale flat near any parents of the married couple.

17 Rent for three-room flats is reduced for these couples from $750 to $250, monthly.

18 Minister of National Development, *Straits Times*, National Day Supplement, 9 August 1995.

19 The general election was held in January 2002.

20 In some of the central areas, the lessees are certain that they can get market prices that are better than the compensation, if they chose to sell the flats.

References

Chiu, R.L.H. (2000) 'Housing reform in a marketised socialist economy: the case of Shanghai', *Urban Policy and Research*, 18 (4): 455–68.

Chua, B.H. (1997) *Political Legitimacy and Housing: Stakeholding in Singapore*, London: Routledge.

—— (2000) 'Public housing residents as clients of the state', *Housing Studies*, 15 (1): 45–60.

Koh, T.T.T.B. (1967) 'The law of compulsory acquisition in Singapore', *The Malayan Law Journal*, 35: 9–22.

Lai, A.E. (1995) *Meanings of Multiethnicity: a Case Study of Ethnicity and Ethnic Relations in Singapore*, Kuala Lumpur: Oxford University Press.

Lim, L.Y.C. (1989) 'Social welfare', in K.S. Sandhu and P. Wheatley (eds) *Management of Success: Moulding of Modern Singapore*, Singapore: Institute of Southeast Asian Studies: 171–200.

Ooi, G.L. (1990) *Town Councils in Singapore: Self-Determination for Public Housing Estates*, Singapore: Institute of Policy Studies Occasional Papers No.4/Times Academic Press.

Power, A. (1993) *Hovels to High Rise: State Housing in Europe since 1850*, London: Routledge.

Tan, A.H.H. (1996) 'Housing aspirations must be rooted in reality', *Straits Times*, 2 July.

Tay Boon Nga (1992) 'The Central Provident Fund: operation and schemes', in L. Low and T.M. Heng (eds) *Public Policies in Singapore: Changes in the 1980s and Future Signposts*, Singapore: Times Academic Press: 264–84.

Tremewan, C. (1994) 'Public housing: the working class barracks' in *The Political Economy of Social Control in Singapore*, London: St Martin's Press: 45–73.

Wong, A.K. and Yeh, S.H.K. (1985) *Housing a Nation: 25 Years of Public Housing in Singapore*, Singapore: Housing and Development Board.

Woodiwiss, A. (1998) *Globalization, Human Rights and Labour Law in Pacific Asia*, Cambridge: Cambridge University Press.

5   Housing and regulation theory

Domestic demand and global financialization

Alan Smart and James Lee

Introduction

One challenge for housing studies is to understand the linkages between the economic, political and social dimensions. Much of the analysis of housing focuses on only one of these categories, with at best ad hoc linkages with the others. While not the only viable strategy for increasing our comprehension of their interrelations, the contribution that regulation theory can offer is the one adopted in this chapter. One of the main advantages of regulation theory for our project is its emphasis on the instability of capitalist economies which require non-economic 'fixes' in the form of political and social interventions to maintain stability and growth, providing explicit links between the three dimensions. A major disadvantage is that little research has been carried out by regulationists specifically on housing. This chapter makes a modest contribution to this task by first reviewing work that has been done on housing in regulation theory, and then attempting some further steps by adapting ideas derived from Robert Boyer's work on finance-led growth regimes. The majority of regulationist examinations of housing emphasize the contribution that governmental housing subsidies make to enhancing effective demand for consumption. We suggest that globalization and other dimensions of social change in recent decades are creating a new situation for housing and its roles in promoting growth and political stability. We then use a brief case study of some recent changes in the housing sector in Hong Kong, where real estate is arguably more central to the political economy than in almost any other territory, to examine the impact of financialization on some recent housing issues.

Regulation theory: an outline

Michael Aglietta, a pioneer of regulation theory, in a recent essay asserts that the 'hypothesis that underlies the regulation approach' is that: 'capitalism is a force for change which has no inherent regulatory principle; this principle is provided by a coherent set of mechanisms for social mediation that guide the accumulation of capital in the direction of social progress' (Aglietta 1998: 62).

A *regime of accumulation* is a 'systematic organization of production, income, distribution, exchange of the social product, and consumption' (Dunford 1990: 305). For most of history, power and the ability to command labour and allocate resources served to organize cooperation. By contrast, capitalism is a distinctive regime of accumulation in that large proportions of activity are organized by formally equal individuals contracting to buy and sell products for profit and provide labour for wages. However, unregulated capitalism generates various crises which cannot be resolved endogenously, that is, by purely economic mechanisms.

Regulationists argue that crises are commonly caused by imbalances of power between those who control capital and employees since this may result in insufficient demand for the production increases that are necessary for continued growth. Overproduction and underconsumption lead to declining profits and recessions. The mechanisms which overcome such conflicts are the *mode of regulation*: 'a set of mediations which ensure that the distortions created by the accumulation of capital are kept within limits which are compatible with social cohesion within each nation' (Aglietta 1998: 44). For example, building public housing not only meets demand, but also influences the cost of labour and transfers public funds to private contractors, subcontractors and suppliers, who employ local citizens and purchase local resources. Increased demand may generate a virtuous circle where growth is stimulated for a time.

Particular modes of regulation, however, generate pressures which lead to new crises. Regulationists have described a variety of Fordist regimes of accumulation that appeared after World War II. In general, Fordism was characterized by the development of large corporations with high profits based on near-monopoly conditions, collective bargaining and the development of a unionized working class with middle-class powers of consumption, fine-tuned with Keynesian macro-economic management techniques and government redistribution (Aglietta 1980).

By the mid-1970s, Fordist regimes in the developed countries and their accompanying modes of regulation had apparently exhausted their capacity to increase enterprise profit margins, and with the drop in corporate profitability began their systemic collapse. Enterprises and governments undermined the previous Fordist institutions through intensified competition, offshore investment and the outsourcing of work, fostering what is now thought of as 'globalization'. A new regime of flexible accumulation is widely believed to be 'epitomized by "flexibility" … in labour processes and labour markets, in the production process, in consumer markets and corporate hierarchies' (Tickell and Peck 1992: 196).

While production and accumulation have become more flexible and global, Tickell and Peck (1995) argue that new modes of regulation adequate to the task of providing stable underpinnings for the increasingly flexible and mobile production and financial institutions have yet to be developed. It may be, though, that our expectations of what an adequate flexible mode of regulation might look like are excessively biased by our experience of the unusually coherent and nation-based Fordist era, so that we cannot recognize what is emerging. Without necessarily envisaging a long-term 'grand compromise', continued growth in the fourth quarter of the twentieth century provides evidence that many nations have managed to achieve a 'spatio-temporal fix' which temporarily stabilized accumulation regimes 'by establishing spatial and temporal boundaries within which the relative structural coherence is secured and by externalizing certain costs of securing this coherence beyond these boundaries' (Jessop 2000: 335). Decommodifying and recommodifying housing is one example of such a fix, but so is selective importation of cheap labour, or maintaining a selectively permeable border between Hong Kong and the rest of China (Smart 2001).

In the following section, we examine the role of housing in supporting both accumulation and the stabilization of economic growth. Its role varies by place and time, and has been used in rather different ways. We begin with accounts of the role of housing in Fordism, and then move to the less certain ground of how its role is changing after Fordism, and particularly in the context of the heightened porosity of borders where the profits from expanded local demand do not necessarily accrue to local producers, and where states find it increasingly difficult to control flows across their borders (Jessop 2000: 350).

Regulationist accounts of housing

Housing is a major component of both consumption and production within domestic economies. It may have significant implications for export competitiveness as well, since high housing costs may inflate wages. Policies that promote the expansion of housing production have played an important role by both increasing effective demand for increased production and responding to societal tensions created by capitalist development. Much of the literature that touches on regulation and housing emphasizes variation in national modes of social regulation, such as whether the promotion of housing construction has emphasized subsidies to consumers (as in western Europe) or the promotion of private mortgages (as in the United States).

However, Robert Boyer has argued that the contemporary world economy is increasingly dominated by global finance and short-term investment flows. In this situation, state policies encouraging the construction of housing, whether through direct provision, producer subsidies, or mortgage subsidies, do not have the same effects as they had in Fordist regimes of accumulation. Developed Fordist economies (in which mass production was matched with practices that produced a mass domestic consumer market) were much more self-contained than they are at present, so that investment in increasing domestic consumption largely benefited domestic producers.

With globalization, there is more cross-border 'leakage' of the profits from state support for consumption. At the same time, property corporations have become much more global in operation, while securitization of mortgages and rental revenues has heightened the financialization of the sector (Sweezy 1997). There has been little attention to the real estate dimension of these issues in regulation theory.

Housing provision was an important, but understudied, component of the Fordist expansion of domestic demand. Florida and Feldman (1988: 188) have argued that 'US Fordism was inextricably tied to suburbanization which enhanced consumer demand and set the preconditions for a temporary cycle of self-reinforcing growth'. New Deal programmes attempted to make private home-ownership available to larger segments of the population through government mortgage guarantees and road-building programmes that made the development of cheaper land at urban peripheries feasible. Promotion of suburban housing development functioned as a 'mechanism to channel effective demand and thus to complete the productivity-wage-consumption circuit of US Fordism' (Florida and Feldman 1988: 196). A large increase in savings in the postwar period (from $32 billion to $109.1 billion between 1940 and 1960) provided the initial pool of capital for the housing boom, which mobilized consumption through the expansion of debt. Residential mortgage debt increased from $17.7 billion to $208.7 billion between 1946 and 1965, facilitating a shift to home-ownership for more than 60 per cent of the population (Florida and Feldman 1988: 196).

The promotion of home-ownership has also been argued to 'inculcate capitalist values of individual property ownership' (Kennett 1994: 1019) which provides ideological support for the system at the same time as it encourages hard work (including overtime and second jobs) to support the expanded consumption demands it generates. Suburbanization and the subsidization of private housing provided the US government with an alternative to the social democratic institutional fixes adopted in Europe with their greater emphasis on public housing and the social wage (Florida 1986; Florida and Jonas 1991; Kennett 1994). Both paths tended to promote a shift to a 'more home-centered culture and a suburban lifestyle based on patriarchal social relations ..., the "family" wage, and consumption of an ever-growing range of consumer durables by a working-class experiencing increasing living standards' (Forrest and Kennett 1997: 343). While certain groups, particularly ethnic minorities and immigrants, were often left out of the general increase of prosperity, the general tendency was towards greater inclusion of the working class (Forrest and Kennett 1997).

Kennett (1994: 1020) argues that class conflict has been a major influence on housing interventions and is a crucial element of explanation of how these interventions vary from one state to another. While social housing and the promotion of private home-ownership both serve to increase demand, their economic and social outcomes can be quite distinct. Assets built up in private housing, particularly during periods when housing prices regularly increased, can provide an important basis for the emergence of a property-based growth regime, particularly if housing equity is leveraged in order to 'play the markets'.

The collapse of the Fordist system in the advanced capitalist economies since the 1970s has modified the role of housing. Kennett (1994: 1026) quotes Wollmann as suggesting that in Germany 'housing policy has ceased to be part of the "social net" for low income people and has turned instead into an investment to assist financially the households with high income'. Competition for investment and for the most highly skilled individuals in the rapidly growing financial and high-technology sectors has encouraged gentrification-friendly policies and the exclusion of those who don't fit with the 'image' of aggressive global cities. Restructuring has tended to 'reinforce social divisions internationally and at the level of the nation-state with a shift towards greater inequality and a greater acceptance of much higher levels of unemployment, poverty and homelessness' (Kennett 1994: 1029). Many believe that the inclusive tendency associated with Fordism has been reversed, and exclusion of those without skills valued in 'knowledge-intensive' economies has become more prevalent (Forrest and Kennett 1997). As pointed out above, globalization has meant that domestic demand is less crucial for economic growth, particularly in smaller export-oriented economies, so that the utility of public subsidy for housing has decreased.

While Kennett's suggestions are useful starting points, her emphasis on the competitive strategies of political elites doesn't examine far enough the economic dimensions. Valuable as a starting point, much more needs to be done to fully comprehend the position of housing and real estate more generally in these new contexts.

The increasing centrality of global finance and associated business services in current regimes of accumulation has heightened the importance of the key nodes in which these activities are concentrated and which serve to coordinate global flows: global cities such as New York, London, Tokyo, and to a lesser extent Hong Kong (Meyer 2000). Sassen (1991) has argued that the shift to a global city role is associated with sharp increases in economic polarization, with a dual labour market divided between the corporate elite and the low-paid service workers who serve them in restaurants and retail outlets, and work for them as domestic servants. More generally, Jessop and Sum (2000: 2296) argue that cities and other localities have had to become more entrepreneurial through creating 'local differences to capture flows and embed mobile capital'. The position of housing and real estate in the circuits of financial capital (e.g. Mitchell and Olds 2000; Olds 2001) have not been adequately brought into the picture.

Depending on the kind of strategies adopted, the roles that housing may play in the refiguring of place and space to attract scarce resources (whether investment, skilled labour, tourists, or research institutes) might vary considerably. The small portion of a metropolis that is actively used by the elites, while important in these processes, is only one component of the broader dynamics which operate differently in working class suburbs or the urban fringe. Emphasis on the two poles in global cities has resulted in neglect of the impact on the mass of the population in the middle classes, which Forrest and Kennett (1997) argue have become more differentiated and subject to risks and uncertainties unfamiliar during the Fordist expansion. The end of general and reliable inflation of housing prices has also subjected them to new risks, and in some cases negative equity has crimped consumer demand.

In the next section, we turn to ideas about financialization and finance-led regimes of accumulation. These approaches have the merit that they bring the question of financial assets into the core of the analysis, even if housing has not yet been a key part of these accounts. One of our arguments in the next section will be that given housing and real estate's great importance to national and particularly urban economies, their specificities need to be brought into these theoretical projects.

Financialization and housing

Other than an occasional aside, for example Boyer's (2000b: 313) mention of the possibility of the transmission of speculative bubbles between stock and real estate markets (particularly apparent in the Silicon Valley), there has been little attention given to the impact of financialization on housing and vice versa. Boyer (2000b) argues that the stability of a finance-led growth regime depends on a sufficiently large property-owning population where returns on equity become more important than returns on labour. This might preserve a sufficient level of consumer demand to support growth. Real estate equity is still a much larger proportion of total equity for the middle classes in the US and Britain than is personally-managed share equity (as opposed to pension funds) (Byrne and Davis 2001), and often provides the financial basis for stock purchases. A comprehensive understanding of the dynamics of financialization ultimately cannot neglect real estate. The effects of real estate costs also, of course, can have critical effects on the 'real economy' of production costs, and influence a city's ability to maintain its position as a centre for the concentration of business services and corporate headquarters.

Financialization is related to a shift towards the 'ecological dominance' (Jessop 2000) of finance in the aftermath of Fordism. A shift away from corporate finance based on the retention and reinvestment of revenues towards equity finance, combined with the rise of global financial actors such as pension funds, has resulted in a heightened emphasis on 'shareholder value' and short-term rate of return in financial decision-making (Lazonick and O'Sullivan 2000). A critical driver of change in finance-led regimes of accumulation is that the rate of profitability demanded by investors tends to increase, and institutions are transformed in order to meet this demand, or else lose out to competition from other firms or nations. This situation is commonly thought to be characteristic of post-Fordist conditions and one of the main threats to sustainability in the absence of new modes of regulation: the competitive 'drive to the bottom' erodes the demand that expanded production ultimately requires. Boyer suggests two main potential outcomes in terms of demand:

> Result 1: When equity effects are well developed and if the financial markets lead to a generalization of investment behaviour determined largely by profitability, then a virtuous system of financial growth can be said to exist. In this system, raising the profitability norm does have a favourable effect on demand ... Result 2: If, on the other hand, financialization occurs in an economy which is still dominated by wage-earning social relations, where the wage is the essential determinant of the mode of consumption, raising the profitability norm has a contrary negative effect.
>
> (Boyer 2000a: 127)

In the second case, financialization leads to destabilization (Boyer 2000a: 131). If wages are still a much greater component of total domestic demand, then restructuring through down-sizing of the workforce may have counterproductive results (note that this analysis is based on the assumption that demand is primarily domestic, rather than international, an assumption that is reasonable enough for the US, but inappropriate for small open economies such as Hong Kong). However, if property-based incomes are greater than wages, then growth may be consistent with the kinds of changes that the push for increased rates of profit tends to generate (Froud et al. 2000). Boyer (2000a: 135) suggests that at present most nations do not possess the necessary conditions for a stable financialized/equity-based economy. In their absence, financialization does indeed tend to lead to the kinds of financial instability seen in recent years in most developing economies (Lin 2000; Sum 2002). The only likely exceptions Boyer identifies are the United States, Britain and Canada, where wealth 'in stocks and shares in relation to households' disposable income is in fact particularly great' (Boyer 2000a: 135).

There is a long tradition of studies of wealth accumulation through home-ownership and its impact on social relations (e.g. Lee, E.W.Y. 1999; Forrest et al. 1990; Kemeny 1992). What these studies do, and which is absent as yet in the examination of financialization in regulation theory, is to carefully examine the concrete activities of ordinary people, and how capital gains may influence their decision-making and attitudes. Recently, the 'wealth effect' (the idea that returns on investments encouraged increased consumer spending despite apparently negative savings rates) has received considerable academic and practical attention. A debate within the US Federal Reserve about it

> could have a big impact on what the Fed does about interest rates in the months ahead. On one side is Chairman Alan Greenspan, who believes that the surging stock market overheated the economy by inducing consumers to spend newfound paper wealth. On the other side are wealth-effect skeptics [who] believe that what really matters for spending is the 'income effect': low unemployment and rising pay.
>
> (Miller 2000:52)

Empirical studies of the wealth effect are still showing very mixed results (*The Economist* 2001).

Financialization implies that subsidization of local consumption may become less important for fostering growth. If a major portion of the benefits of increased local consumption go to outsiders, and if such expenditures reduce an economy's competitive standing, the results may actually be negative for growth and profits. With the decline of the advantage of housing strategies that promote growth through the subsidization of local consumption, the role of housing in regimes of accumulation seems likely to change. The exact character of this transformation, however, is as yet very poorly known. Kennett's analysis is one of the few explicit arguments that we have in this field. She argues that increasingly societies and cities must compete for mobile capital, whose agents are demanding conditions within cities that fit both their productive demands (world-class telecommunications infrastructure, for example) and their lifestyle preferences. Key employees prefer to be transferred to cities with culturally rich and vibrant urban neighbourhoods filled with gourmet and ethnic restaurants, cultural institutions such as museums and top universities, and potentially lucrative real estate investment possibilities.

Globalized accumulation has not created a 'borderless world', but rather has begun to replace the heavy predominance of domestic economies and national territories under Fordism with a mosaic 'composed of multiple, partially over-lapping levels that are neither congruent, contiguous, nor coextensive with one another' (Brenner 1999: 53). Within this reterritorialized mosaic, states (particularly the advanced capitalist ones) continue to have crucial impacts on processes of change, but they can no longer maintain the same kind of control within their territories that they once did. These changes are related to accumulation strategies 'through which globally oriented capitalist firms are attempting to circumvent and restructure the nationally organized systems of social, monetary, and labor regulation that prevailed throughout the Fordist-Keynesian regime of accumulation' (Brenner 1999: 64).

The more exposed a territory is to the global economy, the more it needs to be able to exploit economic niches in the global arena. While there are still a wide variety of niches, two of the most desired at present are to become a centre for global finance and the provision of business services or to become a key node in the network of knowledge and technology intensive industries that operate around the world. However, regulationists argue that there is no one single best way to organize a regime of accumulation. Instead there are multiple workable solutions to the contradictions and crises, and which ones will be most effective in a particular situation depend in part on the nature of prior institutions (Boyer 2001). This suggests that even if it is true that the role of housing in capitalist economies is changing as a result of globalization and financialization, the kinds of changes that we can expect will vary considerably between different contexts. In the next section, we attempt to illustrate this thesis with a case study of the role of real estate and housing in recent changes in Hong Kong's regime of accumulation. Hong Kong is a useful case study, we suggest, because as a small, liberal city-state it has never been able to rely on domestic consumption to drive economic expansion. Furthermore, real estate has for a long time been a central preoccupation of investors, government and citizens alike. While these characteristics do not make Hong Kong a 'typical case', as an extreme case of the tendencies we have been discussing it does offer the possibility of serving as an 'early warning system' for the implications of trends that are less well developed in most other localities.

Hong Kong: the centrality of real estate

Very little can be understood about Hong Kong without keeping in mind the scarcity and high cost of land. Although to a considerable extent the result of mountainous topography combined with rapid population increase in a territory of just over one thousand square kilometres, the cost of land has also been strongly influenced by government practices. The high cost of land, and the substantial increases between 1985 and 1997 also contributed to the loss of competitiveness of manufacturing enterprises located in the colony and has been accused of producing a 'casino' mentality that encouraged speculation in pursuit of quick profits.

Before 1953, housing concerned the Hong Kong Government only indirectly, for example through its impact on public health and morality. More generally, though, land was a central preoccupation throughout the colony's history (Chun 2000; Smart 1989). Monopoly of land ownership by the Government, which made land available for development on the basis of long-term leases (after auction or treaty) combined with substantial land-based revenues, ensured the Government's attention.

Between 1985 and 1997, land sales accounted for an average 7.6 per cent of total Government revenues, rising from a low of 1.0 per cent in 1984/5 to 13.5 per cent in 1996/7 (Lee 1999: 164). While substantial, revenues that indirectly accrue from real estate magnify the sector's importance further. Investment in property accounted for an average 68 per cent of gross fixed capital formation between

1980 and 1987, and private revenues related to real estate (property development, construction and ownership of premises) amounted to 30 per cent of GDP in 1996 (Tse and Ganesan 1999: 69), so that profits and income tax related to the real estate sector expand the total. The housing industry was one of the main drivers of economic growth in the 1990s (Fung and Forrest 2002). Land-related revenues have helped keep Hong Kong's tax rates low and competitiveness ratings high, despite the very high cost of living, itself largely a result, directly and indirectly, of high land prices. Hong Kong's largest companies, accounting for about 40–50 per cent of the capitalization on the Hong Kong stock market, are primarily property developers (Tse and Ganesan 1999: 71; Mitchell and Olds 2000).

One result is that the relationship between the large property development corporations and the Government is of great importance to understanding Hong Kong's regime of accumulation. Carolyn Cartier (1999: 189) argues that the Hong Kong planning system's 'ability to control development, especially on individual sites, has been, depending on perspective, flexible or relatively loose, if not effective'. She suggests that this situation prevails (despite the governmental monopoly on land ownership) because 'it has been in the state's direct interest to facilitate property development' (Cartier 1999: 189). The six main developers build on average 40–50 per cent of new residential and office properties (Tse and Webb 2000). Many of Hong Kong's developmental policies and practices can only be understood as resulting from the greater political influence of commercial interests compared to industrialists (Chiu 1996; Tang et al. 2000). Although some manufacturers were large employers, the sector as a whole was characterized by a myriad of small and medium enterprises, with an average workforce of only 17 in the 1970s (Smart 1992). The most influential tycoons were generally in the areas of trade, finance and real estate (Fung and Forrest 2002). A February 2001 survey found that 75 per cent of respondents believed that the Government's housing policy mainly served developers rather than the poor, and 31.6 per cent thought that policies were entirely for developers' benefit (Kong 2001).

The maintenance of public budget surpluses and profits for large corporations has been unusually reliant on the state of the real estate market. Between the 1984 signing of the Sino-British Agreement to return Hong Kong to Chinese sovereignty and the actual handover in 1997, the property market was remarkably buoyant, producing record real estate prices throughout the 1990s, peaking in 1997. The 1997 prices were seen as too high by the Government, since they created costs of doing business in Hong Kong that were among the highest in the world, threatened Hong Kong's status as a regional financial centre, and generated 'unhealthy' speculation in ever-increasing housing prices at the cost of 'productive' investment. High real estate prices had an impact on every aspect of Hong Kong's society and economy, accelerating the transfer of manufacturing into China to take advantage of cheaper land as well as abundant low-wage labour, convincing individuals that property investment was the main way to get ahead, and eventually producing a spillover of Hong Kong's hot real estate markets into investments in apartments across the border in Shenzhen where prices were much lower, especially for second homes or for those who couldn't afford to buy in Hong Kong (Moy 2000). Several interventions to stabilize the market were of only modest effect, but the Southeast Asian financial crises that started in July 1997 brought the Hong Kong property market down with a crash: an estimated 50 per cent drop in average prices. As of July 2002 prices remained substantially below the peak levels.

Initially the Government's actions exacerbated the property slump. The new Hong Kong Special Administrative Region Chief Executive, Tung Chee-hwa, announced in his first speech in his position on 1 July 1997 a target of 85,000 new housing units annually (Chiu 1999). The sharp increase was planned in order to 'alleviate the impact of the high prices on both people's livelihoods and HKSAR's economic competitiveness' (Lee 1999: 953). Many property analysts and investors considered this level of production excessive, and believed that it contributed to the property slump. The target was first silently dropped, and in 2000 the Administration publicly acknowledged that the target was not being pursued.

Other government interventions that were directed at helping Hong Kong out of the sharp economic downturn from mid-1997 have done so through attempts to promote the property market. In some ways, this might have been inevitable, given the centrality of real estate to Hong Kong's growth regime. Consumer demand dropped sharply in Hong Kong after the property slump, contributing to serious deflation, and the Standard Chartered Bank argued that this was the result of a higher level of consumer debt in Hong Kong than elsewhere in the region. Personal loans as a percentage of nominal GDP was 55.8 per cent in Hong Kong in 1998, compared to 20.7 per cent in South Korea, 33.6 per cent in Singapore and 40.9 per cent in Taiwan. The ratio for Hong Kong had increased from 40.6 per cent in 1995, and seems clearly associated with the increase in housing prices until 1997. The average household in Hong Kong had total outstanding loans of HK$367,000. The effects were more wide-ranging than this, however, because small and medium firms tended to rely on the proprietor's real estate holding as collateral for loans needed to do business, and with the slump, liquidity dried up rapidly. Small and medium firms have been a major force in Hong Kong's economic dynamism (Smart 1999), and their inability to access credit seriously hampered economic recovery. Investment in Hong Kong fell 24.4 per cent between the first quarters of 1998 and 1999 (Bank of East Asia 2000).

A variety of interventions have attempted to rescue the real estate market since 1997. For example, when the Administration bought US$15 billion worth of Hong Kong shares in order to prop up the stock market, 60 per cent of these were property related, a proportion higher than the sector's weighting in the stock market (Sum 2002). In March 2001, the mortgage ceiling for new apartments was raised to 85 per cent from 70 per cent, after a previous increase to a maximum of 90 per cent had been limited to resale flats. The original restrictions had been put in place before 1997 to discourage real estate speculation, particularly on units still under construction. The mortgage loans above the 70 per cent level were provided by the Government's Hong Kong Mortgage Corporation. The managing director of Ricacorp Property indicated that the move 'would favour property developers more than home buyers, for whom there would only be a change in the mortgage provider' (Chak 2001a). Financial aid for those who were unfortunate enough to buy real estate in the two years prior to the housing slump, and thus suffer from negative equity (Hong Kong law prevents them from simply walking away from their investment), has been suggested at various times. The Secretary for Treasury Denise Yue recently ruled out doing so, stating that to do so would give rise to 'moral hazard' and would encourage excessive risk taking. 'It would induce people to be less cautious in future when they make major investment decisions. They will have a mistaken belief that if anything goes wrong, the Government will come in and help them out' (No 2001). Nothing was mentioned about the moral hazard of Government support for the large property development corporations.

Governmental decisions, or at least public legitimations of those decisions, are thus clearly related to expectations about how housing and real estate prices will affect the economy more generally. The outcome of efforts to use housing to influence the economy are thus mediated by the decisions of individuals and households. Most regulationist research has been carried out at a macro level, and the relation between institutions and individual responses tends to be assumed rather than demonstrated through empirical research. This is unfortunate for a number of reasons, since it allows analysts to assume humans act as some kind of *Homo oeconomicus* making rational responses to governmental interventions and yet simultaneously being subject to the hegemonic influences of dominant ideas. To avoid functionalism, the agency of ordinary subjects of regulation must be the subject of analysis just as much as the decisions of powerful elites (themselves usually hidden behind reified institutions). In the next section, we provide some excerpts from an interview with a Hong Kong home owner in order to illustrate how the interface between the household and the broader economy operates through expectations and the relative returns to investment versus employment earnings, and the impact of conjunctural events in determining the outcomes.

Hong Kong homebuyers: a case study

Mr Chan was a primary school teacher. He has two sons and a daughter and a dependent mother. They all lived together in a 900 sq ft three-room apartment which they bought in 1998. The family used to live in a small two-room flat in the early 1980s. Mr Chan had a meagre income then, made worse when his wife quit teaching after their second child was born. This changed when they sold their first flat and bought a pre-sale flat in Aberdeen in 1986. They sold their flat in early 1989 and made substantial capital gains. The family left for Canada for three years and returned in late 1992. Making use of the capital gains they bought a bigger flat. When the market was extremely buoyant in 1994 they sold their flat again, making more capital gains, and then rented for a few years. During this time, Mr Chan turned to the stock market. He managed to make handsome profits before 1997 and when the property market slumped after the AFC, he bought the current flat in Aberdeen at a bargain price. From the mid-1980s onward, Mr Chan successfully made his salaried income secondary to his wealth creation from property and equity investment.

> Look at me. A primary school teacher's income would never bring me to where I am now. All through the years I have only been earning very little income. I am not saying I didn't like teaching. I think I was a devoted teacher. But I still needed to make ends meet. … When I sold the flat I bought in Aberdeen I knew we made the right decision. We bought the flat at pre-sale and paid mortgage for one year before we actually occupied the flat. We bought it for $800,000 in 1986 and sold it for $1,500,000 in 1989. It would be impossible for me to save that much money for the rest of my life working as a teacher. That money enabled us to emigrate to Canada. Without that money we wouldn't be so bold as to move out after 4 June.[1] … At school I taught my students to work hard and respect all walks of life. I still believe in this. But Hong Kong is really a rather unique brand of capitalism. It is a system that favors those who hold money and wealth. I have colleagues who refused to get into the housing market and are still renting. I have great respect for them. … But having said that, we must also realize that this is not what is happening 'out there'. The Hong Kong economy, or at least before the Asian financial crisis, is a system favoring property investment, or you can call it speculation if you like. What it really means is that if you are not locked into the system early enough and persistent enough, you will be excluded from it. You would be on the periphery. You will not be able to take part fully. If the government is going to provide everyone with cheap home ownership, I am sure Hong Kong would be a much poorer place. The reason why we eventually returned from Canada was obvious. I think I will always get better returns to my time and effort here. During 1992 the housing market was temporarily struck by the Gulf War and house prices plummeted a bit. We knew it was the right time to act so we bought this not so big flat. It was a very nice flat with a harbor view and it cost us $1.5 million. But having been in Canada we were much more cautious about the market. Things go up must come down! We were right. The government was already talking about ways to cool off the market. This would give it a strong blow if the government was really going to do something drastic. We finally sold our flat in 1994 for $1.9 million. I then began to get acquainted with a number of friends we knew in Canada and also returned to Hong Kong at more or less the same time. They were working

in the stock market. They told me that there would be opportunities for better return if we played the 'returning of sovereignty card'. They were right. I did manage to stay outside of the property market, although at some point during 1997 we were tempted, seeing the astronomic rise in prices again shortly before the handover. But I was firm enough to stay cool. I knew something could go wrong eventually. The market just got mad!

Sum (2002: 74) argues that the growth of Hong Kong as a regional financial centre generated massive inflows of wealth that 'promoted the rise of property investment and speculation not just as a form of business but as a way of life'. Mr Chan makes the lived experience of this situation very clear. He is far from an unusual case, as case studies in Lee (1999) demonstrate. Two serious challenges arose to this mode of growth. First, success itself generated huge increases in costs, particularly for residential and office rental costs and for the wages of professional and skilled staff (Standard Chartered Bank 1999; Tsang 1999: 44). Second, the regional financial crises starting in 1997 cast serious doubts on the viability of reliance on the wealth generated by serving as a regional hub: investment flows dropped sharply and assumptions of unstoppable growth for the region evaporated. Among the most important effects of the crisis on Hong Kong was a 50 per cent reduction in the real estate market (from unprecedented peaks, it must be noted) that 'cut at the heart of Hong Kong's internal "growth" dynamics as this had developed since the opening of China' (Sum 2002: 80). Since so much of Hong Kong's economy, stock market and even household economies had come to rely on the expectation of ever-increasing real estate prices (Lui 1995; Lee 1999), the sharp drop had immense multiplier effects and generated a deflationary trend and a sharp increase in unemployment and decrease in economic growth. The slump reduced the share of property-related revenues in total government income from 35 per cent in 1996/7 to 15 per cent in 1998/9 (Standard Chartered Bank 1999).

Sum (2002) identifies two competing strategies that were formulated in response to the crisis. One would build on and enhance the regional financial role by combining hub functions with a new emphasis on the knowledge economy. The second strategy was less prepared to abandon the manufacturing sector and instead promoted technological upgrading that would intensify research and development, the creation of brand-name goods, and an emphasis on technologically-intensive manufacturing. The first strategy was promoted by commercial and financial capital interests, the second by industrial capital.

Subsequent policy initiatives by the Hong Kong Administration have tended to adopt elements of both strategies. This was particularly clear in the Chief Executive's 1999 Policy Address. To become a 'world-class city' which was not only a major Chinese city but also the 'most cosmopolitan in Asia', Hong Kong would have to 'turn increasingly to innovative, knowledge-intensive economic activities, make the best use of information technology, reduce our costs further to enhance our competitiveness, and restructure our economy in the most advantageous directions' (Chan 1999). The upgrading of the workforce, partially through excluding low-skilled potential immigrants who have family ties in Hong Kong and promoting the importation of highly skilled mainlanders (Smart 2003) and partly through local training schemes, would be matched by the transformation of the local infrastructure.

In his 1999 Policy Address, the Chief Executive emphasized the need to make Hong Kong a more attractive place for foreign investors and expatriate employees, through improving the environment and enhancing the amenities. The improvement of local cultural and environmental amenities, particularly those that appeal to executives, professionals and investors, is a common part of the policies and practices of cities that are trying to strengthen their ability to compete on the global market for sunrise industries,[2] head offices and business services. Hong Kong has some advantages in this area, but also a variety of demerits, particularly in the form of increasing pollution, overcrowding and congestion. Sassen (1991) has argued that the shift to a global city role is associated with sharp increases in economic polarization, with a dual labour market divided between the corporate elite and the low-paid service workers who serve them in restaurants and retail outlets, and work for them as domestic servants. The extremely sharp increases in income inequality in Hong Kong since 1986 (Lui 1997) fit this pattern very well. The richest 10 per cent received 41.8 per cent of all income in 1996, compared to 1.1 per cent for the lowest decile. The Gini coefficient for Hong Kong was among the highest in the world (ranging from 0.0 for absolute equality to 1.0 for absolute inequality) at 0.571 in 1996, higher than Zimbabwe at 0.568 and not that much below the 'leader', Sierra Leone at 0.629. The highest inequality among the G-7 rich countries is found in the United States with a coefficient of 0.408 (World Bank 2001).

The persistence of reduced real estate prices into mid-2001 despite various governmental efforts to stimulate the market has increasingly focused attention on the public housing sector, and particularly the Home Ownership Scheme (HOS). Public provision is being seen as an important factor in preventing the revival of the private sector so that 'the Government's massive direct presence in the housing market and the competition from all those cheaply priced HOS flats has gradually been squeezing the private sector out of the business' (van der Kamp 2001). The private sector is currently building only a third as much residential space as 15 years ago, and the affordability ratio for private housing is half what it was in 1997 (van der Kamp 2001). The secretary-general of the Real Estate Developers Association (and a member of the Housing Authority) asserted that 'scrapping home-ownership flats would enable private developers to bid for prime land and lead to a fairer use of public resources' (Chak 2001b: 4). Such attacks on the HOS succeeded in September 2001 when the Chief Secretary announced a freeze on new sales and a change towards the provision of loans for purchase of private sector dwellings (Hon 2001).

The HOS programme was itself part of a larger policy to promote home ownership in order to encourage citizens to have a greater emotional and financial stake in Hong Kong, with a view towards stabilizing Hong Kong during the turbulent transition to Chinese sovereignty. With the failure of other efforts to reinvigorate the property market, subsidies to home purchase became widely blamed for the prolonging of the slump. A moratorium and perhaps complete end to the programme came to be seen as a way to restore confidence. As of April 2003, though, the property market has continued to drop. Perhaps two strands of thought revealed by prospective home buyers subsequent to the policy announcement may provide clues to the failure, at least so far, of this latest 'fix'. First, people saw this eleventh hour policy effort as abrupt and desperate and possibly suggested that the Government had lost confidence in the future of the market. The decision was also seen as an attempt to pacify the developers who had been exerting tremendous pressure on the Government. Second, the further drop in the market may not have been a response to the policy announcement itself. Rather, it was a reaction to further interest rate cuts and expectations of an impending recession in the US economy. Pessimism about the global economy has generated widespread feelings that anything the SAR Government does could only worsen the situation. Both the intervention and the reactions of the public have demonstrated our relative ignorance of the micro and macro links between individual households and the world economy, yet assumptions about these linkages are necessary groundings for any governmental efforts to regulate the system. While government interventions have been instrumental in bringing about a mass demand for home ownership, it has so far only succeeded in doing so during a highly inflationary and buoyant period. How these policies affect housing consumption within the context of a long-run global downturn remains largely unclear. The rapid increase in wealth that once (for at least a decade after 1987) appeared to have produced something like Boyer's vision of a stable property-based regime of accumulation seems to have evaporated with the slump in the real estate market. With a more volatile economy and an unstable job market, people are focusing more on the pursuit of a secure wage income rather than depending on income from equity. Work place politics are such that people are more ready to accept jobs which require multiple skills, flexible roles and uncertain income. While the Hong Kong case might not be the most typical to illustrate the relationship between housing and regulation theory, its rise and fall of ownership, the volatility of the property market and the recent risk involved in home ownership and negative equity, do suggest that the individual household's perception also plays a role in affecting the sustainability and maturity of a finance-led growth regime.

Conclusion

We suggested in the introduction that the integration of political, economic and social dimensions of housing is a crucial challenge for housing studies, and that regulation theory might have some advantages in addressing the interface between them. The small number of regulation theorists who have explicitly addressed housing issues have provided some significant insights, demonstrating the importance of varying systems of housing provision in helping to provide institutional fixes for problems that might otherwise undermine continued economic expansion. In the various societies that have been classified as organized in some variant of the Fordist regime of accumulation, governmental subsidies to housing provision, either directly through socialized housing or indirectly through support for mortgages and the infrastructure that facilitated suburbanization, served to generate a huge increase in consumption and also increased inclusion and commitment of the working classes. Globalization and the increased ecological dominance of financial institutions vis-à-vis local institutions have reduced the perceived advantages of subsidizing local consumption. Instead, export-oriented (of either goods or services) competitive strategies have recast the role of housing and real estate.

We have suggested that recent regulationist work on financialization, although largely ignoring housing and real estate issues, provides some clues to a better understanding of their position in contemporary development. Earlier approaches assumed that increasing profits at the expense of wages or employment levels eventually produced a consumption crisis that would curtail continued growth. Boyer's argument is that once a sufficient critical mass of equity among a population is achieved, consumption levels may be able to be maintained or expanded based on returns to property rather than wages. A stable property-based regime would dramatically change the class relations within an economy. So far neglected, equity in housing and other real estate needs to be brought into this analysis, given its status as among the most important financial assets for the majority in most developed economies. Housing markets, however, have their own distinctive dynamics, influenced not least by the way in which they are permanently fixed in place, unlike the more mobile and liquid assets that Boyer has concentrated on.

In order to explore the implications of financialization for housing studies, and vice versa, we provided a short case study of Hong Kong, a locality where real estate has been unusually central to economics, politics and social life. The nexus between powerful private sector interests and governmental decision-makers is significantly mediated through property issues, and efforts to promote the recovery of the post-1997 real estate market have been a continuing feature of policy choices in the last few years. We suggested that there has been a tendency among regulation theorists to 'read off' the social and cultural implications of changes in the regime of accumulation and mode of regulation, to assume congruence, rather than to examine how individuals and households respond to financialization. A case study of one household illustrated how the centrality of real estate affected their decision-making, and how the increased importance of real estate equity compared to wages worked out at the micro level. These issues are of crucial importance, as debates within the Federal Reserve and elsewhere about the impact of the 'wealth effect' (and its corollary in the wake of financial meltdowns such as the one occurring after 11 September 2001) clearly demonstrate.

Hong Kong illustrates the ways in which either high or depressed housing prices can cause serious challenges for a growth regime. Rapid and continual growth between 1984 and 1997 produced huge difficulties for those struggling to find affordable housing, forced manufacturers to seek lower cost production platforms outside of Hong Kong, and turned investment and energy into real estate speculation. The sharp drops after 1997, however, have also hurt manufacturers, particularly small and medium enterprises, since their collateral for working capital was often real estate based, and the reverse of the wealth effect, negative equity, has resulted in price deflation for goods and services, causing great difficulties for local companies and producing unemployment levels not seen since the 1960s.

The latest in the series of attempted 'fixes' for this situation has been the attack on the Home Ownership Scheme, itself the product of a previous effort to stabilize Hong Kong's economy and society in the troubled transition to Chinese sovereignty. Alleged to be at least a contributing factor to the failure of all efforts to restore housing inflation, hence exacerbating many of Hong Kong's other problems, restrictions on the programme, perhaps its eventual ending, are hoped to restore demand and confidence. Whether or not this will succeed remains to be seen, but it does provide a clear indication of the confluence between government, the property tycoons, and home owners suffering from negative, or at least decreased, housing equity, and the way in which this nexus powers important policy decisions. The initial lack of success suggests that the efficacy of interventions during periods of housing deflation may be severely limited by the note of desperation they may transmit, producing the opposite of the intended effect, and by the state of the global economy.

Acknowledgement

We wish to acknowledge the funding support from the Governance in Asia Research Centre (Centre for Comparative Public Management and Social Policy). Project number: RCPM 994: *Economic Downturn and Home Ownership: An Exploratory Study on How Households Cope with Owner-occupation after the Asian Economic Crisis in Selected Asian cities.*

Notes

1 The 1989 Tiananmen June 4th Massacre.
2 Referring to information technology and knowledge-based economic activities.

References

Aglietta, M. (1980) *A Theory of Capitalist Regulation: The US Experience*, London: New Left Books.

—— (1998) 'Capitalism at the turn of the century: regulation theory and the challenge of social change', *New Left Review*, 232: 41–90.

Bank of East Asia (2000) 'The world-city challenges', *Economic Analysis*, February: 1–3.

Boyer, R. (2000a) 'Is a finance-led growth regime a viable alternative to Fordism? A preliminary analysis', *Economy and Society*, 29: 111–45.

—— (2000b) 'The political in the era of globalization and finance: focus on some regulation school research', *International Journal of Urban and Regional Research*, 24: 274–322.

—— (2001) 'The financialization of capital: an interpretation along "regulation" theory', paper presented at the workshop on 'Regulation in East Asia's Mode of Development', Taichung, Taiwan, 18–20 April.

Brenner, N. (1999) 'Beyond state-centrism? Space, territoriality, and geographical scale in globalization studies', *Theory and Society*, 28: 39–78.

Byrne, J. and Davis, E.P. (2001) 'Disaggregate wealth and aggregate consumption: an investigation of empirical relationships for the G7', *National Institute of Economic and Social Research Discussion Papers*, Number 180. Online available http://www.niesr.ac.uk/index.htm.

Cartier, C. (1999) 'The state, property development and symbolic landscape in high-rise Hong Kong', *Landscape Research*, 24: 185–208.

Chak, M. (2001a) 'New-flat loan ceiling lifted to help buyers', *South China Morning Post*, Internet edition, 2 March 2001, www.scmp.com.

—— (2001b) 'Subsidized flat sales "no longer necessary"', *South China Morning Post*, 29 June: 4.

Chan, Q. (1999) 'City must aim to become Asia's most cosmopolitan', *South China Morning Post*, 7 October: 1.

Chiu, R.L.H. (1999) 'The swing of the pendulum in housing', in L.C. Chow and Y. Fan (eds) *The Other Hong Kong Report 1998*, Hong Kong: Chinese University Press.

Chiu, S.W.K. (1996) 'Unravelling Hong Kong's exceptionalism: the politics of laissez-faire in the industrial takeoff', *Political Power and Social Theory*, 10: 229–56.

Chun, A. (2000) *Unstructuring Chinese Society*, Amsterdam: Harwood Academic Publishers.

Dunford, M. (1990) 'Theories of regulation', *Environment and Planning D: Society and Space*, 8: 297–322.

Florida, R. (1986) 'The political economy of financial deregulation and the reorganization of housing finance in the US', *International Journal of Urban and Regional Research*, 10: 207–31.

Florida, R. and Feldman, M. (1988) 'Housing in US Fordism: the class accord and postwar spatial organization', *International Journal of Urban and Regional Research*, 12: 187–210.

Florida, R. and Jonas, A. (1991) 'U.S. urban policy: the postwar state and capitalist regulation', *Antipode*, 23: 349–84.

Forrest, R. and Kennett, P. (1997) 'Risk, residence, and the post-Fordist city', *American Behavioral Scientist*, 41: 342–60.

105

Forrest, R., Murie, A. and Williams, P. (1990) *Home Ownership: Differentiation and Fragmentation*, London: Unwin, Hyman.

Froud, J., Haslam, C., Johal, S. and Williams, K. (2000) 'Shareholder value and financialization: consultancy promises, management moves', *Economy and Society*, 29: 80–110.

Fung, K.K. and Forrest, R. (2002) 'Institutional mediation, the Hong Kong residential housing market and the Asian Financial Crisis', *Housing Studies*, 17 (2): 189–207.

Hon, M. (2001) 'Drastic market changes force strategy rethink', *South China Morning Post*, Internet edition, 4 September 2001, www.scmp.com.

Jessop, B. (2000) 'The crisis of the national spatio-temporal fix and the tendential ecological dominance of globalizing capitalism', *International Journal of Urban and Regional Research*, 24: 323–60.

Jessop, B. and Sum, N. (2000) 'An entrepreneurial city in action: Hong Kong's emerging strategies in and for (inter) urban competition', *Urban Studies*, 37: 2287–313.

Kemeny, J. (1992) *Housing and Social Theory*, London: Routledge.

Kennett, P. (1994) 'Modes of regulation and the urban poor', *Urban Studies*, 31: 1017–31.

Kong, L. (2001) 'Housing scheme rethink urged', *South China Morning Post*, Internet edition, 27 February 2001, www.scmp.com.

Lazonick, W. and O'Sullivan, M. (2000) 'Maximizing shareholder value: a new ideology for corporate governance', *Economy and Society*, 29: 13–35.

Lee, E.W.Y. (1999) 'Governing post-colonial Hong Kong: institutional incongruity, governance crisis and authoritarianism', *Asian Survey*, 39: 940–59.

Lee, J. (1999) *Housing, Home Ownership and Social Change in Hong Kong*, Aldershot: Ashgate.

Lin, G.C.S. (2000) 'State, capital, and space in China in an era of volatile globalization', *Environment and Planning A*, 32: 455–71.

Lui, H.K. (1997) *Income Inequality and Economic Development*, Hong Kong: City University of Hong Kong Press.

Lui, T. (1995) 'Coping strategies in a booming market: family wealth and housing in Hong Kong', in R. Forrest and A. Murie (eds) *Housing and Family Wealth: Comparative International Perspectives*, London: Routledge.

Meyer, D.R. (2000) *Hong Kong as a Global Metropolis*, Cambridge: Cambridge University Press.

Miller, R. (2000) 'How real is the "wealth effect"?', *Business Week*, 3685: 52.

Mitchell, K. and Olds, K. (2000) 'Chinese business networks and the globalization of property markets in the Pacific Rim', in H.W. Yeung and K. Olds (eds) *Globalization of Chinese Business Firms*, Basingstoke: Macmillan.

Moy, P. (2000) 'SAR may fuel rise in Shenzhen flat prices', *South China Morning Post*, Internet edition, 6 July 2000, www.scmp.com.

No, K. (2001) 'Denise Yue rules out financial aid for homeowners', *South China Morning Post*, Internet edition, 14 March 2001, www.scmp.com.

Olds, K. (2001) *Globalization and Urban Change: Capital, Culture and Pacific Rim Mega-Projects*, Oxford: Oxford University Press.

Sassen, S. (1991) *The Global City*, Princeton: Princeton University Press.

Smart, A. (1989) 'Forgotten obstacles, neglected forces: explaining the origins of Hong Kong public housing', *Environment and Planning D: Society and Space*, 7: 179–96.

—— (1992) *Making Room: Squatter Clearance in Hong Kong*, Hong Kong: Centre of Asian Studies.

—— (1999) 'Flexible accumulation across the Hong Kong border: petty capitalists as pioneers of globalized accumulation', *Urban Anthropology*, 28: 373–406.

—— (2001) 'Unruly places: urban governance and the persistence of illegality in Hong Kong's urban squatter areas', *American Anthropologist*, 103 (1): 30–44.

—— (2003) 'Sharp edges, fuzzy categories and trans-border networks: managing and housing new arrivals in Hong Kong', *Ethnic and Racial Studies*, 26 (2): 218–33.

Standard Chartered Bank (1999) 'The economic impact of an influx of immigrants on Hong Kong', *Viewpoints*, 17 (February): 1–5.

Sum, N. (2002) 'An entrepreneurial city in action: emerging strategies for (inter-) urban competition in Hong Kong', in J. Logan (ed.) *The New Chinese City: Globalization and Reform*, Oxford: Blackwell.

Sweezy, P.M. (1997) 'More (or less) on globalization', *Monthly Review*, 49: 1–5.

Tang, B., Choy, L.H.T. and Wat, J.K.F. (2000) 'Certainty and discretion in planning control: a case study of office development in Hong Kong', *Urban Studies*, 37: 2465–83.

The Economist (2001) 'Saved! Are the finances of American consumers in better shape than people fear?', *The Economist*, 23 June: 72.

Tickell, A. and Peck, J.A. (1992) 'Accumulation, regulation and the geographies of post-Fordism: missing links in regulationist research', *Progress in Human Geography*, 16: 190–218.

—— (1995) 'Social regulation *after* Fordism: regulation theory, neo-liberalism and the global-local nexus', *Economy and Society*, 24: 357–86.

Tsang, S. (1999) 'The Hong Kong economy: opportunities out of crisis?', *Journal of Contemporary China*, 8: 29–45.

Tse, R.Y.C. and Ganesan, S. (1999) 'Hong Kong', in J. Berry and S. McGreal (eds) *Cities in the Pacific Rim: Planning Systems and Property Markets*, London: E. & F.N. Spon.

Tse, R.Y.C. and Webb, J.R. (2000) 'Public versus private real estate in Hong Kong', *Journal of Real Estate Portfolio Management*, 6: 53–60.

van der Kamp, J. (2001) 'Poor housing idea past use-by date', *South China Morning Post*, 30 June: B18.

World Bank (2001) *World Development Report 2000–2001*, Washington, DC: World Bank.

6 Housing diversity in the global city

Sophie Watson

In the mid to late 1980s I published two books, *Housing and Homelessness: A Feminist Perspective* (1986) and *Accommodating Inequality* (1988), for which the research had been undertaken earlier in that decade. Central to the argument of both of these books was a focus on the marginality of the non-traditional household in the housing system, which, I suggested, derived from the centrality of the traditional nuclear family to housing access, production and design in the housing systems of the two countries on which the book focussed – the UK and Australia. Up until this time the majority of housing provision in the public and private housing sectors had been developed for the traditional family household on the assumption that this form represented the majority of households. Thus in the public sector flats and houses were developed with two to three bedrooms and family households received priority in allocations. Single households were marginalized in this sector. In the private sector similar assumptions prevailed and single women in particular, because of their generally lower incomes, had difficulties gaining access to private finance. At the time these books were seen to break new ground and were even contentious in some quarters. Now 15 years later, as predicted then, to argue that the diversity of households in the global city is considerable, and should thus be a central focus of policy debate and housing provision, is a far less provocative claim.

In this chapter I want to look first at the social and economic changes which have complicated the more normative household structure of the early post-war period. Many of the changes that have taken place in the West as a result of processes of globalization, industrialization and de-industrialization, feminist movements, and changing social demography find their parallels in the East. However, the pace of change – particularly in relation to the strength of the traditional family and patriarchal gender relations – has in some ways been less dramatic. There are though strong indications that similar issues are beginning to be of concern in the countries that comprise Asia. In the second part of the chapter I consider briefly how this diversity has been addressed in various countries both at the broad-brush level of policy debate and provision. I conclude by suggesting that there is still a long way to go if large numbers of households are not to remain inadequately provided for, or homeless, in the global city.

To begin, then, with the impact of globalization. Over the last three decades there have been huge population shifts between countries with growing numbers of people moving from one country to another in search of work – economic migrants, in search of a new life away from a repressive regime – namely political refugees, or to rejoin family members. These shifts have had a significant impact on housing in many cities of the world. Cities concentrate and express ethnic and cultural diversity. Many of the migrants to global cities represent the other side of globalization to its more common face as the concentration of finance capital, wealth and power. These are the people who live on the other side of the tracks from the smart gentrified lofts, or the expensive apartments which have proliferated on the water fronts of the global cities developed for households with incomes in the top 10 per cent. Often these also are the hidden employees of the global city – the cleaners who clean the offices at night or the night security men. As Sassen (1998: xxxi) puts it: 'While corporate power inscribes these cultures and identifies them with "otherness" thereby devaluing them, they are present everywhere'. But many of these 'other' cultures live on the margins and in poverty and

> the disparities, as seen and as lived, between the urban glamour zone and the urban war zone have become enormous. The extreme visibility of the difference is likely to contribute to further brutalization of the conflict; the indifference and greed of the new elites versus the hopelessness and the rage of the poor.
> (Sassen 1998: xxxiii)

This is not to suggest that all migrants are poor, unemployed or low paid, but many are. This is a fragmented and kaleidoscopic picture with spaces of power bordering spaces of exclusion. But as private housing has become more and more extortionate in many global cities, for many it represents an impossible dream.

As far as social or public housing is concerned, the fact that many such households do not meet the residency requirements and are not registered on housing waiting lists for public housing in those cities where public housing is available is one problem. In the UK, for example, current housing legislation (Housing Act 1988) provides an avenue for some of these households to be defined as homeless and in priority need of housing, yet the lack of housing means either little hope of a permanent allocation or, where housing is allocated, potential hostility from others who see such homeless households as jumping the queue. Migrant households are also diverse in form: single households or extended households, and changing or transient. The lack of flexibility in the housing system mitigates any easy solution. As far as the private housing system is concerned, many migrants are poor or on low incomes, are in unstable employment and have no record of saving or banking histories to reassure lenders of their ability to repay loans. Let us now look at some evidence to substantiate these claims.

A number of countries – Australia, the USA, Canada, New Zealand – have actively encouraged immigration over several decades. These countries were initially established from European settlement and traditionally reflected European values, norms, forms of government and politics, and housing was usually constructed according to Anglo-European assumptions also. The large influx of migrants from non-European countries has raised new and challenging questions for housing providers, to which I shall shortly return. In Asia the highest level of immigration is to Malaysia, with almost one million foreigners on the census in the early 1990s, while Singapore had some 300,000 migrants, and Hong Kong, Korea and Taiwan had approximately 100,000 foreign workers (Borja and Castells 1997), though these numbers are fluctuating all the time. Emigration from Latin America to the United States has had a huge impact on that country particularly in Los Angeles, where in some parts of the city new migrants outnumber the longer established population. Worldwide there has been a marked increase in the numbers of those described as refugees, from an estimated 2.5 million in the early 1970s to 27.4 million in 1994 (UNCHR 1991). In Europe particularly, the addition of asylum seekers swell these figures considerably – for example there were 680,000 in 1992. Countries which traditionally accepted few migrants are also not immune to these trends. Thus, for example, in 1993 Sweden received almost 59,000 immigrants of whom two-thirds were refugees, while one third entered on the basis of family reunion (Inglis 2001: 22). Over half were from non-Nordic countries with 40 per cent from outside Europe (OECD 1995: 119). In the same year Canada's foreign born population had reached 16.2 per cent while Australia's first generation migrants constituted 25 per cent of the population (Inglis 2001: 24). As a result of the political, economic and demographic changes over the last 50 years only 10–15 per cent of countries can be described as ethnically homogeneous (Connor 1994), with ethnic diversity being particularly marked in western Europe and the USA.

Another crucial factor in the increasing diversity of households is the decline in the traditional patriarchal family. The impact of industrialization for nearly two centuries in the West has gradually shifted the place of the family, as specialized institutions, such as schools, hospitals and welfare institutions, have supplanted or supplemented the family's traditional role. By the late twentieth century further changes had occurred as these patterns encountered the impact of changing gender relations. In his recent work *The Power of Identity* Castells (1997) goes as far as entitling one of his chapters 'The End of Patriarchalism' to capture the powerful shifts in gender relations that have occurred over the last thirty years or more. Though I do not share his optimism that the deeply embedded patriarchal power relations which have characterized most societies have been seriously challenged in many quarters, there is no doubt that there has been a sea change in gendered expectations and practices, in women's consciousness and thus in many arenas of social, economic and political life in many parts of the world. In large part this can be attributed to the success of women's movements since the early twentieth century, particularly since the late 1960s, and to a lesser extent other movements for sexual freedom such as the gay liberation movements. As a result there has been a massive increase in the participation of women in higher education and paid employment giving women greater independence in relation to men and their own families of origin. At the same time women's ability to control their own fertility and child bearing, again only in some parts of the globe, through contraception and abortion, has had a profound effect on patterns of family life.

There are, however, differences between the East and the West, with more dramatic changes having occurred in the USA, Europe, Australia and Canada. Mason *et al.* (1998: 5–7) highlight three differences in the impact of modernization on family change. The first difference that they identify between the USA and East Asia is that of family values. Here they contrast the values arising from Confucianism with what they see as the individualistic values of the West. In contrast to an emphasis on individual choice Confucian values promote filial piety, loyalty and obedience to the family. Second, they argue that gender inequality, although universally present prior to industrialization, was more strongly embedded in East Asian families than in North American families. Traditionally the family line passed only through men, and daughters became members of their husbands' family through marriage. This system gave sons great importance as preservers of the family line (Tsuya and Choe 1991), augmented the power of sons in the household and promoted the obedience and compliance of women. The third trend they identify is the rapidity of demographic transition in the two regions. While the transition from high fertility and mortality rates to low ones has been taking place gradually over more than a hundred years in the USA, in East Asia these transitions have occurred very rapidly with family size plummeting from five or six children to one or two children in a very short period. One effect of this is the rapid aging of the population.

In some countries these shifts have led to new legislation, such as equal opportunity legislation, equal pay and affirmative action legislation – notably in the USA, Canada, Britain, Australia and various European countries and Scandinavia particularly. There has also been a reform of divorce laws in many countries, as formal state religion has declined in significance – again more commonly in Western countries, with the result that there has been a dramatic increase in divorce and separation and less and less social expectation of an enduring partnership through life. Thus, between 1971 and 1990, for example, there was a percentage increase in relationship breakdown of 113 per cent in Canada, 104 per cent in the UK, 157 per cent in Mexico, 100 per cent in France, and 50 per cent in Italy (Castells 1997: 140). If we look at the proportions of the female and male population over 18 years old who are divorced we find the following comparisons: 1.8 per cent women and 0.9 per cent men in Japan, 0.9 per cent women and 0.7 per cent men in South Korea, and 9.3 per cent women and 7.2 per cent men in the USA in 1990 (Inoue 1998: 22).

Similarly the percentage of women who have never married by the age of 24 is also on the increase – a trend which is visible in industrialized and less industrialized countries alike (Inoue 1998: 145). For example, in Indonesia from 1976 to 1987 there was a 36 per cent increase, in Sri Lanka a 58 per cent increase, in Colombia a 39 per cent increase, in Kenya a 32 per cent increase, in Spain a 59 per cent increase, and in the USA a 51 per cent increase. In Japan late marriage is more common for everyone leading to an increase in lifelong single persons: the percentage of never married people who are over 18 years old is 37.0 for men and 34.3 for women, compared to equivalent figures of 25.8 and 18.9 in the USA. This disinclination among young Japanese to marry is seen by many to indicate a serious danger for the continuity of the family system. Another social demographic shift is the growth in childless couples including those who decide not to have children, couples whose children have grown up and gay couples.

These social and cultural shifts have led to a massive growth in diverse family forms including a growing number of single parent households, usually female headed, and single households, and a growing number of reconstituted families which include parents with children from earlier relationships as well as children from the new partnerships, and so on. This increase in single parent households is also evident across most countries with single parent households comprising 9.2 per cent of all households in the early 1970s in Australia, 8.0 per cent in the United Kingdom, 10 per cent in the former USSR, 12.5 per cent in Thailand, 11.5 per cent in Morocco, and 14.7 per cent in Peru, with respective increases int the 1990s to 14.9 per cent, 14.3 per cent, 20 per cent, 20.8 per cent, 17.3 per cent and 19.5 per cent (Inoue 1998: 148). Another factor contributing to the growth of single parent households, particularly in poorer parts of the world, is the necessity of men having to leave the family home to find employment in another area. Commonly men migrate from country areas to the city to find work, but this is also a growing issue in inter-country migration.

The significant increase in single households is a result of a number of factors. First more and more people choose to live alone for longer periods with less pressure to form permanent partnerships at an early age. Second, single households form as a result of relationship breakdown. Third, growing longevity is beginning to present enormous housing challenges across the globe. In Western countries there are a number of issues. Where older people are homeowners on low incomes, problems can arise when the dwelling starts to deteriorate or fall into a state of disrepair. In time this can lead to an overall deterioration of the housing stock and a hidden form of housing poverty amongst older people. In some countries poorer older households have been reliant on the public sector; this is particularly the case for women who represent the majority of older single households. Where the public sector has been cut back, as in the UK, these households have fewer options and become vulnerable to homelessness in old age. Another hidden group of the older housing poor are in the private rented sector where costs are often high and security and standards are low. The housing of older people is thus an area of growing concern for housing policy makers.

In the East the housing of older people is also squarely on the agenda, though the contours of the problem differ. In Japan the population is already one of the oldest in the world and soon to become older (Ogawa and Retherford 1997). As Mason *et al.* (1998: 5–7) argue 'this rapid aging of the population poses serious problems for intergenerational income transfers and the care of the elderly'. In many countries the traditional family structure has incorporated the notion that the care of older people is the responsibility of their offspring. As a result there is little in the way of existing welfare provision in many countries for this group. As the traditional family starts to break down, with an associated decline in the marriage rate and an increasing desire for independence among younger people, older people are becoming increasingly vulnerable. In their study Hong and Buyn (1998) found that women in South Korea were far less likely to give primacy to intergenerational obligations than men and expressed a far stronger discontent with traditional family arrangements. If this trend continues the impact on older people will be considerable. Already there was evidence of an increase in poverty levels amongst this group in recent years (Hong and Buyn 1998: 190).

Given that the housing stock in most countries has traditionally been produced for, and allocated to, the nuclear family many of these non-traditional households have faced exclusion or marginality. Women headed households, which now comprise one third of the world's households (Moser and Peake 1987), have been shown to be particularly affected in this respect with an estimated 70 per cent of the world's 1,300 million poor being women (UNDP 1995). As I have argued elsewhere (Watson 1988) housing policies in many countries have failed to take account of this phenomenon and discrimination towards women on the basis of their low incomes or lack of formal or full time employment is a pervasive pattern (Borja and Castells 1997: 50–1); while Moser and Peake (1987) have shown that the methods of access to public or subsidized housing often discriminate against women involuntarily due to their being less well informed with less access to sources of information and being restricted in space and time due to child care responsibilities. Women face a further problem with dwellings designed in such a way that their needs, which derive from their domestic responsibilities, are not accommodated (Hayden 1981). Thus, for example, the cooking and cleaning area is often treated as a leftover space in many residential projects in developing countries (Borja and Castells 1997: 53), with the result that an estimated 70 million women suffer respiratory and other health problems from high levels of pollution produced by kitchen stoves (Shegal 1995).

Housing diversity – the response

There is no way in a chapter of this kind that a complete picture of different policy responses to this growing phenomenon of household diversity can be given. What is possible is to signal some significant responses that have occurred at the level of public policy in various countries. First, the question of ethnic/racial diversity. At an international level the United Nations now attaches considerable importance to ethnicity and pluralism which is reflected in the recent inclusion of a study of multicultural and multi-ethnic societies (Inglis 2001) in UNESCO's Management of Social Transformation Program. As the director of the Program, Ali Kazancigil, put it: 'multiculturalism … is of prime interest to UNESCO, in so far as it embodies the ideal of reconciling respect for diversity with concerns for societal cohesion and the promotion of universally shared values and norms'. Other international organizations such as the Council of Europe have articulated a similar commitment, reflected, for example, in the adoption in 1994 of the Framework Convention for the Protection of National Minorities.

Inglis (2001: 19) has argued there are various different policy models associated with multiculturalism which have been developed to deal with ethnic/racial diversity: the assimilationist model which envisages the incorporation of ethnic minorities; the differentialist model which minimizes contacts with ethnic minorities; and the multiculturalist model which envisages that individuals and groups can be fully incorporated into society without losing their distinctiveness or being denied full participation. My argument here is that it is crucial that countries adopt a multicultural approach to housing and urban policies, if conflicts are to be avoided and if the plurality of housing needs are to be met.

There are some countries which have actively adopted a national policy of multiculturalism. Notable amongst these are Canada, Australia and Sweden, where policy initiatives have included language, educational and employment policies. There have been fewer initiatives at the housing and urban policy level, indeed some of the tensions of living with diversity have been most visible in the spaces of the city. Taking Australia as an example, in a study of planning for diversity in Sydney (Watson and McGillivray 1994) we found that conflicts had emerged where migrant households had used their homes for small businesses or industries, thereby contravening local planning regulations, or had constructed houses which challenged dominant housing design norms. Thus, for example, houses were built to cover the entire block of land associated with the dwelling, which contrasted with the usual practice of placing a dwelling in the middle of the block allowing for space for a garden/yard; while public housing was shown to be inappropriate to the different cultural practices of various groups – for example, it faced the wrong way, there was no room in the dwelling to practise religious rituals, or the dwelling was unable to accommodate extended families. These and other such conflicts led us to conclude that local, state and national housing authorities needed to develop culturally sensitive housing policies. These arguments have begun to be incorporated into the policy agenda in some localities.

In Britain, the Joseph Rowntree Foundation has supported a number of research projects which have examined the social and economic experiences of minority ethnic groups. Though these groups do not form a homogeneous mass at which policies can be directed in equal measure there are some general points which have emerged from this research which Kusminder Chahal has brought together (2000). The first shared characteristic is high levels of poverty: over half of African-Caribbeans and Africans and over a third of South Asians live in districts with the highest rates of unemployment, while people of Pakistani and Bangladeshi origin represent the poorest groups of virtually every measure. Second, all minority groups experience racist victimization particularly where families are isolated from social networks, and there is a lack of social support from agencies, family and friends. Targeting resources on council estates does not solve the problem since the most disadvantaged areas for minority groups are of mixed tenure. The studies have highlighted several issues including: 1) the need for a) greater involvement of minority groups in regeneration projects b) an improved information base of localities and better targeted policy initiatives c) a greater awareness of diversity and difference at all stages of policy and practice; 2) the importance for some minority ethnic families to retain a culture and identity which is different and protected from the British way of life; 3) the importance of tackling racist victimization which restricts choices about housing, lifestyle and engagement within the wider community. More specifically: 1) area regeneration policies need to be spread across tenure groups within neighbourhoods where minorities live and 2) because deprivation cuts across tenures renewal programmes and area regeneration of deprived estates does not benefit all minority groups living in inner city housing equally. This implies a range of different approaches to home improvement, renewal and regeneration and a more active involvement of ethnic groups in the planning and implementation of programmes.

At the housing industry level, ethnic and racial diversity has become profitable. In 1998 The National Association of real estate agents in the USA (Nevada Association of Realtors 1998 October newsletter) introduced a training programme entitled 'At Home with Diversity: One America' in order to give agents the marketing skills to assist them in selling properties to what was perceived as a growing number of multicultural and minority buyers. The programme was developed in cooperation with the US Department of Housing and Urban Development as a response to the rise in homeownership amongst minority households: 42 per cent of the overall rise in homeownership between 1994 and 1997 (NVAR 1998: 1), though minority households still only constituted 17 per cent of all homeowners. Overall, the rate of homeownership for Black people is 46 per cent, for Hispanics 43 per cent, compared to 66 per cent for White households

(US Census Bureau 1998). As the chair of the NVAR's Equal Opportunity and Cultural Diversity Committee put it:

> It makes good business sense. Persons from many different racial and ethnic groups are becoming major players in the housing market. Practitioners who do not tap all these markets stand to lose a lot of different customers, clients and money. This is an important social and bottom-line business issue.
>
> (NVAR 1998: 2)

The groups being targeted here are clearly not those marginalized in the global city in part time, insecure and poorly paid employment.

Again at the industry level, there is a growing recognition that addressing household diversity makes good economic sense – as long as households with the ability to pay are those targeted. An article in the *Puget Sound Business Journal*, Seattle, USA (Fina 1998) entitled 'Wave of diversity sweeps downtown housing' captures many of the trends in the housing industry response that can be witnessed in any number of cities – particularly the more wealthy global cities. The author begins:

> It wasn't long ago in Seattle when the only choice in downtown living was new building or old building. Wall colours were white or ivory. Carpet choice was tan or beige. Urban chic was a guy sleeping on your doorstep and industrial funk was something happening under the kitchen sink.

This was the period of gentrification of the downtown where buildings were designed to appeal to the masses. She continues:

> By the mid-1990s, however, downtown's vitality became more of a reality and projects that didn't fit the conventional moulds started to appear. In a period of three years we saw the development of projects as diverse and upscale as Harbor Steps apartments, the industrial theme Banner Building condominiums, the renovated lofts at 210 Third Avenue, and Waterfront Landing condominiums.

This is the high end of the market but what is distinctive and new is the diversity of housing products aimed at niche markets. On the basis of focus group research and sophisticated market analysis, developers are designing projects to meet the needs and desires of different groups. This shift from broad market appeal to market segmentation is a new trend.

To return to Seattle, the Harbor Steps 1997 second stage development drew on feedback from the tenants of their first development in 1994 to design housing more suited to the renters' desires. These, they discovered, were no longer primarily the 20–30-year-old single urban professionals. Rather – deploying the new metaphors of the housing market – there was a great influx of 40–50-year-old 'empty nesters' – so called – and senior citizens, which signalled to the developers a shift from what they defined as 'necessary renters' to 'lifestyle renters' (p.2). As a result large studios, penthouses and townhouses with sports courts, a meeting room and a library were all available in one project. In Vancouver where this trend has been in place for a decade amenities usually associated with the suburbs, such as parks and schools, along with amenities more traditionally associated with city centres, such as theatres and restaurants, have increasingly appeared in the downtown area. As the author concluded, Seattle downtown with its diversity of housing types will soon 'see such diverse groups as baby boomers, empty nesters, seniors, and echo-boomers enjoying the urban lifestyle together' (p.4), while the neglected market in downtown is for traditional families with children.

Far less attention is paid to low income groups, in particular those headed by women. Given that the private market is inevitably market led, it is left to government agencies to respond to household diversity at the low income level. Though public housing authorities in social democratic countries have responded to the housing need of single parents, with the growth in countries like the UK in housing associations and housing cooperatives, research has consistently shown that these households are allocated the poorest quality housing, often in locations that are ill served by services, local employment opportunities and transport (Schmink 1986; Watson 1988). Over the last two decades with the shift from Keynesian welfare state models to mixed private-public initiatives, or even greater levels of privatization of the public stock, access to secure low income housing has diminished. In some countries, nevertheless, community activism and feminist movements have precipitated the creation of various cooperative housing ventures where individual empowerment and control are central to the ethos of these housing initiatives. More such projects are needed on a global level. Given that the home is also the site of employment, particularly in developing countries, restrictive planning legislation has become in many cases the main cause of the economic deterioration of many resident families (Moser 1993). This is not to support the appalling living and working conditions of many such women, but it is to argue for a recognition that industrial and services zoning in residential areas could ease the burdens of urban family life and pave the way for a more flexible relation between household and more formal economies. Housing provision for women also needs to be located within a more flexible and dense transport structure than that more typically geared to the regulated working day of traditional male employment. Overall the complexity and fragmentation of many women's lives in most parts of the world is not well accommodated in traditional planning systems which are predicated on stable employment and family patterns.

In conclusion, household diversity is here to stay in the global city. What this necessitates is a more flexible and responsive housing system which recognizes this diversity across a number of levels. In particular, minority ethnic and racial groups and women headed households are particularly disadvantaged in the housing systems of most countries. Low income and thoughtfully designed housing provision which offers a range of dwelling types, carefully linked in with employment, transport and other services, continues to be a pressing issue for governments to address. Though the private sector is beginning to recognize this market niche, and can meet diverse housing needs at the higher income level, social, public, cooperative and other forms of housing initiatives need to be expanded to address the problem. Furthermore it is not enough for housing agencies to provide a diversity of good quality affordable housing; different housing constituencies need to be involved centrally in the housing process from design to allocation, in order for housing to become a space of empowerment rather than marginality and exclusion.

References

Borja, J. and Castells, M. (1997) *Local and Global: The Management of Cities in the Information Age*, London: Earthscan Publications.

Castells, M. (1997) *The Power of Identity*, Oxford: Blackwell.

Chahal, C. (2000) 'Ethnic diversity, neighbourhoods and housing'. Summary paper F0110, York: Joseph Rowntree Foundation.

Connor, W. (1994) *Ethnonationalism: The Quest for Understanding*, Princeton: Princeton University Press.

Fina, R. (1998) 'Wave of diversity sweeps downtown housing', *Puget Sound Business Journal*, 20 November: 1–2.

Hayden, D. (1981) *The Grand Domestic Revolution*, Cambridge, MA: MIT Press.

Hong, M. and Buyn, Y. (1998) 'Inter-generational relations in South Korea', in Mason, K., Tsuya, N. and Choe, M. (eds) *The Changing Family in Comparative Perspective: Asia and the United States*, Honolulu: East-West Centre.

Inglis, C./MOST Report (2001) *Multiculturalism: A Policy Response to Diversity*, Paris: UNESCO.

Inoue, S. (1998) 'Family formation: Japan, South Korea and the US', in Mason, K., Tsuya, N., and Choe, M. (eds) *The Changing Family in Comparative Perspective: Asia and the United States*, Honolulu: East-West Centre.

Mason, K., Tsuya, N. and Choe, M. (1998) 'Introduction', in Mason, K., Tsuya, N. and Choe, M. (eds) *The Changing Family in Comparative Perspective: Asia and the United States*, Honolulu: East-West Centre.

Moser, C. (1993) *Gender, Planning and Development*, London: Routledge.

Moser, C. and Peake, L. (1987) *Women, Human Settlements and Housing*, London: Tavistock.

NVAR (1998) *Newsletter of the Nevada Realtors Association*, Nevada: NVAR.

OECD (1995) SOPEMI: *Trends in International Migration Annual Report 1994*, Paris: Organization for Economic Co-operation and Development.

Ogawa, N. and Retherford, R.D. (1997) 'Shifting costs of caring for the elderly : back to families in Japan – will it work?', *Population and Development Review*, 23 (1): 59–94.

Sassen, S. (1998) *Globalisation and it Discontents*, New York: The New Press.

Schmink, M. (1986) 'Women in the Urban Economy in Latin America', in Schmink, M., Bruce, J. and Kohn, M. (eds) *Learning about Women and Urban Services in Latin America and the Caribbean*, New York: Population Council.

Shegal, N. (1995) *Women, Housing and Human Settlements*, New Delhi: Ess Publications.

Tsuya, N. and Choe, M. (1991) *Changes in Intrafamilial Relationships and the Roles of Women in Japan and Korea*, Research Paper series no. 58, Tokyo: Nihon University Population Research Institute.

United Nations Commission of Human Rights (UNCHR) (1991) *Resolutions and Reports. Summary of Discussions on Human Rights of Migrants*, Geneva: UNCHR.

UNDP (United Nations Development Programme) (1995) *Human Development Report*, New York: Oxford University Press.

US Bureau of the Census (1998) *Census Statistics*, Washington, DC: Bureau of the Census.

Watson, S. (1988) *Accommodating Inequality*, Sydney: Allen and Unwin.

Watson, S. and McGillivray, A. (1994) 'Stirring up the city: housing and planning in a multicultural society', in Gibson, K. and Watson, S. (eds) *Metropolis Now: Planning and the Urban in Contemporary Australia*, Leichhardt, NSW: Pluto Press.

7 The making of home in a global world
Aotearoa/New Zealand as an exemplar

Harvey Perkins and David Thorns

Introduction

Recent debates about the future shape of urban life have been dominated by questions of 'globalisation'. Social scientists have asked whether the world is becoming increasingly homogenized and dominated by common patterns of urban life. They have also examined the degree to which local differences are maintained in this process. A useful approach to study these global-local interactions is to interpret the ways they play themselves out in local settings. One such setting is the 'home'. This chapter therefore identifies some of the key theoretical ideas about house and home in a more 'global' world and discusses what can be learnt from a grounded, qualitative study of the meaning of home currently underway in Aotearoa/New Zealand.

Aotearoa/New Zealand, and its closest neighbour Australia, are migrant post-colonial European settler societies in which particular ideas about the home and building form have had a continuing influence upon the design and use of space. Davison, the Australian social historian, recently observed that:

> Home was thus both an idea and a place, an object of affection located far away, in the homeland from which most colonials had come, and near at hand, in the houses which they had built in the new country. These new homes were shaped by pressures of both emulation and avoidance: a desire, on the one hand, to reproduce loved and familiar styles and patterns of life; and, on the other, to escape the crowding and poverty of houses which were no longer home-like.
>
> (Davison 2000: 6)

Many of the migrants who came in the nineteenth and twentieth centuries to New Zealand and Australia were manual workers without previous experience of land and house ownership. Indeed this was one of the attractions of migration. The places they came to were often short of accommodation so many acquired land and built or at least assisted in building their shelters, which over time became houses. This has led to a deeply-rooted tradition of ownership and a strong commitment to 'do it yourself' house design, building and maintenance. These characteristics, as we will see later, are ones that are still valued parts of the contemporary activity of homemaking in both Aotearoa/New Zealand and Australian society (Dingle 2000).

The chapter has four sections. The first addresses the question of how globalisation is both changing the nature of the world and challenging our ways of understanding social relations. The second explores the nature of house-home relations and how they have been analysed. The third draws upon recent empirical work in Aotearoa/New Zealand studying the 'making of home' and the final section examines the policy implications that flow from the analysis of house-home relations for urban planning and management.

A global world?

Sennett in a recent discussion of 'street and office' argued that flexible capitalism associated with the present global age 'disturbs identities based on place, that sense of "home", of belonging somewhere in the world' (Sennett 2000: 176). Further, Urry (2000: 2), in challenging sociology to grapple with the realities of the twenty-first century and the greater mobility that now characterizes social relations, sees future sociology engaging with the 'diverse mobilities of peoples, objects, images, information and wastes and of the complex interdependencies between, and social consequences of these diverse mobilities'. The analysis of the meaning of house and home thus sits at the centre of a series of significant debates about globalisation and the nature of identity.

Constructing the meaning of 'home' is central to the ways in which social relations are constituted via interpersonal and location-specific social processes. Structuring our living spaces both physically and socially is of crucial importance in this process and has been the subject of many urban planning debates. Recently, this has, for example, been reflected in the emergence of simplistic neo-traditional 'new urbanism' and 'smart growth' models of urban design (Katz 1994; Southworth 1997). These models, as did those in the past, focus on how spatial design can change or reshape social practices. They are, however, very culturally specific, reflecting largely American experience and are overlain by prescriptive values, many reflecting a nostalgic or romantic view of 'community' and past spatial arrangements (Perkins *et al.* 2003; Talen 1999).

In working through arguments about space, home and globalisation and their respective impacts upon individual and local identity it is important both to be clear about the conceptual issues involved and to ground the analysis so that it does not lose touch with the reality of contemporary lived experiences.

In these terms, globalisation is a troublesome term. Its use is often vague with largely negative connotations about the obliteration of difference and the homogenisation of different aspects of life and the resulting loss of national identities, cultures and traditions. Many see this as an extension of 'colonialisation and Westernisation' leading to the domination of non-Western societies through a new form of imperialism (Roberstson and Khondker 1998). Globalisation is also used to refer to both process and outcome (Urry 2000). In the first instance the term identifies a growing interconnectedness and commonality of experiences. These are tendencies and processes that are ongoing, however. The outcome is not assured and there is not yet a single global economy, polity or society. The second instance of the use of globalisation is as a noun, implying that it has already occurred and that the world is now one 'global society'. This argument is linked to the debate about the 'end of history' and the arrival of the final 'global' stage of development. Such a conclusion appears to be premature, however, and is insufficiently cognizant of the vitality and extent of resistance to aspects of globalisation that exists.

In the literature there is also a strong emphasis on globalisation as largely an economic phenomenon. A 'strong' version of the argument sees first a shift over time from nationally based economies to those that are international, though here companies are still based within a nation state. The final stage is the 'global economy' dominated increasingly by Trans-National Companies less tied to territory and in their most extreme form operating as 'virtual' companies not requiring any spatial reference point (Waters 1995). In this new world, national level processes are of secondary importance and the new global markets are seen as uncontrollable by single national governments. Thus the significance of the nation state is eroded. The strong reading of economic globalisation underplays the strength of international bodies and institutions such as the International Monetary Fund, World Bank, Organisation for Economic Co-operation and Development, the G8, the United Nations and its various constituent bodies, and the activities of Non-Governmental and Community Based Organisations. It is because these economic and political organisations are connected to the interests of individual groups of nation states rather than Trans-National Corporations that they have some capacity to exert control over the operations of such companies (Hirst and Thompson 1996). The strong reading also underestimates the impact of protest movements such as those associated with peace, the environment and free trade.

An alternative reading of globalisation to the one above has focused on culture rather than economics. It too revolves around arguments about homogenisation and again illustrates both process and outcome views. Proponents of this reading argue that the world has become 'compressed' and that we are dominated by the information and entertainment media, which feed us all a common diet of television, films and advertising. New forms of communication including electronic fax, Internet, email, and the World Wide Web are also influential here. Again the dominance of the Trans-National Corporations such as Microsoft and McDonald's have had a profound effect upon both how we communicate with each other and what and how we eat. Our knowledge of events around the world is now both greater and more instant – so we all can share in the action without leaving the comfort of our armchairs. This homogenisation is seen as an aspect of Western or more often American domination of the world, changing habits, taste, and culture into a globalized sameness (Ritzer 1998).

Irrespective of the definition of globalisation to which one subscribes, interpretations of house and home are not immune to global shifts. The analysis of house-home relationships therefore raises significant globalisation-related theoretical and empirical issues. These require researchers to study both the material and symbolic aspects of global change and to think of globalisation as a process creating diversity. In studies of house and home a variety of examples may be advanced to illustrate the interrelationships between house, home and global connections. One of these is the increased international mobility of people and the weakening of national borders (Held *et al.* 1999). The degree to which mobility is chosen rather than forced is an important influence in shaping how 'home' is reconstructed in new locations. This in turn is influenced by local factors such as the past history of housing and urban development and the values embedded in the landscape (Perkins and Thorns 1999; Marsden 2000). Another important example of connections between globalisation and the home is being manifested through the use of the World Wide Web which is having an influence on the promotion and sale of houses. It is now possible to log on to real estate sites and take a virtual tour through the listed properties not only in your own home town but increasingly around the world. How extensive this practice is remains to be systematically examined. The Web also influences the design and remaking of the house in new ways; people can access trends and changes in design and decoration from many sources and adopt them in their own houses. A further indicator of global influence is the strength of the 'lifestyle' and 'home decorating and design' magazines and television programmes featuring refurbishment and renovation to one's house and garden. In New Zealand, for example, British and US television programmes and magazines are influential in this regard. It is issues such as this that have recently been raised in debates in the housing studies literature and it is to those debates that we now turn.

The meaning of house and home

The social scientific debate in housing studies about the house-home relationship and the meaning of home emerged in the 1980s and was largely concerned with houses as material objects and as agents of wealth accumulation. In societies where home owning predominates, the houses individuals and families occupy are a major source of wealth. The investment in property and the generally favourable growth in property values has encouraged a belief that investing in property is a safe way to accumulate for retirement and old age and a way to increase wealth as fast if not faster than through alternative investments and even, at times of property price inflation, than through the 'job' market (Thorns 1992; Badcock 2000). Findings such as this came from work conducted in Britain, Canada, USA, Australia and New Zealand and reflected the fact that these were all home owning societies in which house prices rose substantially through the 1960s and 1970s.

The 1990s saw the development of a sustained critique of this early work. Critics argued that the symbolic value of the home was not well analysed in this work. Feminist scholars also drew attention to its limitations (Winstanley 2001). They argued that greater attention needed to be given to the ways the meaning of home was created and influenced questions of identity. The work of Marcus Cooper (1995) and Iris Young (1997), among others, reaffirmed the need for people to have their own space – without this they suffered a loss of dignity and capacity to take part in everyday social life. Such work links to the ongoing public struggle for housing rights and a 'place to call home' in many parts of the world where tenure systems do not provide for all to have security and where homelessness is an ongoing issue (UNCHS 1996).

The housing studies debate did not incorporate all aspects of social scientific writing about house and home. One way of categorising that literature is according to the ways in which space and/or place are written about (Figure 7.1) (Perkins *et al.* 1998 and 2001). These include space as something that is natural and/or built, often contested, divided around private and public ownership and use. Another major division is around the question of the economic values attached to space and the symbolic. Further variations exist with respect to the way space is spoken about and the language used to describe it and people's relationships to the spaces they occupy and use.

An important issue arising here is the distinction between space and place with respect to the home: space is something we occupy and in its many configurations influences the way we live, and place is something we construct. The idea, therefore, that home is simply 'an ideological construct created from people's emotionally charged experiences of where they happen to live' (Gurney 1990: 26) needs to be rejected. Homes as special kinds of places are thus material *and* social constructions involving the use of space but their nature and form are not determined entirely by spatial considerations. We can and do reconstruct our homes as spaces and places over time with changes to our life course and circumstances.

The making of home is an active social process in which people consciously engage. It is not something that happens once but is something that is continually

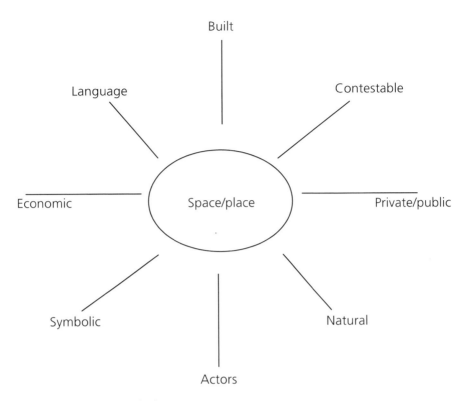

7.1 Home, space and place

being constructed and negotiated and re-negotiated. During our fieldwork people talked to us about the ways in which they constructed a sense of their 'ideal' and sought to achieve this using multiple strategies. Some of these involved the physical remaking of their houses and gardens whereas for others it was about moving to different houses and locations. Other strategies included the establishment of relationships between our respondents and a range of agencies, public and private: designers/architects, tradespeople, local authority planners and building administrators, central government housing agencies, real estate agents, landlords and financial institutions. In order to explore these questions further the case study material will now be discussed.

Case study – Aotearoa/New Zealand

In this part of the chapter a grounded analysis of the making of home drawn from ongoing research within Aotearoa/New Zealand is presented. In developing the theme of the significance of cultural context, reference will also be made to work on Australian 'homemaking'. The making of home is characterized as being a processual and dynamic activity involving negotiation, resistance and resignation. It is significantly influenced by cultural and social practices – context is, therefore, very important. The ongoing research in Aotearoa/New Zealand into the meaning of house and home allows an exploration of the dynamics of this process and the interrelationship of individual life journeys and wider contextual influences. The major ones identified have been shifts in the urban planning environment, economic opportunities and lifestyles together with the significance of the global re-imaging of 'home' through the growing range of 'lifestyle' magazines and related media which assist in the shaping of consumption and 'taste'.

The research has been conducted in Christchurch, a city of 325,000 residents in the South Island of New Zealand. The city currently has a growth rate of 0.3 per cent per annum, and is suburban in character with relatively low-density urban development, with the majority of the population living in separate houses rather than multi-occupancy or high rise dwellings. The work to date has entailed the creation of four data sets as well as theoretical and conceptual work. The first data set is an analysis of the new planning framework that has been put in place with the passage of the Resource Management Act (1991). This together with the Amendments to the Local Government Act (1989, 1996) and the Building Act (1991) provide the context within which neighbourhoods and housing are constructed in New Zealand cities (Perkins and Thorns 2001). The second set is an analysis of lifestyle magazines which is being used to explore the relationship between popular media and New Zealanders' houses and homes. The third component of the study is an analysis of the Christchurch housing market over the last two decades to provide an analysis of the overall context within which housing decisions can be located. Part of this analysis is focused on the ways real estate agents characterize housing within the city. The final component is an intensive interview study of some 41 households. Each interview took place over two sessions. During the first session, which was audio-taped, participants were asked to talk about their housing history and the lives of household members as they interact with each other and their houses and gardens. During the second session, which was audio- and video-taped, participants were asked to interpret the form and contents of their houses and gardens, room by room, outdoor space by outdoor space, and also talk about their interrelationships between themselves and the properties they occupy. The focus here was primarily on the physical form of the house and its contents but inevitably the intimate connections between physical form and social life were captured. Participants were selected to cover a range of tenure, dwelling and location variations from one bedroom rented rooms in a boarding house, to public and private rented accommodation, through to detached, privately owned and occupied houses at the upper end of the housing market. The rest of the chapter draws most heavily upon the interview component of the study.

Making of home

Housing stories

The interviewing approach adopted was to get people to tell their housing stories. They were asked where they were born and raised, when they left their parents' home, and about their first house or flat and when they moved on. They were also questioned about their housing tenure shifts and the importance of moving into home ownership if this was part of their housing history. In the telling of their housing stories it became very clear that homemaking is an ongoing and contingent activity. It also became clear that housing was seldom the central narrative. Most of our respondents took the house as a physical entity for granted. It was embedded in narratives about family, work and leisure. Home was the interweaving of all these in a special place – one which provided a secure physical space for social activity and interaction.

The various people interviewed were positioned at different points in their life course. Some were in their 30s and articulated a view of home that was about aspirations – how they would develop their sense of home. They talked about their ideal home and this included talk about the symbolic, material and economic aspects of homemaking. In this regard, the strategic purchase of a town house was for some a way of getting started on the home-ownership ladder and a stepping stone to the ultimate dream of the peri-urban lifestyle block.

> It's just a nice place to live in [town house, inner city] but it's time to move on – had enough ... served its purpose ... when we moved in here we were always going to moving on ... we wanted a town house for two years and it's two so time to move on. We would like to move to a more rurally kind of setting; we'd probably like to build a new house.
>
> (Interview data)

Other first home owners among our respondents articulated a different view. For them buying a first house was about establishing roots and being settled. The house was made to fit the household's needs. The initial choice was not just about the house but also about the neighbourhood. Here family connection and familiarity were important factors.

> We were married, and we bought this house, so this is the same time we were getting married, we bought it to live in forever.
>
> (Interview data)

Our respondents in mid-life told of how they were preoccupied with getting by. Paying the bills, organising and ferrying children to myriad activities and coping with economic uncertainty shaped their stories. Particularly apparent was the pressure of work in a climate of uncertainty. Employment was the overpowering preoccupation for many and was demanding more and more time – often at the expense of family and leisure activities.

> I think … with his job it has been very time consuming … we are going to walk this year because I am going to make sure that we do. Got a lot to answer for this job. … It's getting more and more to answer for all the time Sucks but um, so we're going to um make sure we go, we get out. Because we used to go out nearly every weekend, up the hills, or somewhere, you know. I think it's important that we get away from the house.
>
> (Interview data)

Members of this mid-life group were less idealistic and ambitious and more resigned to their situation with respect to both the symbolic and material aspects of home.

The third group were those in their 60s and 70s, mostly retired from the workforce and more able to look back reflectively upon their lives. They told a more rounded story of their housing journey. The ups and downs of life, the successes and failures displayed within homes where pictures, paintings, furniture, ornaments, tools and recreational equipment in the garage were all significant markers of their housing journey.

At the outset of the research we had been interested in the idea of a 'housing career' but the variety of housing journeys discussed by our respondents suggested that this idea failed to fully encapsulate their life experiences. Given the variety of housing journeys that we encountered the analysis of these in terms of a 'housing career' did not appear to meet the reality of the lived experiences. One of the consistent themes was the disruption to plans rather than the achievement of plans. The vagaries of the job market, the making and remaking of relationships, mobility between places, local, national and international, all serve to change the trajectories of the housing journey. Although some may have aspired to a 'housing career' alongside an 'occupational career' few achieved this.

In all cases mobility has been a part of our respondents' lives. For some it has involved moving from one country to another whereas for others it is internal mobility. The narratives revealed a conscious move to achieve goals as well as forced mobility. One such example was the Dutch couple who migrated to Aotearoa/ New Zealand in 1952 from Indonesia where because of political changes they were no longer able to stay. Returning to the Netherlands was not an option so they came to New Zealand.

> We decided to go to New Zealand. I saw a film, and I saw Auckland with sailing ships … it attracted me and my husband – and so we decided to apply.
>
> (Interview data)

They lived initially at the north of the South Island and worked on a farm and told of some of the problems they had as migrants coming to a new country and being faced with language and other differences and their attempt to recreate the familiar in the things they brought. Later moves took them to Christchurch and an eventual shift into a different job and their own house and at this point they considered that they had 'made it' within Aotearoa/New Zealand society.

Home ownership

In New Zealand and Australia one of the features that has enabled people to exercise some degree of control over their living spaces is the high level of owner occupation. The commitment to home owning is deeply ingrained and has become a significant aspect of the culture of both societies. In government policies and in popular ideology, home ownership has been continually presented as virtuous and beneficial. New Zealand public policy has had a long history of support through loan schemes, the State Advances Corporation, special saving schemes and the ability to capitalize family benefits (Davidson 1994). Most of these schemes were disestablished as part of the economic and social reforms of the 1980s which encouraged a move to greater reliance upon targeted benefits, usually through an income supplement and market provisions (Thorns 2000). The raft of supports for owner occupation were seen by feminists as being patriarchal with fewer women than men sharing access to home ownership and the prevailing rhetoric emphasising the 'male' as the breadwinner and owner of the household (Ferguson 1994; de Bruin and Dupuis 1995). The ideology underpinning home ownership also remained remarkably consistent throughout the twentieth century. It emphasized the way in which this form of tenure aided in the creation of stable, secure, thrifty citizens. Elements of those views are still prevalent and one writer recently put it: 'Owning your home in New Zealand is considered almost a birthright, a New Zealand tradition, a culture of home owning so embedded in the national psyche that it assumes its own momentum' (Ansley 2001: 18 and 20).

In the 1991 census 73 per cent of the population lived in owner occupied housing: 39 per cent were paying a mortgage and 34 per cent were freeholders. The figures five years later had reduced only slightly to 36 per cent and 32 per cent respectively despite rising costs of owner occupation. More significantly, however, if the pattern in the 18 to 30-year-old group is examined this shows a steeper rate of decline. Further the data show that the patterns of ownership across Maori and Pacific Island people are different with much higher rates here of rental (see Table 7.1).

In 1996, 70 per cent of New Zealanders were owner occupiers.

The proportion of freeholders increases with age with over 83 per cent of the over-60s being owner occupiers. It was in the past certainly seen as a *rite de passage* to adulthood to become an owner (Dupuis and Thorns 1996 and 1998). Ansley commenting in 2001 writes:

Table 7.1 Occupancy of dwelling 1991, 1996

People	All population (%)		Maori (%)		Pacific Island (%)	
	1991	1996	1991	1996	1991	1996
Owned with mortgage	39.4	36.7	40.4	37.6	38.9	33.6
Owned without mortgage	34.2	32.3	14.9	12.8	8.1	8.4
Not specified		1.5		1.0		1.3
Total owned	**73.6**	**70.5**	**55.3**	**51.4**	**47.0**	**43.3**
Rented	23.1	25.6	44.7	46.8	50.9	54.3
Not specified	3.3	3.9		1.8	2.1	2.4
Total	**100.0**	**100.0**	**100.0**	**100.0**	**100.0**	**100.0**

Source: Statistics New Zealand – Population census 1991 and 1996.

> Literally, for most, owning remains the only route to substance. 'It was the first thing I did when I left University' says Levy. Once you have owned your own home it is very hard not to own one any more.
>
> (Ansley 2001:21)

While the attachment to home ownership is still strong, its attainment for the rising generation is becoming increasingly fraught with increased uncertainty in the job market and the introduction of such things as student loans and consequent debt (Winter and Stone 1998). As one of our participants observed:

> Just from a straight financial point of view, there's much more to gain out of buying your house and having a mortgage coz at least then the money's yours, or you're not giving it away each week. Like, just say I bought this house, and I had a mortgage. I'd be paying it off each week. I'd be working towards something. At the moment I'm not. Um I'd like to do that really, you know (laughs). I waste too much money to do that, so you know coz I'd have to save up a deposit.
>
> (Interview data)

Here the questions of investment and setting a target for life are being reflected upon as well as the rival demands on ready cash and commitment.

Choice, constraint and doing it yourself

The choice of the house – to be turned into a home – has long been the subject of research amongst both sociologists and geographers with models of choice being largely favoured which reflect stages in the life cycle (Rossi 1959). We see evidence in our fieldwork of both 'choice' and 'constraint'. The intersection here of economic and social factors is crucial. As we noted above the ways that people have been affected by shifts in employment through restructuring have resulted in life course changes, pressures on relationships, changes in work and also housing locations. Attempts to reconcile lifestyle ambitions with the realities of current opportunities lie at the centre of much of the shifting of house and the reconstructing of the space in which people live. One of our respondents put it this way:

> We decided we wanted to have a house, a townhouse, didn't we, coz we wanted something close to town, no maintenance … as [I'm] not really a handyman, so we couldn't really look at getting an older place coz it would cost us too much to fix up and we sort of had a certain amount of money to spend, didn't we, and we were looking around and thought oh no, we'll have to stay and save more money and we saw this place and we decided well we may see if we've got enough money.
>
> (Interview data)

If they can afford it, people often move to achieve their desired housing changes, but if they can't they work on their existing house and garden to achieve their version of the 'dream' home. Here one aspect of New Zealand's housing is an asset. It appears possible to change houses if one has a modicum of income, skill and access to the technology of the do-it-yourself culture – tools, workshop, etc. We have been intrigued by the well developed workshops possessed by many in our sample. They have extensive sets of tools and equipment built up over the years as part of the lifestyle they have fashioned (Hopkins 1998). The workshop serves not just a practical role, in terms of do-it-yourself maintenance, but it is also an integral part of shaping leisure patterns, gender roles and identity. It is important not to overstate this point, however. An increasing number of New Zealanders are abandoning the do-it-yourself culture. Amongst our participants those who for a variety of reasons depended on professionals either to help them with or take complete charge of their house building or renovation reflected this change.

Popular media

Homemaking can also be about difference and style. Here our analysis of the media and real estate advertising has been of value. Tastes are being shaped and reshaped through the print and visual media; here particularly the impact of global cultural shifts can be seen. Evidence from fieldwork shows a direct influence between ideas presented in such media and the ways in which New Zealanders think about, build, remodel and maintain their houses.

I browse through magazines. I probably should read more really because I think it does keep you up to date. But I think they're quite a luxury thing really … I enjoy reading.

(Interview data)

Looked through magazines. We knew what we wanted … and sort of basic layout and then we looked through a few. A few magazines and then just hunted around to see what equipment we want in it [kitchen].

(Interview data)

While some of the material presented is quite prosaic – what's available, where to get it and how to use it – much of it may be characterized as 'dream-making'. Exotic products and overseas designs (some totally unsuited to New Zealand's climatic conditions and its building codes) are introduced to readers. One of our participants spoke of how they had planned and built on an additional room:

We decided all our lighting, we wanted lighting and how we wanted it. Um flooring, we determined what we wanted. It was the first time in Christchurch that I think they'd done an oak floor. They'd bleached, limewashed. It was the first time [name of firm of architects] had been involved in a floor like this, but we'd seen it in magazines overseas. … It was experimental but, its come up well.

(Interview data)

We read a lot of … architectural magazines which we subscribe to.

(Interview data)

Here there was certainly the connection with the overseas magazines and a desire to be innovators or taste makers within their housing. Also they had the financial capacity to carry out their ideas. For some the magazine images may well be beyond their financial capacity and they seek solutions from the 'imitative' product range in the same way that 'fashion' in clothes provides both the designer labels and the 'popular' versions from the chain stores.

Global influences are part of taste making. There is a degree of universalism in the trends created by common access to images and products reflecting the global nature of the marketing of design and decoration and building materials. The media attempt to establish particular values about what is appropriate for home owners with money to spend. Questions of distinction and taste, while not absolutely explicit, form an important sub-text in this material. The material is pitched at the upper and middle levels of the market and as with fashion items often cheaper 'look-alike' models and solutions appear to enable a broader range of social groups to adopt the latest trends. In a popular television programme 'Changing Rooms' people 'decorate' the rooms of their neighbours' houses with the aid of a professional interior designer. In one recent show the designer simulated solid stone blocks by using a special kind of chalk on the wall. In such programmes people are introduced to elements of contemporary 'designer culture' and their tastes can be modified.

The analysis of popular house and garden media also displayed a concern with changing lifestyles and living arrangements. Writers and advertisers felt there was a need for a diversification of types of room in the house, as home offices, granny flats and space for teenagers became part of what the 'modern family' needs.

> Today's family patterns are much more democratic and free flowing – and for many families the old models of home layout no longer fit.
>
> (Lifestyle Magazine Database)

> Today, if you've got $350,000 plus to spend on a dwelling for the clan … you're more likely to want a home office. You may also like a fancy fridge which delivers ice cold water at the push of a button; possibly a lift, if you're planning to stay into your golden years; a super duper security system complete with video-phone; under floor heating, and a temperature-controlled wine cellar.
>
> (Lifestyle Magazine Database)

This material illustrates the emphasis that is found in many of the advertisements upon technology and the notion of the smart house where you can exercise 'finger tip control' over your environment through the application of ever more sophisticated devices (see http://www.ihome.com.au/html/have/index.htm).

The advertising material in the popular media often glosses over the employment difficulties facing many New Zealanders and suggests that they have more control over their lives than is in fact the case. A good example of this is where writers suggest 'small offices in homes become more popular as more people opt for self employment and turn their backs on air-conditioned office buildings, the popularity of the home office is on the rise' (*Lifestyle Magazine* Database). In our interview material an alternative story was told about the home office. In many cases the existence of this new room in the house resulted from labour market restructuring which ended the secure job and turned a number of people into self employed contractors, who in some cases then sold their services back to their former employer. The office, once provided and paid for by a corporate entity, now became a cost borne by a recently redundant worker. The material also fails to reflect the gendered nature of the use of space within the home and with respect to the creation of the home office. In a number of cases it was found that the male partner had a designated space whereas the female partner was more likely to 'work' in a variety of spaces and had little in the way of autonomous space (Winstanley 2001).

Changes to family and the life course are prominent and the recognition that families now are very different is a recurring theme in the popular media: 'you can't plan for the typical family because there is not one' – we are told (*Lifestyle Magazine* Database). So the chances are 'that grandparents will be sharing the same space as their offspring in the future. … Some people will build their older children a special wing with a small lounge and kitchenette' (*Lifestyle Magazine* Database). Adjustment to change is dealt with by reworking the spaces of the home and money is clearly not an overwhelming limitation in these scenarios. Again the reality is a little different. A number of our respondents discussed the limited adjustments that they could make and reported that they had discussed changing their homes but decided that they could not afford it. Those with more resources had embarked on changes to their houses, with some using professional designers and builders to help them while others used a do-it-yourself approach.

Meaning and symbolism

The spaces of the house are, therefore, not 'neutral' in a symbolic sense. They are usually occupied by particular household members and the level of negotiation over use of these spaces varies from the resigned – 'it's his space, what can you expect?' – to the idea that in the long term democratic mediation will resolve such dissonance. It is through such negotiation, though often operating at the level of the taken-for-granted, that spaces in the house and garden are given meaning. That meaning and related social interaction is often captured in stories household members tell about house and home.

The home is made through the drawing together of the stories of the family, friends and pets – the memories of whose lives are displayed through their creative and other activities.

> I see your house as your personal domain. Like all the photos and things we have around. And all our junk up and down stairs, they're just our own personal memory things really. That's how I see, that's how I see a home. As long as it's comfortable and it's functional, and people can come in and feel comfortable. That's us really, you know.
>
> (Interview data)

The links to past generations are there in the photographs and family memorabilia that have been passed on through inheritance. More recent life experiences are captured through such things as design of the house and the artefacts in each of the rooms and the plants and trees within the gardens. One respondent told us about the importance of the 'walk-in pantry' because it was 'what my wife always wanted'. For others it was the links between inside and outside, or something they had seen in a magazine, book, while travelling or at friends' houses.

Most artefacts and possessions within the house have a story attached to them and are there as reminders of events and people who have been significant to the life course of the individual and/or family. Many talked about the garden as being a place where family, friends and places visited are incorporated into the landscape produced – so as with the house itself, the garden captures and enshrines memories and serves to shape the identity of the occupants.

The home as a symbolic creation is the reflection to a degree of the personalities of the people within them. As we argue above, homemaking is about relationships and negotiation. It is about constructing the sense people have of 'self'. It is thus also a cognitive activity in which all occupants play some part. It can be a process of potential conflict as well as agreement.

> Well we both work through ideas. We found we both wanted to do it, we'd both try and get visually sort of in concert, try and do it together. And we actually, I mean we were very fortunate we both have a very similar view and outlook on, on things so we don't really ever have any problems.
>
> (Interview data)

> It's a joint thing. … Normally I perhaps would go looking, and if I saw something … I mean I would say to M … because M doesn't like shopping, come and see something I think I like it. And that's really how we, generally buy. It would be no good really if I saw something … like a lounge suite or carpet and really liked it and brought it home – if he didn't like it as well. … Well he wouldn't like it and that's it. And I don't see the point of having a row over it.
>
> (Interview data)

Not all the stories that were told were of 'friendly' negotiations. The most serious ruptures occur when relationships break down and disputes emerge over what belongs to each partner. Similarly, when new relationships are formed there is a new process of homemaking that takes place and people deal in different ways with the past. Some dispose of the memories of the previous home whereas for others elements of the past are incorporated into the present. In resolving this, we saw again the importance of negotiation. This reinforced the idea that homemaking is an activity which extends through life rather than something which is done once and for all.

> He had the house. Yeah, his parents bought him a house, which is supposed to be … that's a sore point. It was supposed to become our house because we paid the mortgage jointly and put in a new kitchen and everything like that. When I left him his parents said, it's in our name, bye. So about 60,000 dollars gone there. I'm actually fighting it at the moment with my lawyer, because I

135

just told him about it in passing and he turned bright red and was absolutely furious. And said let's try and do something about this.

(Interview data)

In yet other cases clearly negotiation breaks down and is replaced by conflict and litigation.

Policy issues and challenges

The main discussion in this chapter has been around the everyday lived experiences of people in 'making their homes' in a changing and global world. This at first sight might seem to be a long way away from the pragmatics and constraints of urban policy and planning. There are, however, some significant linkages that can be made. At the beginning of the chapter we made reference to the growth of the neo-traditional 'new urbanism and smart growth' movements within urban planning and design. These movements both, in slightly different ways, seek to recreate a 'community' through integrated design. One of our conclusions is that forming a community is as much about relationships as it is about design. In all cases our research highlighted that the first thing people did when they moved into a new location was to 'make the location theirs' through changing or modifying the property (house and land). Over time they continually rework the use they make of spaces. This is a dynamic and ongoing activity. Community formation is also about relationships between people and place and is similarly a dynamic, contingent and ongoing activity. Unless this dynamic is fully incorporated into the thinking of the 'urban designers' then the 'smart designs' of the year 2003 and beyond will be little different from those of earlier years where neighbourhood balance and integration were to be the result of design solutions to correct failed urban growth strategies.

In respect to design issues there is a need to incorporate diversity and flexibility into both house and subdivision design. Human social life is messier than often conceived by planners and those who would impose order upon neighbourhoods and communities. Such local social arrangements that are fashioned amongst and between people in the city are often fluid and change over time. With increased mobility, both spatial and social, and the access to both real and virtual 'communities' the networks within which people can locate themselves are likely to become more varied. The impact of these changes upon both the house and neighbourhood need to be further explored. The research underpinning this chapter suggests, however, that even in a 'global' world local space is significant and is a key building block in the crafting of identity.

The analysis of the chapter further suggests that the development of housing policy needs to give greater attention to the significance of 'place' for the formation of identity. The need for secure tenure is necessary for social engagement. The opportunity for autonomy that owner occupation provides was strongly endorsed by the New Zealand participants – this reflects the local culture and tenure preferences. In other countries, however, the same need has been expressed but met through different solutions. Secure occupancy of a place of your own provides the setting from which people can build their relations with each other, with residential neighbourhoods and with their work and leisure settings. This means that the right to housing should be a fundamental human right. Achieving this affordably and in ways that meet the needs of a given population will continue to be one of the key debates within housing policy.

Conclusion

In returning to the issues surrounding global-local relations and the ideas of Sennett and Urry we think it is necessary to be cautious about the assumptions they make about the impact of global mobilities upon the significance of 'home'. Place and locality are still important – even for mobile people. For our respondents, mobility appears to have been something, which at least within their lifetimes, has *always* been a feature of housing experience. They experienced a continuing tension between mobility and place making. The home is thus still the central locale for the majority of people and they create this place in dynamic and ongoing ways. It is never finished because it is the site in which relationships are continually re-fashioned.

Acknowledgement

We gratefully acknowledge the support of the New Zealand Foundation for Research, Science and Technology who provided funding for the research upon which this chapter is based.

References

Ansley, B. (2001) 'Home truths', *New Zealand Listener*, 20 January: 18–23.

Badcock, B. (2000) 'Home ownership and the illusion of egalitarianism', in P. Troy (ed.) *European Housing in Australia*, Cambridge: Cambridge University Press.

Cooper, M.C. (1995) *House as a Mirror of Self*, Berkeley: Conari Press.

Davidson, A. (1994) *A Home of One's Own: Housing Policy in Sweden and New Zealand, From the 1840s to the 1990s*, Stockholm: Almqvist and Wiksell International.

Davison, G. (2000) 'Colonial origins of the Australian house', in P. Troy (ed.) *European Housing in Australia*, Cambridge: Cambridge University Press.

De Bruin, A. and Dupuis, A. (1995) 'The Implications of Housing Policy for Women in Non-Nuclear Families'. Paper presented at the Eighteenth Conference of the NZ Geographical Society, University of Canterbury, Christchurch.

Dingle, T. (2000) 'Necessity the mother of invention', in P. Troy (ed.) *European Housing in Australia*, Cambridge: Cambridge University Press.

Dupuis, A. and Thorns, D.C. (1996) 'Meaning of home for older home owners', *Housing Studies*, 11 (4): 485–501.

—— (1998) 'Home, home ownership and the search for ontological security', *Sociological Review*, 46 (1): 24–47.

Ferguson, G. (1994) *Building the New Zealand Dream*, Palmerston North: Dunmore Press.

Gurney, C. (1990) *The Meaning of Home in the Decade of Owner Occupation: Towards an Experiential Perspective*, Working paper 88, School of Advanced Urban Studies, University of Bristol.

Held, D., McGrew, A., Goldblatt, D. and Peraton, J. (1999) *Global Transformations: Politics, Economics and Culture*, Cambridge: Polity Press.

Hirst, P. and Thompson, G. (1996) *Globalization in Question*, Cambridge: Polity Press.

Hopkins, J. (1998) *Blokes and Sheds*, Auckland: HarperCollins.

Katz, P. (1994) *The New Urbanism: Towards an Architecture of Community*, New York: McGraw-Hill.

Marsden, S. (2000) 'The introduction of order', in P. Troy (ed.) *European Housing in Australia*, Cambridge: Cambridge University Press.

—— (2001) 'A decade of reflections on the Resource Management Act 1991 and urban planning in New Zealand', *Environment and Planning B: Planning and Design*, 28 (5): 639–54.

Perkins, H. and Thorns, D.C. (1999) 'House and home: looking in on New Zealanders' culture, sense of identity and sense of place', *Housing Theory and Society*, 16: 124–35.

—— (2001) 'A decade on: reflections on the Resource Management Act 1991 and urban planning in New Zealand', *Environment and Planning: Planning and Design*, 28 (5): 639–54.

Perkins, H., Thorns, D.C. and Winstanley, A. (2003) 'Nostalgia, community and new housing developments: a critique of "new urbanism" incorporating a New Zealand perspective', *Urban Policy and Research*, 21 (2): 175–89.

Perkins, H., Winstanley, A. and Thorns, D.C. (1998) *The Study of 'Home' From a Social Scientific Perspective: an annotated Bibliography*, House and Home Project, Canterbury and Lincoln Universities, p.58.

Ritzer, G. (1998) *The McDonaldization Thesis: Explorations and Extensions*, London: Sage.

Robertson, R. and Khondker, H.H. (1998) 'Discourses of globalisation', *International Sociology*, 13 (1): 25–40.

Rossi, P. (1959) *Why Families Move: A Study of the Social Psychology of Urban Residential Mobility*, Glencoe: Free Press.

Sennett, R. (2000) 'Street and office: two sources of identity', in W. Hutton and A. Giddens (eds) *On the Edge: Living with Global Capitalism*, London: Jonathan Cape.

Southworth, M. (1997) 'Walkable suburb? An evaluation of neo-traditional communities at the urban edge', *Journal of the American Planning Association*, 63 (1): 26–44.

Talen, E. (1999) 'Sense of community and neighbourhood form: an assessment of the social doctrine of new urbanism', *Urban Studies*, 36 (8): 361–80.

Thorns, D.C. (1992) *Fragmenting Societies?*, London, Routledge.

—— (2000) 'Housing policy in the 1990s – New Zealand: a decade of change', *Housing Studies*, 15 (1): 129–38.

UNCHS (1996) *An Urbanizing World: Global Report on Human Settlements*, Oxford: Oxford University Press.

Urry, J. (2000) *Sociology Beyond Society: Mobilisation for the 21st Century*, London: Routledge.

Waters, M. (1995) *Globalisation*, London: Routledge.

Winstanley, A. (2001) 'Housing, home and women's identities'. PhD thesis, University of Canterbury, Christchurch.

Winter, I. and Stone, W. (1998) 'Home ownership off course?', in J. Yates and M. Wulf (eds) *Australia's Housing Choices*, Brisbane: University of Queensland Press.

Young, I.M. (1997) *Intersecting Voices: Dilemmas of Gender, Political Philosophy and Policy*, New Jersey: Princeton University Press.

8 Home-ownership in an unstable world

The case of Japan

Yosuke Hirayama

Introduction

The housing system in Japan has been focused on the expansion of home-ownership. From the end of the Second World War through the 1970s, the inflow of population into urban areas and a rapid increase in the number of households put increasing stress on the demand for housing, which led to an acceleration of housing mass-construction. The macro-economy developed at a striking pace, resulting in an increase in the middle-class whose employment and income were stable. There was a cycle in which the mass-construction of owner-occupied housing stimulated economic growth and this growth, in turn, expanded the acquisition of owner-occupied housing. To own housing was an effective means of acquiring an asset since land and housing prices continuously and rapidly rose. Middle-class family households of 'a couple with child(ren)' formed the social mainstream. That middle-class people had a family, obtained their own house and accumulated an asset was regarded as contributing towards social stability. The conservatives have been in power for most of the post-war period and their housing policy has been concerned with promoting the mass-construction of owner-occupied housing backed by strong connections with the construction industry and private developers.

The housing system which encouraged home-ownership developed under conditions of economic growth, an increase in the middle-class and the dominance of family households in the population. Japan today, however, has entered a period of rapid and profound restructuring, with shifts from a growing to a destabilized economy, from state intervention to a deregulated market, and from a united to a fragmented society.

The condition of the housing system has changed drastically. The 'bubble economy' appeared in the latter half of the 1980s and burst at the beginning of the 1990s. Since the bubble collapsed, there has been a serious and longstanding recession and income and employment have been destabilized. Housing and land prices have dropped sharply for the first time since the end of the war. The safety of owner-occupied housing as an asset has been undermined. The population structure is undergoing dramatic changes signified by a rise in the elderly and a decline in the birth rate. The construction, real estate and housing industries have been continuously exerting political pressure on the government to deregulate the housing market. The direction of the housing system is becoming progressively less clear in this emerging uncertain society.

This chapter will examine the change in home-ownership in Japan today. The first part shows that the housing system has been centered on expanding owner-occupied housing provision. The second part explains that the economic and social conditions for home-ownership have changed rapidly. Recent trends in the owner-occupied housing market and the policy responses are explored in the third part.

Japan's home-ownership system

Housing construction and economic growth

Japan achieved extraordinarily high rates of economic growth after the Second World War. The average growth of GDP was 10 per cent from 1955 to 1973, when the oil crisis occurred. Despite the recession in the early 1970s, the economy recovered quickly and continued to grow until the bursting of the bubble economy.

One of the elements which supported this economic growth was the mass-construction of housing. There was a great shortage of housing after the war until the first half of the 1970s. A large part of the housing stock was lost in the war-devastated cities. Approximately 4.2 million housing units, over one fifth of the total number of existing units, were needed immediately after the war. The number of households increased substantially and there was rapid urbanization. The average annual increase of households swelled from 185,000 in 1950–5, to 466,000 in 1955–60, to 682,000 in 1960–5, and to 758,000 in 1965–70 (Izu 1999: 6). The proportion of the population in urban areas rose from 37.7 per cent in 1950 to 63.9 per cent in 1960, and to 72.1 per cent in 1970.

Housing construction was considered as an 'engine' for economic growth. In the 1960s, the housing industry began to expand and to increase housing construction. Over 90 per cent of housing investment came from the private sector and housing-related industries came to have an important position in the macro-economy. The rate of housing investment remained at a high level throughout the 1970s, at between 7.2 per cent and 8.9 per cent of GDP (Ministry of Construction 1996: 19). And large-scale housing construction has been a prominent feature in Japan up to the present time. The number of new starts per 1,000 people was 3.27 in Britain in 1993, 5.13 in Germany in 1992, 4.42 in France in 1992, while it was as high as 12.02 in Japan in 1993 (Sumita 2000: 33).

Housing construction has been promoted by an ethos of 'scrap and build'. There has existed a system in which demand is maintained by the repetition of construction and demolition, which in turn supports economic growth. The rate of demolished units to new starts was 35.6 per cent in the period 1968–73, 50.4 per cent in 1983–8 and 53.4 per cent in 1988–93. By comparison, in Britain the comparable figure for the period 1981–91 was 7.7 per cent and in Germany 11.1 per cent (1980–9) (Izu, 1999: 43).

Housing policy to promote home-ownership

The post-war housing policy was systematized in the 1950s. Its core consisted of the so-called 'three pillars'; the HLC (Housing Loan Corporation) Act in 1950, the Public Housing Act in 1951 and the HC (Housing Corporation) Act in 1955. The HLC, which is a state-run agency, mainly provides individuals with a long-term and low-interest loan for the building and acquisition of their own home. Public housing, which is constructed, owned and managed by local governments and subsidized by the central government, is for low-income people at a low rent. The HC was founded as an agency of the state to construct rental housing and condominiums for middle-income households in large cities.

Among these 'three pillars' of the housing policy, the government has particularly and constantly emphasized the HLC's low-interest loan (Hirayama and Hayakawa 1995; van Vliet and Hirayama 1994). As shown in Table 8.1, the level of owner-occupied housing remained at around 60 per cent between 1963 and 1998. Though urbanization and household formation rapidly increased up to the latter half of the 1970s, the level of home-ownership was inhibited due to the measures used to accelerate housing acquisition. The ratio of private rental housing has been the second highest at around 25 per cent. However, private rental housing has not been supported by housing policy. The ratio of public housing and HC housing has been very low at around 5 per cent and 2 per cent, respectively.

Home-ownership policy was implemented as a means to accelerate economic growth. Private banks, which had concentrated on capital provision for enterprises in the period right after the war, began lending for acquisition of owner-occupied housing in the 1960s. Households who acquired a house utilized the HLC and a bank loan combined. The HLC's low-interest loan withdrew capital from family finances, expanded the bank's financial market, and stimulated private housing investment. Housing construction had a significant economic ripple effect on the steel, cement and lumber industries. Households which purchase a new house also usually buy new furniture and electrical appliances. In other words housing investment has significant multiplier effects. By raising housing demand the conservative administration made itself more politically secure since the construction industry, the housing industry and real-estate developers were its main supporters.

Table 8.1 Housing tenure in Japan

Year	Owned houses (%)	Public rented houses (owned by local government) (%)	Public rented houses (owned by public corporation) (%)	Private rented houses (%)	Company houses (%)	Total (including tenure not reported) (number)
1963	64.3	4.6		24.1	7.0	20,374,000
1968	60.3	5.8		27.0	6.9	24,198,000
1973	59.2	4.9	2.1	27.5	6.4	28,731,000
1978	60.4	5.3	2.2	26.1	5.7	32,189,000
1983	62.4	5.4	2.2	24.5	5.2	34,705,000
1988	61.3	5.3	2.2	25.8	4.1	37,413,000
1993	59.8	5.0	2.1	26.4	5.0	40,773,000
1998	60.3	4.8	2.0	27.3	3.9	43,892,000

Source: Statistics Bureau, 1963 Housing Survey of Japan, 1993 Housing Survey of Japan and 1998 Housing and Land Survey of Japan.

With the oil crisis in the early 1970s as a turning-point, housing policy became more of a measure to stimulate the economy, putting more stress on encouraging people to buy their own houses with the HLC loan. Of housing construction funded publicly, the ratio of houses with the HLC loans increased from 56 per cent in the 1971–5 fiscal year to 84 per cent in the 1991–5 fiscal year (Table 8.2).

With the exception of the oil crisis period, land and housing prices in Japan continued to rise at a rapid pace until the bursting of the bubble economy. This rate was far in excess of general price and income growth (Table 8.3). The economic stimulation programme created a large amount of investment for the housing market, acting to rapidly push up prices. By the middle of the 1970s, it had become difficult for ordinary workers to buy their own homes. So the HLC repeatedly increased the loan limit to improve lending conditions. In 1978 the terms of repayment for wooden houses was extended from 18 years to 25 years and for non-wooden ones from 25 years to 30 years. The Step Repayment System in which the amount of repayments was set at a low level for the first five years was introduced in 1979. A cycle was created in which the improvement of lending conditions encouraged house acquisition, expanded demand for owner-occupied housing and boosted housing prices. When it became difficult to acquire a house, lending conditions were again improved.

Social mainstream and home-ownership

The social mainstream was represented by middle-class family households of 'parents and child(ren)' who owned a house. There was an assumption that home owners

Yosuke Hirayama

Table 8.2 Housing new starts (thousand units), 1961–2000

Fiscal year	Housing by housing loan corporation A	Publicly funded housing of other types B	Publicly funded housing C=A+B	Private housing	Total N	A/C*100 (%)	A/N*100 (%)
1961–65	392	400	792	2,684	3,476	49.5	11.3
1966–70	697	816	1,513	4,522	6,035	46.1	11.5
1971–75	1,154	902	2,057	5,784	7,840	56.1	14.7
1976–80	1,967	636	2,604	4,658	7,261	75.6	27.1
1981–85	1,994	538	2,532	3,360	5,893	78.8	33.8
1986–90	2,085	482	2,567	5,562	8,129	81.2	25.7
1991–95	2,653	503	3,157	4,161	7,318	84.1	36.3
1996–00	2,171	491	2,662	3,929	6,591	81.5	32.9

Source: Ministry of Construction.

Table 8.3 Land price index and other economic indicators, Japan, 1955–85

	1955	1960	1965	1970	1975	1980	1985
Land price index of six largest cities	100	303	1,038	1,832	3,836	5,844	7,817
Land price index of the whole nation's built-up area	100	280	768	1,395	2,691	3,231	4,177
GNP index	100	183	371	829	1,678	2,703	3,541
Income index	100	132	215	408	962	1,406	1,735
Consumer price index	100	108	145	189	325	446	511

Source: Japan Real Estate Institute; Economic Planning Agency; Ministry of Labour; Statistics Bureau.

would respect the social order, have a family, bring up children and work hard. The conservative administration pursued social stability through an increase of property owners. They considered that it was possible for the majority to lead a typical life, join the mainstream, and become part of a highly homogeneous society.

People demanded their own housing for various reasons. First, it offered a capital gain because of the continuous rise of land and house prices. People recognized the need to buy housing at an early stage in life in order to build a valuable asset. Second, home-ownership was a means of obtaining social security for old age. The level of public pension, social service and public medical security for older people is low. Moreover, elderly people are often rejected by private landlords who fear that they may cause a fire, fail to pay rent or die without relatives who would take care of various things such as the funeral service. By owning their own homes, people thus hoped to ensure a secure home and a place to live in their old age. Third, there was no way to improve one's housing conditions other than acquiring a house. Housing policy was inclined towards measures to increase investment in owner-occupied housing and did not encompass rental housing. According to the Housing and Land Survey in 1998, an owner-occupied housing unit had a floor area of 121 square meters, and a rented unit had 44 square meters. Fourth, the acquisition of a house was symbolic of being part of the social mainstream.

A 'housing ladder system' for a standard life course was created to support the expansion of home-ownership. This was conceived of as follows: when a family is young, they may rent a house of poor quality as their income is low; as the family matures, their income increases and they can move to a better house; and in the end, the family should be able to purchase a house, and once they own a house, it means they can make a capital gain which enables them to move from a small house to a big house, or from a condominium to a single-family house. Single-family housing in a suburb was located at the top of the ladder and regarded as the 'Japanese dream'.

Housing policy is generally expected to allocate more public resources to those with lower incomes. The policy emphasis on home-ownership resulted in the concentration of public funds on the middle- and higher-classes. The housing ladder system was, however, assumed to address these inequalities because public support for the middle-class for housing acquisition was also considered to improve the condition of housing for the lower-classes through the chain reaction of moves.

Japanese society has achieved rapid modernization after the war. The role of family-resources, however, still plays a great part in the improvement of an individual's well-being. Whether an individual can obtain a house in order to join the social mainstream depends on whether the individual can have help from their family. When young households purchase a house, their parents often financially assist them. Within the family system, an owner-occupied house is not only owned by one generation but also passed down to the next generation through inheritance. There are still many cases where parents and their children's household live in the same house. In such cases, the children's household helps out their parents in house chores and then inherits the house when the parents pass away. The HLC established a housing loan system for two generations in 1980 to enable a child's household to take over its parents' loan (Hirayama and Hayakawa 1995). This system assists housing acquisition by cooperation between different generations rather than by individuals.

Yosuke Hirayama

Japanese society is called an 'enterprise-society'. Employees of major enterprises and their families were core members of the social mainstream. The enterprises played a significant role to supplement the home-ownership system (Ohmoto 1996). Many companies adopted the lifelong employment and seniority system to form the models of 'company as a community' and 'company as a family'. An employee and his family lived their lives belonging to and depending on the company. Major companies had systems of internal saving for housing acquisition and low-interest loans for employees who were buying a house. Employees of large companies were thus in a privileged position with regard to house purchase.

Restructuring of the home-ownership system

The rise of the 'bubble economy'

The economic conditions for the home-ownership system changed drastically because of economic globalization, financial deregulation and the formation of a more competitive business environment. The rise and collapse of the 'bubble economy' played an important role in restructuring the environment surrounding the housing system.

The bubble economy appeared in the latter half of the 1980s. The abnormal upsurge in prices of land and housing started in Tokyo and spread to Osaka, Nagoya, and then all over the country. Measured against the previous year, the price rise of residential land was recorded at 68.6 per cent in the Tokyo area in 1988 and 56.1 per cent in Osaka in 1990 (Figure 8.1). The average cost of housing in the Tokyo metropolitan area increased between 1980 and 1990 from 24.8 million yen to 61.2 million yen for a condominium, and from 30.5 million yen to 65.3 million yen for a ready-built single-family house. Price-income ratios rose from 5.0 times to 8.0 times for a condominium and from 6.2 times to 8.5 times for a ready-built single-family house (Ministry of Construction 1996: 24).

The 'bubble economy' was produced by a complex mix of elements. First, a policy to introduce private capital into urban development was implemented (Hayakawa and Hirayama 1991). The Nakasone administration, established in 1982, deregulated urban planning, disposed of large tracts of national land by auction, and privatized JNR (Japan National Railway) with the sale of a large amount of its land properties. JAPIC (Japan Project Industry Council), which was created by 17 industrial organizations and 110 private companies in 1983, lobbied for the sale of national land and urban planning-related deregulation. Second, as a result of the easing of monetary control, surplus capital which had no place to go was injected into real estate. With the Japan-US trade friction as a background, the Japanese yen immediately appreciated and interest was rapidly slashed after the Plaza Agreement in September 1985. The United States called on the Japanese government to expand domestic demand, which forced Japan to increase expenditure in public works on top of the financial loosening. Third, banks, though they had mainly been financing investment in plant and equipment, increased the amount of finance for real estate as big companies began to obtain capital from equity finance in the 1980s. Fourth, once land prices began to rise, all kinds of enterprises joined real estate-related corporations in a rush to invest in land. Banks, non-banks and insurance companies poured an enormous amount of money into land speculation. Banks and securities companies also created a non-bank organization through which to expand the financing for real estate because the Ministry of Finance did not have authority to investigate non-banks.

More and more households hurried to purchase homes with the continuing high rates of house price inflation. The construction of condominiums increased in the suburbs although previously a move to such locations had been generally associated with house purchase. In the central area of Tokyo, however, the price

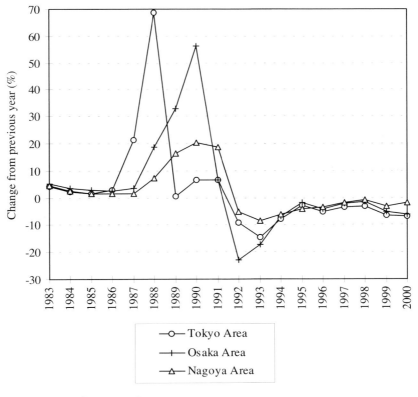

Source: Ministry of Construction.

8.1 Price index of land for residential use

of a condominium with 70 square meters had jumped from 6.2 times the average annual income in 1985 to 14.6 times in 1990 (Fukuda 1993: 17), pushing condominium purchase further out from the central districts.

Under the programme to expand domestic demand, housing policy placed even more importance on encouraging the construction of owner-occupied housing in conjunction with the HLC loans. As the ability of general households to acquire their own houses declined, the HLC repeatedly improved lending conditions. The Supplementary Loan Programme was implemented in 1985. Loan interest was slashed and the size of a supplementary loan was increased in 1986. The loan limit was pushed up and the supplementary amount was again increased in 1987. A policy which added to the initially projected number of houses with HLC loans was implemented every fiscal year.

After the bubble burst

The bubble economy began to collapse in 1989 in Tokyo and land prices started to drop in all cities in 1992. Since then, land prices have been declining (Figure 8.1). The government regulated the total amount of real estate financing in 1990 and introduced a new tax for land holding in 1993, which caused the bubble to immediately burst, rather than dissolving it gradually. The sustained fall in land prices, experienced for the first time since the end of the war, has thrown Japanese society into total confusion.

The bursting of the bubble generated a huge amount of bad debt and brought about a crisis in the banking sector. *Jusens* (housing loan banks) were especially affected. Their anticipated losses were as high as 6.41 trillion yen (US$49.3 billion: $1=Y130) while their estimated worth was only 3.29 trillion yen (US$25.3 billion). The government hesitated to commit public funds to address the bad debts for fear of the political risk, but finally decided to clear such *Jusens'* debt with public funds in 1995. A chain reaction of the collapse of major banks and securities companies, the so-called Second Financial Crisis, began in 1997. The government provided the banking sector with 2 trillion yen (US$15.4 billion) of public funds in 1998 and 7.45 trillion yen (US$57.3 billion) in 1999. There is, however, no sign of the economy recovering because the total amount of bad debts is still on the increase. While the injection of public capital has reduced the existing bad debts, new debts are being generated by the economic stagnation. As of 1999, according to the Financial Investigation Agency, bad debts in total increased from 21.8 trillion yen (US$167.7 billion) in 1996 to as much as 30.4 trillion yen (US$233.8 billion) in 1999 (Watanabe 2001: 21).

Recession has been deeply entrenched since the bursting of the bubble economy. The stability of employment and income has been lost and it is now unclear whether the 'enterprise-society' can be maintained. Many companies are addressing the restructuring by down-sizing and have begun to abandon the lifelong employment system and the seniority system for wages and promotion. Employment is now becoming more mobile and there are more part time workers, agency workers and employees on fixed term contracts. The unemployment rate increased from 2.1 per cent in 1990 to 5.6 per cent in 2001.

Japanese people have been believers in the myth that Japan is an equal society. Income disparities have, however, greatly expanded since the 1980s. According to research by the Ministry of Health and Welfare, the Gini-index of income before tax increased from 0.349 in 1980 to 0.441 in 1994, and the Gini-index of income after tax from 0.314 to 0.361 in the same period. It is rare among today's economically developed countries for income disparity to increase so rapidly in such a short time (Tachibanaki 1998).

A system which expanded home-ownership was effective only under conditions of rising house prices, stable employment and rising real incomes. Even if it was a burden to buy a house, repayments of the loan were expected to ease as income increased and the value of the house rose. However, the value of privately owned houses today is at risk, incomes are not increasing and stability of employment is fragile.

House prices have been continuously falling for the last decade. The price decrease has been most marked in the condominium sector rather than in single-family housing. And among the condominiums it has been more noticeable in older than in new ones. According to the data on condominiums purchased utilizing HLC loans, the average price of a secondhand condominium unit declined from 41 million yen (US$315,000) in 1990 to 25 million yen (US$192,000) in 1999 in the Tokyo metropolitan area, and from 32 million yen (US$246,000) in 1991 to 20 million yen (US$154,000) in 1999 in the Kinki area (Figure 8.2).

Capital losses on condominiums in the major cities have been substantial (see Figure 8.3). In 1991 the average price of a newly built condominium in Tokyo was 51 million yen (US$392,000). This had dropped to 24 million yen (US$185,000) by 1999 indicating a capital loss of some 27 million yen (US$208,000) as of 1999. Similarly, newly built condominiums in Osaka in 1992 cost 45 million yen (US$346,000) on average and their value had dropped to 21 million yen (US$162,000) in 1999 which generated a capital loss of some 24 million yen (US$185,000).

A private research institute has made some provisional estimates of the negative equity on condominiums in the Tokyo metropolitan area (NCB Research Institute 1999). According to these data, the average price of a new condominium was 60.67 million yen (US$467,000) in 1990 and the average loan was 42.47 million yen (US$327,000). Property values were estimated to having decreased on average to 25.62 million yen (US$197,000) and the outstanding balances were estimated at 34.59 million yen (US$266,000) on average in 1997 – a disparity of some 8.97 million yen (US$92,000). In the whole metropolitan area, the number of households who had bought a newly built condominium between 1988 and 1994 was about 280,000. The negative equity generated was

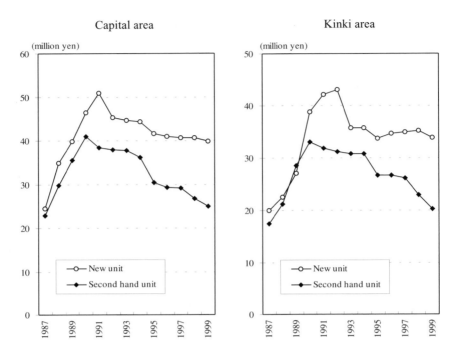

Source: Housing Loan Corporation.

8.2 Condominium prices

thus some 1.4 trillion yen (US$10.8 billion) in total and the capital loss totalled 6.6 trillion yen (US$50.8 billion).

The financial circumstances of households has been generally deteriorating. As shown in Table 8.4, the average balance of savings minus the amount of debt for a household decreased from 8,165,000 yen (US$63,000) in 1991 to 7,760,000 yen (US$60,000) in 2000. The figures for households which have a loan for land and/or housing fell markedly from 2,244,000 yen (US$17,000) in 1991 to minus 1,121,000 yen (US$9,000) in 1995, and to minus 4,158,000 yen (US$32,000) in 2000.

Decline in social homogeneity

Demographic change has also been a destabilizing factor for the housing system. The mass-construction of owner-occupied housing was buttressed by strong demand. Urbanization, however, settled down in the latter half of the 1970s and it is estimated that Japan's population will start to decrease after reaching its peak in 2007. The rate of household formation will also decline. The total number of

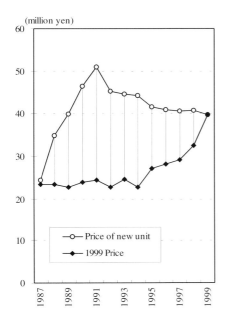

Within a radius of 70km, Tokyo

Within a radius of 50km, Osaka

Source: Housing Loan Corporation.

8.3 Capital loss in condominiums

housing units exceeded the total number of households in the 1970s. Since then, the vacancy rate has been constantly rising – from 7.6 per cent in 1978 to 9.8 per cent in 1993, and to 11.5 per cent in 1998. Housing demand has begun to decline and is expected to fall even more in the future.

The housing ladder system assumed that the social mainstream was represented by family households of 'parents and child(ren)' and that the majority followed a typical life course. The population structure and family composition, however, have been increasingly diversifying, which has been making the system dysfunctional. Social homogeneity has been weakening and the definition of 'mainstream' has been less and less clear.

There has also been rapid societal aging. The proportion of those 65 years old and older in the population has increased from 7.1 per cent in 1970 to 14.6 per cent in 1995, and it is estimated to rise above 25 per cent in the 2020s. The birth rate has also been falling significantly. The number of births per 1,000 of population fell below 10 in the 1990s (Figure 8.4). Japan is one of the nations where an increase in the elderly and a decrease in births are most prominent.

Table 8.4 Balance of savings and debt per household (thousand yen)

Year	Total households			Households with debt for land and/or housing		
	Savings A	Debt B	A-B	Savings A	Debt B	A-B
1988	8,931	2,767	6,164	8,348	7,465	883
1989	9,946	3,254	6,692	9,303	8,300	1,003
1990	10,507	3,401	7,106	10,171	8,675	1,496
1991	11,283	3,118	8,165	11,080	8,836	2,244
1992	11,867	3,105	8,762	10,445	8,607	1,838
1993	12,358	3,587	8,771	11,503	9,991	1,512
1994	12,343	4,052	8,291	11,564	10,962	602
1995	12,613	4,515	8,098	11,125	12,246	−1,121
1996	12,791	4,837	7,954	11,046	13,292	−2,246
1997	12,500	4,977	7,523	10,824	13,881	−3,057
1998	13,517	5,744	7,773	11,814	14,918	−3,104
1999	13,927	6,330	7,597	12,041	15,638	−3,597
2000	13,558	5,798	7,760	10,981	15,139	−4,159

Source: Statistics Bureau.

Social composition has also been diversifying through a rise in those choosing not to marry, postponement of marriage to a later age, and a rise in divorce. As shown in Figure 8.4, the marriage rate has been decreasing and the divorce rate has been increasing since the 1970s. Figure 8.5 shows that the unmarried rates of 25–29-year-old women and 25–39-year-old men have risen since the 1980s.

Those households in the 'a couple with child(ren)' category have decreased and, instead, single households, only elderly households or couples without a child households have increased. Between 1970 and 1995 the proportion of 'parents and child(ren)' in the population went down from 46.1 per cent to 35.4 per cent while the proportion of single households rose from 10.8 per cent to 23.1 per cent. Average family size has fallen. The proportion of households with four and more members decreased from 54.0 per cent in 1970 to 34.1 per cent in 1995.

An increase of so-called 'parasite singles' is one factor in the fall in housing demand and in the weakening of the ladder system (Yamada 1999). Twenty to thirty-four-year-olds living with their parents are defined as 'parasite singles'. Ten million individuals were in this category in 1995. Two-fifths of men and one-third of women between 25 and 29 years old, and one-fifth of men and one-eighth of women between 30 and 34 years old were 'parasite singles'. They enjoy free housing and food and probably have their housework done for them. Believing

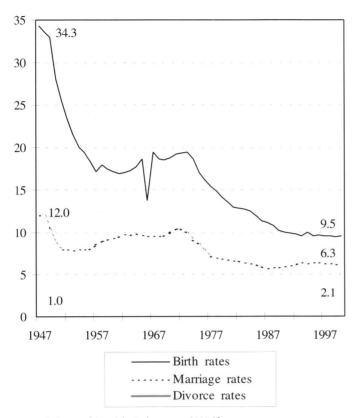

Source: Ministry of Health, Labour and Welfare.

8.4 Trends in birth rates, marriage rates and divorce rates (per 1,000 of population)

that their quality of life will decline if they become independent and get married, they live for longer periods in their parents' house.

The fall in the birth rate has also increased the probability of inheriting parental housing (Hirayama and Hayakawa 1995). This is another element which may discourage house purchase among young people. According to the Housing Demand Survey carried out by the Ministry of Construction in 1993, 30 per cent of young people in rental housing believed they would inherit their parents' housing.

The expansion of owner-occupied housing seems to have been stretched to its limit. The level of owner-occupied housing was anticipated to increase as urbanization stabilized, housing prices fell, low interest rates were maintained and policies to encourage house purchase were continued. In reality, however, the rate has hardly changed, shifting from 61.1 per cent in 1988 to 59.6 per cent in

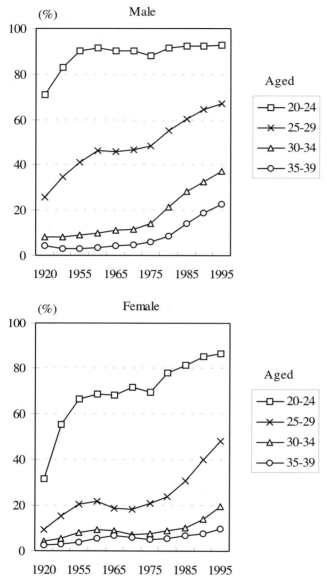

Source: Statistics Bureau, Population Census.

8.5 Unmarried rate by age band

Table 8.5 Home-ownership rate by main earner's age

Age	1983	1988	1993	1998
Total	62.0	61.1	59.6	60.0
−24	7.6	4.5	3.1	3.3
25–29	24.8	17.8	13.0	12.7
30–34	45.5	38.3	31.6	29.0
35–39	59.8	56.6	51.9	48.6
40–44	68.2	66.0	64.2	62.4
45–49	73.1	71.7	70.1	69.7
50–54	77.0	75.1	73.8	73.2
55–59	80.1	79.3	77.1	76.7
60–64	78.3	80.3	79.9	79.1
65–	76.1	76.8	79.1	80.6

Source: Statistics Bureau: 1983 Housing Survey of Japan, 1993 Housing Survey of Japan and 1998 Housing and Land Survey of Japan.

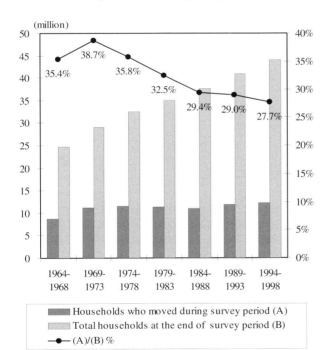

Source: Statistics Bureau: 1983 Housing Survey of Japan, 1993 Housing Survey of Japan and 1998 Housing and Land Survey of Japan.

8.6 Trends in house-moving

Yosuke Hirayama

Table 8.6 The ratio of households with/without housing improvement plan (%)

Year	Households in owned housing		Households in rented housing	
	Households with plans to improve their housing condition	Households with no plan	Households with plans to improve their housing condition	Households with no plan
1978	35.2	64.8	44.1	55.9
1983	28.4	71.6	39.2	60.8
1988	29.0	71.0	36.4	63.6
1993	24.8	75.2	33.5	66.5

Source: Ministry of Construction; Housing Demand Survey.

1993, and to 60.0 per cent in 1998. When we look at owner-occupation levels in terms of the age of the main income earner of the household, the drop in the home-ownership rate among young households is marked (Table 8.5). The combination of increases in the number of single households and 'parasite singles', the postponement of marriage, and the heightened possibility of housing succession have acted to reduce the level of home-ownership. Younger people are more cautious about house purchase as income, employment and property values have become less certain.

There has also been a decrease in housing mobility, indicating a changing pattern of progression through the housing system compared to the past. As shown in Figure 8.6, the proportion of households who moved within the previous five years against the total number of households has fallen from 38.7 per cent in 1973 to 27.7 per cent in 1998. Table 8.6 also shows that between 1978 and 1993 households who planned to improve their housing decreased from 35.2 per cent to 24.8 per cent among home owners and from 44.1 per cent to 33.5 per cent among those living in rental housing.

Lack of direction for the housing system

A diminished, destabilized and fragmented home-ownership market

With the roller coaster-like change in house prices, falling housing demand and weakened social homogeneity, the home-ownership market has become smaller, volatile and fragmented.

Households who bought a condominium during the period of the bubble economy are suffering from a combination of negative equity, the burden of loan repayments and stationary income. Many had anticipated a move to a better condominium or into single-family housing using the condominium as a stepping

156

stone, but this became impossible with the bursting of the bubble economy. The plight of owners is especially serious in the case of the 'suburban bubble condominium'. Families with moderate incomes stretched their financial resources to buy this type of housing during the bubble period. The prices of condominiums in inferior locations have, however, fallen further than other kinds of properties. The owners are forced to continue to repay hefty loans on properties whose value is rapidly declining.

In the prolonged recession, increasing numbers of households are finding themselves unable to repay their housing loans. The number of HLC loans which households have been unable to repay rose from 4,820 in 1990 to 17,757 in 2000. Many households had made use of the Step Repayment System to buy housing during the bubble period. In many cases, however, their income has remained stable or has fallen during the five-year period and they are now faced with much higher repayments with limited resources.

At the bottom of the fragmented market, there has been an increase of very cheap secondhand condominiums priced at less than 10 million yen (US$77,000). These are condominiums with limited floor space and poor equipment built between the 1960s and the 1970s with a very weak market potential. Their prices are rapidly dropping. They are becoming increasingly dilapidated as vacancy rates rise, non-payment of management fees accumulate and the proportions of low-income residents increase.

We are also seeing the creation of new, diversified, but small home-ownership markets in the major cities. In a situation where incomes do not rise and family size is falling, newly built condominiums have included a higher proportion of low-cost units with limited floor space. It has become more necessary for developers to aim not only at conventional family households but also at single people, couples without children and the elderly.

The purchase of condominiums by single women has also steadily increased. Real estate companies which construct and sell condominiums to single women are a recent phenomenon. The participation rate of women in the labour market is on the increase but salary levels, promotion prospects and job security for women are not equal to those of men. The older a single woman becomes, the fewer the prospects she has of moving into private rented housing. As single women are at a disadvantage in the labour and the housing market, they try to secure their future lives and housing through condominium purchase.

There is also the emergence of a small sub market of condominiums for elderly people. Many older, long established home owning households live in single-family houses located in the suburbs. Having finished repaying their housing loans, their living conditions are relatively stable. Some of them, however, wish to return to more central city locations and their single-family house is now too big for them to manage. Living in the suburbs is inconvenient for the elderly although it was an appropriate choice when they were bringing up children.

Land and real estate prices started to rise slightly in 2001 in a few districts in Tokyo – alone among the big cities. This reflects Tokyo's global city status with rising demand for housing among the elite in global enterprises. The prices of such condominiums often exceed 100 million yen (US$770,000). Some American investment banks have begun purchasing real estate in superior locations. There are indications therefore of spatial fragmentation emerging in Tokyo. While real estate prices have risen in a few districts, they remain stable or are continuing to fall in others.

The housing system until the first half of the 1980s had a definite direction. Many people had a family, their income was increasing, and they joined the ladder system with the aim of acquiring their own house and an appreciating asset. People today, however, live in an unstable world. It has become difficult to plan a life course in relation to housing. Younger people have less desire for home-ownership and no longer regard a single-family house in the suburbs as the 'Japanese dream'. According to an awareness survey conducted by *Asahi* newspaper in 2000, the proportion of those who answered 'No desire/intention to own a home' was 48 per cent among those 70 and over, 58 per cent among those in their 60s and 79–85 per cent among those in their 20s, 30s and 40s (*Asahi Shinbun* 1 January 2001). As socio-economic conditions are becoming transient and more complicated, the housing system is losing direction.

Housing policy without a vision

From the 1980s until now, housing policy has been principally about expanding support for home-ownership and promoting the marketization of housing. With the prolonged recession, the construction, housing and real estate industries have been strongly demanding further measures to stimulate the housing market. These measures have included:

- The HLC in the 1990s repeatedly lifted the loan cap to stimulate demand.
- The income criteria for public housing residents was lowered by the 1996 amendment. Public housing was defined as 'welfare housing' and limited to those on the lowest incomes and the elderly. This was to expand the sphere of commodity housing.
- The Building Standards Act was amended in 1998 to relax many regulations. One of the purposes of the amendment was to make it easier to promote redevelopment projects.
- The tax-reduction period for those who bought their own housing was extended from 6 to 15 years in 1999. The maximum amount of tax reduction per family was raised from 1.7 million yen to 5.8 million yen. This had been devised as a measure valid for only two years but was not abolished after the projected period because of political pressure.

- The Ensuring of Housing Quality Act was passed in 1999 to enhance the reliability of the housing market through intensification of the responsibility of housing builders and sellers to maintain housing quality.
- The HC was reorganized into the Housing and Urban Development Corporation (HUDC) in 1981 and again into the Urban Development Corporation (UDC) in 1999. The new UDC was to greatly reduce its housing projects so as not to compete with the private sector.
- The Renters and Leaseholders Act was amended in 2000. Before this amendment, tenants' security of tenure was protected and landlords could not easily request tenants to move. With this amendment, however, it is now possible for owners to rent their houses for a limited period.
- When parents financially supported their child(ren) to buy a house, gifts of up to three million yen (US$23,000) were tax-exempt. This amount was increased to five million yen (US$38,000) in 2001.
- Measures have been introduced to make it possible to convert real estate into small lots of loan bonds in order to attract small investments from individuals. Since the value of land as security has fallen, it has become more necessary for developers to procure capital not only through bank loans but also through equity finance. Although the conversion of real estate into bonds is restricted to office/commercial buildings at present, it will be introduced for housing projects in the near future.

Housing policy until the first half of the 1980s had a clear purpose of improving housing conditions. The goals were transparent: the goal set in 1966 was that housing for all households was to be ensured; the one set in 1971 was that a room for everyone was to be guaranteed; the one set in 1975 was that substandard housing would be eliminated by 1985. Now, however, there are no clear goals in relation to what kind of housing should be provided or what kind of problems should be solved. Housing marketization appears to have become the sole purpose of housing policy.

In relation to the five-year housing construction plan, the Housing and Land Committee reports on the basic course of housing policy for five years. The report in 1980 said:

> Housing is essentially a service provided or allotted in the market. However, various problems can be generated if we leave the matter to the market mechanism in such cases where the market itself fails to function or its function is not fully effective. Therefore, the government is required to intervene adequately in housing provision and allocation to stabilize and improve living conditions for the people.
>
> (Morimoto 2001: 233)

In comparison, the 1995 report declared, 'Housing services should be consumed privately. In principle it should be left to the individual to determine what standard of housing should be enjoyed and what amount of expenditure' (Morimoto 2001: 233). The report went on, 'The role of the free market should be utilized more widely'. The 2000 report declared even more clearly that market forces will be the future determining feature of housing policy (Housing and Land Committee 2000).

The beginning of the twenty-first century has seen the near abolition of the traditional 'three pillars' of housing policy by the central government. The Koizumi administration, established in April 2001, has begun a radical deregulation of the economy and down-sizing of the government sector. It was decided in December 2001 that the HLC and the HC were to be abolished. It is also planned to virtually cease any new construction of public housing for low-income earners. The new administration has removed most governmental interference in housing provision and has put forward a policy to encourage even more rapid marketization of the sector.

Concluding comments

It is a feeling of insecurity that encompasses today's Japan. Because of the destabilization of employment and income, people have become more reluctant to take risks in investment. The interest rate has been kept low for a long time and the government has been investing in public works on a large scale through large-scale issues of national bonds. Business confidence, however, has not recovered and government debt has expanded to a dangerous level. The future of the economy and of society is increasingly uncertain. Many economists released their forecasts about the future on the first day of the twenty-first century (*Nihon Keizai Shinbun* 1 January 2001). There was, however, substantial disagreement among them regarding all the key indexes such as the stock price, the exchange rate of the yen, the economic growth rate, the unemployment rate, spending trends and land prices.

The housing system encouraged the formation of a social mainstream in post-war Japan. Home-ownership for middle-class family households played a key role in defining the mainstream. A society which emphasized a specific direction divided those inside from those outside, creating disparities in housing conditions between owners and tenants, between family households and single people, and between employees of the big companies and others. In today's Japan, the definition of the mainstream has become extremely vague due to the economic stagnation and the decrease in social homogeneity. What this means is not the easing but the rearrangement of social inequality. A society which has lost its direction generates more complex and drifting disparities in relation to variables such as security of employment, the timing of housing purchase and the balance between liabilities and assets (Hirayama 2003). Home-ownership has lost its position as the core of the housing system and no longer symbolizes the social mainstream.

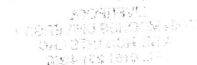

It is not certain at present whether or not a new housing system with a clear direction will be established in such an unstable world. The only thing that is apparent is that the traditional housing system of post-war Japan has already been broken up and will not reappear.

References

Fukuda, Y. (1993) *Tochi no Shohinka to Toshi Mondai [Land Commodification and Urban Questions]*, Tokyo: Dobunkan.

Hayakawa, K. and Hirayama, Y. (1991) 'The Impact of the Minkatsu Policy on Japanese Housing and Land Use', *Society and Space, Environment and Planning D*, 9 (2): 151–64.

Hirayama, Y. (2003) 'Housing Policy and Social Inequality in Japan', in M. Izuhara (ed.) *Comparing Social Policies: Exploring New Perspectives in Britain and Japan*, London: Policy Press.

Hirayama, Y. and Hayakawa, K. (1995) 'Home-ownership and Family Wealth in Japan', in R. Forrest and A. Murie (eds) *Housing and Family Wealth: Comparative International Perspectives*, London: Routledge.

Housing and Land Committee (2000) *Jutaka Takuchi Shingikai Toshin [Housing and Land Committee Report]*, Tokyo: Housing and Land Committee.

Izu, H. (1999) 'Chiiki Kozo no Henka to Jutaku Shijo' [Changes in Regional Structure and the Housing Market], in H. Izu (ed.) *Henbo Suru Jutaku Sijo to Jutaku Seisaku [Transformation of the Housing Market and Housing Policy]*, Tokyo: Toyo Keizai Shinpo Sha.

Ministry of Construction (1996) *Shin Jidai no Jutaku Seisaku [Housing Policy for the New Age]*, Tokyo: Gyosei.

Morimoto, N. (2001) 'Shijo Shugi teki Jutaku Seisaku wo Koete' [Beyond the Market-ization of Housing], *Jutaku Kaigi [Journal of Japan Housing Council]*, 51: 2–5.

NCB Research Institute, Ltd (1999) *News Release*, Tokyo: The Institute.

Ohmoto, K. (1996) 'Kyoju Seisaku no Gendai Shi' [Modern History of Housing Policy], in K. Ohmoto and M. Kaino (eds) *Gendai Kyoju: Rekishi to Shiso [Housing Policy: History and Ideology]*, Tokyo: Tokyo University Press.

Sumita, S. (2000) 'Jutaku Seisaku: Mass-Housing kara Multi-Housing he' [Housing Policy: From Mass-Housing to Multi-Housing], *Kenchiku Zasshi [Journal of Architecture]*, 115 (1462): 30–3.

Tachibanaki, T. (1998) *Nihon no Keizai Kakusa [Economic Inequality in Japan]*, Tokyo: Iwanami Shinsho.

van Vliet, W. and Hirayama, Y. (1994) 'Housing Conditions and Affordability in Japan', *Housing Studies*, 9 (3): 351–67.

Watanabe, T. (2001) *Furyo Saike ha Naze Kienai [Why Don't Bad Debts Disappear?]*, Tokyo: Nikkei BP.

Yamada, M. (1999) *Parasite Shingle no Jidai [The Time of Parasite Singles]*, Tokyo: Chikuma Shobo.

9 Home-ownership and changing housing and mortgage markets

The new economic realities

Peter Williams

Introduction

The imagery of home-ownership is surprisingly static and universalised given the extent to which this tenure has changed over time and varies from place to place. Home-ownership is typically seen as privileged not just because in many (but not all) developed countries the better off are home-owners but also because it is often generously subsidised (and promoted) by government. In that respect, although making a 'false' separation, personal preferences and rationality combine. Although in many developed countries there has been a growth in the proportion of households choosing home-ownership over renting, it is often argued despite the features mentioned above that it is a choice borne out of a lack of alternatives in the rented sectors. The other features strongly associated with home-ownership are a range of closely related risks including policy risk, e.g. where governments take steps which impact upon home-owners or the home-ownership market, house price risk related to falls in property prices, interest rate risk from rises in interest rates and creditor risk related to rises in unemployment and falls in income through loss of jobs, illness or relationship breakdown and the potential loss of the home. Politics may ensure that some of these risks are minimal and others can be offset or mitigated in other ways including insurance – private or government, savings, family assistance, plus of course there is the built-in option of trading down, if and when circumstances allow. Because home-ownership is seen as a tenure of privilege it is suggested it is exposed to policy change under more radical left of centre governments. In reality the picture on this is mixed, some conservative governments, e.g. the United Kingdom, have taken steps to diminish home-owner privileges and some left of centre governments have both protected and enhanced them.

This chapter seeks to explore the ways in which home-ownership has changed over time and is still changing. The chapter is mainly focussed upon the experience of the UK although it does draw upon evidence from other countries (see Perry 2001 and Forrest and Williams 2001 for useful overviews of housing in a range of developed countries). The aim is to try to 'unpack' our understanding of home-ownership and to give a clearer sense of core issues in contrast to the features associated with it at particular points in time and space.

Risk and home-ownership

This greater sense of risk is one of the new economic realities. Home-ownership benefited strongly from both government support and economic growth post-1945. However, globalization of economies, periodic recessions, financial instability and fiscal crises in a number of countries plus demographic change has created a greater sense of uncertainty around home-ownership in recent decades. The emergence of a flexible labour market is one obvious factor in many countries as in different ways is the changing shape of the household unit with an increased incidence of divorce and relationship breakdown and more single person households. The fracturing of what might have been seen as some of the certainties that underpinned home-ownership, e.g. conventional two parent families with stable occupations, has become ever clearer. And given the way home-ownership has expanded in many developed countries there are more households and in more varied circumstances who are exposed to this wider set of risks.

At the macro level, the closer integration of national economies has meant that events in one country are now more closely transmitted to others, not least through the growing dominance and changing fortunes of multi-national companies. Yet, at the same time we have witnessed the emergence of more stable interest rate regimes and a better ability to manage economic volatility. Thus it might be argued that, while the individual home-owning household is now more exposed to a wider range of risks, the overall national economies are in some senses stronger. Interest rate risk is perhaps the most obvious factor which has been reduced (Fernandez-Corugedo and Muellbauer 2002). At the same time low inflation does pose considerable challenges for long-term mortgage debt (Harley and Davies 2001). The debt is eroded far more slowly, exposing the lender (and the borrower) to greater risk regarding default albeit the borrower has more chance that any selected investment vehicle linked to the mortgage has the time to deliver the required return.

What becomes evident from studies of home-ownership in different societies is that beneath what is almost a veneer of similarities there are many structural and cultural differences. Thus the social and political meaning of home-ownership, the risks and rewards associated with it, the expectations of home-owning households, legal and financial structures, the organization of the home-ownership market, the financing of the tenure and its wider impact on both society and the economy all vary considerably and are specific to each country (see Forrest and Murie 1995 covering some of these issues in a range of countries and Osaki 2002 for a recent contribution comparing Japan and the UK).

At the same time, the development of globalised mortgage finance systems and market processes are such that a degree of homogenization is beginning to creep in through the processes and organizations around the market, e.g. via securitization and the creation of secondary markets (see Housing Finance International 2001) or through devices such as title insurance and through global banking regulation (e.g. Bank of International Settlements 2002). Moreover, improvements in transport, greater consumer knowledge and the pre-retirement/ retirement actions of the affluent post-1945 baby boomers (driven not least by concerns with the quality of life and questions about the ultimate value of pensions) are certainly going some way to creating a European real estate market. While we are a very long way from a universalised set of home-ownership market processes and even further from a global home-ownership market there is no doubt that there are tendencies in that direction. And the pace of change is increasing.

UK home-ownership in a comparative perspective

Home-ownership levels and the housing and mortgage markets

The home-ownership market in the UK is now the domain of some 17 million households (about 12 million in 1981), around 60 per cent of whom have a mortgage. There are substantial regional variations in the pattern of home-ownership (and to a degree in the extent of outright ownership reflecting the period in which home-ownership grew in that region). Wales and Northern Ireland have the highest levels of home-ownership and London and Scotland the lowest levels (Wilcox 2002). As a generality, home-ownership in the UK grew rapidly in the 1980s (in England and Wales) and the 1990s (in Scotland) partly fuelled by sales to sitting tenants under the Right to Buy and of course mortgage interest tax relief (MITR). Subsequently, the rate of growth has slowed substantially, reflecting recession, demographic change and, in the late 1990s onwards, house price increases.

Although home-ownership is the dominant tenure in the UK the fact that the rate of home-ownership is lower than in a number of other countries is often overlooked. Ireland, Greece, Spain and Italy are some of the developed countries with the highest rates while France, Germany, Denmark and the Netherlands have some of the lowest rates (Figure 9.1). In reality comparative figures require careful dissection. There is a case for distinguishing rural from urban home-ownership because the former is often linked to small holdings, i.e. to the organization of

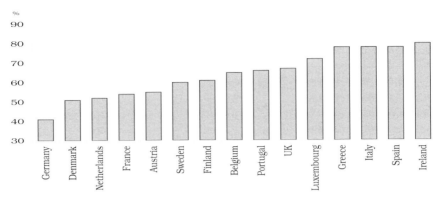

Source: European Mortgage Federation.

9.1 Home-ownership rates

agriculture. Equally the data often mask a substantial second home market with renters also owning homes elsewhere.

In a recent study Holmans (2000) compared home-ownership across four countries (see Table 9.1). It was evident that although there was no major difference between the four countries in 1995, the change over the period 1970 to 1995 had been substantial in some countries and less so in others but in most there was substantial *numerical* growth, e.g. the USA. The proportion of owners with a mortgage also varied greatly from 38 per cent in Australia to 63 per cent in England. As already noted, the Right to Buy had been a significant driver in England while in the USA expansion had taken place on the back of a strengthening economy. In thinking about home-ownership markets we must recognise factors such as the age profile of owners and the extent to which they have mortgages, the turnover in the market and the different policy drivers. All impact upon the degree of vulnerability of the market and home-owners.

In the past, home-ownership in Britain has been viewed as the tenure of the privileged (Forrest *et al.* 1990). Although it is still the case that there is a relationship between income and tenure, home-ownership is now the most mixed tenure in the UK whether measured by income, household type or socio-economic group (Hamnett 1999).

The picture this paints of continued growth and development of home-ownership in the UK masks a series of fundamental changes that have been taking place in and around the tenure. As a generality, home-ownership grew up on the basis of rising incomes and stable families. This is characterised in Figure 9.2 (CEBR 2001). Life was relatively predictable although we should not ignore the growth of working class home-ownership that was often a defensive measure against labour market instability. However, as Figure 9.3 suggests that world has

165

Table 9.1 Long-term changes in the number of owner-occupier households in Australia, Canada, New Zealand and the USA

	Australia	Canada	New Zealand	USA
1970 or 1971				
Owner-occupier households (000s)	2,435	3,640	542	39,886
Per cent of all households	70.0	60.3	68.1	62.9
1995 or 1996				
Owner-occupier households (000s)	4,790	6,700	864	63,544
Per cent of all households	68.9	62.4	70.5	65.0
Change in owner-occupier households 1970–95 (or 1971–96)				
(a) With constant (1970/1) proportion of owner-occupiers (000s)	2,440	2,835	292	21,563
(b) Effect of change in the proportion (000s)	−75	225	30	2,095
(c) Total increase	2,365	3,060	322	23,658
Rate of increase in total households (per cent per year)	2.7	2.4	1.9	1.7

Source: Holmans 2000.

changed substantially. Families, jobs and incomes are now less stable, life expectancy has increased considerably and with the continued growth of home-ownership the likelihood of being an owner-occupier and inheriting a property or the proceeds of a property are now considerably greater.

Alongside these socio-demographic changes have also come major shifts in the macro-economic framework within which home-ownership in the UK operates. In the 1980s the UK inflation rate ran at an average of 8 per cent and the mortgage interest rate was 12.8 per cent. Today inflation is around 2 per cent and the average mortgage interest rate is below 6 per cent (though with limited term discounts much cheaper offers are available, down below 4 per cent). As this suggests households are now paying real rates of interest and with lower rates of house price inflation and less amplified cycles of house price inflation/deflation resulting, there is increased mortgage risk. Households will not see their historic housing debt eroded so quickly by high inflation, thus the period in which they have high debt is increased leaving them a longer period in which they might be both unable to meet mortgage costs and have less capacity to trade out of any difficulties.

These pressures have been intensified in some areas by rapidly rising house prices (and in a few selected areas by the converse – rapidly falling prices) and by the withdrawal of MITR. At its peak MITR cost the government around £8 billion per annum and met around 40 per cent of interest payments due. Although the tax was progressively withdrawn through the late 1980s and the 1990s (under a

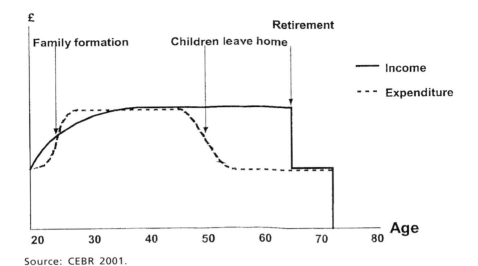

Source: CEBR 2001.

9.2 Life was predictable

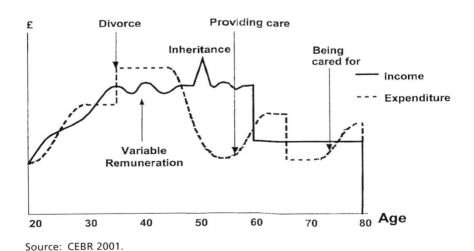

Source: CEBR 2001.

9.3 Now it can be different

Conservative government) it was not finally abandoned until 2000 (under a Labour government). This was achieved without any significant disruption to the market and no major political protest primarily because this was also a period in which the UK moved from a high interest rate environment to a much lower one. This suggests that other countries with similarly generous tax treatment of home-ownership could also use any favourable movement in interest rates to reduce the subsidy. As a generality intervention assistance has declined as the home-ownership markets mature around the world and as governments have sought to target their expenditure more tightly. The UK, Australia and Canada have all abolished tax relief on mortgage interest payments but the USA and the Netherlands continue to give 100 per cent relief at the home-owners highest marginal rate of tax (Freeman *et al.* 1996).

The fall in UK interest rates (and unemployment) over time has had two linked effects. It has brought the cost of borrowing down sharply, leaving lenders (and borrowers in terms of pressuring for) with the dilemma as to whether to increase the multiples applied (i.e. up from three times loan to income ratio – LTI) which in turn has increased demand and through that house prices (see Pannell 2001). The British media has at various times called for lenders to give greater flexibility in terms of the multiples used while at the same time expressing concern that, if interest rates rose rapidly in the future, households would be very exposed (not least because they are relatively highly 'geared' in terms of borrowings in relation to incomes).

In previous periods of rapid house price inflation lenders did increase loan to value ratios but experience in the early 1990s would question the wisdom of that. As Figure 9.4 shows, in the early 1990s the UK experienced a rapid surge in both mortgage arrears and possessions. Interest rates moved up rapidly while unemployment also increased. Debt servicing capacity fell and households got into arrears. As Figure 9.5 shows, in response to rising house prices in the late 1980s lenders had increased the number of high loan to value (LTV) loans. However, experience subsequently showed there was a high correlation between the incidence of arrears and possessions and such loans (Burrows 1998). It is evident from Figure 9.5 that the number of very high LTV loans has diminished in recent years suggesting that both borrowers and lenders have learned lessons. The evidence suggests borrowers have become more cautious while lenders have introduced and developed much more sophisticated credit scoring techniques (imported from the USA) and developed a range of affordability criteria to set alongside the very simple loan to income ratio that previously dominated.

Figures 9.6 and 9.7 provide details of house prices and interest rate changes in a number of European countries. While there are differences regarding house price trends, interest rates have converged reflecting the creation of a European Central Bank and monetary union in Europe. The rate in Greece has now also come closer into line. As a recent OECD report makes clear (OECD 2000), house

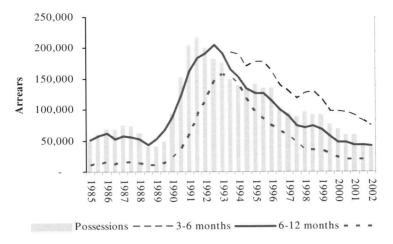

9.4 UK arrears and possessions, 1986–2002

First Time Buyers (excluding sitting tenants)

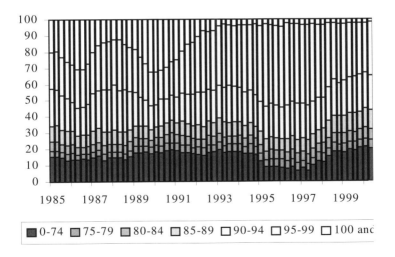

9.5 Loan to value ratios

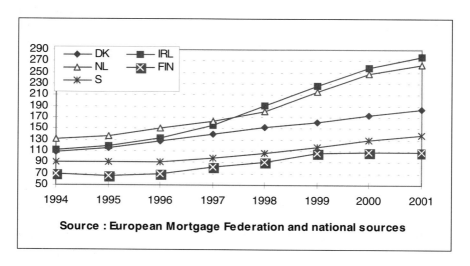

9.6 House prices in selected EU Member States, 1994–2001 (Index 1990=100), Denmark, Ireland, Netherlands, Finland and Sweden

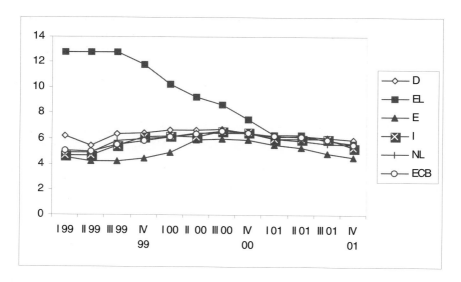

9.7 Selected Euro-zone countries and ECB rate, Germany, Greece, Spain, Italy and Netherlands

price movements have varied quite significantly across the 16 member countries. The greatest price fluctuations have been in countries such as Japan, Spain and the UK but while Japan has seen continuing decline (closely linked to the business cycle), in the UK and Spain there have been rapid real price increases. An *Economist* special report (*Economist* 2002a) has suggested that out of 13 developed economies worldwide the average nominal increase in house prices over the period 1980–2001 was 148 per cent (19 per cent real). Spain had 726 per cent nominal (124 per cent real) and the UK 389 per cent nominal (89 per cent real). As the report notes the Spanish increase partly reflects the way wages in that country rose to converge with European Union norms.

This leads directly to the wealth position of home-owner households. Property is typically the single most important component of household wealth. As Table 9.2 shows, housing assets are currently more important in European countries than in North America and Japan (see also Byrne and Davis 2002). However, this was before the widespread house price boom discussed above which has been largely driven by the low interest rates central banks have set in order to help their economies stave off or recover from recession. Indeed the *Economist* has argued that it is rising house prices and housing market activity and the confidence and consumption it triggers which has 'saved the world' from the post September 11 recession (for a general discussion of the relationship see also Case *et al.* 2001). However, as the editorial notes,

> spending cannot outpace income for ever. House prices have saved America and the world from a deep downturn, but they do not remove the need for consumers to take care over their balance sheets. Homes are only as sound as their foundations.
>
> (Case *et al.* 2001:11)

Table 9.2 Housing as per cent of total household assets

	1980	*1990*	*1995*	*1998*	*Owner-occupation rate (1995)*
	%	%	%	%	%
United States	27	27	23	21	67
Japan	14	8	10	10	61
Germany	–	34	34	32	41
France	44	43	42	40	54
Italy	40	37	35	31	67
UK	40	44	33	34	67
Canada	22	23	22	21	61

Source: OECD Economic Outlook, December 2000.

In Europe, these are overlaid upon substantial national and regional variations in income, well-being and indebtedness. Stewart (2002) has recently charted well-being and exclusion within and between countries in the EU. There are substantial variations with incomes being noticeably higher in the capital regions. The same pattern of variation is also true of indebtedness. A recent study for the EC (Betti *et al.* 2001) highlighted the large number of households across the EU (around 53 million people, 16 per cent of all EU households) that were defined as over-indebted (i.e. having difficulty repaying their loans). The proportion of households over-indebted ranged from 49 per cent in Greece to 11 per cent in Italy (the UK was 18 per cent). Often this was because of loans other than a mortgage though not in Greece. Variations in incomes, social security and access to credit all impact upon the shape and structure of home-ownership across Europe and require substantial disentangling to make sense of it.

The rise in home-ownership and the links with indebtedness, consumption trends and monetary policy are now being given much greater consideration than in the past when many economists disregarded housing market influences on the economy (see, for example, Aoki *et al.* 2002; McCarthy and Peach 2002). *The Economist* (2002b) has begun to track house prices relative to share prices in a range of developed countries. In most countries equities outperform housing though only just in Japan and Britain thus giving even greater justification for the 'flight' into property. This then reinforces the continuing concerns of the monetary authorities about the effects of the withdrawal of stored up housing equity and its impact upon increased consumer spending (Davey and Earley 2001). And as we know, just as there is an upside, so when a recession takes place this can exacerbate the downside.

The role of government

There is a clear tension between continuing to be risk averse and ever more intense market competition that has characterised the UK mortgage market over the last ten years. With lenders losing existing customers to competitors offering discounted mortgages they are under constant pressure to 'stretch' their criteria. This is where better lending techniques have been vitally important, allowing lenders to better assess borrower risk and to demarcate those customers where better lending terms do not mean higher risks. The UK Financial Services Authority (FSA) regulates the lending industry and has laid considerable stress on the need for higher credit standards. It closely monitors lending ratios (see FSA 2002 for an overview of its work and on pages 134–5 a useful comparison with regulators in other countries). The government has added to that pressure through a series of investigations into financial services and a recent inquiry into over-indebtedness.

The management of risk will become increasingly important in the new Bank of International Settlements Basel Committee regime planned for 2007. The Basel

Accord sets a global framework for the management of financial risk that is then implemented through each country's national financial regulator, in the UK's case, the FSA. Under the new Accord currently being finalised the capital adequacy requirements for each lender will be much more closely related to the risk profile of the lending undertaken by that organization rather than an industry average. This will impact upon the competitive position of individual lenders.

Mention has already been made of the role of the UK government in stimulating home-ownership through both the sale of homes owned by local authorities and the reduction of MITR. Although the erosion of support for home-ownership began under the previous Conservative regime, the Labour government elected in 1997 adopted an even more tenure neutral stance to home-ownership. It continued to erode and then removed MITR. It cut back on the development of shared ownership housing, increased Stamp Duty (a transactions tax which has been increased by introducing new higher rates and by not uprating the threshold below which properties are exempt from it) and reduced both grant aid for home improvement and the assistance available to unemployed home-owners. The result is that, even taking into account the continuing relief from capital gains tax for owner-occupied homes and inheritance tax exemptions for estates under £250,001 (2002), home-ownership is now a net contributor in tax terms to the Exchequer (Wilcox 2001).

This notching back of support for home-ownership masks a continuing ambiguity as to the relationship between the UK government (and national governments) and home-ownership. It is evident through many statements regarding the drive to create a more socially inclusive society that the UK government sees increased home-ownership as both a fulfilment of individual choices and preferences and as a powerful self-help mechanism. It has noted, as a generality, that unemployed home-owners get back into the labour market more quickly than unemployed tenants and that home-ownership has a strong positive image, is cheaper in the long term and can facilitate social and geographical mobility (Ford and Burrows 2000). The recent government-inspired debate about asset based welfare put home-ownership at its heart, as has the debate in the USA where this idea was developed (see Stegman, this volume).

However, while there is a desire to see home-ownership grow, the government has reduced its financial support and has begun to explore ways in which current government costs, for example, care costs and housing grants and assistance, can be charged against the value of homes. In other words the government is now moving to effectively 'penalise' households for being home-owners. This reflects the continuing tension both in government and around the Labour Party on redistribution and property ownership. Although owner-occupation is no longer the clear positional good it once was, there is still a strongly held view inside the Labour party that home-ownership equals wealth. However, within the government itself there is a clear view that home-ownership brings benefits to individuals and governments and that it should be encouraged. Aside from being the tenure of choice, the government has noticed that home-owners tend to have better participation rates in the labour force (the reasons for this will of course be many and varied). With policy focussed around work, self-provisioning and self-reliance it is no wonder that the government remains alert to the need to help households both enter and sustain home-ownership.

However, the reality is rather different. Fifty per cent of the defined poor in the UK are home-owners (Wilcox and Burrows 2000). Moreover in terms of targeted personal assistance from the state home-owners get under 10 per cent even though they make up 70 per cent of households. The Labour government has been slow to recognise the extent of home-owner poverty and the tensions around its own policies towards home-ownership and property based wealth. At the same time the government has recognised the extent to which problems in the housing market can impact upon the economy as a whole. In the recession in the late 1980s and early 1990s an overheated housing market spiralled very rapidly downwards as interest rates and unemployment rose. The depth and length of the housing market recession was made even worse by an increased supply of homes due to home-owners making forced sales, lenders selling possessed property and builders offloading unsold new homes (Hamnett 1999). The housing market recession in turn contributed to a worsening of the recession overall, damaging consumer confidence and reducing consumer expenditure with knock on effects across a whole range of sectors. Significantly it was through this process that government began to take a more serious interest in the relationship between housing and the economy.

A specific example of this was the government's agreement with the lending and insurance industries to take a number of initiatives around what was termed 'sustainable home-ownership'. The view was that home-ownership per se had been over promoted by government and that this had contributed to the housing market's exposure to an economic downturn. The incoming Labour government in 1997 pledged to avoid this by encouraging more home-owners to take out private mortgage payment protection insurance (MPPI) and at the same time encouraging more lenders to offer flexible mortgages that would allow households to both overpay and crucially underpay their mortgages, thus giving them a capacity to better cope with fluctuating incomes (Smith *et al.* 2002). It is estimated around half of home-buyers do not have the capacity to sustain their mortgage payments if out of work (the other half have savings and/or another person in work) (Whitehead and Holmans 1999). The take-up of MPPI has increased from around 10 per cent in 1995 to over 23 per cent in 2001. Further growth is anticipated, not least through the inclusion of other types of insurance that can cover mortgage payments.

In addition to expanding take-up, work is underway to see how such private cover might be linked to and incentivised by access to the state's Income Support for Mortgage Interest (ISMI). This scheme provides cover for home-buyers out of work for nine months or more plus immediate cover for specified groups such as the disabled. Although doubts have been expressed as to whether MPPI offers adequate cover and whether it will be possible to create an effective public/private safety net (Ford *et al.* 2001), the UK is perhaps unique in seeking to build a safety net for home-owners. However, that has to be viewed against the backdrop of the UK's more volatile and exposed housing market, e.g. the greater reliance on variable interest rates, a much younger age of entry into home-ownership, the higher loan to value ratio (Ball 2002) and greater general indebtedness. In other countries there is often a requirement for a substantial deposit and interest rates are commonly fixed.

The UK government has also declared its aspiration to improve the housing transaction process and to reduce the costs of borrowing. The UK has one of the cheapest transaction systems in the developed world but it is also one of the slower. The government view is that this slowness encourages failed transactions and 'gazumping', i.e. when the seller fails to proceed on a sale to an agreed purchaser and takes a higher offer from another person. The government proposes to introduce a 'sellers' pack' which will bring all the necessary information for a sale together at a point in time with the expectation this will speed up the transaction. There are differing views as to whether it will work. In other countries the tendency to buy only once and to self build as well as the much greater importance of new build are all factors which make a difference. In house buying and selling as in other aspects of home-ownership there is probably no universal truth!

The government has also set out an aspiration to see the cost of borrowing fall as a consequence of widespread mortgage securitization (see Holmans *et al.* forthcoming). To date most mortgage funds in the UK are raised through retail deposits. This is less common elsewhere. An alternative is to 'sell down' mortgages once issued to investors via a mortgage backed security (MBS). This reduces a lender's exposure to the savings market. The UK is the biggest MBS market in Europe (see Ing Barings 2001) and the second largest mortgage market; Germany is the first.

Table 9.3 Mortgage market

	US	UK	Germany	Japan	Spain
Main lender	s-55%	B-71%	B-28%	G-30%	S-52%
	B-19%	m-23%	S-26%	B-64%	B-38%
	S-12%		m-14%		
Int. type	Fixed	Fixed/var.	Fixed	Fixed	Fixed/var.
Average term	30	25	15	25/30	15
Maximum LTV	75/80	100	80	70/80	80

Source: European Mortgage Federation.

Notes: B = banks, m = mutual building societies, S = savings banks, s = secondary market securitization, G = government.

The structure of the housing finance market in each country is a key factor in the differentiation of home-ownership (Table 9.3). The low interest regime referred to above partly reflects the deregulation of mortgage markets that has taken place across the developed world since the early 1980s and the innovation and competition that has flowed from this. Specialist mortgage lending institutions have declined in significance while more generalised banks have grown. Alongside this there has been a broad move towards the development of mortgage bond and mortgage backed securities markets thus continuing the process of breaking the link between retail savings and mortgages.

The UK is now one of few developed economies where there is no active mortgage bond market (though it is legally possible) albeit there is an active securitization market. There has been a growing appetite for mortgage bonds (where the mortgage assets stay on the lender's balance sheet) and MBS (where mortgage assets pass to a third party), partly reflecting the decline in government bond markets (itself reflecting the decline in public expenditure). The global spread of a developed secondary mortgage market is significant because it allows some lenders not only to diversify their sources and lower the costs of funds but also to reduce their exposure to mortgage risk (see Coles and Hardt 2000; Watanabe 2000).

Having said this the UK mortgage market is one of the most competitive in the world and the margin between mortgages and savings has reduced over a number of years and is currently around 2 per cent although most of that is borne on the savings side (the average between the Bank of England base rate and mortgages is now 0.3 per cent). This competition has not only brought the cost of mortgages down but it has also resulted in a reduction in 'hidden' charges and penalties and more consumer friendly and flexible products. In essence the UK mortgage market has become 'commodified' with the consumer choosing primarily on the basis of price (Walker 2002) and with substantial remortgaging as borrowers 'chase' the lowest rates.

The combination of low mortgage costs and a reasonably strong economy has resulted in housing demand growing. However, supply has weakened with the consequence that house prices have been rising sharply. This has brought pressure on the government to assist first-time buyers and especially those working in public services as well as to ease any constraints imposed by the planning system. Ironically one of the reasons for both increased demand and reduced supply has been the private rented sector. For some years the UK government has been arguing for a bigger rented sector although its own efforts to create a tax vehicle to assist its growth failed. During and after the 1990s recession many younger households opted to rent rather than buy. The proportion of heads of household under 25 who were renting went up from 25 per cent in 1993/4 to over 40 per cent in 2000/1 while the average age of first-time buyers increased from 32 in 1992 to 35 in 2001. More recently the decline of the stock market and the linked fall in pension income has led to a resurgence in the private rented market with many more affluent households investing in second homes to rent. In so doing they were competing with the first-time buyers seeking to buy and in some cases were able to outbid them. The combination of a rise in the number of single person and two person households and the new appetite to invest in rented property has brought increased pressure upon the first-time buyer housing market. At the same time, the pressure to create new supply to overcome these shortages and to diminish price pressures is bringing the government into conflict with existing home-owners. This is especially true in the more middle class and less densely occupied suburbs and small towns in London and the South East of England as the government, through local authorities, seeks to encourage development.

Conclusion

There are substantial variations in home-ownership across the UK, in terms of cost, access, quality and the number, household type and socio-economic status of owners. Most recently the UK has witnessed a growth in the number of local markets where housing demand appears to be static or falling (Bramley *et al*. 2000). This has resulted in a polarised contrast between high demand and rising prices in much of London, the South East of England, the capital cities in the devolved counties plus non industrial county towns and villages, and areas typically in the North and Midlands of England and the more deprived areas of Scotland and Wales where there has been a substantial decline in the local economy and out-migration of population. Such contrasts pose real challenges to government when it seeks to manage the housing market. It requires localised and tailored solutions rather than the use of blunt instruments such as a change in interest rates.

One of the new economic realities in Britain is this more finely grained and differentiated economy and housing market. At the same time running alongside it is a more commodified mortgage market with more national and fewer local lenders. The mortgage system has moved much closer to being consumer demand driven rather than the producer led system which dominated up to the 1980s. Borrowers are now much more likely to move between lenders and products, seeking out what suits them best. They are aided in this by a large and active intermediary broker industry (some 50 per cent of mortgages are sold through them).

The UK's mortgage industry continues to evolve (Walker 2002). The mortgage system is undergoing a process of dis-intermediation, i.e. being broken up into component parts, with specialist suppliers taking on specific functions, e.g. mortgage administration or arrears management. Some lenders have taken the view that there is more profit to be made from mortgage selling rather than mortgage origination and have themselves become primarily intermediaries selling other lenders' products. At the same time the arrival of a number of US banks and specialist lenders has acted to open up a new 'sub prime' market and to hasten the organizational and technological changes (e.g credit-scoring systems and sophisticated computer-based mortgage administration) touched on above. The sub prime market relates primarily to the so-called 'credit impaired', e.g. persons who had previous history of mortgage arrears and the self-employed. This market was developed by US lenders with more sophisticated mortgage credit scoring techniques (itself a product of the 'nationalised US mortgage market via the former government secondary mortgage agencies Fannie Mae and Freddie Mac (see Wallison and Ely 2000)) and using securitization techniques to pass the risk off their balance sheets. UK lenders have now identified these markets as less risky and better business prospects than previously.

A changing economy that is continuing to adjust to a lower interest rate/inflation regime, the growth of the service sector, the decline of traditional industries, intensifying global competition and a more flexible labour market provide a vital backcloth against which to view the ways the housing and mortgage markets have developed in recent years. Both have changed significantly. The mortgage market has the potential for further substantial change. The cyclical nature of the housing market will continue but perhaps in a slightly dampened form. It is less clear whether the potential expansion of home-ownership from the current 69 per cent will take place and how the balance between owning and renting will play out. However, as home-ownership has become the 'social norm' and as house prices continue to rise (while pensions and other investments perform badly) we can expect to see continuing demand. Even if there are only small relative gains there will be continued numerical expansion due to the growth in household numbers.

As all housing studies show there is no such thing as a universal housing system. This selective review has considered a number of features of housing and mortgage markets around the developed world. In part it has been selective because of the difficulty in getting comparative data. Although there is a great deal of information on individual countries, detailed cross country comparisons on housing and mortgage markets are rare (three of the very few empirical studies are Diamond and Lea 1992; Lea 2001; and Freeman *et al.* 1996).

The UK has witnessed a century of growth in its home-ownership market. At the beginning of the twentieth century home-ownership was the tenure of less than 10 per cent of households. By the end of the century it was close to 70 per cent. What might happen in the twenty-first century? Could the UK witness another 'tenure' revolution? At this stage it looks unlikely, not least because there is now a far more developed institutional framework around home-ownership than there was a hundred years ago. However, that must always remain a possibility and there can be no doubt that the character of home-ownership will change over the decades ahead, reflecting further maturing of the market, equity release, the growth of the single person market, second homes and a stronger rental sector. There may also be some growth. The possible trajectory of the UK market will not be universalized, anymore than is the case at present. All markets differ substantially.

In recent years there has been a determined attempt to argue that high home-ownership levels are closely linked to high unemployment. Oswald (1999) has put forward a hypothesis arguing that the cost and inflexibility of home-ownership prevents rapid adjustment to employment change and thus creates unemployment. He supports this argument with data from a range of European countries. While there is some support for the argument (see Owen 1999) it is also the case that unemployment is high where home-ownership is low and in the UK home-owners tend to return to work more quickly than tenants. However, this does raise important issues about home-ownership and competitive advantage. There are established links between home-ownership and business start-ups and there is an association between this tenure and wealth, albeit a weak one. We also know from experience that a declining home-ownership market erodes consumer confidence and spending and can contribute significantly to economic decline. We do not know a great deal about how all of that plays out internationally.

The UK, like a small number of other countries, would identify home-ownership with specified risks and has been seeking to mitigate them, as have many home-buyers who have displayed more caution in recent years (that might be less true now in the UK with continuing house price increases). The emergence of relatively stable and low interest rate regimes itself grants considerable security to home-buyers and even though house price rises may slow home-ownership remains, at least relatively speaking, a very safe investment (Trimbath and Montoya 2002). Yet the combination of falling house prices, increased household debt and low inflation does raise concerns which need careful tracking and examination (Pannell 2002; *The Economist* 2002b). The efforts in the UK to develop a more substantial public/private safety net does hold out the promise of a market which could be less disrupted by the economic cycle as does the emergence of more sophisticated mortgage products and mortgage finance systems. They all contribute and given the global rise of home-ownership and the emergence of a mortgage backed securities market, there will be ever more effort focussed around this sector than before (both to protect economies and households).

At the same time we are seeing more competition between tenures, reflecting the increased diversity of housing markets and labour markets. This will change over time, reinforcing the simple point that there is no natural level of home-ownership in any country (beyond saying it is the level which reflects consumer demand and ability to pay including government assistance). The slow emergence of a framework for a global home-ownership market will continue through this century and may in itself contribute to a universalising process. If government debt continues to decline (a big if) and mortgage debt becomes a universally traded substitute then this market will continue to be a focus of attention. Although we remain a long way from a global home loans market and indeed even regionalized as opposed to national markets there are moves in this direction (especially within the European Union).

As the market grows in significance so there may be a need for national and supra national governments to play a greater role in managing the home-ownership market. Primarily that will be through interest rates but given the variations which exist this may also require more individualized solutions country by country. The UK's current attempts to deal with failing housing markets are a case in point. All this suggests we have to become far more analytically (and policy) sophisticated, mapping home-ownership in a much closer and more sensitive way and abandoning ideas of universal truths. Governments that make the simple assumption that home-ownership is a solution to housing problems will be sadly mistaken. It is a tenure that understandably has problems of its own and these will change and develop over subsequent decades. The imagery of home-ownership has tended to be static; the reality is far more complex. As economies and markets evolve so will the home-ownership market. Predicting the trajectory of that market in one country is difficult enough. To attempt to do it on a bigger scale is close to impossible. However, we should remain close to the detail and continue in our attempts to construct a wider and more sophisticated picture.

Acknowledgements

I am grateful for comments given at the conference on Managing Housing and Social Change and for the advice and guidance of the editors. The views expressed in this chapter are mine alone and not those of my employer, the CML in London.

References

Aoki, K., Proudman, J. and Vlieghe, G. (2002) 'Houses as Collateral: Has the Link between House Prices and Consumption in the UK Changed?', *Economic Policy Review*, May: 163–77, New York: Federal Reserve Bank of New York.

Ball, M. (2002) *RICS European Housing Review 2002*, London: RICS.

Bank of International Settlements (2002) *72nd Annual Report*, Basel: BIS.

Betti, G. Dourmashkin, N., Rossi, M., Verma, V, and Yin, Y. . (2001) 'Study of the Problem of Consumer Indebtedness: Statistical Aspects', ORC Macro for DG Health and Consumer Protection, European Commission, Brussels.

Bramley, G., Pawson, H. and Third, H. (2000) *Low Demand Housing and Unpopular Neighbourhoods*, London: Department of the Environment, Transport and the Regions.

Burrows, R. (1998) 'Mortgage Indebtedness in England: an Epidemiology', *Housing Studies*, 13 (4): 5–22.

Byrne, J. and Davis, P. (2002) 'A Comparison of Balance Sheet Structures in Major EU Countries', *National Institute Economic Review*, 180: 83–95.

Case, K., Quigley, R. and Shiller, R. (2001) 'Comparing Wealth Effects: The Stock Market versus the Housing Market', Cowles Foundation Discussion Paper No. 1335, Cowles Foundation for Research in Economics, Yale University, New Haven.

CEBR (2001) *Housing Futures 2010*, London: Centre for Economics and Business Research.

Coles, A. and Hardt, J. (2000) 'Mortgage Markets: Why US and EU Markets are so Different', *Housing Studies*, 15 (5): 775–83.

Davey, M. and Earley, F. (2001) *Mortgage Equity Withdrawal*, CML Research, London: CML.

Diamond, D. and Lea, M. (1992) 'Housing Finance in Developed Countries: An International Comparison of Efficiency', *Journal of Housing Research*, 3 (1).

The Economist (2002a) 'Going through the Roof', 'The Houses that saved the World' and Editorial, *The Economist*, 30 March, London: 11, 77–9.

—— (2002b) 'As Safe as What?', and Editorial, *The Economist*, 31 August, 63–4 (article) and 12 (Editorial).

Fernandez-Corugedo, E. and Muellbauer, J. (2002) 'Modelling Consumer Credit Conditions in the UK'. Paper presented at the European Network for Housing Research Conference, Vienna.

Financial Services Authority (2002) *Annual Report 2001/02*, London: FSA.

Ford, J. and Burrows, R. (2000) 'Labour Market Influences on Attitudes to Home-Ownership in Britain; an Analysis of the British Social Attitudes Survey Data', Discussion Paper, Centre for Housing Policy, University of York, York.

Ford, J., Burrows, R. and Nettleton, S. (2001) *Home-Ownership in a High Risk Society. A Social Analysis of Mortgage Arrears and Possessions*, Bristol: Policy Press.

Forrest, R. and Murie, A. (eds) (1995) *Housing and Family Wealth; Comparative International Perspectives*, London: Routledge.

Forrest, R. and Williams, P. (2001) 'Housing in the Twentieth Century', in Paddison, R. (ed.) *Handbook of Urban Studies*, London: Sage.

Forrest, R., Murie, A. and Williams, P. (1990) *Home-ownership: Differentiation and Fragmentation*, London: Unwin Hyman.

Freeman, A., Holmans, A. and Whitehead, C. (1996) *Is the UK Different? International Comparisons of Housing Tenure*, CML Research, London: CML.

Hamnett, C. (1999) *Winners and Losers; Home-ownership in Modern Britain*, London: UCL Press.

Harley, E. and Davies, S. (2001) 'Low Inflation; Implications for the FSA', Occasional Paper 14, London: Financial Services Authority.

Holmans, A. (2000) *Home-ownership, House Purchases and Mortgages: International Comparisons*, CML Research, London: CML.

Holmans, A., Karley, K. and Whitehead, C. (forthcoming) 'Mortgage Backed Securities in the UK: Overview and Prospects'. Report in preparation for the Office of the Deputy Prime Minister, London.

Housing Finance International (2001) 'Innovations in Mortgage Instruments, Funding and Processing', *Housing Finance International*, June (entire issue).

Ing Barings (2001) *International Asset Backed Market Review*, Third Quarter, London: Ing Barings.

Lea, M. (ed.) (2001) *International Housing Finance Sourcebook 2000*, Chicago: International Union for Housing Finance.

McCarthy, J. and Peach, R. (2002) 'Monetary Policy Transmission to Residential Investment', *Economic Policy Review*, May: 139–58, New York: Federal Reserve Bank of New York.

OECD (2000) 'House Prices and Economic Activity', *OECD Economic Outlook 68*, Paris: OECD.

Osaki, R. (2002) 'Housing as a Reflection of Culture: Privatised Living and Privacy in England and Japan', *Housing Studies*, 17 (2): 209–28.

Oswald, A. (1999) *The Housing Market and Europe's Unemployment: a Non Technical Paper*, Coventry: Warwick University.

Owen, D. (1999) *Housing: A New Structural Problem for Europe*, UK Economics series, London: Dresdner Kleinwort Benson.

Pannell, R. (2002) 'Affordability – How Much Higher can UK House Prices Go?', *Housing, Finance*, 55: 26–35.

Perry, J. (2001) 'International Comparisons', *Housing Finance Review 2001/2002*, Chartered Institute of Housing and CML, Coventry and London for the Joseph Rowntree Foundation.

Smith, S., Ford, J. and Munro, M. (2002) *A Review of Flexible Mortgages*, CML Research, London: CML.

Stewart, K. (2002) *Measuring Well-being and Exclusion in Euope's Regions*. CASE Paper no 53. London: CASE, LSE.

Trimbath, S. and Montoya, J. (2002) 'A New Kind of Gold? Investment in Housing in Times of Economic Uncertainty', Policy Brief no. 30, California: Milken Institute.

Walker, S. (2002) *The Changing Structure of the UK Mortgage Market*, CML Research, London: CML.

Wallison, P. and Ely, B. (2000) *Nationalizing Mortgage Risk: The Growth of Fannie Mae and Freddie Mac*, Washington, DC: American Enterprise Institute.

Watanabe, M. (ed.) (2000) *New Directions in Asian Housing Finance*, International Finance Corporation/World Bank, New York.

Whitehead, C. and Holmans, A. (1999) *Why Mortgage Payment Protection Insurance? Principles and Evidence*, CML Research, London: CML.

Wilcox, S. (2001) 'Help with Housing Costs', in *Housing Finance Review 2001/2002*, Chartered Institute of Housing and CML, Coventry and London for the Joseph Rowntree Foundation.

—— (2002) *UK Housing Review 2002/2003*, Chartered Institute of Housing and CML, Coventry and London.

Wilcox, S. and Burrows, R. (2000) *Half the Poor, Home-owners with Low Incomes*, CML Research, London: CML.

10 From welfare benefit to capitalized asset

The re-commodification of residential space in urban China

Deborah S. Davis

Introduction

On the eve of the Communist victory in 1949 urban housing was a privately owned asset. Real estate transactions were highly commercialized and residents from all economic strata viewed residential property and land as commodities that could be traded, sold, rented or sublet for a profit. However, after more than three decades of war, urban housing stock was in disrepair and there was an acute shortage of space. Millions camped on the streets or lived in crowded, make-shift hovels. Thus when the new Communist government nationalized urban land in 1950 (Wang and Murie 1999: 58) and presented a socialist property regime where all new urban housing could only be collectively owned, there was little opposition. The minority who already owned their homes were permitted to continue to hold full title to their residence, but for the overwhelming majority, the Communist victory de-commodified residential space and transformed a private, capitalized asset into a public welfare benefit.

In terms of property rights, the communist revolution had created a system of urban tenancy where public agents held the ultimate rights of use, the rights to all financial gain, and the right to sell or alienate the property. Thus with the exception of a small minority of homeowners, urban residents became renters with limited rights of occupancy and no option to become property owners (Whyte and Parish 1984: 82).[1] In 1978, when the Deng leadership jettisoned most of the Maoist blueprint, they also questioned the ideological foundations of the existing urban housing policy and subsequently launched a series of program innovations that by 1999 had re-commodified and privatized most urban housing stock (Li 2000). However, the route by which urban residential property was re-commodified and privatized did not evolve from a simple master plan. Rather like other components of Chinese market reforms, urban housing policy resembled the more general approach that Chinese leaders have aptly described as 'feeling the stones to cross the river' (ZGFDCB 2000a). Marketization began with piecemeal change in a few selected cities and then stalled or accelerated in response to macro and micro-level financial and political incentives. As expected, such incremental change is highly path dependent. As a result, by the time urban housing stock had been transformed from a public welfare benefit to privately held capitalized assets, the pre-reform cleavages between households headed by officials and managers and those headed by production workers and migrants had become more pronounced.

Research on the impact of Chinese market reforms on income inequality have already documented a similar story. As marketization accelerated during the 1990s and collective assets became more fully capitalized, urban income inequality increased and the wage gap between managerial and blue-collar employees widened (Ding 2000; Ruf 1999; Lin and Chen 1999; Lin and Zhang 1999; Sargason and Zhang 1999). Thus trends in urban China generally refute the optimistic expectations inspired by the first years of rural decollectivization (Nee 1989). Instead as Guo Xiaolin (1999: 84) has noted when quoting Douglass North (1994): 'Institutions are not necessarily or even usually created to be socially efficient; rather they, or at least the formal rules, are created to serve the interests of those with the bargaining power to create new rules.'

Is there any reason to expect that privatization of a public asset such as urban housing would follow a different trajectory or have different consequences? To date most scholars have answered in the negative (Chen and Gao 1993; Khan and Riskin 1998; Mei 1998; Pan and Liu 1994; Rocca 1992; Zhou and Logan 1996). In China some scholars have argued that privatization of urban housing stock may actually be the very *best* example to illustrate how those in positions of workplace authority whether in industrial or not-for-profit enterprises (*shiye*) have reaped a disproportionate share of newly privatized housing stock. For example CASS sociologist Mi Xiaohong (1999) concludes that because market reforms increased managerial autonomy and redistributive control over collective assets, the retreat from socialism gave local level leaders throughout China *unprecedented* freedom to commandeer collective assets for themselves and their relatives. Specifically, Mi (1999) argues that housing reform was an ideal site for cadre abuse because housing reform 'allowed ... a safe and secure (*anquan*) location in which to use power for private gain' (*shi yixie ganbu huodele yiquan mousi de anquan kungjian*).

Unlike deliberate asset stripping of productive assets which was clearly illegal, the differential access to newly privatized housing assets was *only* unfair and therefore could proceed with little censure or intervention from officials outside the enterprise. Moreover, urban dwellings in contrast to valuable industrial assets were distributed throughout urban China and could be effectively used or capitalized by any person regardless of age, education, or occupation. For these reasons the re-commodification of urban housing stock offered a more widely distributed opportunity for those in positions of enterprise authority to reap personal gain than asset stripping in a steel smelter or in a workshop of high speed weaving machines.

However, the inequalities of the new urban property regime cannot be explained simply by invoking the now conventional explanation of path dependency. To fully understand the social consequences of re-commodification we need to disaggregate property rights into several constituent parts and then follow the marketization of each component. Previous work on China's success with sub-optimal clarification of property rights in agriculture and industry, for example, have demonstrated the analytic value of distinguishing ownership into rights of use or control, rights of return or income, and rights of alienation or transfer (Putterman 1995; Walder and Oi 1999). In this study of the social consequences of marketization of urban housing stock I use this tripartite division of use, return, and alienation plus a fourth – right of occupancy – to clarify how the several phases of urban housing reform redistributed one of urban China's most valuable assets to the increasing disadvantage of production workers and new rural migrants.

Re-commodification of urban housing: an overview

Within a year of Deng's launch of the Four Modernizations in December 1978, the Chinese leadership ideologically embraced the benefits of commercializing real estate and authorized rent increases, sale of use rights to sitting tenants and the creation of the first real estate development company (Lee 1995: 125; Wang and Murie 1999: 142–3; ZGFDCB 2000b: 7). A year later the first consortium (*jituan*) of real estate developers appeared and overseas Chinese could again purchase full ownership rights to newly built apartments in selected cities (ZGFDCB 2000b: 7; Wang and Murie 1999: 132). Despite these significant departures from communist ideology, in practice, there was almost no immediate impact on the existing urban property regime. Even through the mid-1990s, it remained uncertain whether Chinese urban residents – as opposed to overseas Chinese – would ever have more than occupancy and use rights. In fact, during the 1980s and early 1990s, despite the ideological re-legitimation of private ownership, the most distinctive changes in urban housing were publicly financed building projects that by 1995 had rehoused two thirds of the urban population in collectively owned flats distributed as a workplace welfare benefit (*fuli fang*) (see Table 10.1). Even after marketization intensified during the 1990s, it was only in 1999, that the full bundle of property rights was privatized and commodified. Let me now review in more detail how this uneven re-commodification of the different rights claims created a residential property regime that benefited both past and current managers in public enterprises.

Table 10.1 Percentage of housing units built in each decade

	Before 1949	1950s	1960s	1970s	1980s	1990–95
National	7%	4%	6%	16%	46%	20%
Beijing	7%	13%	12%	14%	43%	15%
Shanghai	24%	5%	3%	11%	44%	13%
Tianjin	13%	5%	5%	13%	52%	12%

Source: *1995 Quanguo renkou chouyang diaocha ziliao*, Beijing: Zhongguo renkou tongjichubanshe 1997: 630–2.

1980–92: legalization of ownership, commodification of land use rights, experiments selling use rights

After 1980, urban China experienced the greatest building boom in Chinese history. By 1992, most non-migrant families had moved into new homes and average per capita living space nearly doubled (ZGTJNJ 1999: 349).[2] However, despite a variety of municipal level experiments with selling apartments to sitting tenants (Bian *et al.* 1997: 223–50; Jia 1998; Lau 1994; Lee 1988), more than 80 per cent of all new construction during the first 12 years of housing reforms was rented through workplace benefit programs. The pathway to a new home, therefore, continued to be through enterprise housing offices and those in search of better accommodations remained supplicants rather than customers (Davis 1993: 50–76). Equally note-worthy was that even as the quality and size of residential quarters greatly improved, few urban residents assumed any additional financial burdens and rents continued to average less than 5 per cent of monthly income[3] (Tong and Hays 1996; Lee 1995: 126; Wang and Murie 1999: 137) (see Table 10.2).

Hidden from the view of most urban residents, however, the central and municipal governments were taking steps for full commodification and marketization of urban housing assets. We cannot know if the architects of these shifts during the 1980s explicitly knew that they had laid the foundation for a fundamental shift in the urban property regime, but with hindsight, it appears that these changes created the legal and administrative foundations for the subsequent capitalization of real estate markets after 1998. Most important were legislation to re-commodify land leases and the creation of provident funds and other mortgage instruments that facilitated individual purchases of complete property rights.

Since 1949, the Chinese Communist Party (CCP) had consistently opposed private ownership of land. Within less than a year of their victory, the new central government nationalized all urban land. As a result when urban properties were confiscated or transferred to public ownership, previous owners received compensation for the estimated value of buildings but not for land (Wang and Murie 1999: 56). So rapid and complete was the elimination of a land market that

Table 10.2 Monthly expenditure on rent and utilities

Year	% on rent	% on utilities
1992	2.1	3.8
1993	2.5	4.1
1994	2.7	4.0
1995	2.9	4.1
1996	3.1	4.5
1997	3.5	5.0

Source: Cheng Siwei (ed.) (1999) Zhongguo Chengzhen Zhufang Gaige, Beijing: Minzu yu Jianshe Chubanshe: 471.

Notes
Because average consumer expenditures were generally less than 90 per cent of consumption expenditures after 1995, the percentage of income spent on housing was even lower than the percentage shown in this table.

the regime effectively made land a non-cost in budgeting for urban construction for the next 40 years. Some scholars have even concluded that as late as 1986 state enterprises and agencies were forced to resort to 'black market transactions' in order to handle the land exchanges between collective owners necessary to realize the ambitious state building programs (Wang and Murie 1999: 126).

In 1986 outsiders finally saw a substantial departure when they learned of the first legal land sale to foreign investors in Shen Zhen. Later that year the State Council established a new State Land Administration Bureau (Li 1999). Clearly, Beijing was evaluating the best means to monetize land values and establish new institutions for land exchange and sales. The next obvious steps toward further marketization came two years later when the National People's Congress (NPC) amended the constitution to allow transfer of land use rights (LURs) and revised the 1986 Land Management Law to allow paid transfer of LURs. The major turning point came after a 1990 ordinance allowed cities to sell long term leaseholds by negotiation, tender, or auction and to retain 60 per cent of the profit[4] (Wang and Murie 1999: 127–8). Over the decade of the 1990s, a wide range of new legal and financial procedures further routinized sales of LURs. But even as early as 1992 the floodgates had opened and sales in that one year were eleven times greater than those in 1991 (Chen 1998).

Creation of new financial instruments that would facilitate individual borrowing and purchase of market rate housing complemented the changes in land policy. Several large cities created new financial institutions to facilitate individual purchases (China Daily 7 January 1991: 1; Beijing Review 17 January 1991; RMRB 26 May 1991: 8; RMRB 1 January 1992: 2). Shanghai under the leadership of Zhu Rongji led the way by establishing the first provident fund for home purchases in May 1991. Guangzhou followed in April 1992 (Lau 1994).

Deborah S. Davis

1993–7: marketization and an emergent property regime

In November 1993, the third National Housing Reform pressed for a faster pace of commodification and in July 1994 the State Council outlined procedures for selling off public rental flats to sitting tenants throughout the entire country (Mi 1999; Wang and Murie 1999: 158). The official goal for 2000 was for 60–70 per cent of urban couples to have purchased a self-contained flat of 56 square meters at a price equal to five times their combined yearly income. New owners would purchase use rights in perpetuity, could bequeath ownership to others, and use the property as collateral for loans. After five years of owning the use rights, they would obtain full title to the property with the right to sell. However, if put up for sale, the public or state agency that had originally owned the building, retained the right to buy the home back at its original price or (alternatively) share in a portion of any profits. After 2000, only impoverished non-migrant households would be eligible to rent subsidized, public housing (Wang and Murie 1999: 158).

In February 1995 the State Council launched the *Anju Gongcheng* program that – among other initiatives – called for mandatory contributions to housing provident funds as a primary means to promote home ownership of self-contained flats among low and middle income families (GWYGB 1995: 70–3). Subsequent banking reforms to develop mortgage and loan instruments further strengthened the financial and legal infrastructure for popularizing home ownership (GWYGB 1997: 810–15 and 1412–17).

Nevertheless, despite these measures from local and central governments to increase the levels of home ownership, the majority of urban residents remained public tenants who enjoyed low cost and secure use-rights to their greatly improved residential space. In 1997 rents averaged less than 4 per cent of household income (Li 1998; ZGTJNJ 1998: 328–9) and only a third of residents held some form of title to their homes, a mere gain of 10 per cent over ownership levels of 1983 (Mi 1999; Davis 1993).

1998–9: full capitalization and a windfall to sitting tenants

Finally in 1998, came the decisive break with past practice. In the spring Zhu Rongji spoke repeatedly in favor of full commercialization and in July the State Council promulgated Circular No. 23 that announced as of December 1998 no enterprise would be allowed to sell employees' housing below construction costs. Within six months, market rates were to prevail and except for a small minority of families in economic difficulty, there would no longer be any welfare housing (*fuli fang*) in Chinese cities (GWYGB 1998: 679–82). Thus in one abrupt pronouncement the central government abandoned all ideological reservations they may have had to full scale privatization and attention shifted to accelerating the number of urban residents with full ownership rights across the entire nation.[5]

As one would expect, the old system of welfare housing did not entirely disappear on 31 December 1998. Below-cost 'fire sales' to sitting tenants continued, as did pre-construction 'distributions' to employees who had never purchased a home and to those employers deemed eligible for additional upgrades. Nevertheless the main story for 1998–9 was a fundamental break with past practice of the central government and widespread enthusiasm among residents to enter the housing market. Thus for example a Gallup poll in fall 1998 reported that 18 per cent of respondents in Chengdu, 16 per cent in Beijing and Guangzhou, and 15 per cent in Shanghai planned to buy a home within the next 12 months (Miller 1999). A spring 1999 survey in Guangzhou, Xian, and Wuhan indicated that 25 per cent expected to purchase a home in 1999. Results from two surveys at the end of 1999 suggested that in metropolitan China, home ownership had become the norm. One survey of the fourteen largest cities in December 1999 reported that 72 per cent of all (non migrant) households reported some type of ownership.[6] Another done in Beijing, Shanghai, Guangzhou, Chengdu, Wuhan, and Xian reported that among those earning 2,000 RMB per month, 70 per cent expected to purchase in the next year if they had not already done so. Even 35 per cent of those who earned 500 RMB or less per month had similar expectations (China Daily 2000).

Over the course of 1999, policies to legalize the resale of the recently sold public flats and expand the role of commercial banks in underwriting individual loans completed the process of commodification.[7] Most critical to this final stage toward full capitalization were the Temporary Procedures (No. 69) issued by the Ministry of Construction on how to deal with the resale of the collectively owned flats (*gongfang*) and low cost housing (*jingji shiyong zhoufang*) that had been sold to sitting tenants at highly subsidized prices. Signed on 22 April, these procedures went into effect 1 May (GWYGB 1999: 1005–8). Henceforth anyone who held full rights to their home, regardless if they had purchased the home privately or through a subsidized sale of their original *gongfang*, had the right to sell the property and to retain all after-tax profits.

In fact owners of *gongfang* had been selling their occupancy and use rights for several years, but May 1999 marked the point at which the central government fully legitimated privatization of this former public good on a nationwide scale and thereby commodified rights of transfer or alienation. By December 1999 the government announced that 70 per cent of all new housing had been sold directly to individuals rather than to municipal housing offices or state enterprises, and that half of all cities had lively secondhand markets for the individual sale of former *gongfang* (ZGFDCB 2000c). Nationwide only 40 per cent of the publicly built flats continued as rentals, and in many places – for example the city of Chongqing and the Provinces of Zhejiang and Guangxi – less than 20 per cent of urban *gongfang* remained as collective property (ZGFDCB 2000c).

As a result of these policy shifts of 1998 and 1999, the old system of welfare housing became defunct. Subsidized sales continued in some cities through the summer of 2000, but by December 1999 the bulk of urban housing stock had become fully capitalized, alienable individual assets (Li 2000; ZGFDCB 2000d).[8]

Urban housing reform and emergence of new urban property rights regime

From the early 1980s through the late 1980s, urban China had a dual track property system. On Track I were those who had purchased their homes before 1949 or those who had purchased commercially built homes after 1980. In Chinese documents these owners were considered to hold 'complete property rights' (*quanquan*). This meant that they had the right of occupancy, the right to extract financial benefits, the right to dispose through resale and the right to bequeath it to others.

On Track II were those who had purchased their homes after 1983 at heavily discounted rates from the housing stock owned by their employer or municipality. Initially these Track II owners did not have 'complete property rights' but only the use-rights (*shiyong quan*). Initially they could neither rent nor sell it to anyone but the original seller. They could, however, bequeath the home to their heirs. As reforms progressed, those on Track II were promised full property rights after five years and told they would have full discretion both to rent or sell their apartment. However, the conditions by which any profits would be retained usually required payment to the original seller and/or right of first refusal. Purchase of use-rights therefore gave sitting-tenants the possibility of reaping financial gain through future sales and guaranteed that the property could be passed on to any heirs designated by the owner. As explained in the popular press, urban residents could now purchase *rights of occupancy*, *rights of use*, *partial rights to extract benefits*, and *partial rights of disposal*.[9]

The State Council's July 1998 circular ended the treatment of urban housing as a de-commodified welfare benefit. The 1999 reforms legitimating the re-sale of the recently privatized collective assets clarified the rights to extract benefits or to alienate. Therefore in terms of legal reform, as of May 1999 a new private property regime had replaced the partially privatized system of the late 1980s and early 1990s. Henceforth all who had bought occupancy and use-rights to their former *gongfang* could purchase the rights of income and transfer. Once these rights were purchased the owners could then sell their apartment and put 95 per cent of the sale price toward a down payment or purchase of a flat with the full bundle of property rights.

These policies of 1998 and 1999 ended the dual track ownership system of the earlier reform era and potentially put all owners of urban housing on the same legal footing. In practice many who had only bought – or only been eligible to buy – the cheaper and less complete use-rights chose not to immediately become full owners. And some who enjoyed spacious apartments at very low rents continued to stay out of the market. As a result, the domestic property regime of 2000 is best described as segmented into four groups: (1) owners with full ownership rights, (2) owners with only occupancy and use-rights, (3) renters with long term occupancy rights who rent public quarters, and (4) renters with only short term occupancy rights who rent on the private market (Zhongguo Xinxi Bao 19 January 2000: 1).[10]

In terms of bundles of property rights, one can identify a clear hierarchy of tenancy and ownership that reflects privileges from the pre-reform era as well as favorable conditions at the time of purchase. At the top of the hierarchy are those who owned their homes in 1949 or have purchased full property rights (*quanquan*). At the end of 1999 approximately 40 per cent of non-migrant residents fell into this category. A year later as a result of the new availability of loans, I would estimate that 60 per cent of non-migrants have purchased full property rights and that half of those without full rights will secure them in their life times. Given that official surveys disregard the tens of millions of urban residents who have recently emigrated from rural villages and now constitute between 20 per cent and 30 per cent of the urban population, I would estimate that as of December 2000 slightly less than half of all urban residents held the full bundle of property rights if we include both migrant and non-migrant households.

The second position in the hierarchy of tenancy is held by those that have purchased use-rights. They control their living space and in some cases can legally rent out all or part of their residence. They can also bequeath these rights to their heirs. At the end of 1999 approximately 32 per cent of non-migrant residents fell into this category. However, as a result of easier access to long term loans, over supply of empty flats, and fears of real estate inflation in 2000, I would estimate that by December 2000 the percentage of non-migrants in this category fell to less than 20 per cent. If one includes migrants, the percentage falls to approximately 12.5 per cent of all urban households.

At the bottom of the tenancy hierarchy are those who rent. In general they have no property rights; however, those holding certificates of permanent urban residency (i.e. urban *hukou*) who rent collectively owned flats through their employer or the city real estate bureau do have long term rights of occupancy and in some cases also have first right to purchase if their rental unit goes on sale (Minzuyu Fazhi 2000). By contrast those renting on the market have only short term right of occupancy. At the end of 1999 approximately 23 per cent of non-migrants were still renting collectively owned apartments and 95 per cent of migrants and 4 per cent of non-migrants were renting on the market. Twelve months later I would estimate that the percentage renting collectively owned flats fell, while the percentage renting on the market did not change. Thus if we include all residents, regardless of their migrant status, approximately 37.5 per cent of all urban households remained renters as of December 2000.

Winners and losers in the new urban property regime

When one goes beyond general survey results and turns to individual housing histories, one can see how incremental, enterprise controlled extension of property rights exacerbated pre-reform inequalities by favoring managerial cadres over production workers. One reason, as Mi Xiaohong and Guo Xiaolin have noted, was that during the extenuated process of commodification, managerial staff both designed and implemented the subsidized sales of collective property. They selected the properties to be sold and decided on the prices. Thus through December 1997 when most urban housing – new and old – was still distributed or sold through bureaucratic channels controlled by enterprise leaders or government officials, production workers were least able to shape how public assets would be distributed to private hands.

Since January 1998 I have visited more than 100 homes in Shanghai and Shenzhen to interview residents about the housing conditions of their family. During these interviews, all of which took place in the homes of the respondents, I have been able to have broad ranging discussions about the route individuals followed to establish the current tenancy as well as plans they had for relocating or making a home purchase in the near future. Particularly revealing were 25 home interviews I did in Shanghai in the twelve months after Guofa No. 23 required that all but the very poor pay market prices for new housing. I will now draw on these interviews to explain how the incremental and unevenly paced processes of partial commodification followed by abrupt capitalization in 1999 worked to the disadvantage of households headed by men in blue-collar jobs.

Among these 25 households, 13 managers and 2 blue-collar workers had purchased some form of ownership. However, in all but one case – a salesman from Anhui who went to work for a US Joint Venture – they purchased their home with substantial assistance from their employers. Equally noteworthy were the situations of the five professionals and managers who still rented. In each case the family had decided to keep renting because the husband had not yet worked out the best bargain with his employer. The three managers lived in spacious homes that they rented from their employer, but before they took advantage of buying the use-rights of their *gongfang* they were holding out for more space in an equally good location. The two professionals, a doctor in his mid-thirties and a magazine editor of 50 lived in more crowded, lower quality flats. But they too had decided against purchasing new apartments subsidized by their units because they preferred the location of their current rentals in the center of the city. The doctor, who was renting a room in the large garden apartment that his wife's grandfather had once owned, was struggling (along with his wife, father-in-law, mother-in-law and brother-in-law) to have a city real estate bureau relocate a retired municipal official who had been housed in their home during the Cultural Revolution. Once this non-family member had moved out, the family would then be able to re-purchase their home at a heavily discounted price and both his unit and his wife's unit would be involved in calculating the amount of discount based on their rank and years of service.

By contrast only two of the seven households headed by a manual worker were owners. One had bought the use-rights to a 26 square meter flat in 1994 for 10,000 *yuan*. As a three-generation household of five they felt cramped in the two small rooms, but because the husband's employer was in economic distress, the wife had retired, and both their son and daughter-in-law were working partial shifts, they had given up planning another purchase. Instead the mother spoke most hopefully about her married daughter who lived with her in-laws, husband, and teenage daughter in an old cottage which the city had 'promised' to condemn. After the city demolished the cottage, the city would then allocate them two new rental units. The daughter and her husband were unlikely to be able to afford the new market value of the use-rights, but at least their housing problems would be solved.

The second worker who had been able to purchase her home also had been forced to give up an earlier plan to improve the family's accommodation. In earlier conversations in 1995 and 1997 she had told me that they were waiting for her husband's employer to offer them a new flat, to which they would then purchase the use-rights by transferring occupancy rights to their two room flat and a room they had rented for their children in another district. However, after the husband retired, they lost their chance for help from his enterprise and simply bought the use-rights of their current home for 9,000 *yuan* in 1999.

Interviews with five other blue-collar workers who still rented in July 1999, revealed similar limitations. None of these men and women looked to their employer to upgrade their housing situation and all said their only hope was if their current residence were slated for demolition by the city. Four of these five families lived in self-contained apartments built in working class neighborhoods during the early 1980s. By 1999 the interiors were shabby and parents and adolescent children shared one room. Three spoke bitterly of their decision to move to their current apartments claiming that if they had remained in their old cottage or tenement instead of moving in the early 1980s, they would now be better compensated when the hovel was condemned. And in fact, the one working class family who rented a new spacious apartment was precisely an example of a family that had not been relocated in the first wave of demolition. Not incidentally, the reason they had been able to hold out for the better apartment was that the original home in the city center had been in a better neighborhood. Thus because they initially had superior accommodation they were later rewarded more generously when the city did claim the family's home.

Disparities in family resources also reinforced the disadvantage production workers had in the workplace. For example when white-collar respondents described how they planned to upgrade their housing conditions, they cited family as well as employer resources as part of their strategy. Ten of the eighteen managers and professionals mentioned homes other than their current residence on which they had full or partial occupancy or use-rights. Moreover, two had been able to have their employers subsidize new home purchases without having to move other family members out of the original apartment which the unit had earlier rented or sold to them. By contrast none of the working class households had additional property claims nor were they able to get their employers to advance them new resources unless they renounced all claims on their current residence. Instead, several even looked enviously at their siblings who had remained in the family's hovel into the 1990s and berated themselves for having been so 'unlucky' as to have been allowed to relocate in the 1980s.

Thus whether professionals and managers were describing to me their current or past housing situations, it became clear that the majority could claim housing assets beyond their immediate need. As a result, even when they were renting they had the option of treating housing resources as a tradeable asset, and when housing became a fully capitalized asset they reaped substantial financial gain. By contrast, no working class respondent had rights to anything other than their current residence and because they did not receive the same upgrading of residential space during the first phase of reforms as did managerial staff, even when they could afford to purchase full property rights, their property was of substantially less market value.

In the early phases of reform, when city dwellers behaved as supplicants importuning enterprise housing authorities to improve their living conditions, need and seniority were as important as occupational status in determining which households were rehoused. As a result the new housing distributed during the 1980s did not immediately advantage white-collar over blue-collar families. But starting with the early sales of use-rights in 1993, working class families began to fall behind their better-paid white-collar neighbors who outranked them in the workplace. First the cost of purchasing use-rights imposed a relatively heavier financial burden, and second as the reforms accelerated manual workers became less able to make multiple claims on enterprise assets or bargain for larger discounts on purchase price (Lee 1999). In the mid-1990s managers and professionals – but not workers – could negotiate with their employers to upgrade their housing. Then when it became possible in 1999 to fully capitalize the use-rights, managers and professionals found themselves in possession of more valuable, better quality homes.

Conclusion

By the end of the 1990s housing reforms had commercialized a substantial share of urban real estate and popularized the ideal of home ownership. But despite the language of market exchange most buyers had paid less than 15 per cent of market value (China News Analysis 1998). Moreover the wealthier the family the higher the absolute value of the subsidies. Khan and Riskin (1998) have even estimated that as of 1995 the richest 10 per cent owned 60 per cent of private housing assets and a similar estimate has been made for the late 1990s.[11]

Overall among long time urban residents – as opposed to the rural majority or new migrants to the city – home ownership had been made possible through both intensive and extensive bureaucratic intervention. Nevertheless by routinizing the expectation of home ownership among city dwellers and by creating a national system for privatizing publicly built housing, the reforms of the late 1990s created a fundamental break with the social welfare property regime that had prevailed in China's cities between 1956 and 1989. In short the partial re-commodification – even when dependent on massive state spending – served as a catalyst for granting urban residents the full range of property rights over domestic space.

The process by which this commodification was achieved, however, discriminated against blue-collar employees. Moreover materials collected on urban China after 1996 suggest that the inequities increased as marketization accelerated. Thus while early reforms had the potential to create a more transparent and universal metric that could benefit all residents, later reforms to capitalize housing stock as a personal asset favored managerial and professional staff. As a result privatization of this former welfare benefit laid the foundation for residential segregation by economic class and undermined the relative equality of lifestyle that had prevailed in earlier years.

While less heated than the debate over consequences of the privatization of the means of production or the commodification of labor, scholars have disagreed about the consequences of privatizing a consumer good like housing. For example Peter Marcuse (1996) presumed that the logic of property rights for consumer items, and specifically for housing, differed from that for means of production. Szelenyi and Kostello (1996) by contrast concluded that the key to understanding the trajectory of the new property rights regime is not whether reform privatizes consumption or production but rather the extent and timing of the marketization. When market reforms are local, everyone benefits, but when the markets penetrate so deeply and widely that capital accumulation becomes possible then former cadres and current managers gain disproportionately. The material presented here suggests that in urban China, as in Eastern Europe, capitalization and the legitimization of the rights of alienation are the critical steps for creating a domestic property regime where blue-collar workers with little authority in the workplace are systematically less successful than managers and professionals in gaining title to the most valuable welfare good of the previous public goods regime.

Notes

1 As opposed to rural China where villagers could own and sell their homes throughout the Communist era, in urban China the percentage of owners fell steadily until it stabilized at about 15 per cent in the late 1970s.

2 In 1980 urban households averaged 3.9 square meters per capita; by 1992 they averaged 6.9 square meters.

3 In 1985 a newly created Office of Housing Reform under the State Council advocated selling off use-rights to sitting tenants in 160 large cities and 300 medium sized towns, and in 1986 Zhao Ziyang advocated market rates. In February 1988 the first National Urban Housing Reform Conference endorsed a plan to raise rents and make their ultimate goal full commercialization (*shangpin hua*) of urban housing stock. Subsequently the Ministry of Construction, which had become the key administrative actor for urban housing reform, issued detailed regulations for property exchange among individuals and businesses.

4 The ordinance allowed cities to sell leases of 40 years to those who would build for commercial use, 50 years for educational use, and 70 years for residential. Forty per cent of the income went to the central government, 60 per cent to the city. Soon after foreign real estate investors were encouraged to go beyond modest partnerships and capital from outside China began to have a major impact on the quality and quantity of urban construction (Wu 1992: 198).

5 For example, in 1996 53 per cent of newly built housing space was sold to individuals, both foreigners and citizens. But more than half of those individual purchases were in Guangdong (23 per cent), Shanghai (10 per cent), Jiangsu (9.5 per cent), and Zhejiang (8.7 per cent) (Mei 1998).

6 The survey reported that 39.8 per cent of respondents had full ownership (*suoyouquan*) and 32.1 per cent had ownership of use-rights (*suoyong quan*). Another 4 per cent rented privately and thus less than 25 per cent of respondents still rented dormitories (*sushe*) from the city or their employers (Zhongguo Xinxi Bao 19 January 2000: 1).

7 First the central government issued a series of documents that took housing reform to the next level by elaborating financial instruments that supported twenty year home mortgages and clarified the rules for capitalization of use-rights through resale. Document No. 43 of the Construction Ministry addressed a range of practical problems encountered by individuals in selling their former *gongfang* and also reiterated the need to end all discounts after January 2000. Between February and April there were a variety of decrees from the central government to facilitate home mortgages. In February Banking Bill No. 73 announced that qualified borrowers could henceforth take out mortgages equal to 80 per cent of the sale price. In March State Council Decree No. 262 issued new guidelines on creating and withdrawing deposits from Provident Funds and in April Banking Bill No. 129 announced that new guidelines for handling loans for building low cost housing would be in effect immediately (GWYGB 1999: 310–11, 268–71 and 852–4).

8 By December 1999, a State Statistical Survey of 150,000 urban residents reported that nearly 70 per cent of urban households held individual property rights (*geren soyou quan*). We of course need to note that the 15–25 per cent of the urban population who were migrants still registered in their home villages and fell outside these surveys. But because the majority of these migrants rented housing at market rates, if one added migrants to the totals, the percentage of owners would fall but the percentage of those purchasing residential space on the market rather than drawing work place benefits would rise.

9 These four rights were already circulating on the advertising pages of *Xinmin Wanbao* in February 1998.

10 A survey in China's 14 largest cities in fall 1999, reported that 72 per cent of households now hold some form of ownership and the most typical (40 per cent) situation is to hold full property rights. Next most frequent (32 per cent) are those who have purchased hold use-rights, while 23 per cent still rent public housing and 4 per cent rent from private landlords.

11 The same point, but with different data, has been made by Wang and Murie 1999: 170–201 and Chen 1999.

References

Bian, Y.J., Logan, J., Lu, H.L., Pan, Y.K. and Guan, Y. (1997) 'Work Units and Housing Reform in Two Chinese Cities', in X.B. Lu and E. Perry (eds) *Danwei: The Changing Chinese Workplace in Historical and Comparative Perspective*, Boulder: Westview.

Chen, X. (1998) *Shehuixue Yanjiu*, Beijing: Shehuixue yanjiu zazhishe.

Chen, X.M. (1999) 'Zhongguo zhufang shichang', paper given at conference on urban housing reform, Zhongshan University, April 1999.

Chen, X.M. and Gao, X.Y. (1993) 'China's Urban Housing Development in the Shift from Redistribution to Decentralization', *Social Problems*, 40 (2): 266–83.

China Daily (2000) Business Weekly, *China Daily*, 9 January 2000: 6.

China News Analysis (1998) *China News Analysis*, 1619, 1 October 1998: 2.

Davis, D. (1993) 'Urban Households: Supplicants to the State' in D. Davis and S. Harrell (eds) *Chinese Families in the Post-Mao Era*, Berkeley: University of California Press.

Ding, X.L. (2000) 'Illicit Asset Stripping of Chinese State Firms', *China Journal*, 43, July 2000: 1–23.

Guo, X.L. (1999) 'The Role of Local Government in Creating Property Rights', in J. Oi and A. Walder (eds) *Property Rights and Economic Reform in China*, Stanford: Stanford University Press.

GWYGB (1995) *Guowuyuan gongbao* (State Council Gazette).

—— (1997) *Guowuyuan gongbao*.

—— (1998) *Guowuyuan gongbao*.

—— (1999) *Guowuyuan gongbao*.

Jia, Z.W. (1998) 'Zhufang, fanggai, and Laobaixing (Housing Reform and Ordinary People)', *Shenzhen Zhoukan*, 17 August 1998: 6–11.

Khan, A. and Riskin, C. (1998) 'Income and Inequality in China', *The China Quarterly*, 154: 221–53.

Lau, K.Y. (1994) 'Urban Housing Reform in China Amidst Property Boom Year', in J. Cheng and C.K. Lo (eds) *China Review 1993*, 24: 1–35, Hong Kong: Chinese University of Hong Kong Press.

Lee, C.K. (1999) 'Changing Labour Regimes in Chinese Factories', *The China Quarterly*, 157: 52–4.

Lee, F. (1988) 'The Urban Housing Problem in China', *The China Quarterly*, 115: 387–407.

Lee, P. (1995) 'Housing Privatization with Chinese Characteristics', in L. Wong and S. MacPherson (eds) *Social Change and Social Policy in Contemporary China*, Aldershot, England: Avebury.

Li, L.H. (1999) *Urban Land Reform in China*, London: Macmillan.

Li, R.X. (1998) 'Residential Houses Go to Market', *Beijing Review*, 18– 24 May 1998: 4.

Li, X.F. (2000) 'Chengshi Zhumin Zhufang (Housing of city residents)', *Beijing Fangdichan* (monthly), 15 May 2000: 18–22.

Lin, N. and Chen, C.-j.J. (1999) 'Local Elites as Officials and Owners', in J. Oi and A. Walder (eds) *Property Rights and Economic Reform in China*, Stanford: Stanford University Press.

Lin, Y.M. and Zhang, Z.X. (1999) 'Backyard Profit Centers', in J. Oi and A. Walder (eds) *Property Rights and Economic Reform in China*, Stanford: Stanford University Press.

Marcuse, P. (1996) 'Privatization and its Discontents', in G. Andrusz, M. Harloe and I. Szelenyi (eds) *Cities after Socialism*, London: Blackwell.

Deborah S. Davis

Mei, W.C. (1998) '1997–1998 Zhongguo Shangpin zhuzhai jianshe yu zhufang zhidu gaige' (Construction of Chinese Commercial Housing and Reform of Housing System), in *Zhongguo shehui xingshe fenxie yu yuce* (Analysis of Chinese Social Structure), Beijing: Shehui kexue wenxian chubanshe (Social Science Documentation Publishing House).

Mi, X.H. (1999) 'Questions of Fairness in the Development of China's Housing Market', paper presented at conference on housing reform, Zhong Shan University Modern China Research Center, 15–16 April 1999.

Miller, M. (1999) 'City Dwellers Hungry for Durables', *South China Morning Post*, 14 January 1999, Internet edition, www.scmp.com.

Minzuyu Fazhi (2000) *Minzuyu Fazhi*, 7: 60.

Nee, V. (1989) 'A Theory of Market Transition', *American Sociological Review*, 54: 663–81.

Pan, Y.K. and Liu, M. (1994) *Dangdai Zhongguo Jiating Da Biandong* (Great Changes in Contemporary Chinese Families), Enping: Guangdong renmin chubanshe.

Putterman, L. (1995) 'The Role of Ownership and Property Rights in China's Economic Transition', *The China Quarterly*, 144: 1047–64.

Rocca, J.L. (1992) 'Corruption and its Shadow', *The China Quarterly*, 130: 402–16.

RMBR, *Renmin Ribao* (People's Daily)

Ruf, G. (1999) 'Collective Enterprises and Property Rights' in J. Oi and A. Walder (eds) *Property Rights and Economic Reform in China*, Stanford: Stanford University Press.

Sargason, S. and Zhang, J. (1999) 'Reassessment of the Role of the Local State', *China Journal*, 42, July 1999: 77–102.

Szelenyi, I. and Kostello, E. (1996) 'The Market Transition Debate', *American Journal of Sociology*, 101 (4): 1094.

Tong, Z.Y. and Hays, R.A. (1996) 'The Transformation of the Urban Housing System in China', *Urban Affairs Review*, 31 May 1996: 625–58.

Walder, A. and Oi, J. (1999) 'Property Rights in the Chinese Economy', in J. Oi and A. Walder (eds) *Property Rights and Economic Reform in China*, Stanford: Stanford University Press.

Wang, Y.P. and Murie, A. (1999) *Housing Policy and Practice in China*, New York: Macmillan.

Whyte, M. and Parish, W. (1984) *Urban Life in Contemporary China*, Chicago: University of Chicago Press.

Wu, L.C. (ed.) (1992) *Fangchan Jiufen yanjiu* (Research on Real Estate Disputes), Chongqing: Sichuan University Press.

ZGFDCB (2000a) *Zhongguo Fangdichan Bao*, 12 June 2000: 1.

—— (2000b) *Zhongguo Fangdichan Bao*, 27 December 2000: 7.

—— (2000c) *Zhongguo Fangdichan Bao*, 1 March 2000: 1.

—— (2000d) *Zhongguo Fangdichan Bao*, 19 April 2000: 1.

ZGTJNJ (1998) *Chinese Statistical Yearbook*, Beijing: Zhongguo Tong Ji Chu Ban She.

—— (1999) *Chinese Statistical Yearbook*, Beijing: Zhongguo Tong Ji Chu Ban She.

Zhou, M. and Logan, J. (1996) 'Market Transition and the Commodification of Housing in Urban China', *International Journal of Urban and Regional Research*, 20 (3): 400–21.

11 Banking the unbanked

Connecting residents of social housing to the financial mainstream

Michael A. Stegman

Introduction

In today's economy, it is increasingly important to have access to a basic bank account and mainstream financial services (Summers 2000). Without bank accounts, families often pay high fees – as much as US$15,000 over a lifetime – to check cashers and other fringe bankers to conduct basic daily financial transactions (Hawke 2000). More importantly, banking status has profound implications for families' long-term self-sufficiency. People with bank accounts are more than twice as likely to hold savings as are people who are unbanked and are more likely to add to their savings on at least a monthly basis (Dunham 2001, cited in Kim 2001). In fact, controlling for income and other factors, lower-income individuals with bank accounts are 43 per cent more likely than those who are unbanked to have positive net financial assets of any kind. Indeed, for more than half the unbanked (54 per cent), their only asset is their car (US Department of Treasury 2000). This is why community advocates and US policymakers should be concerned that, despite the longest economic expansion on record during the 1990s, 10 per cent of all American families – including 25 per cent of African Americans and Hispanics, a quarter of all families with incomes under $20,000, and nearly half of all families moving from welfare to work – have no bank accounts (Kennickell *et al*. 1998).

The problem of growing financial exclusion and asset-deprivation has global dimensions, and is closely tied to the themes of this book. For instance, one in every six adults in Britain – around 2.5 million people – does not have a bank or building society current account, and British households are becoming increasingly asset-poor (Meadows 2000). The ratio of British households without any assets doubled between 1979 and 1996, and 50 per cent of all people have less than £500 of disposable financial wealth.[1] More than 80,000 adult Glaswegians are also 'unbanked' – '16.5 per cent – compared with 15 per cent for Scotland overall, and 8 per cent for England and Wales' (Levine 2000). As in the US, minority groups in Britain are more vulnerable – people of Indian, Pakistani or Bangladeshi origin are twice as likely as white people not to have an account (Meadows 2000).

Financial exclusion is also a problem in Eastern Europe. According to one account, only 54 per cent of Poles are active users of banking services (in 1998) (*Cards International* 27 September 2000), while about one-third of Hungarian households are unbanked, including a quarter of all households in Budapest, and 45 per cent in outlying villages (*European Banker* 2000).

While the incidence of so-called cash deserts, or neighborhoods without convenient access to banks, is generally greater in core cities and remote rural communities, residents of social housing in various locations are also more likely to be unbanked. Confirming the link between this chapter and the larger themes of this compilation, research sponsored by the Britannia Building Society recently pointed out that:

> People who live in local authority or housing association housing are roughly twice as likely not to have an account than otherwise similar people who are owner-occupants. ... Those without accounts, although the same as those who have them, are likely to be part of social networks concentrated in social housing in major urban areas where the predominant form of money management is cash, and where use of mainstream financial services is relatively uncommon.
>
> (Meadows 2000: 2)

This chapter traces the rise of financial exclusion in the US and abroad, and discusses how a decision designed to save the taxpayer money by delivering government benefits electronically, has the potential to improve people's lives by helping them open a bank account and bringing them into the financial mainstream. The chapter begins with an overview of the US government's transition to electronic funds transfer (EFT), including the factors that motivated this policy, and its current status. This is followed by a discussion of global trends in the banking sector, marked by a decline in the number and concentration of commercial banks, and the explosive growth in the number of 'fringe banks', most notably check cashing outlets and payday or money lenders. This latter, parallel banking system increasingly serves, and preys upon, the poor and financially disenfranchised, including residents of social housing. Policies that complement the transition to EFT and support more asset-based social policies are then discussed in the next section.

With the government transition to EFT potentially increasing the commercial viability of low-income consumers to private-sector commercial banks, the next section describes several innovative banking products and strategic alliances entered into by commercial banks that are designed to bring more unbanked people into the financial mainstream. The chapter concludes with a call for closer links between government EFT programs, asset-based social policies, and financial institutions' strategies to profitably develop the lower-income market, including that consisting of residents of social housing.

The significance of the move to EFT

In my book, *Savings for the Poor* (Stegman 1999), I suggest how a cluster of new public policies – most importantly, the federal transition to electronic funds transfer (EFT) or the delivery of government benefits through direct deposit – present new opportunities for financial institutions to better serve unbanked and marginally-banked populations in the United States, and to help people save. Because of EFT, the Treasury Department has undertaken several initiatives to stimulate the development of new, low-cost banking products for unbanked federal benefit recipients. As part of this transition, Congress has also required all fifty US states to convert their food stamp programs to electronic payment by 2002, using point-of-sale (POS) terminals at participating retailers. And, while not required by law, more than forty states have added their emergency cash assistance programs to the plastic food stamp cards so that welfare benefits will be accessible at ATM and POS networks.

Although the move to convert millions of benefit checks to electronic payments was begun to save American taxpayers money – as much as $100 million a year according to one estimate – EFT could be the first step toward greater financial independence for millions of low-income Americans. If partnered with financial literacy and savings initiatives for working people, EFT could help the poor build assets and become a critical link in the nation's transition from entitlement programs to policies that promote and reward work, self-sufficiency, and wealth accumulation.

The transition to EFT is not limited to the United States. For example, the Australian government makes 6 million welfare payments by electronic transfer each fortnight (Westbury 2000a), and ambitious plans are underway in Great Britain to make the transition to EFT between 2003 and 2005. Like the US, the driving force in Britain is cost-efficiency rather than individual empowerment. Excluding actual benefit payments, administrative costs – including security, printing, postage, and payment of a fee to the Post Office – amount to

> 79p a payment for girocheques (around a million payments a week) and 40p for each order book counterfoil (around 14.5 million payments a week). By contrast, payment by credit transfer is very cheap – only 1p a time according to the Department's estimate.

> (Husband 2001:1,3)

Conversion to direct deposit of social security benefits in Britain, including the creation of a 'universal bank' that would be operated by the British Postal Service to serve low-income individuals who are poorly served by commercial banks, 'would save taxpayers an estimated £540 million a year' (Husband 2001; *The Economist* 2000). Another important motivation for a Post Office-run bank is to make up some of the £400 million in lost revenues from the posting of benefit checks that will no longer be necessary when electronic welfare delivery is put in place. While officials were still working on the details when this chapter was written, it is expected to offer accounts through which holders can pay bills, withdraw money from cash machines and receive electronic payments.

The future of commercial banking

As suggested in the introduction, campaigns to reduce the number of unbanked and expand financial literacy and savings incentives come at a time when access to financial services for low-income families has become increasingly problematic. The interplay of many factors – among them the deregulation of interest rate ceilings in the 1980s, new technology, and growing competition from non-depository institutions – has led to a significant decline in the number of financial institutions in the United States and abroad, and has driven banks to charge for services that they formerly subsidized with cheap, regulated deposits. In the US, for example, the number of federally insured banks and thrifts declined by 43 per cent over the last fifteen years, and the number of credit unions fell by 19 per cent in the 1990s (Stegman 1999; FDIC). At the same time, the banking industry is restructuring to focus on higher-income markets.

Thus, while the total number of banking offices has increased by 29 per cent during the last twenty years – nearly all of this growth has occurred in middle- and high-income areas – low-income neighborhoods in the US saw a 21 per cent decline in branch facilities (Avery *et al.* 1997).

The same forces at play in the US are also changing the global banking landscape. In Australia, for example, an average of five branches per month are closing in regional and rural New South Wales alone (totaling 137 in NSW over the last two years) (Westbury 2000b), while in Great Britain, over 4,500 bank branches have closed in the last decade, and consolidation is still underway. In April 2000, Barclays announced 172 branch closings, according to one account, putting businesses at risk and increasing social exclusion in disadvantaged communities (Benham 2000: 7).

Growing competition with non-banks such as money market funds and mutual funds, and technological advances have also been important factors in the move to fee-based banking. In the twenty-first century, banks in the US and abroad will meet their bottom lines more by charging fees for specific services than by living off the interest spread between taking deposits and making loans. This trend, which has important implications for lower-income consumers, is already discernible.

By October 1997, some 35 per cent of the total revenue for American banks came from fees, almost double the proportion in 1980 (*Economist* 1997). In practical terms the results of this phenomenon are higher transaction fees, charges for speaking with a live banking representative instead of an automated voice response telephone unit, or higher minimum balance requirements. For example, 'the cost of using another bank's automated teller machines has nearly tripled in the past four years to $2.86 (US) up from $1.01 in 1996, when ATM surcharges were first allowed in most states' (*Washington Post* 30 March 2001: E02).

Wells Fargo, which recently merged with Norwest Bank, now gives checking account customers three free calls into its automated-voice-response telephone lines and then charges 50 cents for each additional call. To speak to an agent to shift funds or ask questions, customers are charged $1.50 per call (Perman 1998).

Like the other banking trends discussed earlier, the growth of fee-based banking and its implications for small depositors also transcends national borders. In 2000, New Zealand's Commerce Minister called for an investigation into rapidly rising bank fees (*Dominion (Wellington)* 2000), while Industry Canada reports a distressing trend among Canadian banks to require higher minimum monthly balances to qualify for low-cost banking (Prentice 2001). Scotiabank, for example, doubled the minimum monthly balance required to avoid bank charges from $1,000 to $2,000, 'which is the equivalent of an open-ended $2,000 loan to the bank. At five per cent interest, that's a $100-a-year cost to the customer' (Prentice 2001). Despite record profits, 'Hong Kong's biggest lenders, HSBC and Hang Seng Bank, are ending free banking' (*Deutsche Presse-Agentur* 27 February 2001). Punjab National Bank in India has announced plans to increase fee-based income from its present level of 14 per cent of the bank's revenue to bring it closer to the 40 per cent benchmark of foreign banks (*Hindu* 26 December 2000). Similarly, 'Bangkok-based Bank of Ayudhya aims to double its fee-based income to 20 per cent of total revenue over the next few years in order to compensate for the shortfall of income from lending' (*Bangkok Post* 6 October 2000).

The explosive growth of 'fringe banks'

Though less well understood, studied, or regulated, there is a parallel system of financial services providers that primarily serve lower-income working class communities in the US and elsewhere in the world who are benefiting from these global banking trends while putting the poor at risk. The core of this 'fringe banking' industry, as it is commonly referred to by consumer advocates in the US, is a national network of check cashing centers and payday lenders that cash more than 180 million checks a year with a face value of $55 billion (Stegman 1999). A study by the New York Office of the Public Advocate found that a customer with an annual income of $17,000 will pay almost $220 a year at a check-cashing business for services that would cost $30 at a bank (Organization for a New Equality 1998: 5). The Federal Reserve Bank of Kansas City reached similar conclusions: a family with an annual income of $24,000 will spend almost $400 in fees at a check cashing outlet for services that would cost under $100 at a bank. The Massachusetts Division of Banks found that, depending on the customer's income, the costs of cashing a weekly payroll check and writing money orders are 3.2 to 40.5 times more expensive at a check casher than if the customer used a low-cost Basic Checking Account offered under the Commonwealth's basic banking program (Massachusetts Division of Banks 1999). These high fees add up. Over the course of a lifetime, ONE estimates, 'the cost of using a check cashing outlet … is more than seven times the cost of using a basic checking account'(Organization for a New Equality 1998: 5). Reliance on fringe bankers also has serious wealth implications. According to ONE, if the difference in fees saved by using a basic checking account instead of a check cashing outlet were deposited in a standard savings account, a person would be able to save more than $17,000 over an average lifetime of work (Organization for a New Equality 1998: 5).

Sometimes operating in standalone storefront facilities, and sometimes co-located with check cashers, payday lenders are an important part of the parallel banking system. Payday loans are high-interest, short-term sources of credit backed by post-dated personal checks, which borrowers promise to repay out of their next paycheck (Riccobono 2000).

No matter how the size of the industry is measured, the statistics are striking. Where virtually no payday loan outlets existed 10 years ago, industry analysts estimate there are now up to 10,000 of them, with total loan originations of between $8 billion and $14 billion in 2000 alone.[2] At an average of $350 per loan, this translates to between 23 million and 40 million individual payday loan originations in 2000. Experts anticipate that a steady growth in loan demand to about $20 billion a year by 2004 will fuel expansion at a rate of about 100 new payday loan outlets a month across the country (Blackwell 2000; CFSA).

The payday loan industry defends its high fee structure – my state of North Carolina, for example, sets a ceiling of $300 on the amount that can be borrowed at any one time, limits fees to 15 per cent of the amount borrowed (which works out to $45 on a $300 loan), and provides for a maximum term to maturity of 31 days (North Carolina Cash Checkers Act 1998) – largely on the grounds that 'small loans are relatively more costly per dollar to originate and service than are large consumer loans'(Elliehausen and Lawrence 2001: 3). Because, the argument goes, payday loans are one of the few accessible sources of very short-term, *occasional* credit for hard-pressed consumers and are *not* intended to be a source of longer-term credit, the annual percentage rate (APR) is not a fair way of assessing the reasonableness of the cost of a two-week loan. In North Carolina, for example, the median APR for a payday loan in 2000 was 419 per cent.

The most urgent policy and regulatory challenges posed by payday lending relate to the repeated use of such loans. Rollovers occur when a borrower cannot repay a loan that becomes due and so renews it for another short term by paying another fee. Because of the high fees and very short terms, after just a few rollovers, 'borrowers can find themselves owing many times the amount they originally borrowed'(Riccobono 2000: 1).

That rollovers are a widespread problem is documented in audits by state regulators, studies, and academic research. For example, regulators found that 77 per cent of payday loans in Indiana are rollovers, with the average payday customer taking out more than 10 loans per year (DFI 2001). The average customer in California takes out 11 payday loans a year, while repeat usage is even greater in Illinois, where the typical customer averages more than one payday loan per month (PIRGs and Consumer Federation of America 2000). A typical payday loan customer in North Carolina took out about seven loans in 2000, a sizeable increase over the 1999 level of 5.8 loans (North Carolina Check Cashers Act 1998).

The payday loan industry has its counterpart in countries across the globe, drawing its 'customers from groups who find it difficult or inconvenient to borrow from banks and other mainstream financial institutions' (Meadows 2000). The British press has coined a new term – cash deserts – to describe communities in East London and elsewhere where banks have pulled out, forcing small merchants and others to turn to 'cheque-cashing companies to get money, and face commission charges of 10 per cent or more'(Andrew 2000). Another sign of the times is in Bristol, where loan sharks 'take benefit books so they can demand repayment as soon as the benefit is claimed'(*Bristol Evening Post* 9 February 2001: 12).

Abuses in the parallel banking system are also evident in Borneo (Gunsika 2001), in Scotland, where the Office of Fair Trading has launched an investigation into extortionate agreements with money lenders (Hunter 2000: 9), and in the former Czech Republic, where small loans to welfare recipients by money lenders at interest rates of up to 100 per cent per month have become widespread (CTK News 2001).

Reports from Uganda suggest that 'you can't fail to bump into a money lender any 100 metres you walk in Kampala today' (Buwembo 2001), while business is booming for India's money lenders, who are euphemistically known as 'blade' 'since the high rates of interest (of up to 3,650 per cent) are sharp enough to slit your throat' (*Business Line* 2001). The same can be said for Korea's more than 1,400 loan sharks – which account for about one fourth of that nation's 5,200 financial institutions (*Korea Herald* 26 March 2001). Further indication of the prolific growth of the parallel banking system is in Malaysia, where the Federation of Malaysian Consumer Associations recently urged government to expedite approval of a proposed Consumer Credit Act to more effectively monitor money-lending activities' (*Malaysia General News* 2001).

Michael A. Stegman

Complementary policies to EFT

A number of new US policy initiatives that complement EFT promise to further enhance the economics of serving unbanked and under-banked populations. The most important of these involve savings initiatives for working families like those being piloted in Individual Development Account (IDA) programs across the country that are discussed more fully below. Matched savings programs like IDAs can make EFT and related banking initiatives not only more powerful forces for individual empowerment, they can also significantly improve the economics of low-cost account products for banks. A few of these policy initiatives are discussed below.

First Accounts

In December 2002, the US Treasury Department expanded its EFT campaign with the launch of First Accounts, a $10 million pilot program designed to encourage mainstream banks to target the other half of the unbanked – individuals without bank accounts who do not receive government checks. The goal of First Accounts is to move a maximum number of 'unbanked' low- and moderate-income individuals to a 'banked' status with either an insured depository institution or an insured credit union through the development of financial products and services that can serve as replicable models in other communities without the need for ongoing public subsidies (http://www.treas.gov/firstaccounts/).

Recognizing the difficulty that mainstream banks have in reaching unbanked low- and moderate-income individuals, and the importance of achieving scale economies, the Treasury believes that depository institutions are more likely to succeed if they forge strategic alliances with partners who have more direct access to the target market than they do, including employers, labor unions, faith-based organizations and other non-profit organizations whose workers, members, and neighborhoods, respectively, include large numbers of unbanked individuals (Department of Treasury 2001).

Welfare reform

American-style welfare reform is more widely recognized for ending the federally-guaranteed entitlement to means-tested public assistance for impoverished families than it is for legitimizing government's role in helping the poor build assets. The rationale for an asset-based social policy is that assets promote a longer planning horizon by the poor, and a variety of positive attitudes and behaviors, including household stability, community involvement, and political participation (Mills *et al.* 2000).

Welfare reform not only led to new rules that liberalized asset limits – North Carolina, for example, raised its limits from $1,000 to $3,000 – but it also encouraged savings by promoting Individual Development Accounts, or IDAs. IDAs are special savings accounts for low-income families and are restricted to the first-time purchase of a home, to higher education, and to small business capitalization. IDAs are like tax advantaged retirement accounts (commonly referred to as 401(k)s, after the section of the tax code that created them), except that IDAs provide an incentive to save by matching account holders' deposits instead of giving them the kind of tax breaks that are incorporated into 401(k)s. Participants are usually required to complete financial education courses provided by non-profit organizations as part of the IDA programs (Corporation for Enterprise Development 1998: 1). The welfare reform law also permits states to use their welfare block grants to fund IDAs and account balances in eligibility determination for all means-tested federal benefits (Corporation for Enterprise Development 1998: 1). A total of thirty-one states have enacted legislation to support IDAs, with most of this legislation occurring since 1995 (Corporation for Enterprise Development 1998: 5).

Welfare reforms and asset building strategies are also under discussion in Europe. Press reports from France, Germany, and Italy suggest widespread recognition that soaring welfare budgets cannot be sustained (Crooks 2000). A recent public opinion poll found 'majorities in Germany, Italy and Spain supported the option of privatizing their social security retirement, while the French narrowly rejected the idea' (Crooks 2000: 2). Reforms in the United Kingdom are also focused on driving people off benefits and into work (MacLeod 2000), a new form of means-testing, which the Labour Party refers to as 'progressive universalism' (Watson and Miles 2001), and a new emphasis on asset-building.

Individual Development Accounts (IDAs)

The most important thing that banks and communities should know about IDAs is they are proving that, with appropriate support and incentives, poor people *can* save. Two-year results from the nation's largest national demonstration in fourteen US communities found that participants with incomes at about 130 per cent of the federal government's poverty-level income are saving an average of about 3 per cent of their income, or $24 a month (Schreiner *et al.* 2000). Another study of eleven IDA programs showed that average account balances per participant were $903, including both deposits and accrued match, ranging from a high of $2,361 in Raleigh, North Carolina, to a low of $362 in Chicago (Mills *et al.* 2000: 63).

And IDA savings don't just displace savings families would otherwise accrue. For example, Stegman and Faris estimate that overall the median participant in a national IDA demonstration saved $117 more than they would have saved had they not enrolled in an IDA program (Stegman and Faris 2001). The mean savings increment is almost two-and-a-half times greater – $285. The evidence suggests not only that low-income people can save, but that the resources offered by IDA programs are effective in helping people get into the habit of saving. These include financial education, peer support and encouragement, an accessible and cooperating financial institution, and financial inducements in the form of matching funds.

The Assets for Independence Act (AFIA) enacted by the US Congress in October 1998 authorizes $125 million in federal funds to support local IDA programs over a five-year period (Community Opportunities, Accountability and Training and Educational Services Act 1998). After appropriating $10 million a year for AFIA in FY 1999 and 2000, in response to local program successes, Congress appropriated $25 million for AFIA in FY 2001 (US Department of Health and Human Services 2001).

Congress has not yet passed the proposed Savings for Working Families Act (SWFA), which authorizes $5–$10 billion in federal tax credits for financial institutions and private sector investors to set up, match, and support IDAs at financial institutions (http://thomas.loc/cgi-bin/query/D?r106:1/temp/~r106CxPREY). Under SWFA, savings from any source would be matched on a one-to-one basis, up to $500 per person per year. Financial institutions would be reimbursed for all matching funds provided, and for some of the banks' program and administrative costs (Corporation for Enterprise Development 2001). However, there continues to be strong bipartisan support for a national IDA program that would be funded on the tax side of the federal budget, and renewed efforts to pass SWFA are continuing.

As suggested above, interest in IDAs is also strong in Great Britain, with proposals focusing on children's savings accounts. One plan under study would include a state deposit of about £1,000 into a savings scheme for every child at birth, at a cost of £700 million a year (Grice 2001). Another would apportion £1,000 to every newborn baby and match savings contributions on a ratio of three-to-one for lower-income families. A third option would give a lump sum to young adults when they reach 18 and match the individual's contributions rather than those of their parents (Sherman 2001).

Programs to reduce the digital divide and help residents in social housing build assets

Most germane to the themes of this volume are two promising programs aimed at increasing the computer literacy and online access of residents of US social housing and motivating them to increase their labor market activity by dedicating earnings-induced rent increases to resident savings accounts.

Neighborhood Networks (NN)

Launched in 1995, NN is a community-based initiative by the US Department of Housing and Urban Development (HUD) that has thus far created more than 800 multi-service community technology centers in social housing. Tailor-made to fit each local community, NN centers open the doors – both on-site and via the Internet – to an infinite array of job opportunities, social services, microenterprise possibilities, and educational programs (www.hud.gov/nnwaboutnn.html). While not directly linked to any government-sponsored banking initiative, because they provide online access, Neighborhood Network centers are a portal to a menu of electronic banking and financial education opportunities that increase the commercial potential of the social housing market to mainstream financial institutions.

The Family Self-Sufficiency (FSS) program

Created in 1990, FSS is an employment and savings incentive program for low-income families that receive either tenant-based rental assistance (housing vouchers), or who live in social housing (Sard 2001: v). The program is a combination of

> case management services that help participants pursue employment and other goals, and of escrow accounts into which the public housing agency deposits the increased rental charges that a family pays as its earnings rise. Families that complete the program may withdraw funds from these accounts for any purpose after five years.
> (Sard, p.v. paper can be accessed at: http://www.cbpp.org/4-12-01hous.pdf)

Despite the fact that not all local housing authorities participate in the program, and not all social housing residents who enter the program complete it, the results are quite impressive. According to HUD, as of November 2000, almost half of the participants who had been enrolled in FSS for 12 months or more had positive escrow balances, which averaged about $2,400. Even more impressive is the finding that these families were 'adding to their accounts at the average rate of about $300 per month' (Sard 2001: vi). Furthermore, the families that 'successfully completed the FSS program between the fall of 1999 and November 2000 received escrow funds averaging nearly $5,000 per family'(Sard 2001: vi).

Innovative products for the unbanked

In the course of our research, we identified several account products that target the unbanked, which suggests that the industry is beginning to explore the commerical potential and behavior of this underserved market. Save for one technologically-advanced product introduced by Standard Bank of South Africa, none have achieved the degree of market penetration necessary to capture scale economies and demonstrate commercial viability. The following brief descriptions of some of these products document the current state of practice and, hopefully, will encourage others to take a hard look at the business potential of serving the unbanked. As indicated above, some of these products are built around technology, while others are off-the-shelf products that are delivered through community development partnerships. Still others blend the products and services of fringe and conventional banks to help unbanked customers through the transition into the financial mainstream.

Technology-based products

Banco Popular's Acceso ETA and Acceso Popular accounts

As part of the federal government's campaign to convert more government checks to direct deposit, the Treasury Department created a new, low-cost account called the Electronic Transfer Account, or ETA. The department hopes to attract unbanked recipients of Social Security and other federal benefits to open ETAs and then sign them up to receive their federal benefits by direct deposit.

To encourage banks to offer ETAs, the Treasury Department compensates financial institutions $12.60 for each new account that is opened. This one-time fee is intended to fully offset institutions' account set-up costs. Among the ETA's features are:

- Maximum cost of $3.00 per month;
- Minimum of four cash withdrawals and four balance inquiries per month, to be included in the monthly fee, through any combination of proprietary ATM transactions or over-the-counter transactions;
- Access to the institution's online point-of-sale (POS) network, if available;
- No minimum balance, except as required by state or federal law;
- Account to be interest-bearing or non-interest-bearing, at the discretion of the financial institution;
- A written monthly statement. (Financial Management Service 2002)

The transition to direct deposit of federal benefits is much slower than the government had hoped. In the first year, only about 5,000 people had opened an ETA account. However, one particular bank – the $18.4 billion asset of Popular Inc., Banco Popular de Puerto Rico – has distinguished itself as a model provider of high tech banking services to unbanked individuals who receive government checks (Daigle 2000).

As of 31 October 2000, Banco Popular (BP) had opened more than 3,000 ETA accounts, which is more than 60 per cent of all ETAs opened by all US banks (Daigle 2000; US Department of Treasury 2000). BP attributes its success to three factors: (1) serving the unbanked is a long and honored tradition of the People's Bank of Puerto Rico – its 2001 business plan calls for converting an additional

35,000 unbanked individuals; (2) it uses its most sophisticated technology and delivery systems to create low-cost, *and* low-risk accounts for financially marginalized populations, including debit cards without checking privileges to prevent overdrafts; and (3) despite low account service charges – ETA charges are limited by the Treasury to $3 a month – Banco Popular invested more than $100,000 in a marketing campaign and provided financial incentives to employees for every ETA account they opened during the early months of the campaign.

Tracking Treasury's First Accounts program discussed above, BP has also created a companion account for other unbanked individuals, called Acceso Popular. Unlike its ETA product, the electronic Acceso Popular account includes a savings component. To simplify account management, reduce risk to both the bank and the account owner, and to avoid overdrafts, Acceso Popular provides for no check writing privileges or off-line credit transactions. Also, unlike Acceso ETA, this account features a savings plan option that permits the automatic transfer of a pre-specified amount of money each pay period from the transaction-side of the account into the savings-side.

Acceso Popular account holders have electronic access to the transaction purse through ATM and POS terminals, but to discourage savings withdrawals on impulse, there is no electronic access to the savings purse – all withdrawals have to be made in person at a bank branch. Introduced in March 2001, Banco Popular opened more than 59,000 Acceso Popular accounts by the end of the year, with fully half of the account holders having activated the savings component, giving further evidence that, once they enter the banking system, poor people are able to save.

Standard Bank of South Africa's Auto E-Bank

According to an analyst at McKinsey and Company, Standard Bank of South Africa is defying 'the conventional wisdom of the financial-services industry: that the low-income market is at best marginal, at worst disastrous' (Moore 2000). The bank created its E-Bank (later renamed E-Plan) program in the 1990s to serve a growing market of low-income, largely illiterate wage-earners who could no longer receive their pay in cash because of growing crime problems (Moore 2000). When employers switched to paying employees by check or direct deposits, Standard Bank was flooded by waves of unbanked customers (Moore 2000). Operating exclusively through a 'fingerprint-secured' debit card system and ATM network that is programmed to give operating instructions in each of South Africa's eleven official languages, costs per outlet are 30 per cent to 40 per cent below those of traditional branches (Moore 2000). ATM technology greatly reduces the delivery and service expenses of transactions and sales (since there is no back office) and the bank minimizes unit cost of its ATMs by using education and incentives to maintain high transaction volume (Moore 2000). E-Plan grew to around 340,000 accounts by 1996. By 1999, the number of E-Plan accounts had grown to 2.6 million, with around 50,000–60,000 new accounts opened each month (Moore 2000).

Fleet Bank Boston Financial's CommunityLink (CL)

Not all electronic banking initiatives are aimed at the unbanked. Because an online transaction costs just a fraction as much as an over-the-counter branch transaction, financial institutions are developing marketing strategies and pricing policies to encourage more of their customer base to migrate from branch-based to online banking. One particularly interesting effort, called CommunityLink, is being implemented by Boston-based Fleet Bank to encourage lower-income account holders – a more difficult market to reach – to move to online banking.

CL is a comprehensive community economic development initiative that is being implemented in up to five neighborhoods within Fleet's footprint and is intended to stimulate wealth creation by providing greater access to online financial services in low and moderate income (LMI) communities (Moore 2000). To participate in CommunityLink, households must have an annual income under $50,000 a year (with a priority going to households under $40,000), have a minimum of a Fleet Savings or Checking account in good standing for at least six months, currently not own a personal computer in the home, and be willing to participate in ongoing training and ongoing surveys.

In an effort to reduce the technology gap CL is providing state of the art computer hardware, software, and Internet services to the homes of up to 3,000 LMI customers at no cost, along with the necessary training and technical assistance to help people get online.[3] Like One Economy, through this technology, CL will provide local information and culturally appropriate content to the pilot communities to increase their knowledge and to maintain an ongoing customer relationship with them, using Fleet's online financial services and products.

Given the importance of the Internet as a cost-effective delivery channel and the fact that 'the "easy" markets of well-educated, affluent knowledge workers are already wired up', it is probable that first-mover advantages can accrue to the institution that figures out how to best connect with CommunityLink's market segment (Cavanagh 1999: 5).

Community development banking partnerships

Chicago CRA Coalition and Bank One's Alternative Banking Program (ABP)

'The Coalition, which is convened by the Woodstock Institute … developed an agreement with Bank One when it purchased First Chicago Bank NBD in 1998' that included a pilot program 'to promote deposit services to unbanked customers' (Williams 2000). Rather than a separate product,

> the Alternative Banking Program (ABP) incorporates into standard Bank One products features similar to a model lifeline account, including: $10 to open an account, minimum balance as low as $0 ... unlimited check writing, unlimited use of Bank One ATMs, and some free teller transactions, depending on the account.
>
> Bank One [also] conducts financial literacy workshops in cooperation with community partners to demonstrate cost savings over check cashers, improve financial management skills, and increase trust ... with mainstream financial institutions. Although applicants with a credit history must have suitable credit scores, people with no or borderline credit may also open accounts. In exchange for more flexible credit criteria, the bank established some modest restrictions on the ABP. However, after one year, account holders can apply to upgrade to traditional account[s].
>
> (Williams 2000: 5,17)

Shore Bank's Extra Credit Savings Program

The nation's pre-eminent for-profit community development bank, South Shore Bank (SSB), and the Center for Law and Human Services created the Extra Credit Savings Program to encourage unbanked working poor to save a portion of their sizeable Earned Income Tax Credit (EITC) refunds by providing them with low-cost savings accounts (Beverly *et al.* 2000). Between January and April 2000, the Tax Counseling Project of CLHS offered free tax preparation assistance to EITC-eligible individuals two nights a week at an SSB branch (Smeeding 2000). On these evenings, SSB bankers invited individuals to join the ECSP. Those who chose to participate opened no-fee, no minimum balance savings accounts and arranged to have some portion of their 1999 federal tax refunds directly deposited into the accounts. Funds in these accounts earn a market rate of interest, and include a no-fee ATM card for those who desire one. To encourage savings and discourage early withdrawals, participants receive a 10 per cent bonus on any funds remaining in their account at the end of the year (up to a maximum bonus of $100 per account-holder) (Beverly *et al.* 2000). Over the first two years of the program, this innovative partnership has attracted more than 200 account holders and initial deposits of $200,000 (Shore Bank and the Center for Law and Human Services 2001).

The Big Issue and Bank of Scotland banking for the homeless partnership

'Not surprisingly, homeless people are almost entirely excluded from banking services, yet they are among the most at risk of assault and robbery living as they do on the streets or in dangerous hostels' (*Guardian* 2001). This is why the efforts by the Big Issue-Bank of Scotland partnership are so exciting. Set up in 1991 to give homeless people the chance to make an income, Glasgow-based Big Issue 'campaigns on behalf of homeless people and highlights the major social issues of the day' (www.bigissue.com/home.htm). Six years ago, The Bank of Scotland enabled Big Issue vendors and other homeless people to use its easy cash, no-frills accounts by accepting Big Issue vendor badges as proof of identity to open a bank account. But homeless people weren't making full use of the services because they were embarrassed to go into 'posh' bank branches, and embarrassed to be depositing small amounts of money – £1 or £2 at a time – in such places. This led to the creation of Grand Central Savings – a 'branch' of the Bank of Scotland for the exclusive use of homeless people, based in the Big Issue in Scotland's Glasgow headquarters. In its first two weeks of operation nearly 60 homeless people opened bank accounts, and the organizers are confident that there will be 200 within the year.

Transitions to mainstream banking

Union Bank of California's Cash & Save program

Union Bank's Cash & Save is a hybrid program that goes beyond check cashing by using education and consulting services to transfer previous check casher users to traditional banking services (Stegman 1999). '[W]ith profit margins ranging from fourteen percent to fifty-one percent at its fifteen locations, Cash & Save [successfully] competes with other check cashing outlets' (Glassman 1996: 80). 'But what differentiates it is the way it tries to bring unbanked customers into the financial mainstream rather than simply exploiting profit from their financial alienation' (Glassman 1996: 80).

> Cash & Save provides a full range of services targeted to lower-income, ethnic markets with large contingents of unbanked workers. While each location provides basic check cashing services – at lower fees than those generally charged by [check cashers] – what really distinguishes Cash & Save from other check cashing operations is the range of banking services that it provides. Under its Money Order Plan, which carries a one-time fee of $10, customers get six free money orders per month plus a 1 per cent check cashing charge. With Nest Egg Savings, a customer can open a no-fee, passbook interest rate savings account with an initial deposit of $10 and a commitment to deposit $25 monthly for at least one year. Cash & Save also offers a basic checking account for … as little as one dollar, a secured credit card for people who are repairing their credit rating, and a direct deposit option for the electronic delivery of government benefits.
>
> (Glassman 1996: 80)

Almost one third of Cash & Save customers converted to traditional banking services in 1997, up from 14 per cent in 1996 (Comptroller of the Currency 1998).

Efforts to reduce the digital divide and encourage online banking

Several efforts are underway to reduce the digital divide, including the Neighborhood Networks program, discussed in the previous section, that targets residents of US social housing. Improved computer literacy and access to the Internet where they live, provides residents of social housing with a convenient and economical pathway to the world of e-commerce, including online banking services.

One Economy

Enterprising businesses and non-profit organizations have also begun to recognize the potential of the Internet to reach, educate and market a variety of goods and services to residents of social housing. One of the more ambitious developments in this area is the creation of One Economy, a national non-profit organization headquartered in Washington, DC whose goal is to 'maximize the potential of technology to help low-income people raise their standard of living and build assets' (www.one-economy.org/aboutus.asp). The core element of One Economy's operation is the construction of a consumer web site called the Bee Hive (www.theBeehive.org) to provide, among other things, low-income individuals with a suite of Web-based products and services focusing on financial services, education, jobs, healthcare, and homeownership that help them build assets and raise their standard of living (www.theBeehive.org/money).

Conclusion

We have a very serious problem with under-saving in the United States. As former Senator Bob Kerrey has said, 'In a global economy, your economic health and security is measured by what you own, in addition to what you earn' (Kerrey 1997: 7). About 30 per cent of American households have no financial assets, and about half of all children in the United States are growing up in families that have no financial assets. Along racial lines, the difference in asset-holdings between whites and African Americans is far greater than the difference in their incomes (Oliver and Shapiro 1995). Under-saving for retirement is another big problem. As it has done for generations of middle- and upper-income Americans, the federal government should create policies that make compound interest work for the poor and help those with lower incomes join the asset-building classes. This is why it is so important to use the transition to EFT as the vehicle for giving lower-income, low-wealth Americans – in Kerrey's words – 'a chance to own a piece of their country'.

By bringing millions of unbanked people into the financial mainstream, EFT can facilitate savings by providing recipients with bank accounts, but alone will not provide them with a concrete incentive to save. We have a golden opportunity to expand EFT's impact by linking it with a national economic literacy campaign and new savings initiatives targeted at the working families of America who don't benefit from existing tax-preferred savings incentives such as individual retirement accounts.

The growing political support for asset-based programs together with the advent of EFT present a critical opportunity for the nation to adopt a full-scale IDA program that will incorporate not only families in social housing, including those who are moving off welfare, but also the working poor. A national IDA program coupled with EFT would help millions of families develop an emergency cushion to help weather unemployment and other short-term setbacks as well as to build their long-term financial strength by investing in homes, job training and small businesses. While it might be possible to create a national program without linking it to EFT, coordinating the two together would improve partnership-building, outreach and education efforts.

There is a clear link between EFT and the banking partnerships discussed in this chapter, and the IDA movement. To succeed, both require strong grassroots support and intensive outreach, education, and training in financial education. Treasury is sponsoring a two-pronged education campaign for EFT; one to a broad array of stakeholder groups emphasizing the benefits of direct deposit, and the other to unbanked benefit recipients on basic finances, including how to maintain a bank account and how to make the best informed choices. Hundreds of local community organizations are helping with the grassroots public outreach efforts (Hawke 1997).

A national IDA initiative could contribute to the success of EFT by providing benefit recipients with a substantial incentive to save. And by increasing the number and size of savings deposits, a national IDA program, such as that envisioned by sponsors of the proposed Savings for Working Families Act, could also improve the economics of low-balance accounts by providing banks with an inexpensive source of longer-term deposits, thereby increasing 'float'.

Finally, while not directly tied to EFT, but important nonetheless, IDAs can help keep hard-pressed workers out of the clutches of exploitive payday lenders if they permit early withdrawals to pay for family emergencies. IDA programs could allow account-holders to make up the difference within a specified amount of time to avoid losing previously earned matches.

Notes

1   Gavin Kelly, 'Welfare: Nest Eggs': 'The Government is listening to new ideas from the US to invest money for each newborn baby as a way of helping people on low incomes save for the future' (*The Guardian (London)*, 7 June 2000: 8).

2 Estimates vary; see, for example, Community Financial Services Association of America, at www.cfsa.net/geninfo.html, downloaded 27 April 2001; Frank J. Diekmann, 'More Questions than Answers: Issues Related to Credit Unions and Payday Lenders Are Almost as Numerous as the People in Line', *Credit Union Journal*, 4 (48), 27 November 2000: 6; Rob Blackwell, 'Warning on "Payday" Partnerships', *The American Banker*, 28 November 2000: 32.

3 Although CommunityLink will include about 100 small businesses, the Request for Proposals (RFP) addresses only the residential customers, which will number about 2,900. Therefore, our research design addresses the impacts of CL on residential customer behavior, banking activities, and related issues.

References

Andrew, J. (2000) 'Banks Meet "Cash Desert" Communities', BBC News, 25 July 2000. Available online http://news.bbc.co.uk/hi/english/uk/newsid_851000/851392.stm.

Avery, R.B., Bostic, R.W., Calem, P.S. and Canner, G.B. (1997) 'Changes in the Distribution of Banking Offices', *Federal Reserve Bulletin*, 83 (9): 2, 18.

Bangkok Post (2000) 'In Brief: BAY Seeks More Fee-Based Income', *Bangkok Post*, 6 October 2000: 2.

Benham, M. (2000) '"Black Friday" as Barclays Axes 172 Banks', *The Evening Standard* (London), 7 April 2000: 7.

Beverly, S.G., Tescher, J. and Marzahl, D. (2000) 'Low Cost Bank Accounts and the EITC: How Financial Institutions Can Reach the Unbanked and Facilitate Saving', paper presented at University of Illinois at Chicago 8th Annual Great Cities Winter Forum and Urban Universities Collaborative Biannual Conference on Chicago Research and Policy: Remaking Chicago, Chicago, 30 November – 1 December.

Blackwell, R. (2000) 'Warning on "Payday" Partnerships', *The American Banker*, 28 November 2000: 32.

Bristol Evening Post (2001) 'Loan Sharks "Take Benefit"', *Bristol Evening Post*, 9 February 2001: 12.

Business Line (2001) 'India: Where 3,650% Interest Finds Takers', *Business Line (The Hindu)*, 8 March 2001.

Buwembo, J. (2001) 'Uganda: Want a Loan? A One-Man "Bank" Will Sort You Out', *The East African (African News)*, 4 January 2001: 14.

Cards International (2000) 'Striving for Pole Position', *Cards International*, 27 September 2000: 14.

Cavanagh, T.E. (1999) 'Community Connections: Strategic Partnerships in the Digital Industries', *Research Report 1254–99–RR*, New York: The Conference Board: 5.

CFSA 'Consumer Demand Fuels Industry Growth', Community Financial Services Association of America. Available online www.cfsa.net/geninfo.html, Dowloaded 27 April 2001.

Community Opportunities, Accountability and Training and Educational Services Act, Pub. L. No. 105–285, §416, 112 Stat. 2772 (1998).

Comptroller of the Currency (1998) *Community Reinvestment Act Performance Evaluation*, 30 March 1998. Available online http://www.occ.treas.gov/cra/crasrch.htm, last visited 15 February 2001.

Corporation for Enterprise Development (1998) *Q & A on the Assets for Independent Act (AFIA)*, 7 October 1998. Available online http://idanetwork.cfed.org/index.php?section=initiatives&page=afi.html.

—— (2001) 'The Savings for Working Families Act of 2001'. Fact sheet can be accessed at http://www.idanetwork.org.index.php?section=policy&page=swfa2k1_summary.html.

Crooks, E. (2000) 'Europe's Citizens Oppose Cuts to Welfare State', *The Financial Times* (London), 19 December 2000: 2.

CTK News (2001) 'Inter-Ministerial Commission Discusses Romany Money-Lending', *CTK (Czech News Agency) National News Wire*, 21 March 2001.

Daigle, L. (2000) 'E-Benefit Accounts Fail to Gain Broad Usage', *American Banker*, 12 December 2000: 1.

Department of Treasury (2001) 'Notice of Funds Availability (NOFA) Inviting Applications for the First Accounts Program', Federal Register, 66 (248), 27 December 2001: 66976.

Deutsche Presse-Agentur (2001) 'Bank Losses Spur 2.59 per cent Fall in Hong Kong Stocks', *Deutsche Presse-Agentur*, 27 February 2001, financial pages.

DFI (2001) *Review of Payday Lending in Wisconsin 2001*, State of Wisconsin: Department of Financial Institutions.

Dominion (2000) 'Union Joins Call for Investigation into Bank Fees', *The Dominion* (Wellington), 20 October 2000: 15.

The Economist (1997) 'Finance and Economics: The Good Times Keep on Rollin': American banks', *The Economist*, 25 October 1997: 83.

—— (2000) 'Squeezing the Banks', *The Economist*, 2 September 2000: 53–4.

Elliehausen, G. and Lawrence, E.C. (2001) 'Payday Advance Credit in America: An Analysis of Consumer Demand' (monograph No. 35), Washington, DC: Georgetown University, McDonough School of Business, Credit Research Centre.

European Banker (2000) 'The Great Unbanked', *European Banker*, 23 October 2000: 14.

FDIC, *Statistics on Banking, Table 103 Number of Offices of FDIC-Insured Depository Institutions*. Available online http://www2.fdic.gov/hsob, last visited 16 February 2001.

—— *Number of Institutions and Offices by Charter Type, FDIC-Insured Savings Institutions, United States and Other Areas, Balances at Year End 1984–1999*. Available online http://www2.fdic.gov/hsob, last visited 5 February 2001.

—— *Table RC-11, Assets and Liabilities of FDIC-Insured Savings Institutions*. Available online http://www.fidc.gov/bank/statistical/statistics/0009/sirc11.html, last visited 4 February 2001.

Financial Management Service (2002) *Fact Sheet: Electronics Transfer Accounts*. Available online http://www.fms.treas.gov/eta/eta-fact.html, accessed 25 July 2002.

Glassman, C.A. (1996) 'Consumer Finance: The Borrowings/Savings Dilemma', *Journal of Retail Banking Services*, Autumn 1996: 80.

Grice, A. (2001) 'Labour to Pledge £1,000 Bond for Children', *The Independent* (London), 2 January 2001: 1.

Guardian (2001) 'Banking on Helping the Homeless', *The Guardian*, 6 March 2001. Available online http://www.society.guardian.co.uk/homelessness/story/0,8150,447421,00.html.

Gunsika, A. (2001) 'Borneo: Caught in the Web of Money Lenders', Financial Times Information, Global News Wire, *Borneo Bulletin*, 7 February 2001. FT-ACC-NO: A20011020711C5-15D-GNW. Accessed on 3/30/01 from Lexis-nexis.

Hawke, J.D. (1997) *Testimony before the Subcommittee on Government Management, Information and Technology of the House Government Reform and Oversight Committee*, 18 June 1997, US Department of Treasury. Available online http://www.ustreas.gov/treasury/press/pr061897.html.

—— (2000) 'Focus on Retail Financial Services to Underserved Communities', *Community Developments* (Fall 2000: 4), Washington, DC: Comptroller of the Currency, Available online http://www.occ/treas.gov/cdd/Fall2000.pdf.

Hindu (2000) 'India: Punjab National Bank to Focus on Fee-Based Income', *The Hindu*, 26 December 2000. Available online http://www.hinduonnet.com/thehindu/2000/12/26/stories/06260006.htm.

Hunter, T. (2000) 'Clamour Grows for Laws to Curb Extortionate Charges for Credit', *The Sunday Herald*, 19 November 2000: 9.

Husband, J. (2001) 'Lloyds Advertises its Account for the Poor in Top People's Papers', *The Mirror*, 14 February 2001: 1,3.

Kennickell, A.B., Starr-McCluer, M. and Surette, B.J. (1998) 'Summary Description of 1998 Survey Results: Recent Changes in U.S. Family Finances: Results from the 1998 Survey of Consumer Finances', *Federal Reserve Bulletin*, 86 (January 2000): 1–29.

Kerrey, B. (1997) 'Who Owns America? A New Economic Agenda', *Assets*, Winter 1997, Corporation for Enterprise Development: 7.

Kim, A. (2001) 'Taking The Poor Into Account: What Banks Can Do To Better Serve Low-Income Markets', *Policy Report*, Washington, DC: Progressive Policy Institute: 2. Available online http://www.ppionline.org/document-Banks080601.pdf.

Korea Herald (2001) 'More than 1400 Loan Sharks Detected Across the Nation', *The Korea Herald*, 26 March 2001.

Levine, T. (2000) 'Bringing Scotland's "Unbanked" to Account', *The Guardian* (London), 1 April 2000: 7.

MacLeod, C. (2000) 'Getting Tougher on Dole Cheats', *The Herald* (Glasgow), 28 November 2000: 6.

Malaysia General News (2001) 'Implement Consumer Credit Act, FOMCA Tells Government', *Malaysia General News*, 5 February 2001.

Massachusetts Division of Banks (1999) *Check Casher Report: Second Annual Study on the Costs of Utilizing Massachusetts Licensed Check Cashers*, March 1999. Available online http://www.state.ma.us/dob/checkrep.htm.

Meadows, P. (2000) *Access to Financial Services*, Britannia Building Society, National Institute of Economic and Social Research.

Mills, G., Campos, G., Ciurea, M., DeMarco, D., Michlin, N. and Welch, D. (2000) *Evaluation of Asset Accumulation Initiatives: Final Report*, report prepared for the US Department of Agriculture Food and Nutrition Service, 2000: 15.

Moore, D. (2000) 'Financial Services for Everyone', 1 McKinsey Q. 125. Available online http://mckinseyquarterly.com, last visited 5 February 2000.

North Carolina Cash Checkers Act (1998) N.C. General Statutes Section Article 22 of Chapter 53.

Oliver, M.L. and Shapiro, T.M. (1995) *Black Wealth/White Wealth: A New Perspective on Racial Inequality*, New York and London: Routledge.

Organization for a New Equality (1998) *Cash, Credit & EFT '99: Reducing the Cost of Credit and Capital for the Urban Poor*, unpublished paper by ONE, the Organization for a New Equality.

Perman, S. (1998) 'Is Bigger Really Better?', *Time Magazine*, 151 (16), 27 April 1998: 56.

Prentice, M. (2001) 'Is Your Bank Charging too Much?', *The Ottawa Citizen*, 4 March 2001: D1.

Public Interest Research Groups and Consumer Federation of America (2000) *Show Me the Money! A Survey of Payday Lenders and Review of Payday Lender Lobbying in*

Michael A. Stegman

State Legislatures, February 2000. Available online http://www.pirg.org.reports/consumer/payday/index.html.

Riccobono, R.M. (2000) *Memorandum for Chief Executive Officers*, Subject: Payday Lending, 7 November 2000, Office of Thrift Supervision, Department of the Treasury.

Sard, B. (2001) 'The Family Self-Sufficiency Program: HUD's Best Kept Secret for Promoting Employment and Asset Growth', Center on Budget and Policy Priorities, April 2001.

Schreiner, M., Sherraden, M., Clancy, M., Johnson, L., Curley, J., Zahn, M., Beverly, S. and Grinstein-Weiss, M. (2000) 'Asset Accumulation in Low-Resource Households: Evidence from Individual Development Accounts', paper for the Federal Reserve System's Second Community Affairs Research Conference: Changing Financial Markets and Community Development. Center for Social Development, Washington University, St Louis, 21–3 September 2000.

Sherman, J. (2001) 'US-Style "Baby Bonds" Planned', *The Times* (London), 12 January 2001.

Shore Bank and the Centre for Law and Human Services (2001) 'Money in the Bank: The Extra Credit Savings Progam': 1–3, Chicago: Shore Bank, Available online http://www.shorebankadvisory.com/resources/moneyinthebank.pdf.

Smeeding, T.M. (2000) 'The EITC and USAs/IDAs: Maybe a Marriage Made in Heaven?', paper prepared for the Annual Conference of the Association for Public Policy Analysis and Management (APPAM), Seattle, Washington, 2–5 November 2000.

Stegman, M.A. (1999) *Savings for the Poor: The Hidden Benefits of Electronic Banking*, Washington, DC: Brookings Institution Press.

Stegman, M.A. and Faris, R. (2001) 'The Impacts of IDA Programs on Family Savings and Asset-Holdings', conference paper, Center for Community Capitalism, University of North Carolina, Chapel Hill, 19 February 2001: 15–16.

Summers, L.H. (2000) 'Helping America To Save More: Remarks by Treasury Secretary L. H. Summers, Choose to Save Forum Washington, DC', 4 April 2000, US Department of Treasury. Available online http://www.treas.gov/press/release/1s524.htm accessed 24 July 2002.

US Department of Health and Human Services (2001) *ACF FY Budget*: 4. Available online http://www.acf.dhhs.gov/programs/olab/testimon/2000/2001budget 020900.htm.

US Department of Treasury (2000) *ETA Providers Compensation Report*, 31 October 2000.

Washington Post (2001) 'Economic Growth Slows to 1%', *The Washington Post*, 30 March 2001: E02.

Watson, R. and Miles, A. (2001) 'The Muddle Way to Welfare Reform', *The Times* (London), 27 March 2001.

Westbury, N. (2000a) 'Helping Hand Like Money in the Bank', *Sydney Morning Herald*, 19 June 2000: 17.

—— (2000b) 'What's in it for Koories? Barwon-Darling Alliance Credit Union and the Delivery of Financial and Banking Services in North-West New South Wales'. A Report to ATSIC, New South Wales, Centre for Aboriginal Economic Policy Research, The Australian National University, June 2000.

Williams, M. (2000) *Community-Bank Partnerships: The Chicago CRA Coalition and Bank One Forge the Alternative Banking Program*, Community Developments, Office of the Comptroller, Washington, DC. Available online at http://www.occ.treas.gov.cdd/resource.htm, last visited 5 February 2000.

12 Social sustainability, sustainable development and housing development

The experience of Hong Kong

Rebecca L. H. Chiu

Introduction

Sustainable development became a buzzword in the West in the 1980s and in the Asia-Pacific region about a decade later. There are contentions and confusions over what is 'development', how it should be achieved, and what should be 'sustained' by sustainable development. Although there is little refutation that there are different strands of sustainability to be considered, such as ecological sustainability, social sustainability, economic sustainability and cultural sustainability, disagreements about the relationships between these different dimensions of sustainability and sustainable development abound. For instance, some may argue that social sustainability, i.e. maintaining existing social norms and introducing changes within social limits, is a social constraint on development, and therefore it is a core element of sustainable development (Munro 1995). Others may define social sustainability as the social conditions necessary to support environmental sustainability which is at the heart of sustainable development, and therefore all social development goals should be considered within the limits of environmental capital (Mitlin and Satterthwaite 1996).

Whatever the definitions for and understanding of sustainable development and social sustainability are, the concepts provide a new perspective or paradigm to interpret and possibly to steer social change. Housing is a basic component of the built environment and social development; examining its development in this new perspective would help understand whether changes or developments of a society are achieving the tenets of sustainable development, howsoever one defines it. In 1999, Hong Kong has made a clear commitment to observe sustainable development although the policy and the implementation mechanism are still in the making at the time of writing . The Asian financial crisis of 1997 and 1998 dealt a heavy blow to Hong Kong's economy, engendering drastic social changes which were beyond the imagination of the Chinese, British and Hong Kong governments in the 1980s when the post-1997 arrangements for the city were negotiated. Housing problems and issues prevailing in the pre- and post-1997 periods are dramatically different (Chiu 1998). There could be many interpretations on the changes, but that by the sustainable development paradigm may provide a longer-term perspective.

This chapter thus has dual aims. Methodologically it attempts to explore the relationship between housing and the social dimension of sustainable development. Empirically it applies the quantifiable components of the methodology to explore the social sustainability of housing development in Hong Kong, noting in particular the changes before and after the critical year of 1997.

Conceptual issues

Sustainable development and sustainability

The concept of sustainable development was first given currency by the World Conservation Strategy in 1980. Its most oft-cited definition is that given by the World Commission on Environment and Development contained in the Brundtland Report in 1987: 'development that meets the needs of the present without compromising the ability of future generations to meet their own needs' (WCED 1987; Trzyna and Osborn 1995). This definition coins the essential components of the concept in simple terms: that of equity within and between generations and that our ability to meet needs is bounded by the limits of the earth. As Mitlin and Satterthwaite (1996) put it: 'the term has become widely used to stress the need for the simultaneous achievement of development and environmental goals' (p.43). A more elaborate definition is further given by WCED: 'a process of change in which the exploitation of resources, the direction of investments, the orientation of technological development, and institutional change are all in harmony and enhance both current and future potential to meet human needs and aspirations' (WCED 1987: 46 quoted in Hediger 2000: 481–2). This extended definition does not only highlight the different facets of development but also emphasizes that they should concur with each other and that sustainable development should be able to meet aspirations not just basic needs.

The real challenge of the sustainable development concept posed to social scientists is to define it in operational terms (see, e.g. Hediger 2000; Munro 1995). Sustainable development as a concept is easy to understand, however, its implications on government policies and individual behaviors are often too complex and fluid to be grasped. Munro's offer of an operational definition, that is, 'the complex of activities that can be expected to improve the human condition in such a manner that the improvement can be maintained' (Munro 1995: 29), does not seem to offer much help. Nonetheless, Munro's deliberation on what 'development' is and what is to be 'sustained' is useful. He suggests that *development* should be inclusive of all kinds of activities and processes that increase the capacity of people or the environment to meet human needs and improve the quality of human life. He further cautions that development should not only include the physical development of the living environment, but also of equal importance are health care, social security, education, nature conservation, and cultural activities, etc. Therefore 'development is a complex of activities, some with social, some with economic objectives, some based on material resources, some on intellectual resources, all enabling people to reach their full potential and enjoy a good life' (p.28).

Defined in this way, it is not difficult to understand why development should be made 'sustainable'. The subsequent questions are of course how can we make developments sustainable, and what are the deterrents or barriers to sustaining developments? These questions bring us back to the genesis of the sustainable development paradigm: the limits of the earth. Given our past and present speed of development, the capacity of the earth to sustain such growth and consumption rates was questioned and cautioned. Hence, 'sustainable' is initially widely used with reference to environmental or ecological sustainability. However, as the debate develops, there are contentions on what is to be 'sustained': is it natural systems or human activities? While it is not easy for developmentalists and environmentalists to come to full agreement, an increasing number of social scientists accept that in addition to 'ecological sustainability', 'economic sustainability', 'social sustainability', and 'cultural sustainability' should be part of sustainable development. Further, the linkages between these different dimensions of sustainability should be fully taken into account, and they should not be isolated from one another (Khan 1995; Goodland and Daly 1996; Mitlin and Satterthwaite 1996; Hart 1999; Williams *et al.* 2000).

Hart (1999), in developing indicators for a sustainable community, cites useful examples to illustrate the need to integrate the economic, social and environmental segments of a society. She argues that economic indicators such as the gross domestic product (GDP) reflect the amount of economic activity but neglect the effect of that activity on the community's social and environmental health. Thus GDP can go up when overall community health may go down. Thus, instead of using median income as an economic indicator, the number of hours of paid employment at the average wage required to support basic needs should be used; and in lieu of unemployment rate, diversity and vitality of local job base should be used (Hart 1999: 9). Hart's work substantiates the similar views expressed earlier by Khan (1995): an appropriate sustainable development index should be developed to measure development in the context of an integrative framework of social, environmental and economic sustainability, rather than relying on the conventional method of GDP. Sustainability thus required a more integrated view of the world. It is within this perspective that sustainable development can be sought.

Social sustainability and housing

Housing as an essential component of the built environment, a constituent of social development, an important economic sector and an entity that uses natural resources (including labour power) and produces energy and waste, its development certainly affects the ecological, economic, social and cultural sustainability of a place. Little research has been done on the interconnections of housing, sustainability, and sustainable development. What is emerging in the literature mainly concerns the environmental sustainability of housing (see, e.g. Bhatti 1994; Rydin 1992a, 1992b, 1996; Chiu 2000a, 2000b; Morgan and Talbot 2000). Not until the other sustainability aspects of housing are adequately researched and integrated, would it be possible to seek a sustainable development path for housing. As the basic function of housing is to provide shelter and it directly affects the quality of life, this chapter therefore chooses to begin a discourse on social sustainability and housing.

There are diverse views on what the concept of social sustainability embraces. Three different interpretations can be distilled from the literature. One interpretation equates social sustainability with ecological sustainability, and hence, analogous to ecological limits, there are social constraints limiting development (Munro 1995). The social constraints are set by social norms. If the social limits are breached, the activity will fail because people will resist. Hence for an activity to be socially sustainable, specific social relations, customs, structure and value have to be maintained. Social changes are therefore slow. This interpretation is challenged since in order to achieve the goals in sustainable development, fundamental changes in social structure are often demanded, and sustainability should not be interpreted just as 'keeping them going continuously' (Mitlin and Satterthwaite 1996: 25).

Another interpretation of 'social sustainability' thus refers to the social preconditions for sustainable development. More precisely they are the social conditions necessary to support ecological sustainability. The basis for this definition is the contention that the rules and values within a social context determine how resources and assets are distributed within the generation and between the future and the present generations (Mitlin and Satterthwaite 1996: 25; Borrini-Feyerabend and Buchan 1997). Thus to achieve ecological sustainability which is at the heart of sustainable development, the social structure, social values and norms must be changed so that they are conducive to the sustainability of the environment. Such an interpretation is environment-oriented.

In contrast, the third interpretation is people-oriented, and it is a more popular definition. It refers to maintaining or improving the well-being of people in this and future generations (Borrini-Feyerabend and Buchan 1997; Pugh 1996; Townroe 1996). The emphases are social cohesion and integrity, social stability and improvement in the quality of life. Thus social sustainability entails reductions in social inequality especially social exclusion, and diminution of social discontinuity or destructive conflicts (Hediger 2000; Polese and Stren 2000). Thus to be socially sustainable, there needs to be equitable distribution and consumption of resources and assets, harmonious social relations and acceptable quality of life. Hence this interpretation of social sustainability echoes with the principles of sustainable development defined by WCED, i.e. equity and social justice for this and future generations.

Among the above three interpretations of social sustainability, the first one offers a less integrated and less dynamic perspective. It does not seem to capture the fluidity of social change and it borrows the ecological constraints concept rather than integrating it with the social dimension. A useful implication from this interpretation is, however, that should sustainable development demand fundamental changes in human behaviour, we have to begin with changing the attitude and values of people, and the process may be a long one.

The second and the third interpretations could be combined to provide a more comprehensive concept of social sustainability. Without the social preconditions to advance ecological sustainability, people of the future generations will be deprived of the physical environment and the resources they need such that they also may enjoy similar living standards as the present generation. More important is the possibility that with tighter resources, it is easier to lead to or to compound social inequity, conflicts and hence social segregation, instability and dissension. Thus social sustainability needs to be environment- and people-centred.

This bi-focal emphasis also applies to the social aspect of sustainable housing development or the social sustainability of housing. Housing is about providing shelter to people, and sustainable housing development should not only cater for the housing needs of this generation but also of those to come. While the primary concern of sustainable housing is to meet the accommodation needs of the citizens, the environment has to be safeguarded from deteriorating to an extent that it diminishes the ability of future generations to meet their housing needs. Further, sustainable housing should not be merely about meeting basic needs, but should also improve liveability (Chiu 1999). Improved liveability does not necessarily mean larger space and more facilities. It may refer to

> ... a shelter which is healthy, safe, affordable and secure, within a neighborhood with provision for piped water, sanitation, drainage, transport, health care, education and child development. Also a home ... protected from environmental hazards, including chemical pollution. Also important are needs related to people's choice and control – including homes and neighbors which they value and where their social and cultural priorities are met ...

Table 12.1 Social sustainability of housing

Social precondition for ecological sustainability	Equitable housing distribution and consumption	Harmonious social relations	Quality of housing and living environment
Values	Housing equity	Landlord and tenant relationships	Internal housing conditions
Habits	Housing standards		
Rules	Affordability	Haves and have-nots relationships	Immediate environment (includes neighborliness)
Life style	Role of the government		
Environmental consciousness	Housing subsidy policies	Influence of the stakeholders	
Regulations			

achieving this implies a more equitable distribution of income between nations and, in most, within nations.

(Mitlin and Satterthwaite 1996: 31–2)

Thus, following from the above tenets of sustainable housing and our previous discussion on the concepts of social sustainability, the social dimension of sustainable housing pertains to: *a) the social preconditions conducive to the production and consumption of environmentally sustainable housing; b) equitable distribution and consumption of housing resources and assets; c) harmonious social relations within the housing system; and d) an acceptable quality of housing and living environment* (Table 12.1).

These four aspects traverse a wide spectrum of social issues. The first aspect involves, for instance, values, habits, rules, life style, and environmental consciousness and regulations. The second aspect would pertain to housing equity and housing standards, affordability, role of the government in housing, and housing subsidy policies. The third aspect may be concerned with the landlord and tenant relationships, the relationship between the haves and the have-nots, and the influence of the stakeholders in the housing arena, particularly that on housing price and rental, possibly involving the empowerment of the less privileged. The fourth aspect is more tangible and may refer to the internal housing conditions and the immediate environment, including its neighborliness. The four aspects are inter-related or even inseparable. Similar to the qualitative and quantitative aspects of sustainable economic development, they cannot be maximized simultaneously in all situations (Barbier 1987). Trade-offs, such as the relief of housing shortage problems requiring the use of virgin land for housing development, are constantly involved. To make appropriate choice over the trade-offs is complex and contentious. A better understanding of the trade-offs involved is nonetheless fundamentally important in providing a knowledge base for the choice.

The assessment of the social sustainability of housing is, therefore, not an easy task. The indicator approach is certainly not applicable to constituents which cannot be quantified, e.g. values, life style, landlord and tenant relationships, and the influences of the stakeholders in the housing system. Benchmarks or normative sustainable standards are also difficult if not impossible to be set for some of the constituents, e.g. the role of the government, the relationship between the haves and the have-nots. Generally the first and the third aspects of social sustainability in housing discussed above are difficult to be measured quantitatively. Qualitative assessments are of course as important as, if not more than, quantitative evaluation. Qualitative analysis often yields deeper insights although more subjective and interpretative elements are often involved.

As a pioneering study, the rest of this chapter will present a preliminary assessment of the quantifiable aspects of the social sustainability of the housing system of Hong Kong. This is very much a research progress report and the author is still in search of benchmarks or normative standards to position the sustainability of Hong Kong's housing system.

The social sustainability of housing in Hong Kong – the quantifiable issues

The indicators

Table 12.2 shows the list of possible indicators to assess the liveability of Hong Kong's housing environment and equity in housing distribution and consumption. One group of the indicators under *liveability* should pertain to the internal housing conditions and they include space standard, degree of sharing, self-containment, and the extent of households living in inadequate accommodation. Ventilation and lighting also directly affect internal housing conditions but data on these two aspects are difficult if not impossible to collect and therefore excluded. The other group of indicators assesses the immediate external residential quality including cleanliness in the neighborhood, access to open space and community facilities, air quality, and noise level. Although the provision of open space and community facilities is subject to planning requirements, similar to cleanliness, the accessibility of these facilities needs to be assessed from the residents' perspective. Likewise, although a statutory limit on noise level is stipulated for residential areas, residents' opinions on whether they feel that they are exposed to excessive noise should be sought. Air quality is more problematic as residents may not be able to give precise and meaningful response. This indicator is therefore dropped.

Rebecca L. H. Chiu

Table 12.2 Indicators for quantifiable components of the social sustainability of housing

	Indicators
Liveability	**Internal housing conditions**
	1 Space standard
	2 Degree of sharing
	3 Self-containment
	4 Inadequately housed households
	External residential quality
	5 Cleanliness in the neighborhood
	6 Access to open space
	7 Access to community facilities
	8 Noise level
Equity in housing distribution and consumption	**Affordability (private housing)**
	9 Price-to-income ratio
	10 Affordability ratio
	11 Rent-to-income ratio
	Accessibility to housing market
	12 Downpayment-to-income ratio
	Inadequately housed household
	13 Extent of homelessness
	14 Extent of squatter settlement
	Accessibility to public housing
	15 Length of the waiting list for public rental housing
	16 Length of the waiting time for public rental housing
	Adequacy of government subsidy in housing
	17 Supply ratio for subsidized owner-occupation
	18 Loan sufficiency ratio
	19 Affordability ratio

On the *equity of housing distribution and consumption*, indicators employed include those which measure affordability, accessibility to the housing market, the extent of homelessness and squatter settlements, the length of the waiting list for public rental housing and the extensiveness and intensity of government subsidy in housing.

Table 12.3 Residential floor area (RFA) per person, degree of sharing and average flat size, 1998–9

	Private domestic	Subsidized sale flat	Public rental housing	Average
RFA/person (m²)				
Hong Kong Island	18.3	14.2	8.9	16.1
Kowloon and New Kowloon	14.1	14.6	8.7	12.0
New Territories	16.7	14.2	8.5	12.8
Average	16.4	14.3	8.6	13.3
Degree of sharing	1.06	1.01	1.02	1.04
Average flat size (m²)	55.7	42.6	30.8	45.0

Sources: Chiu (forthcoming).

Notes
a   Residential Floor Area (RFA) is the aggregate floor area of private housing, public rental housing and HOS/PSPS of the Hong Kong Housing Authority and flats of the Hong Kong Housing Society, measured by different parameters respectively. Internal Floor Area (IFA) is used for Public Rental Housing; Saleable Floor Area (SFA) is used for HOS/PSPS and private housing; Gross Floor Area (GFA) is used for sale properties of the Hong Kong Housing Society.
b   Figures of private housing are as at the end of 1998; figures of subsidized sale flats, HOS/PSPS of the Hong Kong Housing Authority are as at March 1999 while sale flats of the Hong Kong Housing Society are as at the end of 1998; figures of Public Rental Housing, rental flats of the Hong Kong Housing Authority are as at March 1999 while rental flats of the Hong Kong Housing Society are as at the end of 1998; figures of population are as at mid-1998, figures of degree of sharing are as at the end of 1999.

Applying the indicators – a progress report

Liveability

Table 12.3 shows the space standards of different types of housing in the major districts of Hong Kong in the 1998/9 period. As anticipated, the highest space standard was in the private housing of the Hong Kong Island, reaching 18.3 sq m per person. The lowest, 8.5 sq m, is found in the public rental housing of the New Territories. The overall average was 13.1 sq m . These statistics demonstrate the degree of inequality in housing both geographically and across housing types. Inequality in housing conditions is inevitable in a free economy, and the crux of the matter is whether the space standard of the poorest housed meets that of the minimum housing standard (Chiu, forthcoming).

Rebecca L. H. Chiu

Table 12.4 Distribution of households by housing types, 2001

Type of quarters	No. of households	Percentage
Public rental housing	627,339	30.6
Subsidized sale flat[a]	320,122	15.6
Private permanent housing[b]	1,048,968	51.1
Public temporary housing	639	0.0
Private temporary housing[c]	24,997	1.2
Others[d]	29,825	1.5
Total	**2,051,890**	**100.0**

Source: Census and Statistics Department 2001: 68.

Notes
a Includes Housing Authority and Housing Society subsidized sale flats.
b Includes private residential flats, villas/bungalows/modern village houses and simple stone structures/traditional village houses.
c Includes temporary structures such as roof-top structures, contractors' matsheds, nissen huts, derelict boats, huts and places not intended for residential purposes (such as landings, staircases, corridors, etc.).
d Includes staff quarters and non-domestic quarters.

The 110,000 households classified as inadequately housed by the government obviously did not enjoy even the minimum standard (Chiu, forthcoming). For the public rental housing sector, the Hong Kong Housing Authority sets an allocation standard which currently is 5.5–7 sq m per person. The SUSDEV21 study, a consultancy study commissioned by the HKSAR Government to help develop a sustainable development strategy for Hong Kong, points out that 'some households, whilst residing in housing that meets the definition of adequate housing, may not have enough space within their living quarters to achieve a satisfactory living environment' (Government of Hong Kong Special Administrative Region 1999b: 35). Therefore it proposes to include a space standard indicator. However, it does not go further to stipulate a minimum standard that would provide a satisfactory living environment and is within the environmental and spatial capacity of Hong Kong to provide not only for this generation but also for generations to come. This is a thorny issue but until we have sought a resolution the space standard indicator provides no reference to sustainable housing development (information supplied by the Housing Department, November 1999; Hong Kong Housing Society, December 1999; Rating and Valuation Department 1999).

The indicators on the degree of sharing and self-containment are much simpler as the general, acceptable standard in terms of providing a satisfactory living environment is un-shared and self-contained accommodation. However, for some special groups, such as the elderly and the disabled, sometimes shared accommodation with independent internal facilities may be a preferred option. Therefore the degree of sharing shown in Table 12.3 requires further investigation, although apparently the relatively high degree of sharing in the private sector (1.06) was due to subdivision within accommodation units. With further research, it should not be difficult to set an overall maximum standard for the degree of sharing in Hong Kong.

On self-containment, there is no direct and readily available data that can be used. But Table 12.4 provides some reference. At most 25,636 households who lived in public and private temporary housing in 2001 did not enjoy self-contained accommodation. However, shared accommodation within public and private permanent housing usually has to share internal facilities and therefore strictly speaking this type of accommodation is not self-contained. The target of course is to enable every household to live in self-contained dwelling units (Census and Statistics Department 2001).

Apart from the aggregate data collected from secondary sources, the views of residents are also important for understanding the liveability issues. A face-to-face questionnaire survey pertaining to sustainable housing development in Hong Kong was conducted in April 2001. The aims of the survey were to gather residents' views on environmentally sustainable homes and their opinions on the physical quality of their living environment. Three convenient samples of 200 households each were interviewed in the streets of three locations: an old but vibrant district (Wanchai) near the city centre with mixed residential, retail and office use; a public rental housing estate (Wah Fu) in the fringe of the main urban area built in the 1960s; and a subsidized housing estate (Verbena Heights) built in a new town in the mid-1990s with green housing design concepts. It was expected that the choice of the three residential locations would enable the collection of views across a spectrum of living environments of the lower- to middle-income citizens.

The survey results (Table 12.5) show that only slightly more than half (58 per cent) of the interviewees thought that the sizes of their dwellings were adequate. Indeed, 53 per cent of the interviewees lived in flats which were only 400 square feet or even smaller. Nonetheless, a majority of the residents (83 per cent) found that the immediate living environment was clean or very clean. Likewise, an absolute majority (94 per cent) felt that the localities of their residences were safe. Noise was, however, a bigger problem as only 61 per cent reckoned that their dwelling places were quiet or very quiet. There were 2 per cent of the interviewees who felt that the noise problems were intolerable. It is noteworthy that one-fifth of the residents had to close the windows when sleeping in order to reduce the noise level. The accessibility to recreation and retail services scored better however. Most interviewees (91 per cent) could walk to local parks for morning exercises if they wish and almost all (97 per cent) walked to the shops to buy their daily necessities.

Of the three residential locations, residents of Verbena Heights, the first green housing estate in Hong Kong built by a housing association (The Hong Kong Housing Society), were more satisfied with their living environment. More

Table 12.5 Residents' opinons of liveability, April 2001

	Verbena Heights (%)	Wa Fu Estate (%)	Wanchai (%)	All (%)
Size of dwelling				
Very adequate	1	1	3	2
Adequate	65	51	52	56
Not adequate	34	48	45	42
Cleanliness of the surrounding area				
Very clean	11	3	3	5
Clean	88	67	78	78
Not clean	1	30	19	17
Safety of the locality of residence				
Very safe	12	6	5	7
Safe	87	86	87	87
Not safe	1	8	8	6
Quietness of the dwelling place				
Very quiet	16	7	6	10
Reasonably quiet	59	52	42	51
Noisy but bearable	25	38	49	37
Very noisy not bearable	0	3	3	2
Window closed when sleeping				
Yes	13	25	22	20
No	87	75	78	80
Walk to recreational / open space	90	92	93	91
Walk to shops	99	95	99	97

residents from this estate felt that their dwellings were big enough, and that the surrounding area was clean, safe and quiet (Table 12.5). However, residents in the old area of Wanchai had slightly better access to community and shopping facilities. This slight edge might be due to the more central location of Wanchai. The trade-off was more severe noise problems created by the busy traffic. It nonetheless provided a cleaner living environment than the public housing estate of Wah Fu (Table 12.5).

Thus on the whole, space and noise pose the biggest problems in the living environment of Hong Kong. However, due to the high density of population, the economy of scale mitigates the financial viability problems, permitting provision of community and shopping facilities in close proximity to the main housing locations, thus enhancing accessibility of these services. The high density and vibrancy in the old area of Wanchai and professional management of the two housing estates contribute to the low crime rates reflecting that Hong Kong one of the safest cities to live.

Equitable housing distribution and consumption

There were about 740 homeless persons in Hong Kong in 1998 and the number increased to 1,399 in February 2001. While these numbers are small, 108,000 households in the low-income brackets were on the waiting list for public rental housing in April 2000, and the average waiting time was expected to drop to five years at the end of 2001 (information supplied by Council of Social Services, February 2000; information supplied by Housing Department, April 2001; *Ming Pao*, 10 April 2001). However, due to decreased demand for subsidized owner-occupied housing on one hand, and the pressure from private developers to reduce the supply of subsidized housing for sale on the other, more subsidized housing has been transferred to the rental sector since 2000. By October 2001, the length of the waiting list has thus been reduced to 98,000 households. And it is expected that waiting time could be reduced to three years by the end of 2003 (information supplied by Housing Department, November 2001). Hence the economic downturn produced an unexpected positive effect on the housing shortage problems of the lower-income families.

Similarly the Asian financial crisis has also significantly improved the affordability of home purchasers in the housing market because of drastic falls in housing prices. The changes can be illustrated by a few indicators demonstrating the affordability of middle income families to purchase homes in the private market. Based on the income of a household whose income was just beyond the eligibility limit for government subsidy and the price of a small flat (50 square metres) in the extended urban area, the price-to-income ratio, accessibility ratio, affordability ratio and the rent-to-income ratio (see the notes to Table 12.6 for the definitions of these terms) was 9.3%, 2.8%, 69%, and 23% in July 1997 before the Asian financial crisis affected Hong Kong. The same ratios dropped to 4.3%, 1.3%, 31%, and 19% in December 1999, that is, about two years after Hong Kong was hit by the crisis (Table 12.6).

The continued fall in housing prices has improved affordability, and finally led to a more substantial cut in the income eligibility for subsidized owner-occupied housing, reducing from US$4,000 per month in 1999 to US$3,205 per month in 2001. Therefore more households fell out of the subsidy net, but as reflected in

Table 12.6 Affordability in home purchase, 1997–2001

Year	1997	1999	2001 (as in Oct 2001)
Without government subsidy			
Price[a]-to-income[b] ratio	9.3	4.3	4.8
Accessibility ratio[c]	2.8	1.3	1.6
Affordability ratio[d]	69%	31%	28%
Rent-to-income ratio[e]	23%	19%	22%
With government subsidy[f]			
Loan sufficiency ratio[f]	0.5	1.04	1.05
Affordability ratio	55%	25%	29%

Sources: Chiu (forthcoming); Housing Authority (1998, 2000); Rating and Valuation Department (2001); Census and Statistics Department (2001).

Notes
a The price used was a flat of 50 sq. m. (gross) in City One Plaza. The mortgage repayment was based on a loan-to-value ratio of 70 per cent, an interest rate at the prevailing best lending rate, and a repayment period of 20 years.
b Since households with income above the HOS/PSPS eligibility income limit were more likely to purchase housing from the market, the annual income used in this calculation was based on the minimum income beyond the HOS/PSPS income limit. The income limits in 1997, 1999 and 2001 were 33,000, 31,000 and 25,000 respectively.
c It was the ratio between the downpayment (30 per cent of flat price) and annual income.
d It was the proportion of monthly household income used for mortgage repayment.
e The rent of a 50 sq. m. (gross) flat in the New Territories was used.
f It was assumed that the flat was located in Shatin, and was 20 years old and of a size of 50 sq. m. (gross). The mortgage loan was 70 per cent of flat price with a repayment period of 20 years, and the interest rates were best lending rate plus 1 per cent for 1997, but minus 2 per cent for 1999 and 2001. The income level used in the calculation was 20 per cent below the income limit and not the full income limit to reflect the wide range of income levels meeting the income eligibility criteria. The loan size of the Home Purchase Loan Scheme prevailing at the time is used for the calculation.

Table 12.6, these households could still afford housing at market prices. Private housing in Hong Kong thus has become more socially sustainable in affordability terms since the end of 1997. However, due to the poor economic outlook, the improvements in affordability have not increased demand. In fact, effective demand had dropped significantly – by 60 per cent – when transactions in the first half of 1997 and 1998 are compared (Chiu 1998; Chiu forthcoming). Transaction volumes remained at the low levels between 1998 and the present time. Signs of economic recovery emerged in 2001 but unfortunately the September Eleventh Incident in New York and the subsequent war against terrorism sabotaged the hope of economic resurgence at least in the near future.

For lower-middle income families eligible for government subsidies, the afford-ability of home purchase has also improved at the wake of the Asian financial crisis. The ratio between the size of interest-free loans obtainable from the Hong Kong Housing Authority and the down-payment for a flat in the extended urban area was only 0.5 in July 1997, and increased to 1.04 in December 1999 and 1.05 in October 2001. Similarly, the affordability ratio of the families eligible for the housing loan was 55 per cent in July 1997, but decreased to 25 per cent in December 1999, and 26 per cent in October 2001 (Table 12.6). Therefore the depth of subsidy was also found to be adequate in the current property crash conditions (Hong Kong Housing Authority Annual Report, various years and Census and Statistics Department 2000; Chiu forthcoming, and information supplied by Housing Department, October 2001).

Finally, due to the diminished demand for home-ownership on one hand and the government's expansion of subsidy schemes (in order to achieve the home-ownership target of 70 per cent) on the other, the imbalance between the supply and demand of subsidized homes after 1997 has been much reduced. Before 1998, the over-subscription rates of the Home-ownership Scheme were often more than ten times. However, in the past few sale exercises, subscriptions were inadequate to take up all the flats, even though eligibility has been extended to singleton families. In contrast, the quota of the loan schemes was fully consumed as eligible families considered it opportune to take advantage of the plummeted housing prices in the market.

How socially sustainable?

The above quantitative analyses on liveability and equity demonstrate that the housing system of Hong Kong has not reached the tenets of social sustainability but improvements have been continuous. It is ironical that the progress has been more significant during the economic downturn, at least in statistical terms. At present, there is still a segment of the population who do not enjoy the basic housing standards, albeit its size is diminishing due to the continuous and increasing supply of public housing. A total of 98,000 households, involving approximately 310,000 people, are waiting for public rental housing and the waiting time is about three years (except for the elderly) (information supplied by Housing Department, November 2001). Although it is rare for cities to be able to completely eradicate the housing shortage problem or remove substandard housing, the long waiting time for public housing and the presence of substandard interim housing and squatter huts still pose significant housing problems in Hong Kong. Their impact on social relations in the housing system and whether these problems are outcomes of social exclusion are subjects for further investigation.

The government and its agent, The Hong Kong Housing Authority, have set policy objectives and targets to resolve the problems, but the objectives and targets are administratively set without giving due consideration to the goals of sustainable development. For instance, is the current target of shortening waiting time of three years by 2003 a socially sustainable target; is the current space allocation standard of 5.5–7 sq m per person socially and ecologically sustainable? The questionnaire survey identified two major problems in Hong Kong's living environment: noise and insufficient living space. These two problems need not be chronic as the survey also found out that environmentally friendly design helped alleviate or mitigate the problems.

Affordability in the private housing market is not a problem in current depressed property market conditions, but Hong Kong had suffered badly from this problem for almost two decades before the outbreak of the Asian financial crisis in October 1997. At the change of government in 1997, the problem was so severe that the new government placed it at the top of its agenda. The new leadership saw it politically expedient and socially necessary to devise radical solutions to remedy the situation including drastic increase in land supply (Chiu 1998). The unexpected financial turmoil in the region and the economic recession that ensued made these efforts redundant. The primary problem in the housing market confronting the government and the community after 1997 pertains to the poor economic outlook deterring potential buyers from entering the market or improving their homes. However, the structural changes in the housing market brought about by the land supply policy of the new government and the economic crisis may or may not have steered Hong Kong away from the affordability problem in the medium to long term. It is still uncertain whether the affordability problem will re-emerge when the economy recovers. The various subsidy schemes of the Hong Kong Housing Authority provide a safety valve, but those who fall out of the subsidy net often question the equity of the housing subsidy policy especially when subsidy intensifies.

The qualitative aspects which are not included in the above analysis would be subjects of other studies. Some of the issues have been tackled in the extant literature (see, for example, Chan 2000, 2001) though not in the social sustainability perspective. What might be pointed out here is the short span of time since the environmental policy and the sustainable development concepts were introduced in the city. A formal and comprehensive environmental policy was not announced until 1989 and it was in 1999 that the concept of sustainable development was considered a key government concern. The sustainable development strategy and the pertinent government set-up are presently still in the making. Although the community's environmental consciousness has been raised significantly in the past two or three years, the greening of the values, habits and life style of the public still at the rudimentary stage. The preference for the use of recyclable building materials and paying high housing prices for environmentally friendly design are yet to be nurtured. Nevertheless, the Hong Kong Housing Society has already pioneered green housing estate construction and the Hong Kong Housing Authority has been increasingly using more environmentally friendly building materials and design. Recently the government promulgated a number of incentives to facilitate the construction of green homes, such as exemption of balconies and acoustic features from gross floor area calculation. These are positive moves and in the long run will help in developing green values in the community.

Conclusions

This chapter has attempted to define the relationships between sustainable development, social sustainability and housing. A useful finding is that the concept of social sustainability has to be both environment- and people-centred if sustainable development is to be sought. The social aspect of sustainable housing development should follow this bi-focal approach, and four key components of this approach are identified. They are the social preconditions conducive to the building and use of environmentally sustainable housing; equitable distribution and use of housing resources and assets; harmonious social relations within the housing system; and an acceptable quality of housing and living environment. Housing issues under these four components are also exemplified and indicators for assessment are developed for the quantifiable elements. As this is only an exploratory study, further work is necessary especially in the integration of the social sustainability indicators with the other strands of sustainability.

This framework provides a more comprehensive and a longer-term perspective to evaluate and interpret housing developments in Hong Kong. The quantifiable components of the methodology identified the housing problems of Hong Kong and showed that these problems needed to be dealt with in a more holistic manner, involving the social, economic and environmental arenas. The sustainability perspective also challenged the objectives and targets of the housing policies of the government on equity and sustainability grounds. The rapid changes in the housing system brought about by the Asian financial crisis were also interpreted along these two lines. The tenets of social sustainability in housing were particularly useful in this regard as they provide a direction to evaluate these changes. This is, however, only a pioneering study and more work is needed to grapple with the sustainability issues in housing and beyond.

Acknowledgement

This chapter presents some of the findings of the research project 'Sustainable housing development in Hong Kong', funded by the Research Grant Committee of the University Grant Council, Hong Kong.

References

Barbier, E.B. (1987) 'The concept of sustainable economic development', *Environmental Conservation*, 14 (2): 101–10.

Bhatti, M. (1994) 'Environmental futures and the housing question', in M. Bhatti, J. Brooke and M. Gibson (eds) *Housing and the Environment: A New Agenda*, Coventry: Chartered Institute of Housing.

Borrini-Feyerabend, G. and Buchan, D. (eds) (1997) *Beyond Fences: Seeking Social Sustainability in Conservation*, Gland, Switzerland: IUCN.

Census and Statistics Department (1999) *Hong Kong Annual Digest of Statistics 1999*, Hong Kong: Government Printer.

—— (2000) *Hong Kong Monthly Digest of Statistics, January 2000*, Hong Kong: Census and Statistics Department.

—— (2001) *2001 Population Census Summary Results*, Hong Kong: Census and Statistics Department.

Chan K.W. (2000) 'Prosperity or inequality: deconstructing the myth of home ownership in Hong Kong', *Housing Studies*, 15 (1): 29–44.

—— (2001) 'Excluding the disadvantaged: housing inequalities in Hong Kong', *Third World Planning Review*, 23 (1): 79–96.

Chiu, R.L.H. (1998) 'The swing of the pendulum in housing', in L.C.H. Chow and Y.K. Fan (eds), *The Other Hong Kong Report 1998*, pp. 329–52.

—— (1999) 'Housing, environment and the community', in P. Hills and C. Chan (eds) *Community Mobilisation and the Environment in Hong Kong*, pp. 139–160.

—— (2000a) 'Environmental sustainability of Hong Kong's housing system and the housing process model', *International Planning Studies*, 5 (1): 45–64.

—— (2000b) 'Indicators for sustainable housing development in Hong Kong'. Paper presented at the Symposium on Sustainable Development – Co-operation Between Guangdong, Hong Kong and Macau, co-organized by the Guangdong Provincial Association for Science and Technology, The Hong Kong Institution of Engineers and The Macau Institution of Engineers, 3–7 April, Guangzhou, Macau and Hong Kong.

—— (forthcoming) 'Housing in the social development perspective', in R.J. Estes (ed.) *Social Development in Hong Kong*, Oxford University Press: London and New York.

Goodland, R. and Daly, H. (1996) 'Environmental sustainability: universal and non-negotiable', *Ecological Applications*, 6 (4): 1002–17.

Government of the Hong Kong Special Administrative Region (1999b) *Sustainable Development in Hong Kong for the 21st Century – Second Stage Consultation: Study on Sustainable Development for the 21st Century Topic Report 6: Guiding Principles, Indicators and Evaluative Criteria*, Hong Kong: The Government of the Hong Kong Special Administrative Region.

Hart, M. (1999) *Guide to Sustainable Community Indicators*, North Andover, MA: Hart Environmental Data.

Hediger, W. (2000) 'Sustainable development and social welfare', *Ecological Economics*, 32: 481–92.

Hong Kong Housing Authority (1997) *Hong Kong Housing Authority Annual Report 1997/ 98*, Hong Kong: Public Relation Section, Hong Kong Housing Authority.

—— (1998) *Hong Kong Housing Authority Annual Report 1998/99*, Hong Kong: Public Relation Section, Hong Kong Housing Authority.

—— (1998) *Housing in Figures 1998*, Hong Kong: Hong Kong Housing Authority.

Hong Kong Housing Society (1999) *Hong Kong Housing Society Annual Report 1999*, Hong Kong: Hong Kong Housing Society.

Khan, M.A. (1995) 'Sustainable development: the key concepts, issues and implications', *Sustainable Development*, 3: 63–9.

Mitlin, D. and Satterthwaite, D. (1996) 'Sustainable development and cities', in C. Pugh (ed.) *Sustainability, the Environment and Urbanisation*, London: Earthscan Publications Limited.

Morgan, J. and Talbot, R. (2000) 'Sustainable social housing for no extra cost?', in K. Williams, E. Burton and M. Jenks (eds) *Achieving Sustainable Urban Form*, London and New York: E. & F.N. Spon.

Munro, D.A. (1995) 'Sustainability: rhetoric or reality?', in T.C. Trzyna and J.K. Osborn (eds) *A Sustainable World: Defining And Measuring Sustainable Development*, Sacramento: published for IUCN – the World Conservation Union by the International Center for the Environment and Public Policy, California Institute of Public Affairs.

Polese, M. and Stren, R. (eds) (2000) *The Social Sustainability of Cities: Diversity and the Management of Change*, Toronto: University of Toronto Press.

Pugh, C. (ed.) (1996) *Sustainability, the Environment and Urbanisation*, London: Earthscan Publications.

Rating and Valuation Department (1999) *Hong Kong Property Review*, Hong Kong: Government Printer.

Rydin, Y. (1992a) 'Environmental impacts and the property market', in M. Breheny (ed.) *Sustainable Development and Urban Form*, London: Pion.

—— (1992b) 'Environmental dimensions of residential development and the implications for local planning practice', *Journal of Environmental Planning and Management*, 35 (1): 43–61.

—— (ed.) (1996) *The Environmental Impact of Land and Property Management*, Chichester and New York: J. Wiley.

Townroe, P.M. (1996) 'Urban sustainability and social cohesion', in C. Pugh (ed.) *Sustainability, the Environment and Urbanisation*, London: Earthscan Publications Limited.

Trzyna, T.C. and Osborn, J.K. (eds) (1995) *A Sustainable World: Defining and Measuring Sustainable Development*, Sacramento: published for IUCN – the World Conservation Union by the International Center for the Environment and Public Policy, California Institute of Public Affairs.

Williams, K., Burton, E. and Jenks, M. (eds) (2000) *Achieving Sustainable Urban Form*, London and New York: E. & F.N. Spon.

World Commission on Environment and Development (1987) *Our Common Future*, Oxford: Oxford University Press.

13 Urban reform and low-income communities in Chinese cities

Ya Ping Wang

Introduction

Poverty amid plenty is the world's greatest challenge (World Bank 2001). In Europe most countries have followed the strategy of 'liberalization' to pursue economic prosperity in the new global market over the last two decades. This has led to an increase in unequal social conditions among citizens. In most countries, inequalities of income have been growing. In some, the incomes of the richest groups are rising fast, while the incomes of the poorest groups have grown little in real terms, or are even falling (Townsend 1993; Cornia 1999). Neo-liberal economic reform and transition in former socialist states has also resulted in an increasing gap between rich and poor and the polarization of socialist cities (Andrusz *et al.* 1996; Clapham *et al.* 1996; Hegedus and Tosics 1994; Struyk 1996; Szelenyi 1996). An obvious consequence of the new economic order, as observed by Harloe (1996), is the growth of mass unemployment and poverty, together with the process of physical and social exclusion and segregation. In Russia, for example, the World Bank estimated that 25 per cent of households were in poverty in July 1992, rising to almost 32 per cent by summer 1993 using the official poverty line (Clarke 2000). This income disparity and the persistence or growth of poverty have attracted deep concern among academics and government officials (Gordon and Townsend 2000).

China has followed a similar economic development strategy since the early 1980s within the existing political framework and under the control of the Communist Party. Far-reaching economic reforms have been carried out both in rural and urban areas. Similar to the patterns observed in European countries, economic reform in China has had a very uneven effect on the population (Bian and Logan 1996; Logan and Bian 1993). In urban areas industrial restructuring in the state owned enterprise sector since 1992 has increased the number of unemployed people. At the end of 1995, there were 5.6 million people who were registered as 'laid-off' (laid-off, *xiagang*, is a special term in China; it means to become unemployed but the person concerned may receive some subsistence each month from the employer). One year later, this had increased to 8 million. At the end of 1997, the total of laid-off and other unemployed people in urban areas had reached 15 million (Yi 1998). In 1996, it was estimated officially that there were 30 million people living in poverty in cities (Zhong and Wang 1999). This does not include the rural to urban migrants (the commonly cited estimate of their number being around 70 million); most of whom live under very poor conditions. Although the accuracy of these figures is debatable, they do indicate serious social and economic problems in Chinese cities.

Urban poverty has attracted some attention among Chinese academics and officials in the last few years. Some studies were carried out to establish the relationships between unemployment and urban poverty (e.g. Wang 2000; Zhang 1998; Zhu 1998; Zhang 1999). Regional variation of urban poverty, the relationship between poverty and family income, employment types and economic sectors were also the focus of official investigations. However, other problems related to the urban poor were not studied in detail. The nature of low-income communities and the housing conditions of the urban poor are some of the areas that require particular attention.

This chapter looks at the social impacts of urban reform in Chinese cities and assesses the living and housing conditions of low-income communities. It reports the findings from recent fieldwork in Shenyang and Chongqing. These cities were chosen because they experienced significant industrial restructuring and the worst problems of laid-off and unemployment among large Chinese cities. Both cities are located in the inland areas and the impacts from new high-tech and property led urban development were less significant than in the coastal cities such as Shanghai and Guangzhou. The discussion and analysis is based on a research project, funded by the Department For International Development (DFID) UK. The project involved research on policy changes, interviewing central and local government officials and a questionnaire survey of 802 low-income households in the two cities. The chapter aims to uncover the new patterns of social and spatial stratification in Chinese cities; to illuminate the emerging problems of urban poverty; and to evaluate the implications of housing reform policies on low-income communities. Before going to the case studies, the next section will provide an overview of social changes in Chinese cities. This will be followed by two sections, each on one case study city. The chapter will then draw together the findings to reveal common features of urban poverty and the spatial characteristics of the low-income communities.

Economic reform and social change

Economic reform has greatly improved the living conditions of the majority of urban residents in China. However, not every family has benefited equally from this process. Industrial and institutional restructuring in the 1990s resulted in a dramatic increase in the gap between the rich and the poor. In studying the pre-reform urban social groups, Hou (1997) emphasized the important differences between those inside and those outside the state system. With the continuation of Communist Party control and the socialist political system, these differences have been largely preserved. The groups who have benefited most from urban reform have tended to be the core insiders of the state system (such as the government officials) and those with strong links with the government (such as academics and professionals). Those who had traditionally weak links with the state (such as the industrial workers in the state owned and collectively owned enterprises) have benefited less (Wang and Murie 1999 and 2000).

Intensified economic restructuring in the state sector toward the end of the 1990s has broken the social and spatial balance established during the planned economy period. The incomes of white-collar public sector employees including those working in government and administration have increased substantially, while many others have suffered from unemployment. The enterprises, particularly the small and low quality collectively owned factories, were most seriously affected. Table 13.1 gives some indication of the serious unemployment problems in China and the case study cities. Between 1996 and 1999 the total number of persons in employment in China has fallen by 20.8 per cent (about 31 million). In the state sector there was a fall of nearly 24 per cent while in the collective sector nearly half the employment was lost. The national figures covered all urban areas including small towns and special industrial districts. The situation in Shenyang and Chongqing may look better than the national average, but they were among the worst affected large cities. There were increases in the number of jobs in the 'other sectors' over the same period, but the expansion was far from sufficient to compensate for the losses in the state and the collective sectors. The new jobs created also required very different skills from those of the laid-off workers.

The non-skilled industrial workers employed by traditional industries in the state sector, the unemployed, and the majority of collective sector employees are the main groups of poor residents in Chinese cities.[1] In spatial terms the majority of them now can be found in the old traditional housing areas and housing estates associated with bankrupted state enterprises. Most municipal governments have begun to address the poverty problems and established poverty lines based on household income. For those official urban households, whose income fell below the city's poverty line, government or work unit help could be provided.

This emerging poverty problem was the result of a complex social restructuring process. Figure 13.1 conceptualises the social and sectoral changes happening in Chinese cities. It shows:

- reduction of the core and associated groups as a result of the institutional changes. Reform has increased the incomes and benefits of the government employees and at the same time the number of employees in the public sector are in decline.

Table 13.1 Change in the number of jobs in urban areas from 1996 to 1999 (1,000 persons)

			1996	1999	% of change
China as a whole	**Total**		**148,453**	**117,730**	**−21.0**
		State sector	109,494	83,360	−23.9
		Collective sector	29,542	16,520	−44.1
		Other sectors	9,417	17,670	87.6
Shenyang	**Total**		**2,255**	**1,812**	**−19.6**
		State sector	1,396	1,158	−17.0
		Collective sector	668	390	−41.6
		Other sectors	191	264	38.2
Chongqing	**Total**		**2,946**	**2,666**	**−9.5**
		State sector	2,140	1,857	−13.2
		Collective sector	675	477	−29.3
		Other sectors	132	332	151.5

Sources: State Statistics Bureau, 2000; Shenyang Statistics Bureau, 2000; and Chongqing Statistics Bureau, 2000.

- stratification of the working class, particularly between those with jobs and those who were either laid-off or unemployed.
- expansion of the urban poor through contraction in the state sector and the arrival of large numbers of rural migrants.
- expansion of the urban population in the private business sectors, and the social division among them.

These social changes have been accompanied by spatial and residential re-organization. Urban reform policies, which have a direct impact on spatial re-organization, are related to housing. Housing in Chinese cities was mainly provided within a socialist system from 1949 to 1979. In the early 1980s, different housing reform experiments were undertaken. This led to a comprehensive housing reform programme being implemented from 1988 onward. (For further discussion see, for example, World Bank 1992; Kirkby 1990; Chen 1996; Zhou and Logan 1996; Wu 1996 and 2001; Leaf 1997; Zhang 1997; Wang and Murie 1996, 1999 and 2000; Lee 2000; Li 2000a and 2000b; Chiu 2001.) During the first half of the 1990s, large quantities of existing public housing owned by state enterprises and institutions were sold to sitting tenants. Many urban residents have now moved into commercially built housing estates (Wang and Murie 2000; Wang 2001). Along with other reforms, the changes in the welfare housing provision system have had a profound impact on the social and spatial structure of cities. During the pre-reform period, although distinctive functional zones such as administrative areas, industrial areas and commercial and housing areas were planned, the cities

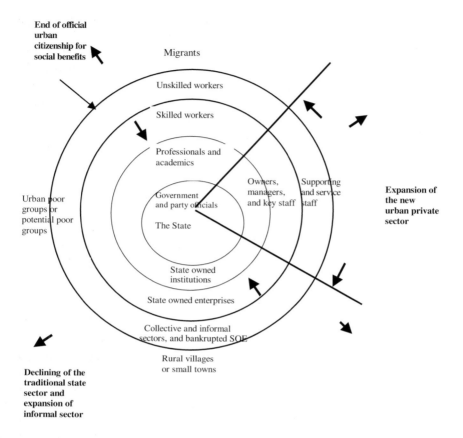

End of official urban citizenship for social benefits

Migrants

Unskilled workers

Skilled workers

Professionals and academics

Owners, managers, and key staff

Supporting and service staff

Government and party officials

The State

Expansion of the new urban private sector

Urban poor groups or potential poor groups

State owned institutions

State owned enterprises

Collective and informal sectors, and bankrupted SOE

Rural villages or small towns

Declining of the traditional state sector and expansion of informal sector

13.1 Urban social groups and changes under reform in Chinese cities

were not divided into different residential areas based on their income levels. There was also no obvious concentration of poor people in particular areas in major cities. Political reliability is still a very important condition for senior party leaders and government officials, but the political classification of residents has become less important as a result of economic reform. Instead, a different social and economic structure has emerged in urban areas, in which communities or neighbourhoods of similar income or status have appeared.

Low-income communities in Shenyang

Shenyang is the political, economic and cultural centre of Liaoning Province in the Northeast Region of China. The municipal administration area is very large (12,980 sq km), while the central urban districts of the city cover an area of 3,495 sq km and the central built-up areas covered 230 sq km in 1999. The total population in the central urban districts was 4.8 million, of which 3.9 million were official non-agricultural urban residents (Shenyang Statistics Bureau 2000). The city was one of the most important industrial cities during the planned economy period, and a base of heavy industry in China. Traditional industries concentrated in the machinery manufacture sector. The open door policy and recent industrial restructuring put great pressure on these old industrial establishments. Many of them became loss-making enterprises. Large-scale unemployment and laid-off workers have been reported in the city in the last few years.

The city has experienced large-scale redevelopment over the last two decades. The urban landscape in the central area is predominantly modern with flourishing shopping and other facilities. The leaders of the municipal government had very ambitious plans for the city. One of the targets was to clear all the major old housing areas by the end of 2000. This proved to be unrealistic. In late 2000, many deprived and run down old residential areas could still be found in the city. These areas were the focus of the research because they were largely associated with the low-income groups in the city. Apart from suburban villages, two major types of low-income communities were identified in the city:

• the remaining traditional housing areas
• housing areas dedicated to state owned enterprises, particularly these related to the factories that went bankrupt or came close to bankruptcy.

Three areas were selected for detailed study on the basis of the size and location. One represents the state owned enterprise housing areas; the other two represent the poor traditional housing areas (Figure 13.2). The following sub-sections discuss the physical, social and economic conditions in each of these areas.

Gongrenxincun area (Workers' Village) in Tiexi

Tiexi (West of the Railway) District is the most important industrial area in Shenyang with a concentration of many large state-owned enterprises. In association with these factories, large areas of public housing were built to accommodate the work force. These housing areas were either dedicated to a particular large factory or as common housing areas for several factories. Gongrenxincun was one of the first public housing estates built in the city in the early 1950s. It offers over 5,000 two to three room flats in three storey buildings. The area was designed at low density with good facilities such as children's playgrounds, nurseries, schools etc. During the planned economy period, these houses provided homes for the privileged officials, managers and senior technical workers. About ten years ago, Tiexi was still one of the richest districts in the city. The development of the market economy resulted in the poor performance and even closure of some of these once important industrial establishments. As a result, houses associated with these enterprises became run down due to the lack of proper maintenance and repairs.

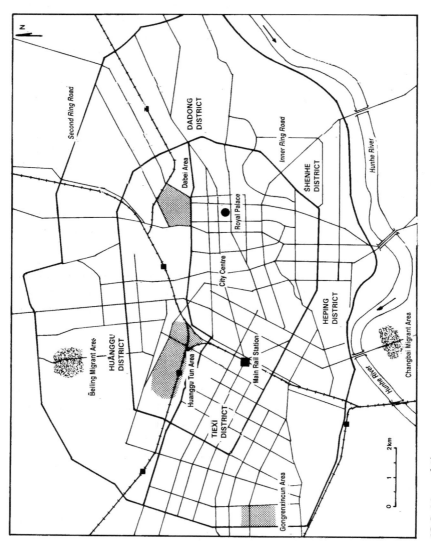

13.2 Map of Shenyang

In 2000 when the area was studied, a large proportion (30 per cent) of the residents in this area had retired. Half of the working age residents were laid-off by their employer. Several factories were permanently closed or in the process of closure at the time, in some cases (such as the Cable Factory) involving several thousand employees. The majority of households living in this estate was generally poor and had a very low income. When it was visited, many laid-off workers sat outside playing cards or chess. A man in his thirties was living in only one room with his wife and son (sharing kitchen and toilet with another family). The room was originally allocated to his parents by the factory, and both his parents had died. He and his wife had worked in a collective work unit, but they had been laid-off recently. Their work unit did not provide much support to the laid-off workers. As they had no other place to go, the factory, which used to employ the man's parents, could not force them out.

Although the income level of the residents in the area was low, the price of the properties was high and no obvious vacancies could be found. The market price of old houses was between 1,000–2,000 yuan per sq metre. (A small flat of 50 sq metres would cost 50,000 to 100,000 yuan. The average wage in the city in 1999 was about 700 yuan per month and most residents in the area had been laid-off.) Because of the work unit ownership, many residents have benefited from housing privatization in this area with nearly half of the households surveyed having bought their house. Another 40 per cent still rented housing from either the work unit or the local authority. Traditional private ownership in this area was very low. Some families had moved into this area when the houses were built in 1952, and had stayed in the same flat there for generations.

Huanggu Tun area

A large poor area around the historical railway station of Huanggu Tun within Yaming and Kejian Sub-District Offices was the second case study in Shenyang. It was a very large area with over 3,500 low quality traditional houses. The area had a long history before the Communist period and private ownership was the dominant tenure. Because it was located near to the industrial area of Tiexi, the majority of the residents were industrial workers. The area also had a small number of temporary residents of rural migrants. They rented the accommodation from local urban families.

Over 24 per cent of residents in this area had retired. An old man who had been living in this area since 1948 recalled his experiences. He had originally lived in another house nearby and moved to the current home 15 years ago. He bought the yard and the two-room house and then built another two rooms within the yard after the family had moved in. He lived here with his two married sons and grandchildren. He considered that his family's living conditions were not very poor compared with many of his neighbours. He had a pension from his work unit, but because the work unit was in financial difficulties he had not received anything for five months. Both of his sons had been laid-off by their employers recently.

Over 55 per cent of the working age residents surveyed in this area were laid-off by their employers. Guangming Lu was the poorest district in the Huanggu Tun area. It consisted of a narrow strip of poor houses between the railway and several larger factories. The area was originally built during the Japanese occupation period (1930s–40s). The 'houses' were small single rooms (*pingfang*), each accommodating one family. The original density was not very high and the open space between two rows of housing was wide. Because of the increase in population residents had made additions at the back and the front of the original room to increase indoor floor space. Parts of the original yard between the two buildings had been covered up. Only a narrow passage of 1–2 metres was left. The basic facilities in the area were very poor, hot in the summer, cold in the winter and wet and muddy during the rain. Traditional family ownership was the dominant tenure in this area. Among those surveyed, more than 76 per cent of residents owned their houses. The others mainly rented from their work units or municipal housing authority. Private rental was very rare.

Because this was one of the poorest residential areas in the city, the municipal government had plans to redevelop it. The demolition had already begun when visited. Timbers and other materials (doors and windows) from the old houses had been collected together by the demolition company for sale. When asked about their views on redevelopment, many residents felt that redevelopment would improve the housing quality in the area, but would require a large sum of money from the residents. 'Without a job, how could one afford to move into a new house back in this area?' Income level in this area was very low. A middle-aged man who was a street cleaner in the area earned 120 yuan a month (less than 20 per cent of the average wages in the city). He was given the job because the local neighbourhood committee knew his family was in real difficulty. Not every laid-off person had this job opportunity.

Dabei area

Dabei, the third case study area in Shenyang, was another of the remaining large poor traditional housing areas. It is located in Dadong, a major industrial district at the east side of the city. The living conditions in this area were similar to those found in the Huanggu Tun area. Most of the core houses existed before 1949. Not much improvement was made apart from the increase in density by additions and insertions. There were about 6,500 households in this area alone with more than 25,000 people. The tenure composition in this area is similar to that in Huanggu Tun, but with a slightly higher proportion of work unit and municipal housing.

Private home ownership was about 62 per cent. Most heads of household surveyed (78 per cent) in this area were industrial workers. A few were low rank government officials (11 per cent). The workers were engaged in different enterprises rather than associated with one particular factory. About half (48 per cent) of working age residents had been laid-off by their employers.

When interviewed, the mood of residents living in the traditional areas was better than that in the New Workers' Village in Tiexi. Many residents in the central traditional areas had got used to unstable jobs and some had never had a permanent public sector job before. Some of them had set up small family businesses at the early stages of the reform. In contrast, the mainstream workers in the state or collective sectors in Tiexi had got used to the comprehensive care provided by their employers and many had found it difficult to get over the shock of being unemployed.

Low-income communities in Chongqing

Chongqing, situated on the Yangtze (Chang Jiang) River in the Sichuan basin, is the major political, economic and cultural centre in the Southwest of China. The new Chongqing Municipality was designated in 1997 and is now under direct control from Beijing. It includes the city of Chongqing itself, four other small cities and 23 rural counties. The total administrative area is 82,403 sq km. The central built-up area was about 175 sq km in 1996 (Chongqing Master Planning Office and Chongqing Urban Planning and Design Institute 1998). The population in the central urban districts was 8.4 million in 1998, of which 3.5 million were official urban residents (State Statistics Bureau 2000). Chongqing was another important industrial city in inland China during the planned economy period with traditional industries including manufacturing, chemicals, steel and textiles. Economic reform and technological changes had made many of these industries unsustainable, and like Shenyang, large-scale unemployment and laid-off workers have been reported in the city over the last few years.

Because of the particular landscape framed by the two large rivers – Yangtze and Jialing (Figure 13.3) – the land use pattern in Chongqing was much more fragmented than in Shenyang. Industrial factories were dispersed at many different locations rather than concentrated in one or two large districts. As a result, poor and traditional housing areas of various standards could also be found in many locations. After some investigation, four sites were selected for detailed study. Three of them were located in the historical central area of Yuzhong District and all were on slopes facing the Yangtze River. The other one was a textile industrial area in Shapingba District. This selection also allows comparison with Shenyang. The following subsections describe these areas.

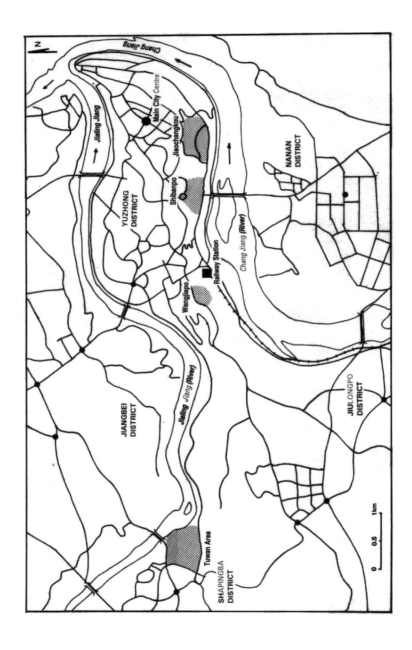

13.3 Map of Chongqing

Jiaochangkou and Shibanpo areas

Jiaochangkou and Shibanpo were two old housing areas less than ten minutes walk from the city central square – Jiefangbei. They were both on steep slopes with very high density, poor quality traditional houses. Because of the central location, both areas were very active in economic terms with small shops and open markets in most major streets. Minor streets in these areas were stairs along the slopes, some of them very narrow. The houses in these areas were also very old with timber, bamboo and bricks as the main construction materials; most had more than one floor. Some houses, which were still occupied, had been marked as 'Dangerous Housing' by the local authority. The fading colour of the official notices indicated that they had been there for a very long time. The infrastructure in the areas was very poor with water pipes running along the walkways and sewage running from open or covered up ditches. Many families had no purpose built kitchen and did their cooking in the street outside their rooms.

The survey found that the major housing tenures included traditional private ownership (64 per cent), private rental (5 per cent), municipal ownership (16 per cent), work unit ownership (11 per cent) and recently privatized housing (4 per cent). The residents of these areas were a mix of original urban families and rural to urban migrants. The original urban residents were generally poor and most without a stable job or they had been employed by the collective sector. The majority (68 per cent) of adults among the official urban residents in these two areas were either laid-off workers or retired persons. The high unemployment rate and the nature of the residents was reflected in the names of new businesses such as *Xiagang Chashe* (Tea House Run by Laid-off Workers) and *Xiagang Banyong* (Removing Company Organized by the Laid-off workers) etc. These names were used to elicit public sympathy.

The majority (78 per cent) of heads of households in these areas were industrial workers. Among them, 85 per cent in Jiaochangkou and 95 per cent in Shibanpo were unskilled workers who had no technical grade. The residents believed that 'anyone who has a connection with the government has moved away long ago. You cannot find anyone still living here who works for the government'. The representatives of cadres in the sample were indeed very low: 3 per cent in Jiaochangkou and 12 per cent in Shibanpo.

Most of the migrants living here either worked as *Bangbang Jun* or small traders along the street selling farm products such as vegetables and fruits. *Bangbang Jun* was a special term in Chongqing, referring to the labourers who helped customers to carry goods at river-side ports, railway and bus stations and outside shops in the city. All of them carried a wood or bamboo bar (*bangbang* in Chinese) and a rope. They could be found in every street in central Chongqing and because of their numbers, they were referred to as an 'army' (*jun*). Despite their low social status, they were extremely useful in a city where other transport was difficult.

Wangjiapo area (Wang Family Slope)

Wangjiapo is located in the western part of the Yuzhong District. Unlike Jiaochangkou and Shibanpo it occupied a more peripheral location and had a much higher level of public housing ownership (70 per cent). It was, however, also on a steep slope facing the Yangtze River. At the bottom of the slope was the main railway station. Before 1949, the area was traditionally a place for the poor in the city. There was a phase of redevelopment carried out in the area in the 1950s and most of the poor houses had been upgraded. On the top half of the slope there were 40 two to three storey brick buildings constructed in 1958 during the Great Leap Forward period by the municipal government. Local residents had been involved in the building process as labour and the government had paid for materials. Residents were the tenants of the municipal housing authority. These buildings only provided single room accommodation with a balcony. These balconies were necessary as a passage and were also used as cooking places by most families. Each room (about 15 sq metres) accommodated a household, some of them three generations. Each building had at least 12 rooms and there were about 700 households in these 40 buildings. The housing authority had not put these houses up for privatization. The rent was about 105 yuan per month.

The lower part of Wangjiapo consisted of about 100 households in mainly privately owned dwellings. The physical condition and facility provision such as access roads, water and sewage were much worse. A resident (a 53-year-old man) living in this area ever since he was a child, recalled that his family used to live by the river. When the railway came, they were pushed up the slope. The original houses were made of bamboo, but they had been eventually replaced with brick walls. Residents were mainly workers in the collective sector enterprises, and most of them were unemployed. Among the adults living in Wangjiapo area, 36 per cent were laid-off workers and 23 per cent retired.

The Wangjiapo area also had some temporary residents. Local residents rented rooms out to the *Bangbangs*. The local neighbourhood committee also tried to generate income from housing provision for temporary residents. An old factory workshop building had been 'refurbished' into small rooms for renting out. The project had a flattering name *Bangbang Gongyu* – apartments for migrants. In reality, they were not apartments at all. Since the original ceiling of the workshop had been very high, the space had been separated into three floors with wood boards. The walls between the rooms were compressed wood-chip board. The corridors were very narrow and dark and the floors and walls were very dirty. There was a disused common cooking area. Each household had its own electricity meter and a common water tap was shared at the outside of the building. Water charges were shared by all residents in the scheme. They either cooked in their room or outside in the corridor. Because of the materials used, the whole building could be burned out in minutes if caught in a fire.

Tuwan area

Tuwan was a textile industrial area in Shapingba District. Two state-owned textile factories were the main employers in the area. They had performed poorly which resulted in many employees being laid-off. About 44 per cent of the adult population surveyed here had retired; another 25 per cent had been laid-off. Only about 30 per cent of working age people had a job at the time of interview. Similar to all the other areas studied, the population was predominantly working class (83 per cent).

Over half of the houses in Tuwan were owned by work units and about 18 per cent of households had bought their houses from their employer through housing reform. Two types of residential areas were found: the factory built housing areas and private housing areas. The private housing areas were on the steep slopes and the residents were quite similar to those found in Wangjiapo. Most residents were very poor. A retired lady described the problems faced by her family. She had four children, all married. Only one was still in full time employment when visited and the others were laid-off. She lived with the youngest son and daughter-in-law, neither of whom had jobs. The main problem for herself was healthcare as she had a serious illness and could not afford to go to the hospital or to see a doctor. She was considering selling part of the house to raise money for her healthcare, although the housing was used jointly by her and her son's family. For many younger generation families in the area, child education was the main problem. If the adults were laid-off, it was very difficult to pay the high costs of education. Residents hoped their child would do well in school and pass the national university entrance examination. When one did pass, however, the family often found it difficult to pay for the high costs. Because of the landscape and rain, local residents reported that landslides were a constant threat.

The factories' main residential areas were at better locations. They consisted of both old and new houses. The older houses were small with many of them only offering single rooms to families. The residents were mainly manual workers from these factories and many of them were retired. They complained about the poor living conditions, maintenance and high charges for repairs. There had been some redevelopment activities in the public housing areas. Older houses had been demolished and new ones built on the site. Not all residents, however, welcomed such changes. *Mofancun* (model workers' village) was one of the old housing areas built in 1953. It offered flats or rooms in two storey buildings. The condition of the buildings was reasonable in comparison to the private housing areas. Because of the relatively large open spaces between houses, residents had built additions at the front of the houses to create more rooms. Most of the residents were retired workers from the factories. The managers of one factory had done a deal with a commercial property developer to redevelop this area. Demolition was underway although some residents had refused to move. Two types of arrangement had been made for the original residents:

- a move back to the new housing when completed and paying part of the cost of the redevelopment;
- a move to other older houses owned by the factory. These houses were generally poor quality and could only be a transitional arrangement.

Not every resident was happy, particularly those poor residents who could not afford the redevelopment costs. The managers put various pressures on these residents to move, including threatening to make their younger family members (son or daughter) unemployed. Some residents had put up big-letter posters to protest against the redevelopment.

Common features of low-income communities

The aim of these case studies is to uncover the economic and social problems and poor living conditions in low-income community areas and to assess the new relationship between employment, housing and poverty in this transitional economy. Although the two cities are located in different regions in the country and each has some distinctive features, some common characteristics can be easily found from the above discussion.

Poor social and economic profiles of the residents

In all these areas investigated, the residents were predominantly poor. Most of them had a very low income from insecure jobs. The economic sectors they engaged in were the poor performing state owned enterprises or collectively owned small industrial factories set up by lower level government organizations such as the Sub-district Committees. Many of these factories had run into trouble resulting in massive unemployment. Some residents from these areas had never had a stable job and those who had jobs before had tended to be manual shopfloor workers. Few senior government officials could be found in these areas. Even the skilled workers had gradually moved out. There was also a high proportion of retired people and rural migrants living in these areas. Figures 13.4, 13.5 and 13.6 indicate some of the general patterns of employment in those areas.

Poor pay and insecure jobs had resulted in low incomes for the majority of the residents in these residential areas. Among the households surveyed, 15 per cent of heads of households had no income and among those who had an income, the average earning per month was 450 yuan, which was much lower than the overall average wage in these cities. (In 1999 average salary was 709 yuan/month in Shenyang and 525 yuan/month in Chongqing (Shenyang Statistics Bureau 2000; Chongqing Statistics Bureau 2000)). Nearly 70 per cent of the households surveyed had an income below the level which divides the bottom 20 per cent of the urban population from the rest. About 35 per cent had a per capita income below the city's official poverty line. In 2000, the social security subsidy line was 195 yuan per person per month in Shenyang and 169 in Chongqing. Households with a monthly per capita income below this line could apply to the municipal social security department for subsidy (Yuan 2000). Among the whole group only 35 households reported to have claimed low-income support from the social security departments.

More than 60 per cent of the households surveyed said that they did not have any savings. Of the ones which had savings, 62 per cent had less than 10,000 yuan and only about 5 per cent (14 households) had savings over 50,000 yuan. With these income and savings levels, it was impossible for these households to buy purpose built new housing from the market to improve their current living condition. About 55 per cent of the respondents reported that there had been no change in income and life standard in the last two years and nearly 25 per cent thought their income and lifestyle had declined. With the rapid increase in average income in these cities, this trend indicates further deterioration in these areas.

Traditional, simple and poor quality houses

In both cities, there were strong linkages between housing quality and the history of the areas. Traditional style, low quality housing is the dominant type of shelter for the urban poor. Apart from the 'New Workers' Villages' in Shenyang and Tuwan Area in Chongqing, other areas had emerged during the first half of the twentieth century before the Communist government. In Shenyang they were the poor workers' districts during the Japanese occupation of the 1930s–40s;

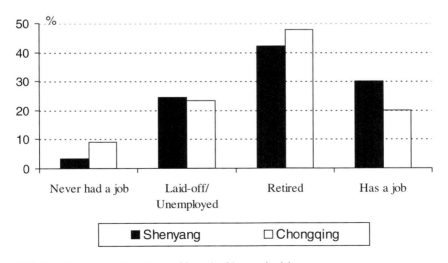

13.4 Employment situation of head of household

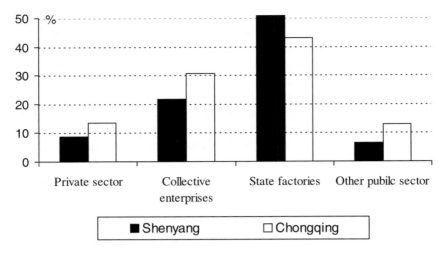

13.5 Percentage of heads of households working for different sectors

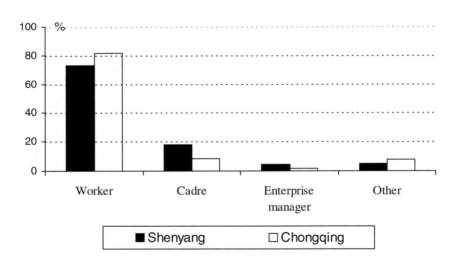

13.6 Occupation status of head of household

and in Chongqing they were poor areas during the same period when the city served as the war time national capital. This historical linkage with urban poverty had been a problem for these areas during the planned economy period and industrial factories and government institutions were often set up in other locations. Only the qualified residents from these poor areas had found jobs in the public sectors and they had also gradually moved out. The remaining population was engaged in the peripheral supporting industries and services (mainly in the collective sectors) in poor employment conditions. Thus these areas had never actually been fully integrated into the socialist cities before the economic reform. They were at the margins of the socialist urban production system though some of them were located near to the centre of these cities. The movement of residents from these areas based on political criteria in the early period was followed by another wave of selective outmigration based on household economic power. Families which made money in new private business were also able to purchase commercial housing in the market, though the number belonging to this category was small.

The findings from the resident survey provide more detailed information on the poor housing conditions in these areas:

- Poor residents lived in old traditional houses. In the survey, 86 per cent of residents lived in houses built before 1980 and 30 per cent before 1949.
- The size of most houses was very small with 60 per cent of them with less than 30 sq metres in floor space and 12 per cent less than 15 sq metres. In Shenyang, over half of the households surveyed lived either in only one room or sharing a room with other families; and in Chongqing the situation was slightly better with more families living in two rooms. About 30 per cent of households had less then 6 sq metres of floor space per person.[2]
- Only about a fifth of households had exclusive access to an internal toilet; more than 30 per cent of households had no kitchen; and 10 per cent of households in Shenyang and 5 per cent in Chongqing had to share water taps with other families.
- About 82 per cent of households surveyed reported no change in their living condition in the last five years; another 4 per cent thought their living conditions had deteriorated; and 81 per cent of the households were dissatisfied with their housing situation.

The survey found that the impact of housing reform in these areas was very limited. As regards to the sale of public sector housing, only 93 (11.6 per cent) households (mainly in the enterprise housing estates) had bought their house through privatization, while about 31 per cent of households still rented their accommodation from the public sector. The housing reform policy which claimed to have the widest impact in social terms was the housing provident fund system.[3] Among the households surveyed, only 129 (16 per cent) had participated in the provident fund (including funds for partners). The central government had promoted various affordable housing schemes since 1995. Theoretically, residents in these poor areas should be the main beneficiary group, but only 21 households identified their houses in these categories. For the majority, housing privatization and subsidy had been irrelevant, although rents in the public sector had increased substantially over the last few years (Wang 2000).

Peripheral locations and low land value

The housing conditions found in the low-income areas in the two cities were not as bad as those found in the slums in many developing countries. They had provided reasonable living conditions to the residents before the take off of the urban economy and the property boom. The conditions had degenerated during the reform period and had become more obvious when major improvements had been made in other areas. Urban renewal had replaced many of the old houses with new modern multi-storey buildings. The ones demolished often included those located in central districts where demand for commercial property was higher and where the redevelopment provided developers with higher returns on their investments. The areas left were those in more peripheral locations with a lower land value. In Shenyang the two large areas of traditional housing were not central enough to attract the investment required. Many smaller areas of older housing located either along the railway lines or near to large industrial factories could still be found. In Chongqing, all the areas identified were located at peripheral locations on steep slopes. The names of these areas, such as Wangjiapo (Wang's Slope), Shibanpo (Slope of Stone Plank), Shibati (Eighteen Stairs), give a good indication of the physical conditions on which these houses were built. Their peripheral location and difficult physical settings also affected their land values. Private ownership, poor residents and a very high population density were other factors which made these places less attractive to large-scale redevelopment. Because of the poor physical and social profiles of these areas, they had become socially excluded areas in cities and the first destination of rural to urban migrants.

Conclusion

Economic reform has brought fundamental changes to Chinese cities. It has modernised the infrastructures and the poor residential images of these socialist cities, and involved improvements in the living conditions of the majority of urban residents. However, not everyone has benefited from this transitional experience. While many of the higher and middle income households now enjoy a lifestyle which was never experienced by ordinary Chinese families in the past, a large group of urban residents has been left behind (Wang 2000). This new social and economic stratification also has important spatial consequences.

In a previous paper on the social and spatial impacts of urban housing reform, we indicated that there was a distinctive division between three different residential zones in Chinese cities – the traditional core, the socialist planned work unit zone and a suburban commercial housing estate zone. Each zone would develop according to different political and economic systems (Wang and Murie 2000). Figure 13.7 presents a revised spatial model, which indicates that the distinctions between those three zones of residence have gradually become less important. Reform and commercial property development have made significant changes to

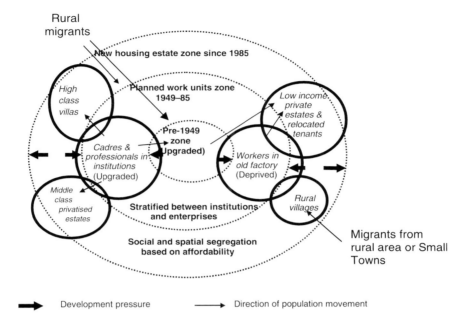

Rural
migrants

New housing estate zone since 1985

High
class
villas

Planned work units zone
1949–85

Low income
private
estates &
relocated
tenants

Pre-1949
zone
(Upgraded)

Cadres &
professionals in
institutions
(Upgraded)

Workers in
old factory
(Deprived)

Middle
class
privatised
estates

Rural
villages

Stratified between institutions
and enterprises

Social and spatial segregation
based on affordability

Migrants from
rural area or Small
Towns

➡ Development pressure   ⟶ Direction of population movement

13.7 Spatial differentiation of residences and fragmentation in Chinese cities

the central and the work unit areas. The differences in living standards and social organization in each housing estate have become important factors in spatial analysis in Chinese urban studies. As this chapter shows, the relatively balanced social equality of Chinese urban societies established during the early stage of Communist control has been broken. The poor and powerless have been concentrated into particular areas in cities. Those communities have been economically and physically marginalised. The traditional poor housing areas, some of which have never really been integrated well within the socialist city, have once again been left out of the first wave of the modernization process. The better-off residents (if there were any) have moved out to other areas of the cities. Those remaining are overwhelmingly poor and old.

Housing has played a very important role in the social and spatial re-organization in Chinese cities. While most government officials, professionals and enterprise managers got their housing either almost free or with a large subsidy from the state, industrial workers and other urban residents, who had never secured a good standard home in the old system, were trapped in the poor traditional housing areas. With the increase in housing prices, they must now have a substantial amount of money to improve their housing circumstances. Property development and urban renewal processes over the last two decades have tended to redevelop the areas with good land value, low population density, and simpler land and property ownership that involved low costs in compensation. The redevelopment process has actually demolished many houses that offered reasonable living conditions. The areas left were mainly the poorest communities with a concentration of the low-income groups. For these people, the only option left for housing improvement has been through municipal supported redevelopment. The common practice has been to invite a commercial property developer to carry out redevelopment with the local government providing policy guidance over price, compensation and quality. The developer can build multi-storey flats and distribute parts of them to the original residents while selling the remaining flats in the market. Internal cross subsidy in price was the main mechanism used to help the original residents. This process sounds favourable to local residents but requires families to pay a large sum of money for a small new flat in the same area. A large proportion of residents were unemployed or had been laid-off and most of them did not have much savings. Many local governments have promoted this type of renewal. It may achieve the leadership's target of image improvement in these cities, but could force many poor residents to spend all their savings on housing when many other household expenses (such as healthcare, education and even food) are more important. When the income gap is increasing and a large proportion of the urban population is still poor, the aspiration to house every family in a purpose built new flat is neither realistic nor necessary.

Similar to the inequality problems outlined at the beginning, the social division and the difficulties faced by the low-income communities are major problems in large Chinese cities. With the increasing pace of urbanization and rural to urban migration, urban poverty will pose a new threat to the future development of cities. It is now imperative to develop proper policies to deal with the social consequences of economic reform. Government should aim to reduce the gap between the rich and the poor and the other negative impacts of urban reform. International research on poverty has led to several policy approaches recently. These include:

> safety nets for the most vulnerable; opportunities for households to increase their assets; assistance to enable people to take advantage of income earning opportunities; provision of basic utilities and services; and the creation of a policy framework, as well as legal and physical context which is favourable to the activities of the urban poor.
>
> (Rakodi 1995: 407)

In order to alleviate urban poverty in China, a pro-poor economic development strategy should be adopted and the government should give more support to the traditional, small and informal business sectors in urban areas. In dealing with poverty and social benefit, an area-based approach could be pursued and an emphasis given to those areas with a concentration of low-income groups and poor quality housing. This will target the poor more directly. Urban redevelopment could focus on the worst areas and should progress slowly to give sufficient support to the poorest families. Future housing reform policies should give more attention to the social aspects of the new housing system. The current distribution of housing benefits could be re-balanced to offer more help to the poor and those working outside the state system.

Acknowledgement

The UK Department For International Development (DFID) supports policies, programmes and projects to promote international development. DFID provided funds for this study as part of that objective but the views and opinions expressed are those of the author alone. During my fieldwork in China I received assistance from many government officials from the Ministry of Construction, Housing Reform Offices in Shenyang and Chongqing. Household surveys were carried out by staff and students under the supervision of Professor Yinzi Dai from Liaoning University and Dr Hao Long fom Chongqing University. Professor Moira Munro and Dr Fulong Wu read drafts of this chapter and made important suggestions for revision. I am also grateful for Ray's comments and careful editing.

Notes

1 The term 'urban poor' was not officially used in China until very recently. An alternative term was 'the medium- to low-income groups'. This referred to the majority of official ordinary employees and their families in the public and private sectors. This official figure for the medium- to low-income group included about 80 per cent of the urban population. More recently the term 'low-income group' was used. This referred mainly to the urban households that required government help.
2 The average housing construction floor space per person for urban areas was 20 sq metres in 2000.
3 A special housing saving scheme for employees. Both employer and employee contribute a percentage of the employee's income to the saving account held by the employee each month. These savings can only be used for housing or retirement pension purposes.

References

Andrusz, G., Harloe, M. and Szelenyi, I. (eds) (1996) *Cities after Socialism, Urban and Regional Change and Conflict in Post-socialist Societies*, Oxford: Blackwell.
Bian, Y.J. and Logan, L.J. (1996) 'Market transformation and the persistence of power: the changing stratification system in urban China', *American Sociological Review*, 61 (5): 739–58.
Chen, A.M. (1996) 'China's urban housing reform: price–rent ratio and market equilibrium', *Urban Studies*, 33.7, 1077–92.
Chiu, R.H. (2001) 'Commodification of housing with Chinese characteristics', *Policy Studies Review*, 18 (1): 75–95.
Chongqing Master Planning Office and Chongqing Urban Planning and Design Institute (1998) *Chongqing City Master Plan 1996–2020*, internal plan document.

Chongqing Statistics Bureau (2000) *Chongqing Statistics Yearbook 2000*, Beijing: China Statistics Press.

Clapham, D., Hegedus, J., Kintrea, K. and Tosics, I. (eds) (1996) *Housing Privatisation in Eastern Europe*, Westport, USA: Greenwood.

Clarke, S. (2000) 'Measurement and definitions of poverty in Russia', in D. Gordon and P. Townsend (eds) *Breadline Europe, The Measurement of Poverty*, Bristol: The Policy Press.

Cornia, G.A. (1999) *Liberalisation, Globalisation and Income Distribution*, Working Paper No. 157, Helsinki: UNU World Institute for Development Economic Research.

Gordon, D. and Townsend, P. (eds) (2000) *Breadline Europe, The Measurement of Poverty*, Bristol: The Policy Press.

Harloe, M. (1996) 'Cities in transition', in G. Andrusz, M. Harloe and I. Szelenyi (eds) *Cities after Socialism, Urban and Regional Change and Conflict in Post-socialist Societies*, Oxford: Blackwell.

Hegedus, J. and Tosics, I. (1994) 'Privatisation and rehabilitation in the Budapest Inner Districts', *Housing Studies*, 9 (1): 39–54.

Hou, X.M. (1997) 'A tentative study on guiding housing consumption and promoting new economic growth', *Beijing Real Estate*, 1: 21–3.

Kirkby, R.J.R. (1990) 'China', in K. Mathey (ed.) *Housing Policies in the Socialist Third World*, London: Mansell.

Leaf, M. (1997) 'Urban social impacts of China's economic reforms', *Cities*, 14 (2): v–vii.

Lee, J. (2000) 'From welfare housing to home ownership: the dilemma of China's housing reform', *Housing Studies*, 15 (1): 61–7.

Li, S.M. (2000a) 'Housing consumption in urban China: a comparative study of Beijing and Guangzhou', *Environment and Planning A*, 32: 1115–34.

—— (2000b) 'The housing market and tenure decisions in Chinese cities: a multivariate analysis of the case of Guangzhou', *Housing Studies*, 15 (2): 213–36.

Logan, J. and Bian, Y. (1993) 'Inequalities in access to community resources in a Chinese city', *Social Forces*, 72 (3): 555–76.

Rakodi, C. (1995) 'Poverty lines or household strategies? A review of conceptual issues in the study of urban poverty', *Habitat International*, 19 (4): 407–26.

Shenyang Statistics Bureau (2000) *Shenyang Statistics Yearbook 1999*, Shenyang: Shenyang Statistics Bureau.

State Statistics Bureau (2000) *China Statistics Yearbook 2000*, Beijing: China Statistical Press.

Struyk, R.J. (1996) *Economic Restructuring of the Former Soviet Bloc: The Case of Housing*, Aldershot: Urban Institute Press.

Szelenyi, I. (1996) 'Cities under socialism – and after', in G. Andrusz, M. Harloe and I. Szelenyi (eds) *Cities after Socialism, Urban and Regional Change and Conflict in Post-socialist Societies*, Oxford: Blackwell.

Townsend, P. (1993) *The International Analysis of Poverty*, Hemel Hempstead: Wheatsheaf.

Wang Y.P. (2000) 'Housing reform and its impacts on the urban poor', *Housing Studies*, 15 (6): 845–64.

—— (2001) 'Urban housing reform and finance in China: a case study of Beijing', *Urban Affairs Review*, 36 (5): 620–45.

Wang, Y.P. and Murie, A. (1996) 'The process of commercialisation of urban housing in China', *Urban Studies*, 33 (6): 971–89.

—— (1999) *Housing Policy and Practice In China*, Basingstoke: Macmillan.

—— (2000) 'Social and spatial implications of housing reform in China', *International Journal of Urban and Regional Research*, 24 (2): 397–417.

World Bank (1992) *China Implementation Options for Urban Housing Reform*, Washington, DC: World Bank.

—— (2001) *World Development Report 2000/2001, Attacking Poverty*, Washington, DC: World Bank.

Wu, F.L. (1996) 'Changes in the structure of public housing provision in urban China', *Urban Studies*, 33 (9): 1601–27.

—— (2001) 'Housing provision under globalisation: a case study of Shanghai', *Environment and Planning A*, 33: 1741–64.

Yi, S.H. (1998) *Urban Poverty in Contemporary China*, Nanchang: Jiangxi People's Publishing House.

Yuan, T.C. (2000) *Report on Current Situation of the Low-income Protection and Social Security for the Urban Resident in Chongqing*. Unpublished internal report of the Chongqing Municipal Social Security Bureau.

Zhang, J.J. (1999) *Informal Institution in the Process of Market Transformation*, Beijing: Archaeological Press.

Zhang, X.Q. (1997) 'Chinese housing policy 1949–1978: the development of a welfare system', *Planning Perspectives*, 12 (4): 433–55.

Zhang, Z.W. (1998) *The Mine Field of Reform, Laid-off and Unemployment*, Zhuhai: Zhuhai Publishing House.

Zhong, M. and Wang, Y. (1999) *The Gap between Two Polars? The Rich and the Poor in Contemporary China*, Beijing: Chinese Economic Press.

Zhou, M. and Logan, J.R. (1996) 'Market transition and the commodification of housing in urban China', *International Journal of Urban and Regional Research*, 20 (3): 400–21.

Zhu, G.L. (ed.) (1998) *Analysis on All Social Strata in Modern China*, Tianjin: Tianjin People's Press.

14 Concluding observations

Ray Forrest and James Lee

In this collection of essays we have explored a number of dimensions of housing and social change. In addressing this broad based theme we have consciously drawn on a range of disciplines and from perspectives rooted in different geographies, cultures and policy regimes. As stressed in the introductory chapter there has been no attempt to force or anticipate a uniformity of message but to use the individual chapters as different windows on the relationship between housing (as policy, as investment, as lived experience) and broader societal transformations. Authors have ranged across the impact of housing policy reforms in China, asset based welfare initiatives in the United States, the meaning of the home in New Zealand and the recession induced fragmentation of home-ownership in Japan. The wide range of topics and policy preoccupations serves to underline the critical position housing plays in a variety of contexts and the complex linkages between housing systems, cultural change, economic reform and restructuring, and demographic developments. As a conclusion to this collection it is appropriate, however, to draw out some of the underlying themes of the book.

Theme 1: privatization and the retreat of the state in housing

Europe, Australasia and the USA were characterized by receding state involvement in public housing and a general instability within different housing systems in the 1980s and this trend has continued through the 1990s and into the new century. In Western industrial societies, the last two decades have continued to witness the slow, uneven but steady progress of government trying to reduce both direct and indirect public expenditure on housing. Many social housing sectors have been progressively transformed from a producer-subsidy approach to a consumer-subsidy orientation. Although the degree and institutional mode in which these expenditure cuts have been realized has varied tremendously across national boundaries, the central tendency has been the restructuring of state sectors in housing through various strategies of privatization. In East Asia the same process also commenced in the late 1980s, with the exception of Singapore where the state housing sector remains exceptionally high, albeit one with rather distinct characteristics. The general trend has been the downsizing or deregulation of public housing sectors. The Asian financial crisis in 1997 and the subsequent collapse of the information technology markets in 2000 have accelerated this process. The ramifications of the economic crisis which emerged initially in Thailand in July 1997 are still being experienced in most East Asian economies. Many of the East Asian nations are still suffering from an extended period of house price stagnation and highly fragile economic prospects. This has created serious knock-on effects for both the production and consumption of housing. On the production side, collapsing construction industries with fewer developments have inevitably aggravated unemployment. This happened in the West in the late 1980s and early 1990s and is now being repeated in East Asia, particularly in the small open economies of Hong Kong, Singapore and Taiwan. As for the consumption side, the property slump and continued economic volatility have produced a much more cautious set of consumers and hence a reduction in overall consumption and effective demand. The common dilemma many governments are now facing is that while on the one hand there is a heavy reliance on the market as the primary mechanism for housing allocation, on the other, it fails to provide the long term confidence necessary for consumers to commit themselves to home purchase. In short, while governments have sought to retreat from or downplay their role in housing provision, the market alternative has also proven to be defective. What then should be the future role for social housing? Lee, Forrest and Tam provide some examples of these policy dilemmas in the East and Southeast Asian context and Hirayama's chapter on development in Japan's home-ownership sector shows how growing economic uncertainty has led to a highly fragmented housing policy. The collapse of the highly inflated real estate sector provoked a salvage operation by the Japanese government which spent some US$15.4 billion in 1998 and US$57.3 billion in 1999 in an attempt to bail it out – unsuccessfully. Chiu's chapter on housing sustainability in Hong Kong takes the discussion one step further. She argues that the heavily market-driven housing strategy cannot be sustainable while a considerable segment of the population in Hong Kong is still not adequately housed. And China's latest housing reform programme suffers from similar difficulties. As Davis' chapter succinctly points out, after two decades of housing privatization, the distribution of housing in China is less rather than more equitable. The sale of former state housing to sitting tenants systematically creates a highly unequal distribution of national housing resources, one which largely favours the managerial and professional class. These inequalities are creating new social tensions. For Chua, to maintain stability, and legitimacy, the state must create a housing sector which is capable of constantly adjusting to manage rising housing aspirations. This requires a very fine-tuned housing ladder where people can continue to transcend and upgrade themselves without resorting to confrontation or violence. These East and Southeast Asian experiences return us to the central question of what prospects remain for the role of the state in housing in the coming decades.

Theme 2: the structure of the housing provision and subsidies

The structure of housing provision is perhaps the more divergent element in any comparisons between East and West. Using the broad framework suggested by Christine Whitehead's chapter, European housing systems are represented by a mixture of dualist and unitary housing systems, with the latter being more prevalent in continental Europe and the Scandinavian countries. In East Asia, it is the dualist model that dominates, even in the case of Singapore where nearly 90 per cent of the housing sector is controlled by the state. Housing subsidies are still relatively selective and concentrate in the public housing sector. The private housing sector is largely unregulated and receives few direct or indirect housing subsidies. The exception is Japan where the state took on an almost monopolistic position in the provision of mortgage finance for homeowners through the Government Housing Loan Corporation combined with direct subsidies in the public rented sector. Since 2001, however, the Japanese government has drastically reduced the role of the Housing Loan Corporation and will allow a progressive takeover of the mortgage business sector by private banks. This will significantly reduce government's role in low interest subsidies and move the Japanese system nearer the more dualistic model of housing subsidies. For other East Asian states such as South Korea, Hong Kong, Taiwan and Singapore, a tenure-specific subsidy policy has always been seen as practically and politically more viable as rent-control generally proved to be ineffective and, as a policy, contrary to free market ideology. Moreover, whilst social housing sectors in Europe have been deeply embedded in the welfare state, many East Asian housing systems are still largely residual in nature. Politically, a tenure-specific policy has been regarded as a safer choice for governments, particularly in an environment of fiscal restraint. Indeed for a long time the development of social housing in East Asia has had much more to do with poverty, resettlement and extreme housing shortages. Housing resources, unlike Europe, are generally targeted at specific income groups and the genesis of many social housing programmes in East Asia lies in the provision of housing for the poorest sections of society. Social ownership for the middle classes has generally been regarded as a progression in housing policy under conditions of economic growth.

Theme 3: home-ownership, economic growth and housing policy

Although widely acknowledged as the preferred tenure in the housing tenure hierarchy, the position of home-ownership at the beginning of this new century is highly varied between East and West. While the real estate market is currently extremely buoyant in most parts of the Western industrial world, East Asian housing markets have suffered tremendously since the 1997 Asian financial crisis. Lee, Forrest and Tam's chapter provides a preliminary assessment of the impacts. They suggest that one of the fundamental issues facing East Asian housing systems is their overreliance on using the housing sector as a source of economic growth. Christine Whitehead's chapter points out that Western economists have long recognized the existence of a positive relationship between housing systems and the wider economy. However, it is the intensity and the extent of its use in East Asia that deserves more of our attention. The dynamics of these housing systems and the state's involvement in them cannot be viewed as a purely unilateral transfer. Meeting housing needs and achieving growth simultaneously are now regarded as important social development objectives. Our collection of essays points to an important trend in housing policy: it is now no longer about whether housing investment leads to growth; it is more about how housing policy should be integrated with economic policy objectives and how an optimal level of public housing should be attained. Various chapters also suggest another trend in the financing of the social housing sector. It is now widely recognized that resources for housing finance from the state are dwindling fast and the chapters in this volume confirm this view. Housing policy, both East and West, is now commonly pursued as a conscious attempt by the state to boost private consumption and economic growth. Peter Williams' chapter suggests that home-ownership in the UK is not simply a choice for the better-off but also a target for preferential treatment in terms of tax advantages and housing finance. The house price boom in the UK since 2001 is seen as providing enormous positive impact on GDP growth, which in turn encourages more home-ownership and wider economic activity. Real and anticipated capital gains from the real estate sector encourage current consumption and a positive expectation of future income streams and purchasing power. In East Asia, the desire for home-ownership comes more overtly as a state policy. Home-ownership policies are almost unquestionably accepted across all East and Southeast Asian societies, although backed by a rather different set of cultural assumptions and motivations. Lee, Forrest and Tam's chapter shows that most East Asian states tend to engage in a home-ownership policy which facilitates capital accumulation for households. As an extreme case, Singapore ties home-ownership in with the social security system where compulsory personal savings from the Central Provident Fund are channelled largely for home purchase. Hence, the government needs to mobilise its policies to ensure future asset appreciation and house price stability, so that people's retirement can bank on future liquidation of their housing assets. The downside of this is the government's deepening involvement in monopolising the housing system. But the Singapore case can be represented as an institutional fix, where social development objectives appear to be in rhythm with economic growth. Hirayama's chapter, however, strikes a warning note to the continuation of a home-ownership policy after the bursting of the Japanese economic bubble in the early 1990s. As we have intimated above, the Koizumi administration has already decided to retreat from its previous involvement in providing low-interest loans for home-ownership which is going to mark a new era for Japanese housing policy.

Smart and Lee's chapter develops a further argument that the unique development of the housing market and the real estate sector in East Asian cities such as Hong Kong provides a primitive analogue of a property-based growth regime whereby income generated might fuel consumption comparable to the income from the stock market and normal wages. The primacy of the housing sector in the economy is clearly reflected in all these debates and this will undoubtedly remain a key area for housing research and policy debate.

Theme 4: the risk of home-ownership

A dominant theme throughout the book has been the higher risk environment for individual home-ownership. In its various forms home-ownership is generally encompassing higher proportions of households. The extent to which these households are vulnerable to shifts in economic, financial and social disturbance clearly varies substantially in relation to sector, income, policy regime and individual circumstances. Hirayama highlights the particular changes in Japan where the promotion of home-ownership, the conventional family form and security of employment for a significant section of the male population have formed what he refers to as the 'social mainstream'. This mainstream is, however, under threat from greater social heterogeneity and economic stagnation. This destabilization of a set of social and economic arrangements which were previously taken for granted has in itself created new forms of home-ownership as developers search for new markets beyond the traditional family. The growth of niche markets catering for singles, women and couples without children is a response to a changing economic context but is itself part of the destabilizing process in which new opportunities for home-ownership arise for groups previously excluded. This higher risk environment for home-ownership is therefore double-edged and is not unambiguously negative in its social consequences. The need for forms of housing provision which cater for a greater variety of household forms and cultural needs is also a central theme of Watson's chapter which highlights market and policy responses to this growing diversity.

However, Williams points to a growth in risks to both home owning households and institutions with policy changes, reduced incomes, relationship breakdown and house price volatility. Savings, family assistance and the growth of state or private insurance schemes are all likely to become more significant as ways of mitigating impacts which could involve the loss of a home. And the formal and informal resources available to different households in this more individualized and privatized environment will be highly differentiated. It is likely that single earner households, and particularly those headed by females and ethnic minorities, will be among the most vulnerable. Policy responses to these developments therefore require recognition by governments that home-ownership is no longer a tenure of privilege but includes households in a wide range of circumstances. Part of this policy and market response may involve a new acceptance of rental forms as a legitimate part of contemporary housing systems – and as a lifestyle choice for some rather than as necessarily a tenure of constraint or transition.

It is also worth noting, as Williams does, that it is not all about growing instability or uncertainty. Low inflation and low interest rates offer a reduction in some dimensions of risk even though they pose problems for both institutions and households in relation to the servicing of long-term mortgage debt. Moreover, the progressive deregulation of mortgage markets offers greater possibilities to consumers to shop around for financial instruments which minimize costs. But while these kinds of developments can be seen as symptomatic of processes of globalization with major financial institutions scouring the world's housing markets for new and profitable opportunities, there is a strong message from this collection of essays that local norms and circumstances remain important. Whether we are referring to the cohorts of owners in Tokyo with entrenched negative equity or the demand 'deserts' in parts of England, what is required are not imported or universal policy responses but, as Williams emphasizes, localized and tailored solutions.

Theme 5: housing and community

Much of what we have said so far emphasizes the significance of the interactions between housing markets and the wider economy. It is important, however, to conclude this collection with a reassertion of the importance of housing as a pivotal element of everyday life, as a key site in the creation of social identity and sense of belonging, and as a primary ingredient in the creation or erosion of social cohesion. The strongest expression of this dimension of housing comes from Perkins and Thorns' account of 'home' as something which is being constantly negotiated and recreated amidst a fluid and changing world. The home and community represent a set of social relationships which are always in transition but which nevertheless offer security and stability. Moreover, as they highlight in relation to the settlement history of Aotearoa/New Zealand, mobility and fluidity are not some novel processes associated with postmodernity and globalization. They have been around for rather longer. There is a constant tension between rootedness and movement in the recreation of home. Local space is not some residual, anachronistic site which is being eroded by the virtual and remote. It is an integral part of a changing world, being actively refashioned and remains significant as a 'key building block in the crafting of identity'.

These local spaces as communities of poor households can also be sites of entrapment and division. They may be cohesive in adversity but increasingly disconnected from the wider society in which they are embedded. This is a growing and apparently intractable problem for many governments, East and West, with a panoply of area based initiatives aimed at alleviating such deeply entrenched and multidimensional inequalities. Two of the chapters in this collection highlight new aspects of these socio-spatial divisions. Wang provides a detailed account of the way in which policy reforms, rural-urban migration and economic restructuring in two Chinese cities, Shenyang and Chongqing, are creating new problems for poor households in poor housing. Echoing Davis' chapter, while an emerging middle class and rich elite in Chinese cities are experiencing a dramatic improvement in their living conditions and lifestyles, another group of the poorer and powerless are being physically and economically marginalized. Housing has been at the core of wider economic reforms but the policies pursued have apparently too often been blunt instruments in which grand plans have overridden an understanding of local conditions and circumstances.

While Wang is concerned with the housing and social consequences of market reforms within a socialist political system, Stegman focuses on making technology and capitalist financial instruments work more effectively for poor communities. It is typically the residents of social housing in major urban areas in north American and European cities who are financially excluded. In these 'cash deserts' fringe banking practices act to further deplete whatever material resources poor households possess. For Stegman, part of the answer to the problem is the use of electronic funds transfer (EFT) in the delivery of welfare payments. In combination with new forms of savings instruments and initiatives such as technology centres in social housing, Stegman argues that EFT can be a powerful tool in enabling poorer households to build a financial asset base.

As a final comment, it is appropriate to reassert the significance of housing in social change. The way in which housing systems operate remains a key determinant of quality of life. And quality of life here refers to both its individual and collective aspects. It is self-evident that housing quality and the wider residential environment are pivotal elements of the daily lived experience. Insecure, badly located and low quality accommodation dominates the grind of daily life for those on the social and economic margins. But how housing is provided and of what quality is a key aspect of wider perceptions and experiences of social justice, environmental sustainability, economic buoyancy and of the extent to which societies are cohesive, or fragmented and divided. Both East and West, the escalating quantities of capital invested in the residential sphere, both individual and corporate, means that with the increasing dominance of home-ownership the fate of both household and wider economies can be fundamentally affected by shifts in the value of the residential stock. Housing then is big business, central to a financialized capitalism and to the consumption regimes which must be constantly refuelled. And in whatever cultural context, it remains one of the most visible and potent determinants of social participation or exclusion.

Index

Index